Documents of Doubt

Documents of Doubt

The Photographic Conditions of Conceptual Art

Heather Diack

MINNESOTA

University of Minnesota Press
Minneapolis — London

Advancing
Art&Design

Publication of this book has been aided by a grant from the Wyeth Foundation for American Art Publication Fund of CAA.

The University of Minnesota Press gratefully acknowledges financial support for the publication of this book from the University of Miami Faculty Publication Fund.

Published by the University of Minnesota Press
111 Third Avenue South, Suite 290
Minneapolis, MN 55401-2520
http://www.upress.umn.edu

ISBN 978-1-5179-0756-3 (hc)
ISBN 978-1-5179-0757-0 (pb)
A Cataloging-in-Publication record for this book is available from the Library of Congress.

Printed in Canada on acid-free paper

26 25 24 23 22 21 20 10 9 8 7 6 5 4 3 2 1

For my two E.T.s

Contents

List of Illustrations

Plates

Introduction
Burning with Contingency

One searing summer day, a shirtless man lay on a sandy beach, an open hardcover book face down on his chest. He is the embodiment of leisure in the glare of the midday sun. The circumstances surrounding this moment are unknown—the banality of it all easily dismissed. And yet, perhaps somewhat surprisingly, the ordinary act I am describing forms the basis of a widely recognized work of art, one half of a now-famous photographic diptych, canonically situated within the parameters of conceptual art, created in 1970 by the American artist Dennis Oppenheim. Though inconspicuous, at least at first glance, this image signals many of the issues that preoccupied conceptual artists in the late 1960s and which continue to elude historical accounts in the present. Titled *Reading Position for Second Degree Burn,* the typewritten text that Oppenheim includes in the gap between the images ostensibly provides enough information to situate the where and the what: *Reading Position for Second Degree Burn. Stage I, Stage II. Book, skin, solar energy. Exposure Time: 5 hours. Jones Beach,* 1970 (Plate 1 and Figure I.1). Presented with the straightforwardness expected of documentary photographs, the image's relay of information is nonetheless somewhat deceptive. Despite the long-winded title, a missing link in this recipe-like reportage sequence remains: why did he do it?

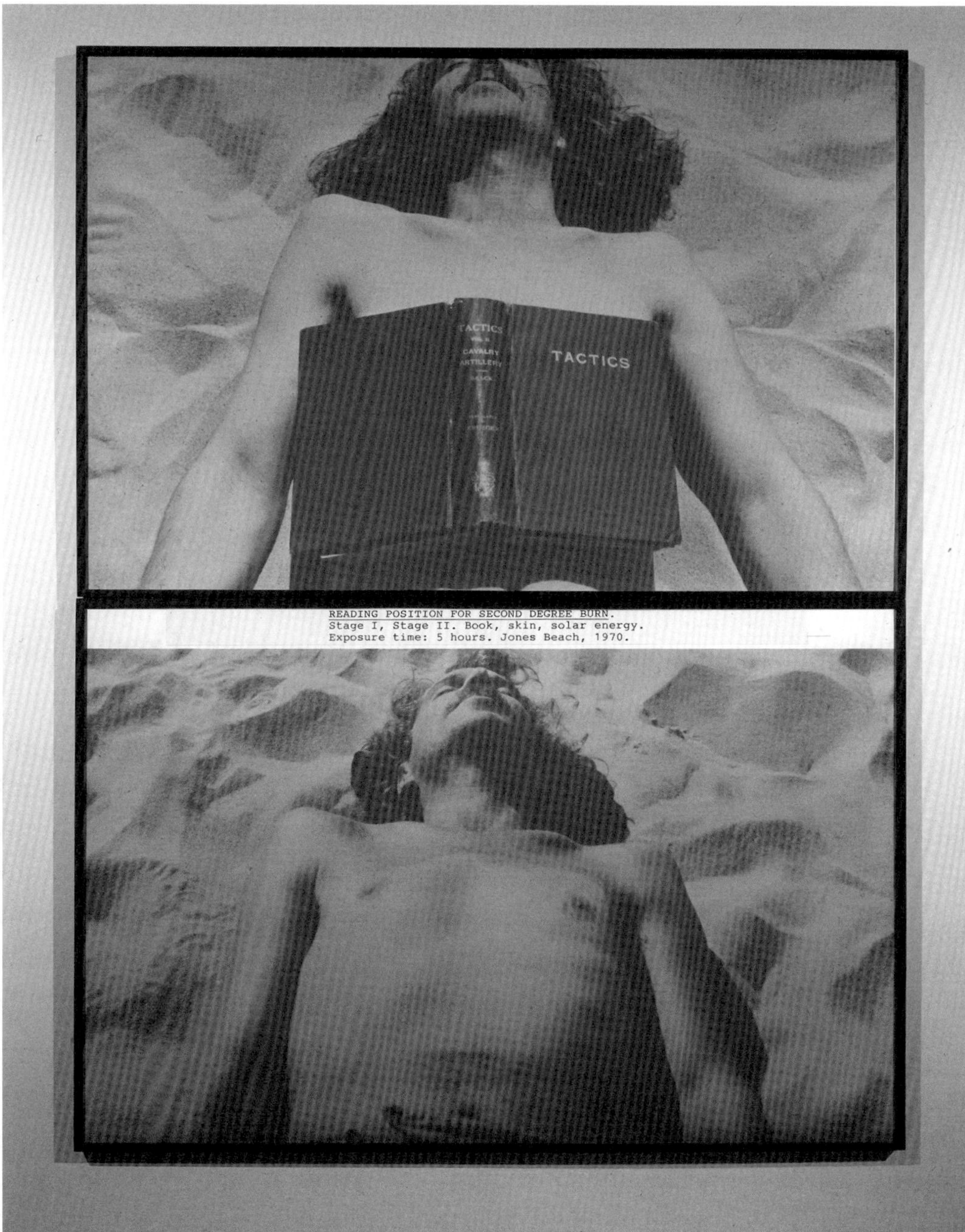

Figure I.1. Dennis Oppenheim, *Reading Position for Second Degree Burn*, 1970. Two-color photographs and black-and-white text drymounted on museum board. Frame (each [black wood]): 41⅛ × 61⅛ × 1½ inches (104.46 × 155.26 × 3.81 cm). Image (each): 40 × 60 inches (101.6 × 152.4 cm). The Museum of Contemporary Art, Los Angeles. Gift of the artist.

Much like cosmetic before and after shots, the second half of the diptych shows perceptible differences from the first, changes the viewer assumes have taken place in the intervening interval. In this photograph, the protagonist, who is the artist himself, reveals a painful sunburn covering everywhere the book was not. His fair skin has become bright red. Where the book had been we find a stark absence. What can we make of this? It seems to be an inside joke,[1] perhaps a playful conceptualist wink toward the interrelation of text and image that was gaining currency as an artistic practice at this juncture. It brings to mind the art historian Douglas Crimp's characterization of the central dilemma and virtue of performance art at the time—the ways in which art was preoccupied with being "in a situation" and "for a duration." As Crimp says, "You had to be there in the seventies."[2]

We were not there on the beach with Oppenheim, but we have the photographs. Now they are faded to a nostalgic warm tone that characterized late-sixties and early-seventies photography, a coveted look currently obtainable through filter options on apps like Instagram. In Oppenheim's photos, however, the images are literally and figuratively sun-drenched. Time has taken its toll, and both the changes between the moments captured in the image and the context of the present need to be distinguished. The innate strangeness of these images is further compounded by the existence of multiple versions of this same piece, each with its own slight variations. The question of what these photographs bear witness to endures. There is something both compelling and frustrating about this mise-en-scène. Oppenheim chose to document the effects of spending five hours lying in the sun in a very particular and somewhat peculiar way. There is something reminiscent of a crime scene in these images, with his body giving the impression of a corpse and notable traces of movement in the sand between the two photographs. Pictorially the foreshortening and Oppenheim's flowing Renaissance-style locks cause *Reading Position for Second Degree Burn* to somewhat absurdly resemble Andrea Mantegna's renowned example of the humanist construction of space in his fifteenth-century painting *Lamentation over the Dead Christ* (circa 1480–1500). The sand emulates the drapery, and uncannily both subjects even possess the same facial hair. Such a morbid comparison seems incongruous given the assumed low stakes of Oppenheim's performance, yet there is something to it, something oddly captivating in its formal echo. That same year, for the *Information* show at the Museum of Modern Art in New York, John Baldessari proposed displaying an actual human cadaver imitating the composition of Mantegna's *Dead Christ* behind a monocular peephole. Though ethical and legal restrictions prevented Baldessari from doing so, both artists, Baldessari and Oppenheim, allude to the contemporary conditions of morbidity and spectatorship in and around 1970. If Kynaston McShine's preface to *Information*'s exhibition catalog is any indication, these conditions were at once abstract and imminent:

> If you are an artist in Brazil, you know of at least one friend who is being tortured; if you are one in Argentina, you probably have had a neighbor who has been in jail

> for having long hair, or for not being "dressed" properly; and if you are living in the United States, you may fear that you will be shot at, either in the universities, in your bed, or more formally in Indochina. It may seem inappropriate, if not absurd, to get up in the morning, walk into a room, apply dabs of paint from a little tube to a square of canvas. What can you as a young artist do that seems relevant and meaningful?[3]

For Oppenheim's part, in place of the pleasure commonly associated with sunbathing, we instead have the suggestion of sacrifice and the evidential body.[4] Oppenheim's photographic documentation of what could tentatively be called an event thus sets a series of conundrums into motion, which begin to surface, emerging slowly and then poignantly like the sear of a second-degree burn.[5]

Oppenheim's *Reading Position for Second Degree Burn* encapsulates the ambivalence and contradiction of the moment and, by extension, of the documentary capacity of the photographic medium. The title of the protagonist's tome is boldly emblazoned across the red cover in classic gold typeface: TACTICS, VOL. II.[6] The book admits itself as the sequel to the original, echoing once more the logic of the multiple and the sequence. The spine is more difficult to decipher, but on closer inspection reads CAVALRY/ARTILLERY. It is a borrowed library book, tattered from circulation, held by multiple anonymous hands. The subject of the book alludes to absurdly anachronistic means—how relevant are cavalry to military strategies in 1970? The very summoning of tactics also calls to mind the question of holding ground or gaining territory, defense or conquest.

Searching this piece, one clue seems to dominate and underpin its internal logic: photography. In these photographs the artist has demonstratively and excruciatingly turned his own body *into* a photograph. The viscerality of the photograph is materialized as epidermis, as the sensitive surface of the body mimics the sensitized surface of the photograph. Oppenheim described this process by reference to the pigments of painting, stating: "I could feel the act of becoming red."[7] The literal solarization of his body, its burning, provocatively replicates the photographic process. We have the writing of light in the flesh, as his stark tan lines define a rectangle shape, the standard geometric form of the photograph—another meta-frame within a frame.

In Robert Slifkin's terms, the second degree is the means by which "the photograph is employed to comment on its own contingency."[8] Describing Oppenheim's photograph as an emblematic exploration of the "paradoxical referential capacity of the photograph," Slifkin contends that the very idea of the "second degree" has been fundamental to contemporary scholarship on photography from the 1960s forward.[9] In the late 1970s Roland Barthes similarly cautioned against the potentials of becoming "maniacs of the second degree," while championing the importance of deconstructing photographic meaning making.[10] Writing about the "manipulation or theatricalization of the real," in an essay titled "Shooting America," featured in the *New York Review of Books* in 1974, Susan Sontag also identified the second degree as the modus operandi of photography and, by extension, surrealist practice.

“Surrealism lay at the heart of the photographic enterprise itself,” writes Sontag, “in the very creation of a duplicate world, of a reality in the second degree, narrower but more dramatic than the one perceived by natural vision.” Sontag attributes the drama she detects in photography chiefly to a straightforward plainness of presentation: “The less doctored, the less patently crafted, the more naïve—the more surreal the photograph was.”[11] This growing suspicion of the acts of doubling and dislocation inherent to the photographic process forms the roots of postmodern art. It also forms the impetus for my present inquiry into the photographic conditions of conceptual art. Acknowledging the deceptive capacity of seemingly plain images and calling attention to their many-layered and often-loaded connections to the complex and highly contingent contexts in which they emerge are precisely my preoccupation across the pages to follow.

In a 1995 essay titled “The Second Degree,” James Meyer also emphasized the logic of reference and removal as an operative principle in conceptual art of the 1970s, citing Mel Bochner as a critical progenitor. Though Meyer does not discuss photography, or indeed even mention Oppenheim, he nevertheless analyzes “meaning-as-such and the discursive conditions of meaning’s production,” as prompted by seriality (or the one-thing-after-another model set in motion by minimalism), which, for him, provide the crucial pivot of conceptualism.[12] According to Meyer, the “second degree” stakes out a “less assured position,” in which deliberation is formative to the notion of conceptual art. I would add that conceptual artists using photography further expand the boundaries of this indecisive space, amplifying the ways it may be understood as phenomenologically inhabited by the viewer. I discuss this in more detail in chapter 1, but for the moment, I return to Oppenheim’s peculiar evocation of the second degree with these nuances in mind.

The possibility of reading Oppenheim’s *Reading Position for Second Degree Burn* as an ordinary day at the beach is incredibly vexed. Indeed, it is impossible to know with any certainty how the piece is supposed to be read. The allusion to the relaxation and escape of beach culture combined deliberately with the graphic and raw results of reckless overexposure stages an undeniable tension. Oppenheim’s evocation of pleasure and pain might seem masochistic, and perhaps on one level it is. However, the piece gains resonance and its potential meaning is deepened if we account for the context of its creation. After all, burning was far from an innocent act; it was endemic to the anxiety-ridden sixties and seventies, and vivid images of acts of burning were pervasive in visual culture.[13] From the bombing of the Freedom Riders bus in Alabama in 1961 to Malcolm Browne’s iconic photo of a Vietnamese monk’s self-immolation in 1963, the documented arson of Los Angeles on fire during the Watts riots in 1965, the frequent appearance of photographs of civilians burning draft cards, and Vietnamese bodies badly burned by napalm strikes, fiery tensions were fast becoming ubiquitous, if not normal.

In the mode of a caption, the title tells us that this is June 1970. The spring of 1970 was an exceptionally turbulent moment in American history, a time when the widespread fear of “becoming red” (communist) lurked beneath the surface, ready to erupt. Beyond burning, becoming red in this context might also be taken as an allusion to tremendous bloodshed in Vietnam. By 1970 the number of American casualties exceeded twelve thousand.[14] Add to this the monstrous death toll for the Vietnamese, with more than two million Vietnamese civilian fatalities recorded before the war's end. On April 29, 1970, the United States began bombing neutral Cambodia, and hundreds of campuses across the United States exploded in protest. On May 4, 1970, the National Guard shot and killed four student protesters and wounded nine others at Kent State University in Ohio. These violent acts have become some of the most recognized events of the time. The photographs of that day are irrefutably icons of the turmoil of the early seventies. The photos, and the brutality and anguish they depict, are not the result of a single instance—either one shot of the camera or of a gun—but a culmination of growing discontent and confusion among American students about the war in Vietnam.

The Pulitzer Prize–winning photograph, by the student photographer John Filo, of Mary Ann Vecchio screaming as she kneels beside the dead body of Jeffrey Miller, circulated internationally and remains an emblem of the disillusionment and violence that pervaded the 1970s. Or, what *Life* magazine decried in its May 15, 1970, issue as "a symbol of the fearful hazards latent in dissent" (Figures I.2 and I.3). The interrelated intensity of these two moments—the U.S. invasion of Cambodia (on the heels of innumerable atrocities in Vietnam, including the My Lai massacre two years earlier) and the excessive use of fatal force against student protesters exercising their freedom of speech—are inextricably connected. Like Oppenheim's correlative before and after, they can be understood as encapsulating a cause and effect sequence, leaving us as viewers with irreconcilable questions that far exceed the parameters of Oppenheim's piece.

Yet what happens if we view Oppenheim's *Reading Position for Second Degree Burn* as tapping into the crisis of this moment and contending with the increasing normalization of unfathomable aggression, as well as the "hazards latent in dissent"? In this way, the latency implied by the photographic processes of concealment followed by development that are pictured within Oppenheim's piece can be thought of in tandem with the emergent radical potential of the medium as well as the visceral implications of latency in everyday life. Though Oppenheim himself was dismissive about the role of photographs, famously denouncing them as "there simply to indicate a radical art that had already vanished. The photograph was necessary only as a residue for communication,"[15] he nevertheless acknowledged the tenuous status of radicality, as well as its contingent and necessary relationship to photography. By reading these images more closely, the possibility of radical art and radical thought, however ephemeral, may still be salvaged. The rawness of *Life*'s cover image strikes anew with affinities to *Reading Position for Second Degree Burn*. Its focus on the body of a wounded student facing skyward, with an open book visibly discarded to his side, creates a tragic echo between the two images. Oppenheim's piece responds both to the implications of becoming red and to the contingencies involved in being read.

More than a simple insider's experience of the moment, Oppenheim's photographs

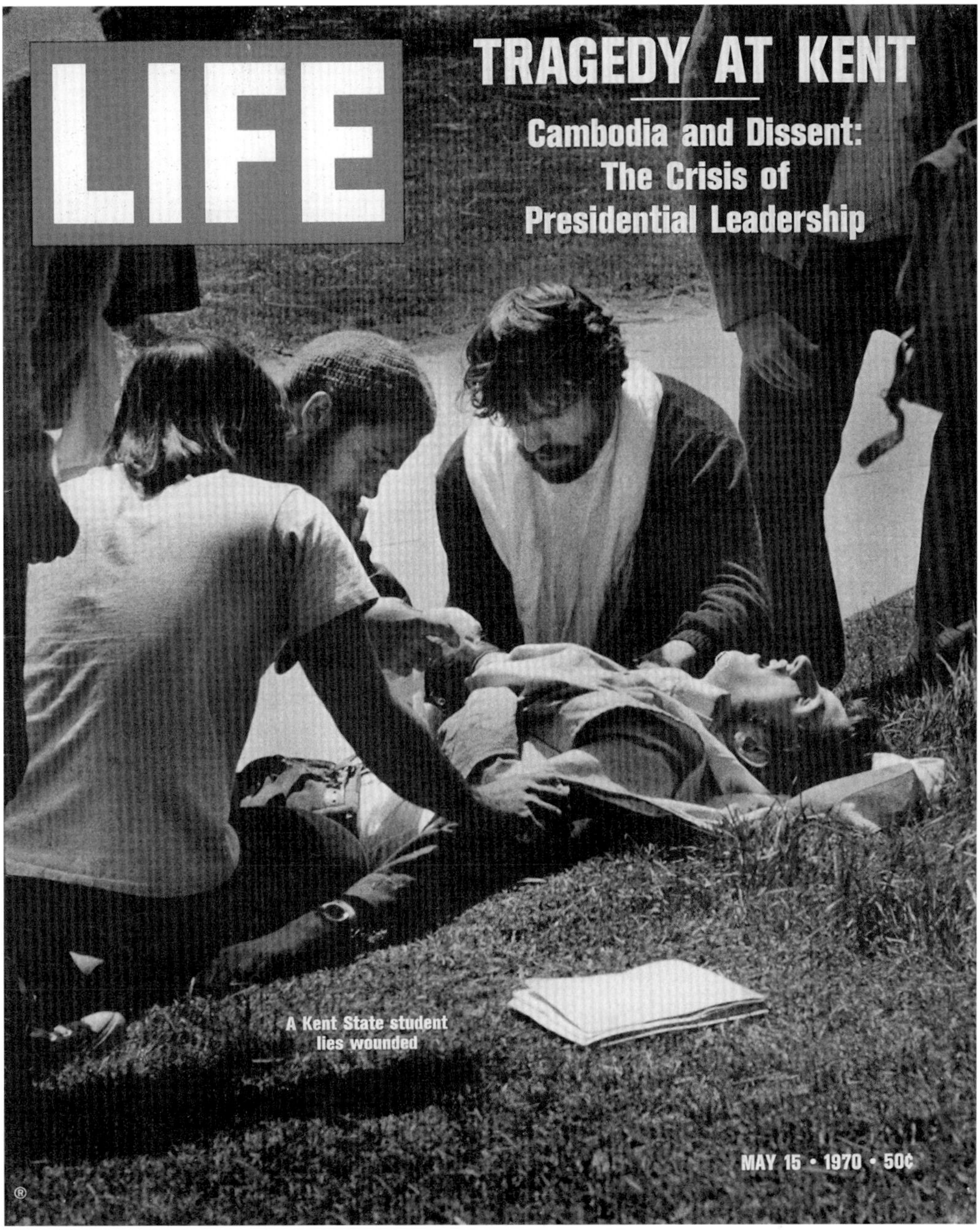

Figure I.2. Cover of *Life* magazine, May 15, 1970. The LIFE Picture Collection / Getty Images.

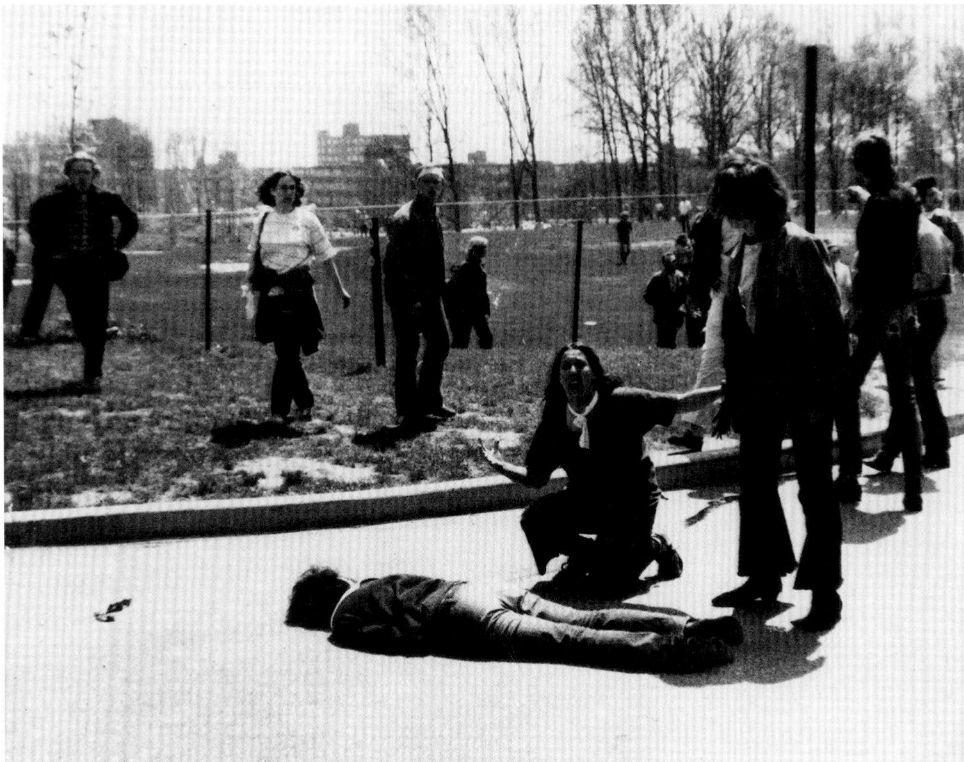

Figure I.3. John Paul Filo, [Mary Ann Vecchio grieving over body of college student Jeffrey Glenn Miller shot by National Guardsmen during an antiwar demonstration, Kent State University, Ohio], May 4, 1970. International Center of Photography. Gift of Jim and Evelyn Hughes, 1998 (57.1998).

lead to provocative possibilities as embodiments of the difficulties of negotiating and articulating a speech act amid this fraught time. Being a bystander was also a precarious position. In its tagline, *Life* magazine agonizes over this paradox, mournfully describing one gunshot victim as "a boy who was just 'there watching it and making up his mind'" (Figure I.4). Even the iconic photograph by Filo is striking in its lack of urgency, as students seem to calmly mill about the fallen body. No one seems hurried, let alone harried (with the exception of Vecchio). Interconnection and indecision are essential themes in the documentation of both the Kent State shootings and Oppenheim's *Reading Position for Second Degree Burn*. In each set of photographs the bodily risk that comes with indecision and passivity are underscored and documented by the camera. Add to this set of events the largely forgotten school shooting at Jackson State in Mississippi only eleven days later. On May 15, 1970, police opened fire with more than 150 rounds of ammunition at a dormitory for female students on this predominantly black college campus. Phillip Lafayette Gibbs, twenty-one years old, and James Earl Green, seventeen years old, were killed. The lack of visibility and collective memory of this event speaks less about the lack of an iconic photograph (for the images of Jack Thornell demonstrate otherwise) and more to the disturbingly uneven politics of race and the varying valuation of life in the United States. Such violence became increasingly ordinary, widely perceived as commonplace. "Being shot is as American as apple pie," explained Chris Burden, in an interview with BBC in 2012, as he reflected on his performance piece of 1971, *Shoot,* during which he was shot in the arm in a gallery. "We see people being shot on TV, we read about it in the newspaper. Everybody has wondered what it's like. So I did it," said Burden.

Viewing Oppenheim's *Reading Position for Second Degree Burn* as a contention to this mode of growing complacency, as a form of oblique protest, testifies to the political, social, and aesthetic challenges of this moment, including the difficulties of bearing witness. Though Oppenheim was not shot, his body is nevertheless used as a palimpsest that reinforces the logic of the photograph in its documentation of both pain and ambivalence, as well as in its material presence. *Reading Position for Second Degree Burn* calls attention to its own conditions. The artist's body is posed as an incarnation or perhaps exaggeration of passive resistance, which is answered by hostility inflicted on the skin. Oppenheim's photographs, like most photographs that come out of conceptual art, present themselves as reticent, as unemotional. Rather than simple avoidance, this could be read as an engagement with the very politics of public emotion at this juncture.[16] Henry Kissinger, then national security adviser and instrumental to President Richard Nixon's Cambodian incursion, succinctly dismissed the student protestors in the aftermath of Kent State, saying, "they were, in my view, as wrong as they were passionate." For Kissinger, the expression of emotion itself was aligned with civil disobedience. Despite the war in Vietnam raging on through 1975, Kissinger would go on to become secretary of state under Nixon and controversially be awarded the Nobel Peace Prize in 1973.

Within the field of art, the succession of movements that emerge after abstract expressionism in the postwar period returned repeatedly to the conundrum of how to locate the work of art in the reality of life, not merely aesthetic reality but cognitive and social realities as well. Perhaps Oppenheim's evocation of the second degree also points to this struggle—the difficulties of being deeply immersed yet removed. This line of thinking summons one of the central crises of this age of information: the economics of attention and the waning of will amid a flood of endlessly eddying media. Upon closer inspection, it becomes unclear whether Oppenheim's photographs are indeed documents of a single day. Is it possible he got a haircut somewhere between the two shots? His tan lines do not match the size and location of the book in the first image. These photographs prove to be anything but straightforward. As a statement of reflexivity, they demonstrate the ways in which the second degree is characterized foremost by distrust and dislocation.

The Vietnam War was popularly referred to as the "living room" war, a euphemism that itself problematizes the politics of proximity and the ways in which the spectacle of war abroad was witnessed from a second degree via media within the comforts of one's home in the United States. An important target for critique in the act of reengaging art and life was indeed the world in which aesthetic pleasure

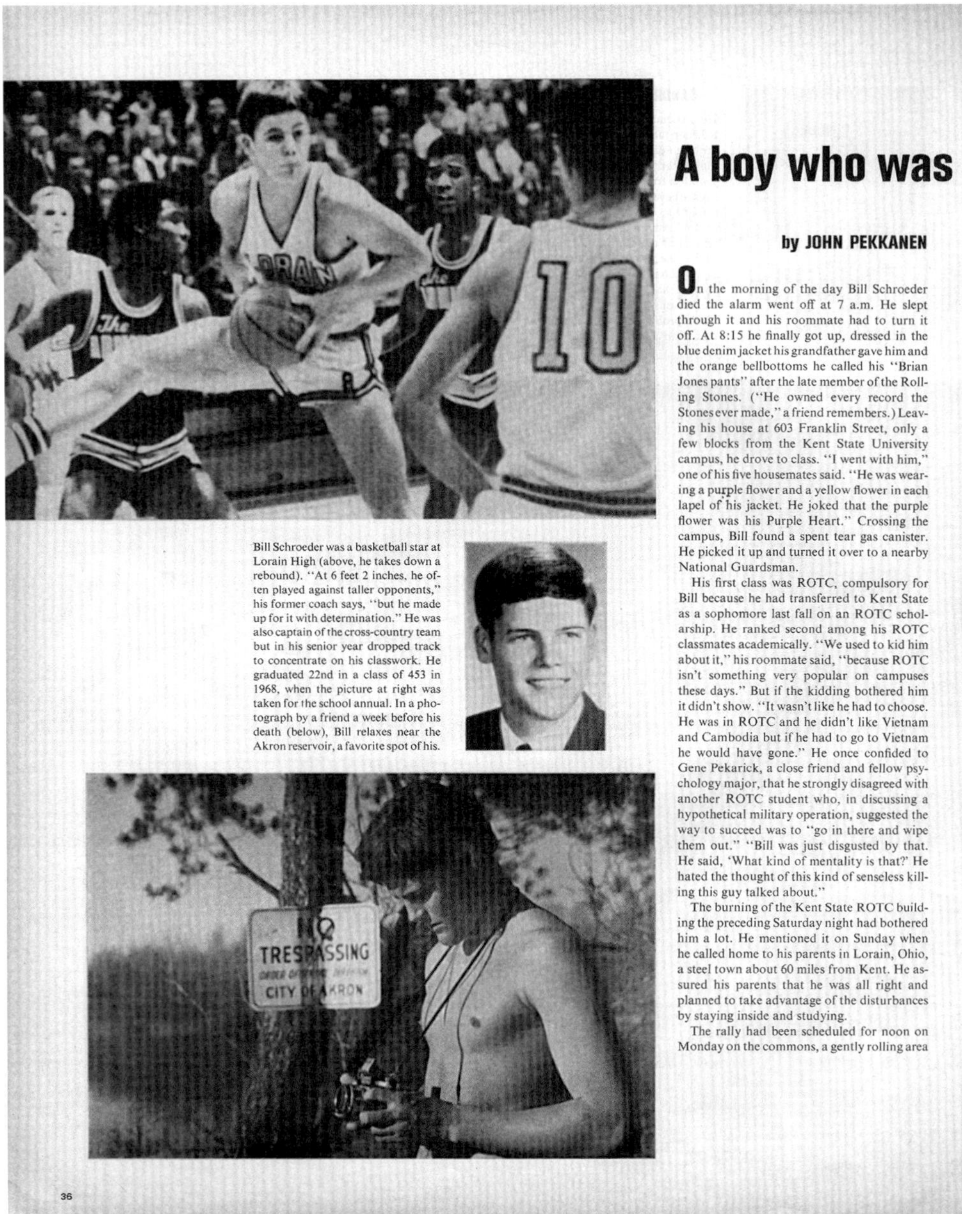

A boy who was

by JOHN PEKKANEN

On the morning of the day Bill Schroeder died the alarm went off at 7 a.m. He slept through it and his roommate had to turn it off. At 8:15 he finally got up, dressed in the blue denim jacket his grandfather gave him and the orange bellbottoms he called his "Brian Jones pants" after the late member of the Rolling Stones. ("He owned every record the Stones ever made," a friend remembers.) Leaving his house at 603 Franklin Street, only a few blocks from the Kent State University campus, he drove to class. "I went with him," one of his five housemates said. "He was wearing a purple flower and a yellow flower in each lapel of his jacket. He joked that the purple flower was his Purple Heart." Crossing the campus, Bill found a spent tear gas canister. He picked it up and turned it over to a nearby National Guardsman.

His first class was ROTC, compulsory for Bill because he had transferred to Kent State as a sophomore last fall on an ROTC scholarship. He ranked second among his ROTC classmates academically. "We used to kid him about it," his roommate said, "because ROTC isn't something very popular on campuses these days." But if the kidding bothered him it didn't show. "It wasn't like he had to choose. He was in ROTC and he didn't like Vietnam and Cambodia but if he had to go to Vietnam he would have gone." He once confided to Gene Pekarick, a close friend and fellow psychology major, that he strongly disagreed with another ROTC student who, in discussing a hypothetical military operation, suggested the way to succeed was to "go in there and wipe them out." "Bill was just disgusted by that. He said, 'What kind of mentality is that?' He hated the thought of this kind of senseless killing this guy talked about."

The burning of the Kent State ROTC building the preceding Saturday night had bothered him a lot. He mentioned it on Sunday when he called home to his parents in Lorain, Ohio, a steel town about 60 miles from Kent. He assured his parents that he was all right and planned to take advantage of the disturbances by staying inside and studying.

The rally had been scheduled for noon on Monday on the commons, a gently rolling area

Bill Schroeder was a basketball star at Lorain High (above, he takes down a rebound). "At 6 feet 2 inches, he often played against taller opponents," his former coach says, "but he made up for it with determination." He was also captain of the cross-country team but in his senior year dropped track to concentrate on his classwork. He graduated 22nd in a class of 453 in 1968, when the picture at right was taken for the school annual. In a photograph by a friend a week before his death (below), Bill relaxes near the Akron reservoir, a favorite spot of his.

36

Figure I.4. "A Boy Who Was Just 'There Watching It and Making Up His Mind,'" *Life* magazine, May 15, 1970, pages 36–37. Copyright 1970 TI Gotham Inc. All rights reserved. Reprinted/translated from *Life* and published with permission of TI Gotham Inc. Reproduction in any manner in any language in whole or in part without written permission is prohibited.

just 'there watching it and making up his mind'

now fresh with the burst of spring. Bill and Gene met after class and instead of going to lunch began walking to the rally. "He went because he was curious to see it. He wasn't a participant and he wasn't just a bystander. He was open-minded. He went there to observe."

As they moved toward the commons there was an edge of confrontation in the air, but no expectation of violence. Bill had earlier told his roommate that he didn't like the prospect of going to class under martial law. But as he and Gene walked past some Guardsmen, Gene said, "I hope none of those guys have itchy fingers," and it was Bill who reassured him. "Don't worry about it. They don't even have clips in their rifles."

They mingled in the rally, along with some 1,000 other students, most of whom shared their frame of mind—curious and a bit angry, but not outraged. "Nobody seems to understand," a student said later, "we just wanted the Guard off our campus. They were making everything worse." The metallic voice of the Guard bullhorn ordered the rally to disperse. Rights of assembly were suspended, it declared, authoritatively, anonymously. "A jeep came up toward us. They kept telling us to disperse. We just scattered and in the confusion I momentarily lost sight of Bill," Gene recalls. "The kids were strung out all over the area."

A cluster of students soon collected, shouting "Pigs off campus" at the Guard. Some of them, perhaps no more than 20, lobbed stones and the Guard responded with tear gas. Students hurled canisters back. The Guard ran out of tear gas and, confronted by a skirmish line of several hundred students, drew together to regroup. Bill was standing about 100 feet from the Guardsmen, between them and the main body of students, when the Guardsmen opened fire. According to Gene, Bill wasn't shouting at the Guard or throwing rocks at them.

Gene, like the others around him, hit the ground. "Some girls had fainted. I looked over and saw a girl lying on the ground. She wasn't moving. It looked like Allison [Allison Krause, one of the four students who died]. I didn't really know her but she went out with a guy down the hall from me. A beautiful, happy girl. Then my roommate came running down the hill shouting at me, 'Do you know who they shot?' I said I think they shot Allison. 'No. They shot your buddy.' I ran up the hill and three people were around Bill. A crowd had gathered and then people moved away to give him room. He was alive and was able to speak. He just said, 'Where's an ambulance?' His voice was weak, like a whisper. An ambulance was nearby but it took another injured student away. About 10 minutes later one came for Bill. As they put him on the stretcher, he moved his leg up to help them. When they drove away I didn't even think he was hurt that bad." Ten hours later the university news service issued a statement: "Schroeder, Wm. K., 19, sophomore, DEAD. Five minutes after arrival."

Tuesday morning, after the National Guard had ordered everyone off campus until further notice, Bill Schroeder's housemates on Franklin Street prepared to leave for home. A group of them came out on the front porch and refused to allow anyone to enter the house. "Don't use our names," one said. "Just say we were a family and one of us was killed."

One of them, who identified himself as Bill's roommate, had known him since junior high school in Lorain and lived a block from his home. Monday night he had gone to the county morgue to make a positive identification of Bill. "We did everything together. Took walks, played basketball. Bill was good at everything he tried. He had a mind, I mean a real mind." Their high school principal said the same. Bill had an A-minus average at Lorain Senior High School and had the highest rating in every attitude category from citizenship to attendance. At Kent State his average was B-plus. "He wanted to get into psychology," his roommate said. "He liked it here. We would spend a lot of nights together just talking, sometimes to 4 or 5 in the morning. He told us once that he really wanted to be a writer. He'd been writing poetry for the last few years but he'd always hide it."

The boy spoke haltingly, unable at times to control his trembling. "Make sure you say one thing if nothing else. Say that Bill was not throwing rocks or shouting at the Guardsmen. It would have never crossed his mind to do that. He was there watching it and making up his own mind about it and they shot him." Then Bill Schroeder's friends went back into the house and began packing his clothes. ■

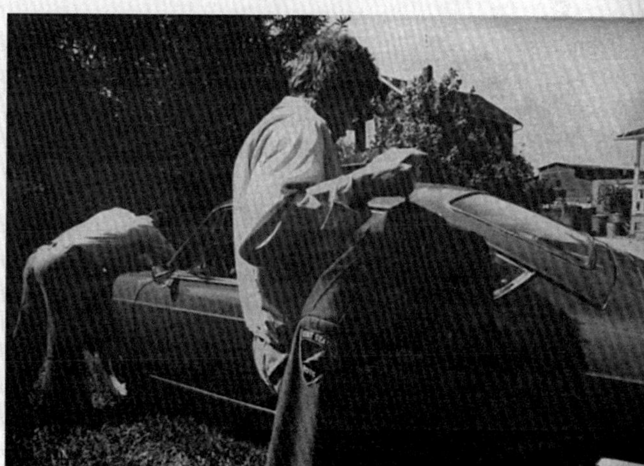

Clearing out Bill Schroeder's room, friends pack his basketball, cowboy hat and ROTC uniform into his car. The uniform went in the rear, just under the peace symbol on the window.

for its own sake came to be seen as an avoidance of, rather than a contribution to, understanding reality. As one critic put it, "In a world tossed by a tumult of cognitive reevaluations, from the Cultural Revolution in China to the Black Panther movement in Oakland, the bestowing of aesthetic pleasure in and by itself seemed less a contribution to reality than a distraction from it."[17] In the face of widespread skepticism and the incomprehensible continuation of the Vietnam War, there was a sense that neither art objects nor images could adequately contend with the reality of pervasive and escalating violence.

The challenge of combining radical politics with prescient aesthetic strategies thus posed a related dilemma. This difficulty partly accounts for the admittedly evasive political positioning in much art of the period.[18] As Tony Godfrey opined about American conceptual artists, "Why, if they were so politically motivated, is there so little direct reference in their works to the Vietnam War or the student riots in Paris in 1968?"[19] For me, this question contextually singes every work of conceptual art, blistering through some photographic works and smoldering beneath others.

Read as a statement about suspended contradictions, a way to materially and conceptually grapple with the anxieties of the moment, *Reading Position for Second Degree Burn* is a feat of endurance. It is simultaneously an investigation into duration exacerbated by its photographic information, which documents the boundaries of both temporal and physical stamina. The second degree can further be understood as a level of questioning—interrogation techniques that are not as intense as third degree but nevertheless mark the body. Following Marshall McLuhan's claim that all technologies are extensions of humans, "medium" here is not limited to the media of mass communication but expands to include media as inquisitive and experimental extensions of the human body. Medium as information—like medium as message—is on display. It points to the generally invisible side effects of technology, including the psychic and social adjustments its users and their society undergo when they adopt each new form. In part, this exemplifies Anne Rorimer's perspective on photography in relation to conceptual art, and the ways in which "the documentary dimension of a work can be enmeshed with its formal, material, and ideational realization."[20] The camera's ability to record any scene or scenario appearing in front of it fuses the performative with the photographic act, underscoring how documentary practices are often linked to photographic staging.

Through this critical lens, the very status of visuality and representation in conceptual art becomes contingent and contentious. Consider Robert Barry's *Inert Gas Series* (1969), for example, as an attempt to unsettle photographic determinism, challenge the photograph's documentary legibility, and revise accounts of conceptual art that attempt to relegate it to an art for art's sake autonomous sphere (Figure I.5). Certainly these issues were in the air at the cusp of the 1970s. They were among conceptual art's central contributions to resisting conventions and, by extension, ideologies associated with visibility; conceptual art practices opened a space of potentially productive ambivalence. I emphasize the words *potentially* and *ambivalence* in this formulation because many instances of conceptual art of course also ran the

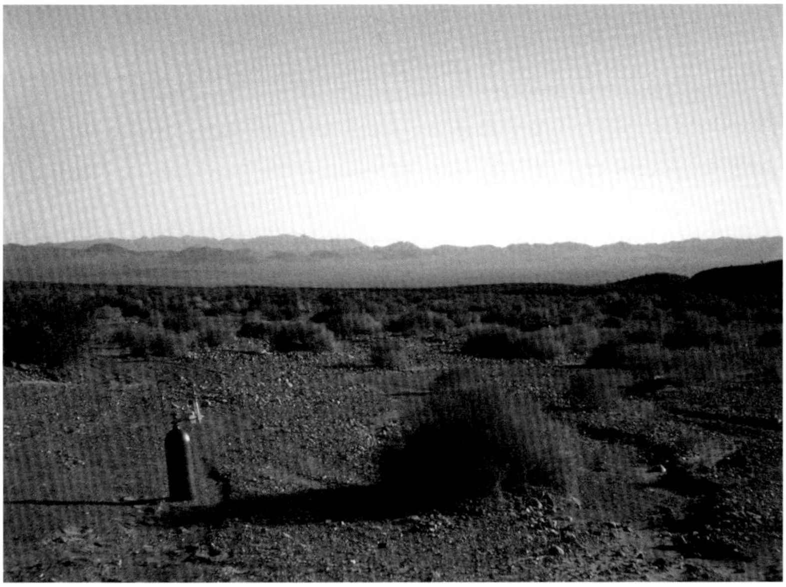

Figure I.5. Robert Barry, *Inert Gas Series: Helium; 2 cubic feet was returned to the atmosphere. Mojave desert, March 5, 1969*, 1969. Courtesy of the artist.

risk of being reinscribed within the narcissistic loop of modernist self-reflexivity. Only through the viewer's active reading can they become something more.

In early March 1969, Robert Barry performed *Inert Gas Series / Helium, Neon, Argon, Krypton, Xenon / From a Measured Volume to Indefinite Expansion* in remote desert locations in Southern California, by releasing various measured volumes of odorless, colorless inert gases into the atmosphere (including helium, hydrogen, neon, and krypton). Once released, the gases naturally expanded and dispersed. Barry then took a photograph to document and ostensibly prove that the action happened. The attendant pictures show inconspicuous expanses of space, unremarkable shrubbery, a blurry mountain range hovering in the background, and indistinct gravel in the fore. Noting the leap of faith it takes to believe these documents, Irene V. Small remarked on how these photographs function as the opposite of bodily evidence. Instead, they "display resolutely empty landscapes occasionally interrupted by a ruptured gas vessel to gesture to the material that had been released."[21] Moreover, despite the dominant claim to understand a project such as Barry's as definitively dematerialized, the artist cleverly subverts this misunderstanding through the emphatically visual and admittedly material means of photography. As Janet Kraynak summarized, through "a seemingly ironic gesture, the work entailed a philosophical and ontological question regarding the very nature of materiality."[22]

Beyond seeing these photographs as tongue-in-cheek plays on the limits of visibility, on what we cannot see despite the photographic evidence, these seemingly banal images of the Mojave Desert may offer something more complex and indecisive. For one thing, they bear a remarkable resemblance to—and seem to anticipate some of the problematics enmeshed in—the practice of documenting land art. For example, a work such as Walter de Maria's *Lightning Field* (1977) in New Mexico seems uncanny in this regard. De Maria's technocratically grandiose project, four hundred stainless steel rods gridded in the high desert, vanishes in front of the camera, becoming nearly imperceptible. That is, unless lightning strikes. This limitation of the photographic image as an effective vehicle to understand the piece, and even the artwork's marked dependence on conditions outside its own control, calls attention to what is actually caught in, and suggested by, the picture at hand. The photograph becomes a site/sight itself.[23] Consider Barry's qualifier, "Inert." In terms of gases, it describes a substance with a perceived lack of participation in chemical reactions. We might also think of an association to the notion of human inertia—as in apathy or inaction—the tendency to remain unchanged. The plainness of the photographs presented suggests as much. But if we consider the other valence of inertia in physics, denoting driven force and constant velocity, contentions and oppositions begin to surface about the photograph and the material contained therein. Though there may be a "perceived lack of participation," immersion and propulsion exist simultaneously.

For the cultural theorist Sianne Ngai, states of aesthetic ambivalence such as the cute, the zany, and the merely interesting productively expose the crucial and pervasive role contradiction plays under the "hypercommodified, intensively informated and networked, performance-driven conditions of late capitalism."[24] These states of ambivalence that avoid conclusive aesthetic judgment bear particular meaning for a consideration of conceptual art, when it is precisely the indefinite category of the "merely interesting" that so much art of the 1960s and 1970s grappled with. This vexation with being between states is nowhere more visible than in artwork that uses photography as its vehicle. Viewed in this light, Barry's title takes on new resonance and is perhaps suggestive of the potential of conceptual art more broadly: *From a Measured Volume to Indefinite Expansion.* Though frequently presented in photographic form as an objective statement of facts, conceptual art effectively problematized the very possibility of either objectivity or fact.

Sontag influentially acknowledged in the early 1970s the ways in which "the practice of photography is now identified with the idea that everything could be made interesting through the camera," simply by virtue of being chosen and photographed. Her damning conclusion was that "this quality of being interesting, like that of manifesting humanity, is an empty one."[25] Still, it bears asking, to what extent did a lack of decisive interest also result from the ever-growing ubiquity of reproduced images, and what are the limits of photographic interest on its own terms? Arguably, in part, "what makes photography uniquely powerful is its ability to express the difficulty—physically, psychologically, emotionally, and aesthetically—of the act of seeing."[26] I would add the act of conclusively understanding, let alone knowing, to the list. In this way, the photograph is indeed marked by its unavoidable contingency.

An analysis of the category of the merely interesting "indexes situations of suspended agency,"[27] in other words, equivocal affects that call attention to a lack of aesthetic power or impact. Oppenheim's *Reading Position for Second Degree Burn* promotes this kind of deferment and contingency. Furthermore, by virtue of their ambivalent ineffectuality, such works of art reveal social conflict through their state of indecision. While the merely interesting might be a weak judgment, it is nevertheless provocative to consider how the proliferation of artworks—characterized as both "mute and indicative" at this juncture—denies the wonder of categories such as beauty and the sublime, in favor of courting deliberate boredom. They also imply "that there is more to see than can be seen, that we have recognized something portentous but at the same time are not sure what it is."[28] Stage 2 in this epistemological sequence engenders a series of discursively powerful questions, including, again: why?

This book is an attempt to grapple with this question. In the following chapters, I analyze the use of photography by select American conceptual artists of the late 1960s and early 1970s in hopes of deciphering the ways in which—despite their frequently banal appearance—the artworks are neither autonomous nor neutral to their context, or to their documentary weight. Indeed, by degrees, each of these photographs marks the burn of its skeptical emergence. As photographs, they frustrate the desire to interpret their meanings as obvious or transparent—they affect a tone of distance while asking to be considered "close to the skin,"[29] and thereby offer a way to ply apart the complex ambivalence and upheaval of the period itself. Deeply enmeshed within the tumult of their moment, such images leave us pondering the indisputable impact and contingency of one's own reading position.

Documents of Doubt: The Photographic Conditions of Conceptual Art is the first single-author book-length study of the unique relationship between photography and conceptual art practices in the United States during the late 1960s. Although many scholars concur that photography became visible as the preeminent medium of contemporary art beginning in the late 1960s, there is little consensus or in-depth study as to how this came about or what is at stake. My aim is therefore to provide a much-needed assessment of the theoretical and aesthetic implications of this historical metamorphosis. I theorize "contingency" in my account in order to address the often contradictory, yet highly deliberate, uses of the medium of photography in and as conceptual art. Exploring early instances of conceptual art in this context, I focus on the intersecting dimensions of materiality, performativity, the social, and visuality, as they resonate specifically and formatively in photography. Taking cues from specific works of art, each chapter demonstrates an act of concentrated visual attention, and, through close readings, I argue for a critical reassessment of the ambivalence proffered by both the appearance and the content of much conceptual art. In so many cases, in ways sometimes subtle and other times absurdly overt, conceptual artists emphasized the gaps between appearance and reality, interrogated the status of the work of art, and engaged the photographic as a way to call attention to these concerns. From beneath the surface of the image or beyond the photograph's frame, the tumult of the Vietnam era—including its profound and irrevocable social, political, and visual effects—emerges repeatedly and is given new analysis in my study. In this way, my methodology is contextualist and, by extension, revisionist.

Why does photography emerge as a vital and disruptive tool for new art making in the 1960s, especially for a group of artists who had no particular background or training in photography? In varying ways, these artists performed conceptual explorations into the formal conditions and limits of photography, probing an aesthetic of indeterminacy, a complicated sense of temporality, and an interest in how meaning itself is created and disseminated. The ideology of capital "D" "Documentary" photography (understood traditionally as providing intelligible insight into significant moments), and the notion of the "document" (as reliable evidence), played central roles in this investigation of photographic meaning. For these and other reasons explored over the following chapters, conceptual art's epistemological questioning of the photograph continues to resonate in the present—as attempts to delineate and search for the possibility of "truth" and meaning persist—in an era overwhelmingly defined by hypermediation and visual anxiety.

During the 1960s and 1970s, photography was not yet firmly established as an artistic medium. Debates over what criteria could allow it to conform to modernist ideals despite its indexical reference to the world—versus how it could sidestep or even overturn the dominance of modernist aesthetics—characterize this period. Photography's ascendancy throughout the late twentieth century and its current privilege as a dominant art form derive partly from the central role it played in the practice of conceptual artists. For these artists, photography offered a discursive space and a way to problematize "documentary" assumptions. I am intent on how, since the late 1960s and early 1970s, artists have pressed and pulled the photograph's status as a document that invariably records the existence of something before the camera, as well as the often evasive difficulty of determining what that subject is. The impasse and occlusion created by the mutable material presence of the photographic object can perhaps be as valuable as the assumed alliance of information and clarity. Indeed, in suggesting an open-ended inquiry, conceptual artists' "motivated and arbitrary" use of photography may also be viewed as an anti-authoritarian gesture through its resistance to closure and an emphasis on contingency.[30]

At the outset of *Camera Lucida* (1980), in his personal quest to deduce "what Photography was 'in itself,'" Roland Barthes immediately marks the photograph's inevitable yet evasive contingency. In his estimation, this peculiar quality sets the photograph ontologically apart from all other images. Beyond noting that "the Photograph mechanically repeats what could never be repeated existentially," Barthes explains that "it is the absolute Particular, the sovereign Contingency, matte and somehow stupid, the *This* (this photograph, and not Photography)."[31] The photograph's idiosyncratic ability to assert its image as reality while remaining open to endless alterations in meaning through its relationship to the world outside the image manifests in all photographs. In this way, photography can be both disarming and unpredictable. The ways conceptual artists approached the photograph shares much in common with Barthes's view of contingency.

Conceptual artists were not the first to doubt the status of the "real" in photography or to investigate the medium's flexibility in an artistic context. Precedents in the photographic activities of the historic avant-garde, particularly in Dada and surrealism, were incredibly influential and play a key role in the narrative to follow. The work of artists such as Andy Warhol, Robert Rauschenberg, Robert Frank, and Walker Evans laid important groundwork for thinking through the photograph's social and aesthetic relation to everyday life. Issues of photographic mediation and materiality, as well as a complicated engagement with the dialectic of immediacy and deferment, recur across the work of these photographers. These precursors spurred conceptual artists to test the extent to which photography was (or was not), in Barthes's terms, "wholly ballasted by the contingency of which it is the weightless, transparent envelope."[32]

In reconsidering the uses of photography under the aegis of conceptual art in the late 1960s, I analyze photography's agile challenge to epistemological limits. I also examine how, despite persistent claims about the medium's imagined inherent indexicality, conceptual artists emphasized experience over exactitude and doubt in place of certainty. Moreover, I argue that photography was crucial to the very notion of "conceptual art." Focusing on the work of Mel Bochner, Bruce Nauman, Douglas Huebler, and John Baldessari, each chapter delves into the significant role of photography in the practice of these artists, and how their turn to photography at this historic juncture marked specific anxieties surrounding art making in the late 1960s. How is it, for example, that at the very moment dematerialization was proclaimed as the dominant mode of contemporary art, conceptual artists were proliferating the use of photography, a medium partly defined by its capacity for multiple reproduction and the possibilities of mass dissemination?[33] In fact, many artists at this time disavowed the role of photography as completely ancillary to the artwork itself. Yet it is precisely in this historical moment that photography was established as art in unprecedented, unforeseen, and enduring ways.

This book addresses the irreconcilable tension between dematerialization and materiality as one of the central paradoxes of photography in relation to, and as, conceptual art. Moreover, through close readings of select works of art, I demonstrate how the changes instantiated by artists at this sociopolitical juncture reveal stubborn beliefs in the photograph while taking the medium to task. Exploring conditions as varied as materiality, performativity, sociability, and visuality, conceptual artists reinvigorated the entwined fields of photographic history and art practice in ways that remain vital in the present. Acknowledging the many correlations between photography and conceptual art brings to light much larger implications. It attests to the ways photography irrevocably altered the fields of art and art history. Indeed, despite the fact that the history of photography often continues to be relegated to a subfield, I argue that the conditions photography brings to bear on viewership and imaging perforce compel all art historical accounts to thereafter also be photographic history.

Through photography, numerous conceptual artists destabilized the major systems of representation in the late sixties by accentuating the importance of ideation without renouncing the value of bodily experience. By making what were largely considered actions rather than objects, these conceptual artists used photography to register a statement against materialism and commodification. Doing so was also a way to investigate how aspects of the performative were essential to the notion of art and central to the pivot of photography. Ultimately, my critical consideration of the photographic conditions of conceptual art traces the movement away from the study of objects and toward a performance of effects in the late sixties. In this way, *Documents of Doubt* is as much an analysis of the photographic conditions of conceptual art as it is of the conceptual conditions of photography.

Doubt over the possibility of ever grasping the true nature of photography can be traced back to its elusive beginnings. Writing in the mid-nineteenth century, even the English inventor William Henry Fox Talbot could not deny the ontological and aesthetic ambiguity of the medium.[34] Despite his adamant ambition to fix the photographic image, Talbot noted in his book, *The Pencil of Nature*: "Though we may not be able to conjecture with any certainty what rank they [photographic images] may hereafter attain to as pictorial productions, they will surely find their own sphere of utility."[35] During the twentieth century, emboldened by the automatist aspects of the medium and the belief in the indexical function of photographic images, confidence was increasingly placed in the idea of the photograph as a neutral representation free from "the fallacies of the human hand."[36] One twist of conceptual art more than a century later was to use photography to counter and question this desire for reassurance. By challenging the notion of the photograph as self-evident, many conceptual artists highlighted not only what we do not know, or cannot know, but also how we might productively *unknow*. In a moment in which "truthiness" (to borrow a term from the comedian Stephen Colbert) is receiving renewed traction, and problematic pronouncements about the realities of living in an era of "post-truth" abound, the need to critically assess the slippery relationship between objective facts, personal beliefs, and visual appearances becomes all the more relevant.

Marcel Duchamp is of particular importance among the precursors to the photographic work of conceptual artists during the social, cultural, and political turmoil of the late 1960s. In part, this is because Duchamp's evocation of chance procedures and his problematizing of nominalist games recur in the work of numerous conceptual artists. It is also because Duchamp's readymades, and his specific conception of them based on analogies to photography, set the stage for thinking through the photographic conditions of conceptual art as well as the conceptual conditions of photography in ways that explicitly question context. Duchamp emphasized how the readymades "were mass produced and to be duplicated."[37] His comment highlights the photograph's kinship with the readymade, since both occupy an ambiguous place in relation to industrial production and reproduction and, by extension, capitalism and modernity.[38] This connection can be read as primarily acquisitive, linked to what Sontag called photography's role as a "defense against anxiety" by accumulating the world.[39] Thinking of photography in this way can be helpful in that it draws attention to some of its key social and political functions. What it misses, however, is the other side of the Duchampian coin and, ultimately, the real source of photography's potential for critique: to read photography beyond its acquisitive mode in order to seriously consider its inquisitive possibilities.

Duchamp's idea of the "snapshot effect" enables a productive affinity between a theory of photography and the practice of the readymade, as well as an entryway into the inquisitive consideration noted above. Recall how Duchamp described the readymade in his notes:

> Specifications for "Readymades" by planning for a moment to come (on such a day, such a date, such a minute), "*to inscribe* a readymade."—the readymade can later be looked for. (*with* all kinds of delays) The important thing is just this matter of timing, this snapshot effect, like a speech delivered on no matter what occasion but at such and such an hour.[40]

The mention of planning emphasizes ideation and touches on one of the central issues of making conceptual art. The echoes of this planning can be heard in Sol LeWitt's influential 1967 text, "Paragraphs on Conceptual Art": "When an artist uses a conceptual form of art, it means that all of the planning and decisions are made beforehand and the execution is a perfunctory affair. The idea becomes a machine that makes the art."[41] Duchamp's analogy to framing time, "a moment to come (on such a day, such a date, such a minute)," describes the apprehension or inscription of the image, a temporal condition that both the photograph and the readymade affect. Duchamp also marks the contingency of the frame that is peculiar and unexpected in the snapshot by his evocation of "with all kinds of delays)." This note suggests how even the instantaneous nature of the snapshot has contingency built in, and how the photograph, like the readymade, is never entirely fixed either temporally, spatially, or conceptually "no matter what." In her now-canonic reading of the "snapshot effect," Rosalind Krauss emphasizes the index as the key link between photography and the readymade.[42] I engage with Krauss's writing on this in more detail in chapter 2. For now, I find that instead of indexicality, what is more striking as a link between photography and the readymade, and thus conceptual art, is Duchamp's emphasis on delay and contingency. Grappling with the commonplace and the aesthetics of indifference, both the readymade and the photograph provoke a fundamental rethinking of the basic relationship between a sign and its referent in a mode that continuously delays any possibility of fixing meaning while pushing for the value of meaning despite its deliberate frustration.

Somewhat ironically, shortly after photography's invention in the nineteenth century, Charles Baudelaire estimated that it was precisely due to its "exactitude,"[43] however contemptible, that the masses would call photography art. In the twentieth century, many conceptual artists (following in the footsteps of surrealism) found photography's imprecise inexactitude its peculiar source of artfulness. Inexactitude and the intellectual seriousness of conceptual art demonstrate the ways such contradictory positions, as instantiated by photography, unhinge the conviction of any given position in aesthetic, political, and social terms.

In 1976 the critic Nancy Foote noted that "oddly enough, conceptual art has never been plagued with accusations that it belongs on photography's side of the tracks, *yet* the condition in which much of it could or would exist without photography is open to question. Photographs are crucial to the exposure (if not the making) of practically every manifestation of conceptual type art."[44] Foote's allusion to tracks, and the possible implication that photography resides on the wrong or rough side of the tracks, intrigues me. It is my proposition that renegade disruption, however subtle, forms a central characteristic of the legacies and practices of conceptual art, and is a crucial feature of photography itself. The continued prevalence of doubt as a vital attribute of, and photography as the principal medium of, contemporary art in the present makes the case all the more convincing: "If conceptual art lives on today it is not because of the transmittance of any orthodoxy" but because of "its aporias, mistakes and misrepresentations."[45] In the spirit of Bochner, we could add misunderstandings to this list. Photography and conceptual art compose a web of inseparable (though often elusive) interdependent supports. Articulating the unruly photographic conditions of conceptual art in the following chapters is therefore an attempt to grasp the radical exchange between a malleable medium and a mutable movement.

In the last two decades, a growing body of art historical writing has addressed issues in conceptualism, yet a scholarly absence remains.[46] Though artists, critics, and art historians have acknowledged visual, material, and theoretical contradictions within the history of conceptual art, few have followed through with sustained close readings of specific projects in order to mine the inconsistencies and the influential role of photography.[47] Jeff Wall, for example, in what has come to be one of the most significant texts on the historicization of conceptual art, let alone photoconceptualism, states that "many of conceptual art's essential achievements are either created in the form of photographs or are otherwise mediated by them."[48] I agree with Wall on this point. However, while he contends that "photography realized itself decisively as a modernist art in the experiments of the 1960s and 1970s," I argue, by contrast, that the significance of most uses of photography under the aegis of conceptual art is located precisely in its break from the purity of the modernist paradigm.

What Wall explains as the failure of conceptual art to rid itself of depiction and of "its ties with the Western picture,"[49] leading to the restoration of these categories in the 1970s, I understand as Wall's own blinding attachment to the aesthetic, an attachment that homogenizes the diverse and often-opposed strategies of conceptual art. This is a position that needs to be critiqued all the more strongly at present, especially in light of publications such as Michael Fried's *Why Photography Matters as Art as Never Before* (2008).[50] Fried seeks to affirm Wall's argument and reinstate his own theory of high modernist painting from *Art and Objecthood* (1967) as the inheritance of contemporary photographic practice. According to Fried, photography "matters as art" because of its intrinsically self-reflexive mechanism. In other words, as a medium it epitomizes the criteria of medium specificity that would, in Fried's words, "extricate the work from its entanglement in everyday contingency and indeterminacy."[51] However, neither Wall nor Fried adequately questions the paradoxical resistances photography performs.[52] This critical occlusion is yet another symptom of the modernist aversion to theatricality perpetually characterized by Fried. By contrast, my project highlights the unpredictable performativity of photography as a conceptual medium and as an artistic matter inextricably entangled with everyday contingency and indeterminacy.

My take on this nexus is much more akin to that of John Roberts, who, in his essay "Photography, Iconophobia, and the Ruins of Conceptual Art" (1997), argues that "photography was the means through which conceptual art realized its exit from modernist closure as practice."[53] If there is a failure in conceptual art, it can be productive and, in some cases, a deliberate failing at that. Moreover, the status of failure itself in conceptual art is indeterminate. By challenging Clement Greenberg's elision of self-criticism with self-certainty, I continue the argument put forth by Donald Kuspit: "Greenberg's quest for the grail of self-certainty fails not simply because it is false from the start, but because it is facile in its method. It handicaps the uncovering of uncertainty as a necessary if not sufficient condition for creation by giving art a historically readymade goal."[54]

It is precisely in the face of the ostentatious certainty and solemnity espoused by Greenbergian modernism and continued by the writings of Fried and Wall that Bochner, Huebler, Nauman, Baldessari, and other conceptual artists responded with ironic wit, brazen doubt, and often deliberate evasiveness. Among conceptual art's central epistemological critiques lay its multiple and disparate efforts to dissolve the autonomy of art. The use of photography by such artists intensified this critique, partly by radically altering artistic conditions of production and consumption, as I explain further, and by exploring the medium's palpable duplicity. The photographic conditions of conceptual art enact a postmodernist sensibility characterized in the literary theorist Ihab Hassan's words:

> "openness, heterodoxy, pluralism, eclecticism, randomness, revolt, deformation . . . ambiguity . . . perversion . . . unmaking, decreation, disintegration, deconstruction, decentrement, displacement, difference, discontinuity, disjunction, disappearance, decomposition, de-definition, demystification, detotalization, delegitimization."[55]

My study considers these attributes in varying and specific artistic projects of the Vietnam War era to demonstrate the expanded implications of such work and how the conditions of uncertainty and contingency mark both conceptual art and photography.

Low Resolution

Photography has been deemed revelatory since its invention. Well before nineteenth-century debates surrounding combination printing and its attendant accusations about the deceitful image, photography was praised as revealing what previously had been hidden from the human eye. This exposure had both aesthetic and scientific significance, purportedly allowing humans to understand the minutiae of movement and biological form, as well as to appreciate the beauty previously invisible in "the everyday." Investments in photography's essential veracity as a medium, as a kind of truth-sayer, exist at its inception and account partly for the late twentieth-century announcement that photography has been executed by the digital.

I argue, however, that skepticism rather than assurance is central to the photographic principle. It is the potential instability and uncertainty of the photograph that underscore its power. The historic moment that best displays this realization in terms of artistic practice is conceptual art of the late 1960s, during which an overlap between discourses of art and science were taken up, and the question of the "real" hinged on the aesthetic and the sociopolitical. The years 1966 to 1973 mark a moment in which many artists embraced photography's unique semiotic limbo as a way to productively challenge authority, disciplinary boundaries, and artistic autonomy. This was often achieved through subversive humor, leaving one with questions that, in provoking a new way of thinking, were infinitely more valuable. The artists' emphasis on aporetic thinking and the negation of finitude also points to the fact that if photography discloses any sense of truth, it nevertheless remains in flux and uncontained. Photography reveals a process of being with beginnings and endings that continuously remain uncertain, delayed, and unfixed.

This book offers both an analytic and philosophical questioning of how the photograph's epistemological and ontological challenges manifest within specific conceptual art practices, and how this juncture functions as a defining moment in the larger understanding of the photograph in contemporary art. Pivoting on the discrepancy between what we "know" and what we perceive, I engage one of the essential problematics of photographic documentation. In the context of 1960s minimalism, objectivity was paramount. The pervasive hope was that creating a work that was anti-illusionistic and uninflected would sidestep the pitfalls of subjectivity. In similar terms, many conceptual artists claimed the photographic medium as literal, direct, transparent, and ultimately unmediated. In many unexpected ways, however, the turn to photography upended the notion of objectivity. The photograph's unavoidable links to perspectival manipulation and the distortion of the lens, for example, as well as the troubling gaps between the real and representation, obstinately interfered with fantasies of so-called pure information. Indeed, as Robert Smithson explained, as opposed to direct experience, photography inevitably altered our ability to perceive without it: "I think, perhaps ever since the invention of the photograph, we've seen the world *through* photographs and not the other way around."[56]

The many-layered and acutely paradoxical promise of photography as an evidentiary practice is one of the many productive conundrums of early conceptual art. Evoking photography as both contingent and excessive, the medium becomes an inassimilable eruption in logical thinking. Because the photograph has no single temporality, it is figured as a space of resistance to science, and to traditional concepts of art, logic, and progress, not simply in imaginary terms but in fundamentally ontological ones. The photograph's complex temporality contributes to its essential irrationality and leads to doubt partly because of the impossible desires for presence and certainty that are repeatedly projected onto the photograph.

Photography has puzzled many. While Barthes remarked that "because of its indexical condition, its status as a physical trace of its referent, the photograph is, of course, intrinsically documentarian, possessed with a unique evidential power: 'the Photograph's essence is to ratify what it represents.'"[57] He complicated the issue in the next breath by admitting the insecurity of his first proposition, stating that though "the Photograph never lies," nevertheless "it can lie as to the meaning of the thing, being by nature tendentious."[58] Barthes's comment on the tendentious aspect of the photograph can productively be connected to Sigmund Freud's writings on humor and the human negotiation of irrationality.[59] The influential Austrian psychoanalyst's definition of a "tendentious joke" in opposition to the "innocent joke" demonstrates striking affinities with the irrational underpinnings of the photograph. A "tendentious joke," according to Freud, is a joke that displaces some form of aggression and seeks to fulfill a repressed urge. In other words, "tendentious jokes safely give voice to what cannot be spoken directly out loud," and "as displacement mechanisms, tendentious jokes function as a safety valve for aggression."[60] The photograph as a displacement mechanism is analyzed at length throughout the following pages and often in conjunction with the device of humor as a way to disrupt the security of rational thinking and commonplace conventions.

As previously mentioned, one of the central claims of early conceptual art was its insistence on "dematerialization," despite its intense reliance on the material and materiality of photography. Yet another way to discuss conceptual art during the sixties and seventies was as "anti-object art." The discourse of anti-object art was a proposition surrounding the problems of objectivity, an attempt to find the place of the subject within the social while confounding presumptions of scientific objectivity. The claims made for anti-object art revealingly parallel a fundamental reformulation of the sculptural object. Ultimately, I interrogate photography and conceptual art's joint contribution to this redefinition and the expansion of the field of possibility within art historical discourse, art criticism, and emergent artistic practices. I investigate the ways in which the emphasis on meaning making is placed onto the spectator as active participant, particularly concerning both the nature and the culture of knowledge. Each artist's work under consideration here is put in historical context, not simply in terms of the art world, emergent contemporaneous discourses of art history, and the history of photography, but also in relation to the integral political and social events of its time.

A radical shift occurs in the late 1960s, when a number of "minimal" artists, including Robert Morris, Huebler, Nauman, Oppenheim, and Bochner, turn to photography, a medium inextricably linked to the logic of both the icon and the index. This goes directly against the minimalist demand that art be anti-iconic and antirepresentational. These artists' documents enact an opening of dialogues about the role of the object and of phenomenology that were not considerations of other photographers of the time. Through a wide array of approaches, each of these practitioners drew strategic attention to the politics embedded in constructs of representation and interrogated photographs "as an ideological function to critique."[61] This was a way to tactically confront the cultural confinement described by Smithson as the context of living within the unrelieved social crisis that plagued the late 1960s through to the mid-1970s.[62] *Documents of Doubt* is therefore an argument against reading the uses of photography in conceptual art as an extension of high modernist logic. This book demonstrates that these particular photographs are defined by their insistence on aporias and even misrepresentations within established expectations for art and visual culture. Though conceptual art has no stable set of positions, I argue for conceptual photography's critical impact by considering photographic rupture as a strategy for confronting conventional ways of looking, framing, and depicting that were increasingly understood as orchestrating systems of hegemonic control.

The political persists. Even when works of art seem disconnected from worldly realities, or when artists seem to turn away from the pressing issues of the day, it is remarkable how the political nevertheless permeates. In her precise and persuasive account of artistic labor in the work of artists including Carl Andre, Robert Morris, Lucy Lippard, and Hans Haacke, Julia Bryan-Wilson notes the striking lack of direct reference to the conflict in Vietnam in much American art of the time and how, "although adversarial politics were frequently made palpable in the art of this era, those politics could also be veiled or difficult to decipher." Even in "forms not legibly antiwar in any conventional way," Bryan-Wilson demonstrates, this apparent absence can be mined in important critical ways.[63] My approach here is inspired by such scholarship. While strains of conceptualism were indeed pointedly political—including the work of Fred Lonidier, Adrian Piper, Martha Rosler, Allan Sekula, and numerous others—further forms of social and political engagement were being investigated in conspicuous and inconspicuous ways.

Remarkably, amid the volatility of 1960s America, a significant body of conceptual art emerges that appears blank-faced, indifferent, and even apathetic. Reading these works anew as cyphers of their context, understood with and against the tensions of their time rather than apart from them, reveals more than initially meets the eye. Widespread acceptance of one of conceptual art's dominant narratives—that the idea is always more important than the object or the image—has led too many art historians to neglect the act of looking closely at the artwork itself. Turning our attention toward the objects and images of conceptual art thus rewards by expanding our understandings of the ideas that were indeed at stake.

That said, recent thematic and monographic studies of conceptual art have contributed to a more expansive understanding of artistic practices of the late 1960s. In addition to Alexander Alberro's *Conceptual Art and the Politics of Publicity* (2003) and Bryan-Wilson's *Art Workers: Radical Practice in the Vietnam War Era* (2011), in particular, I want to underscore the contribution of Liz Kotz's *Words to Be Looked At: Language in 1960s Art* (2007) and Frazer Ward's *No Innocent Bystanders: Performance Art and Audience* (2012).[64] Though these scholarly works do not take up photography specifically as a subject of inquiry, each offers an insightful account of art in the wake of late-sixties social transformations in ways that have informed my own thinking on the matter.

Two recent publications similarly attest to the importance of my area of study and the need to critically revisit the uses of photography in the late twentieth century. These are Joshua Shannon's *The Recording Machine: Art and Fact during the Cold War* (2017) and Kate Palmer Albers's *Uncertain Histories: Accumulation, Inaccessibility, and Doubt in Contemporary Photography* (2015).[65] Emphasizing the concept of factualism, Shannon presents a compelling account of how photography and other visual arts including painting and land art were altered by their engagement with realism around 1968. Though Shannon and I share an interest in analyzing the new attention given to surface appearances during the Cold War era, my study focuses explicitly on photography under the aegis of conceptualism as a distinct move away from the culture of fact and toward multivalent contingency. Perhaps closer to my project thematically is Albers's *Uncertain Histories,* which discusses the aesthetics of doubt and its relation to photography in particular. Though Albers's argument does not exclusively frame this element in terms of conceptual art practices, but rather with regard to artistic projects that use accumulation and archives as a means to question the way histories are collected and understood, it nevertheless resonates with my commitment to recognizing the importance of uncertainty as a productive and critical artistic category.

Documents of Doubt makes no claim to a comprehensive history. Indeed, the very ambition to do such a thing runs counter to my central argument. And though there are other artists whose practices could amply be thought through in relation to the questions posed across the chapters that follow, the four central artists chosen here were selected for the specific, and often peculiarly, rich, multivalent, and problem-driven case studies they proffer. Though they may seem in some ways to be the usual suspects, all four being white male artists with well-established narratives surrounding their work and its reception, I believe that my approach in these pages suggests new and unexpected connections. A lack of resolution and ultimate contingency marks each artist's art practice, and I explore these facets in depth. Despite the privileged position of Bochner, Nauman, Huebler, and Baldessari in the art history of the period, criticality and contextual questioning are oddly absent in much writing about them. In many instances, their work has been taken as a given. Against such static views, in a near analogy with the photograph, I suggest ways to rethink their fixity and pry further into their overlooked complexities. As mentioned earlier, through a close analysis of a single artist's work in the moment of the late-sixties United States, each chapter engages a particular photographic condition, moving sequentially through issues of materiality, performance, the social, and visuality.

Beginning with the work of Bochner in chapter 1, "Material Witness: Mel Bochner Takes Photographic Measures," I examine the transient reality of photographed objects and photographic objects, particularly as concerns their material life. Analyzing the indexical function of photography and questioning normative frames of art segue into how Bochner investigated the ideal of measurement as an objective standard through analogy with the photograph. Bochner's experiments with photography were indeed short-lived, yet their material and theoretical implications continue to resonate in the world of contemporary art practices, particularly in the ways they propose a corporeal investigation of photography that is vital, unpredictable, and indecisive. I chart Bochner's move from minimalism to conceptual practice specifically through photography. What began as a desire for order became the systematic undoing and confounding of all order, as Bochner realized the degree to which he could not control the photographic object. Stating emphatically, "I realized that the physicality of the objects I was making interested me less than the types of order I was imposing," Bochner crosses a trajectory from materialism through conceptualism that ultimately abrogates modernist rule.[66] Tracing his critical engagement with the duplicity of photography from *Surface Dis/Tension* (1968) and *36 Photographs and 12 Diagrams* (1966) to *Misunderstandings (A Theory of Photography)* (1967–70), I seek to systematically unpack Bochner's claims for photography and art more broadly while working through the philosophical questions they jointly pose. Bochner had other people take many of his photographs for him, as did many of his peers. This decision signals yet another challenge to long-established traditions of the hand of the artist and of technē. Bochner initially saw photography as a mode of "objective" creation, as a means toward scientific neutrality. I consider the influence of scientific discourse, bureaucratic language, and other pseudo-empirical systems in Bochner's early photographs, underscoring their significant impact on the proliferation and meaning of conceptual art at this time.

Like Bochner's, Nauman's use of photography was also brief, yet those early photographic experiments shed light on the artist's later projects while expanding the paradigm of what conceptual art is and what a photograph might be. Chapter 2, "Pressing the Point: Bruce Nauman Performs with and against the Frame," discusses the multiple ways in which Nauman engaged photography as a way to analytically, conceptually, and aesthetically accentuate the theatrical dimension of the work of art, making literal situations not only self-reflexive but also representationally subversive. Playful images such as *Bound to Fail* or *Self Portrait as Fountain* (1966–67/1970) pose serious artistic and intellectual questions under the guise of humorous scenarios. Through a close reading of photographs from 1966 to 1970, I argue that Nauman contributed to the experimental framework of performance art at a pivotal historic moment in order to take the trace, otherwise known as the index, to task, thereby disavowing the dominant discourse of conceptual art. As mentioned above, though conceptualism was very much concerned with self-reflexivity, it was not associated with medium specificity in the ways heralded by modernism. Rather, by using an intermedia approach, Nauman's evocation of bodily experience under the rubric of photoconceptualism ultimately denies the vital "dematerialization" of the work of art announced by much conceptual art—and by Lucy Lippard's early reading of conceptual art—by contrast insisting on the essential corporeality of conceptualism.[67] Nauman's prescience calls attention to the difficult relationship between social reality and the work of art, and the role of photographic mediation in its semblance and dissemblance.

In chapter 3, "Everyone Who Is Anyone: Douglas Huebler and the Social Capacity of Photography," I undertake an in-depth analysis of photography as a network of communication that not only reflects but also shapes sociopolitical and cultural boundaries. Though photography was the most visible material manifestation of conceptual art in the late 1960s and early 1970s, the majority of conceptual practitioners nevertheless denied the role of the medium on the work itself. Instead, skeptics wrote photography off as a means rather than an end, as a transparent document of the "dematerialized" work rather than the work itself. Huebler's photographs poignantly register the anxiety surrounding this misperception by deliberately intervening into the pivotal role of photography not simply in conceptual art but in social and economic ideology more broadly. Huebler notes the deceptive transparency of photography's claim to truth-value through strategic investigations of objectivity, portraiture, and mapping.

In effect, Huebler used photography to systematically unravel systems. For example, his *Variable Piece #70: 1971 (In Process) Global* (1971), with the stated intention "to photographically document . . . the existence of everyone alive," played on the humanistic and hegemonic desires embedded in the instantaneity and apparent objectivity of the photographic image while exposing the failures of the medium's democratic ideals. Proposals such as his "anti-documentary documentary" highlight the double negative process that formulates his practice. Importantly, Huebler's project cleverly shifts the emphasis from photography's acquisitive capacity to its inquisitive potential, using accumulation itself as one of his key strategies. Addressing what Siegfried Kracauer described in the 1920s as the "blizzard," the "flood," and the "assault" of mass media photographs, Huebler similarly invests the manic omnipresence of the photograph in the 1960s and 1970s with redemptive potential.[68] Kracauer's thesis, like Huebler's, is based on a paradox. Writing that "in the illustrated magazines, people see the very world that the illustrated magazines prevent them from perceiving,"[69] Kracauer suggests that seeing is not the same as being critically conscious of what one sees, and that somehow through the overaccumulation of photographs, a radical recognition of overrationalized society could and would occur. This chapter is a close reading of Huebler's practice both in the face of and alongside select moments in the history of photography, including the infamous

Family of Man exhibition (1955), in order to interrogate the place of the subject in the social within the established criteria of documentary and art photography during this critical historical juncture. It extends my argument against popular histories of conceptual art's dematerialization and photography's transparency.

In his review of Seth Siegelaub's groundbreaking *January 5–31, 1969* conceptual art exhibition, Gregory Battcock wrote, "There's nothing to see, and that's why it's great." Assumptions about what it means to be "visible" hound conceptual art practice, its perception, and its historicization. Chapter 4, "This Is Not to Be Looked At: John Baldessari and Photography's Insistent Visuality," explores this fraught dynamic and questions the ideologies of "seeing" as they were engaged by Baldessari. Violence is omnipresent in Baldessari's practice. Sometimes it is tacit, sometimes repressed, but nevertheless always there. With this undercurrent in view, I assess the condition of visuality in Baldessari's use of the photographic in relation to contemporaneous social and political events, and aesthetic conventions. Though there is a popular desire to read Baldessari exclusively from a crowd-pleasing perspective (the title of his Los Angeles County Museum of Art / Metropolitan Museum of Art retrospective in 2011 was, after all, *Pure Beauty*), I excavate his works for something more complex if insidious, particularly in the ways they grapple with the construction of, and injunctions against, the act of looking. In addition to weighing the stakes of visuality in political terms, chapter 4 also addresses one of the most significant yet least explored antinomies in the legacies of photoconceptualism: the tension between subversive humor and the notion of a constrained and analytic approach. Though these categories are not aesthetically or philosophically exclusive, they have nevertheless been pitted against each other as contradictory, in a manner that parallels the theorization of photography as a mediator either of authorial control or of artistic agency since the 1960s. The tendency to regard Baldessari's artwork as an amusing one-liner is reassessed here under the premise that there is indeed more than meets the eye. Nearly all of Baldessari's photoworks pivot on ruptures in logic and gaps in legibility, using photography to suggest wholeness yet expose its limits and unknowns, thereby serving as a comic reversal of Joseph Kosuth's declaration that the purest definition of conceptual art is its investigation into the foundations of the "art" concept, and that humor has no place in "serious" art. This chapter seeks to productively reveal the playful seriousness of humor in photoconceptualism and to carefully consider the implications of visuality in relation to visibility and representation.

Documents of Doubt analyzes conceptual photography as a network of communication that not only reflected but also shaped sociopolitical and cultural boundaries. Throughout the book I acknowledge and investigate conceptual photography's significant movement away from a consideration of objects and toward a performance of effects, away from thinking about products and toward thinking about processes. Conceptual art emerged in the late 1960s as the first global art movement, and the first art movement in which photography took center stage. This is not a coincidence.

The broadening of artistic definitions and boundaries at this time, and the various challenges to aesthetic preconceptions and theoretical models, were inextricably connected to a new emphasis on photography. Moreover, the movement's protagonists consisted of a generation of artists considerably altered by communication systems and the increased mobility of people and images, along with the disorienting sense of contingency that comes along with such displacement and dispersion.[70]

One
Material Witness
Mel Bochner Takes Photographic Measures

Weathered and worn, crumpled and creviced, Mel Bochner's *Surface Dis/Tension* (1968) confronts the viewer foremost as an object in space (Figure 1.1). Hung from the wall, it looks like a segmented topographic map, torn from its source, disorienting rather than directing. Far from a specific object in Donald Judd's sense, this work oozes with ambivalence. Posed as a black-and-white investigation of the grid, both in structure and in ideology, Bochner's manipulation of the photographic print takes on a life of its own. Just under six square feet, the scale is corporeal. That this is, in fact, a photograph, albeit mounted on a board cut to its contours and presented in sculptural form, suggests the many layers of contradiction to be pulled apart. In the undulating lines of this shaped silhouette, we have a close-up, replete with a subtle surfeit of detail.

The epidermis of photography preoccupied Bochner in the late 1960s in ways that were both physical and conceptual. The artist confesses, however, that it was seemingly without his own volition that he plunged into the medium, citing that his conceptual practice had "become about photography without wanting it to."[1] *Surface Dis/Tension* tenders a revealing example of the artist's hypnotic interest in

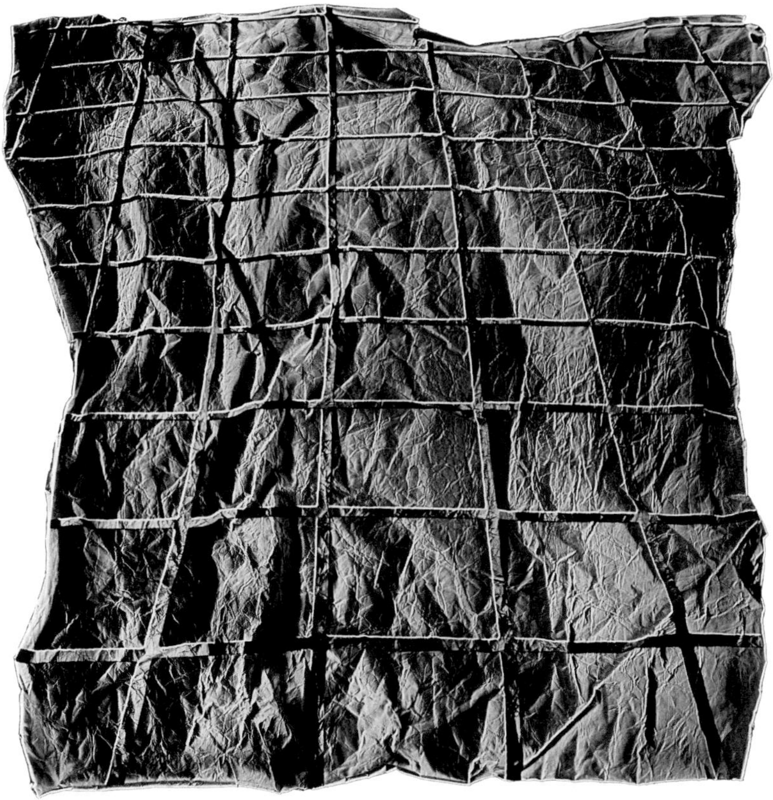

Figure 1.1. Mel Bochner, *Surface Dis/Tension*, 1968. Silhouetted gelatin silver print mounted on board, 72 × 68 inches. Courtesy of the artist.

the medium's vitality, its resistance, and its permeability. Bochner began by soaking an earlier work in water, his photograph *Perspective: One Point (Positive)* (1967) (a picture of a rigidly taped-off grid atop a table). The photograph remained immersed until the top layer of silver salts could be delicately removed from the dissolved paper support. Afterward, this fragile "surface" was hung to dry on a line, absorbing various traces of its own pliancy in the process. Bochner then rephotographed this veil of his earlier photograph, or what Scott Rothkopf has insightfully referred to as its "flayed skin."[2] This was followed by printing the image anew, as both a positive and a negative on the same piece of paper, stratifying iteration upon iteration. By slightly shifting the position of the paper in the middle of the two-part printing process, Bochner interrupted the photograph's coherence and cohesiveness yet again, and achieved a look of high-contrast solarization, giving the surface its textured appearance.[3] The furrowed perspectives of *Surface Dis/Tension* expose the contingency of the membrane of the photograph itself. Bochner recounts that "they were the first place where I thought of acting on the photograph as an object which bore no relationship to something which took place outside the photograph."[4] In this way, Bochner combined a dismantling of academic linear perspective with the deconstruction of the physical body of the photograph, calling attention to how dependent these structures are on outside support for their credibility, let alone legibility. Somewhat unintentionally, he also evoked a series of distended meanings embedded in photography that would prove formative for his later experiments in conceptual art, as well as for other artists working in a similar vein, including Ellen Carey, Walead Beshty, Eileen Quinlan, and James Welling, to name only a few.

The present chapter examines Bochner's experiments with photography in the late 1960s as a way to think through the material life of conceptual photography.

From the tension between photography's illusionism and minimalism's physicality to the contradictory poles of opacity and transparence, Bochner delved deeply into the many permutations embodied by photography. Though the window of time the artist dedicated to the medium was brief, it sheds significant light on the ontology of photographic images and the discursive roles they played as potential evidence in art and mass culture in the United States at this time. After addressing Bochner's early use of photocopies, I analyze select examples of photographic thinking and photographic embodiment, finally arriving at his infamous *Misunderstandings (A Theory of Photography)* (1967–70). Photography, like language and paint, Bochner's work reminds us, is inevitably a nontransparent form: it relies on a shared or public discourse to be read; it retains inherent opacities. More than a hermeneutic, interpretive contest over different meanings, Bochner's measured approach exposes a contest within photography over the very possibility of meaning itself.

Visible Things on Paper

Though many conceptual artists initially turned to photographic reproduction in the late 1960s as a way to fulfill an ambition for direct information via neutral recording, such aspirations inevitably failed. Photography fulfilled neither Lucy Lippard's notion of dematerialization nor the utopian promise of "demediatized" communication proposed by Luis Camnitzer. For Camnitzer, "demediatization" was a neologism used to mark the ways conceptual artists strove to "send messages through no-loss information systems."[5] Despite the high hopes of many conceptualists for direct and comprehensive information, however, the role of media in art and the world more broadly became only increasingly complex, if inconspicuous, and thus more difficult to assess. Any information (visual, textual, or otherwise) that passed through media inevitably experienced losses and gains. Nevertheless, the implications of this dematerialized and demediatized desire and their correlative disappointments have significant relevance to the ways photography influenced conceptual practice. This chapter begins by charting the shift from minimalism to conceptual art at this juncture and then exploring the lingering place of phenomenological considerations within reproducible media. By analyzing the role of reproducibility, display, and mediatization, I argue for the crucial and inescapable *lack* of immediacy or wholeness generated by conceptual approaches and suggest ways in which such strategies continue to influence media studies and contemporary art. A deeper understanding of the contradictions of immediacy and physicality, as well as the ways they are built into photography, and by extension conceptual art, will lay the groundwork for the discussion of Bochner's early experiments with photography.

The year 1966 marked the ascendance of minimalist art in New York. Judd's first exhibition opened at the Leo Castelli Gallery, Sol LeWitt premiered his now-famous white cubic lattices at the Dwan Gallery, and Carl Andre debuted *Equivalents I–VIII* at Tibor de Nagy Gallery, his first "brick show." Works of art that would become monolithic signatures of the movement were seen for the first time. Concurrently, numerous large-scale group exhibitions attempted to consolidate the minimalist zeitgeist and raise essential questions about the nature of three-dimensional art. We have, for example, *Art in Process: The Visual Development of a Structure* at Finch College, the group show *10* also at the Dwan Gallery, and, the most critically influential of all, the Jewish Museum's pivotal *Primary Structures: Younger American and British Sculptors* exhibition. Curated by Kynaston McShine, *Primary Structures* received extensive coverage in both *Newsweek* and *Life,* thereby bringing minimalist art to the larger public's attention. These artists were, according to McShine, "impelled to test primary definitions and basic aesthetic issues."[6] Late 1966 is of course also the year that has been invoked repeatedly as the touchstone for the emergence of another key movement of the late twentieth century—namely, conceptual art and its watershed exploration of the effects of two-dimensional reproduction and the transmission of information. Though these two movements have been pitted against each other in some accounts, or understood as a progression or lineage by others, in fact the spaces in which they overlap are most compelling. Seen together, minimalism and conceptualism provoke important questions about how seriality, repetition, and reproduction formed a shared ethos.

Not coincidentally, the emergence of conceptual art is frequently anchored to a particular exhibition in 1966 (Figures 1.2, 1.3). Acknowledged by Benjamin H. D. Buchloh as "probably the first truly conceptual exhibition (both in terms of materials being exhibited and in terms of presentational style)," this exhibition paradigmatically demonstrates how minimalism and conceptual art wove together.[7] I am referring to *Working Drawings and Other Visible Things on Paper Not Necessarily Meant to Be Viewed as Art,* organized by Bochner at the School of the Visual Arts, New York, and presented between December 2 and December 23 of that decisive year. On this occasion, Bochner compiled and photocopied one hundred pages of studio notes, working drawings, diagrams by artists including Eva Hesse, Dan Flavin, LeWitt, John Cage, Judd, and others, as well as pages from *Scientific American,* notations from serial music compositions, mathematical calculations, and other "paraphernalia of the production process," shown as photocopies of the "originals."[8] Bochner made four copies of each photocopied page before sorting the information into four separate binders so that each featured four identical sets of one hundred photocopies. Each binder was then placed on an individual pedestal in the gallery, lined up in an even row.[9]

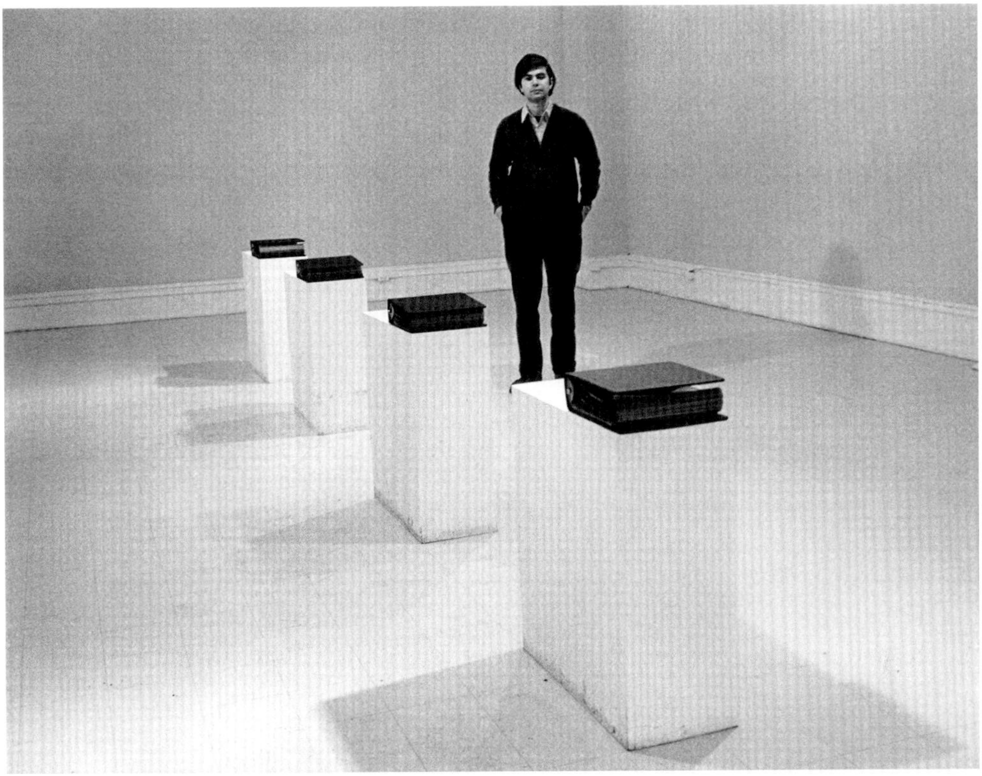

Figure 1.2. *Working Drawings and Other Visible Things on Paper Not Necessarily Meant to Be Viewed as Art,* installation view. Organized by Mel Bochner at the School of the Visual Arts, New York, December 2–23, 1966. Four identical loose-leaf notebooks, each with one hundred xerox copies of studio notes, working drawings, and diagrams collected and xeroxed by the artist, displayed on four sculpture stands; size determined by installation. Collection of Museum of Modern Art, New York. Courtesy of the artist.

Among the many iconic images of art in the late sixties, the installation views of this exhibition stand out. The photographs document and have variably shaped the collective memory and proceeding historicization of this transitional moment in late-sixties American art. Crucially, *Working Drawings* proposed a dynamic model of conceptual art based foremost in "process" and, by extension, emphasizing the "development" of an idea.[10] Echoing LeWitt's statement that "in conceptual art the idea or concept is the most important aspect of the work,"[11] Bochner's exhibition highlighted "planning and decisions." Importantly, *Working Drawings,* though not explicitly concerned with photography, nevertheless points to a central kinship with photography, perhaps suggesting that LeWitt's "idea [that] becomes a machine that makes the art" might be a camera.[12] With the seemingly simple gesture of photocopying, Bochner marked the photographic processes of documentation, reproduction, repetition, and seriality at the genesis of conceptual art.

Without money to frame the drawings, Bochner resorted instead to mechanical reproduction, using a photocopy machine in the art history department to reduce or

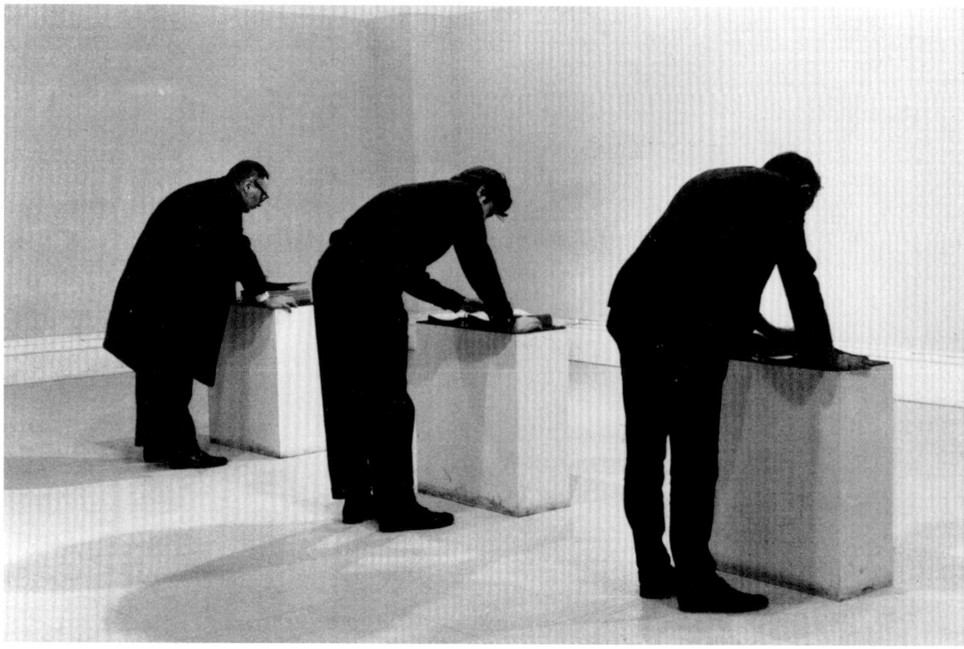

Figure 1.3. *Working Drawings and Other Visible Things on Paper Not Necessarily Meant to Be Viewed as Art,* installation view. Organized by Mel Bochner at the School of the Visual Arts, New York, December 2–23, 1966. Four identical loose-leaf notebooks, each with one hundred xerox copies of studio notes, working drawings, and diagrams collected and xeroxed by the artist, displayed on four sculpture stands; size determined by installation. Collection of Museum of Modern Art, New York. Courtesy of the artist.

enlarge the drawings to scale as a way to create a uniform collection of copies. This act had no art world precedent before 1966. Seth Siegelaub's famed exhibition *The Xerox Book,* for example, did not take place until 1968. Since then, however, the plain presentation of *Working Drawings* has become ubiquitous in the world of contemporary art, even spurring replica exhibitions and multiple homages, in such disparate locations as Estonia, throughout Germany, and the United States. In Bochner's "original" gesture, four copies of the bound volume were presented, each mounted on one of four white plinths that were table height and arranged in a straight row, not haphazardly resembling an installation of minimalist art, though admittedly something more like four I-beams as opposed to Robert Morris's famed three *L-Beams* (1965).

The height of the pedestal itself engaged with phenomenological experience and arguably positioned the viewer in a mode of engaged deliberation. Specifically, the viewer had to hunch over to see the piece, thereby explicitly involving the individual body's physical interaction in this project seemingly intended for the "conceptual" mind. The distance between viewer and work would become foregrounded, as would the inevitably embodied experience of art. This awareness intentionally denies the viewer comfortable mastery of the work. As opposed to the modernist pleasure suggested famously by Henri Matisse's early twentieth-century ideal of art as "something like a good armchair, which provides relaxation from physical fatigue," Bochner kept his viewers on their toes, slouching and wincing to make sense of the piece before them.

The format of the work as presented in booklike binders forced viewers to acknowledge their position as "reader." The overwhelming multiplicity of works contained in each volume further challenges the omnipotence of any individual author or the ability of any viewer to perceive the piece with any sense of definitive immediacy. This resistance later motivated other works by Bochner, including *Misunderstandings (A Theory of Photography)*, which I turn to shortly. For the moment, I would like to emphasize the arduous expectations set up by *Working Drawings* as a precedent. Fully experiencing the exhibition demanded attention, because the binders each contained one hundred diverse projects, and it would be an intensive commitment to thoroughly peruse them. Moreover, with four books on four separate plinths, it was not clear if their contents were identical unless one took the time and energy to riffle searchingly through each. Resisting any expectation of easy satisfaction, Bochner posed what he refers to as "the viewer's dilemma": in other words, the frustrating predicament in which the viewer must decide whether to invest the necessary time to truly look.[13] On this point James Meyer has remarked, "To view them standing up is exhausting—an impossible feat."[14] Moreover, "Bochner, in his inaugural work, did not aim to please"; by contrast, "he made the viewer *uncomfortable*."[15] This impossible expectation and its attendant discomfort are plainly visible in the photographs from the show, which capture viewers bending over plinths, shuffling through pages, furrowing to decipher meaning. One can imagine how this lack of ease would make the viewers/readers acutely conscious of the gap between themselves and the seemingly inexhaustible work of art. Despite being physically present, one would surely feel at a remove. In this sense, the exhibition was premised foremost on issues of distance and the frustration of being out of reach, from the conditions of the work to the related contingency of experience. In other words, even the possibilities of viewing or reading become precarious. Perhaps searching might be the more appropriate description of the engagement proposed by *Working Drawings*. In many respects, this exhibition embodied the mediation of experience performed by photography. For, despite being directly before the thing itself, the object nevertheless remains elusive. Delay and indecision are embedded in the project's title from the outset—these drawings are "working," as though they are incomplete as such, interminably *in process*; furthermore, the subtitle's ambivalence is undeniable. Though we have aesthetic objects before us, the title reminds us that these are nevertheless "visible things on paper not necessarily meant to be viewed as art." The extant object is thus beside the point, instead allowing the format or medium itself to take center stage.

The shift in valence from photo*copy* to photo*graphy*, yet another kind of writing with light, is worth exploring in more detail. While the photocopy machine, and arguably the larger *Working Drawings* installation, gave Bochner a segue to photographic thinking via an emphasis on "copies," these two communicative devices are intrinsically different. Kate Eichhorn's *Adjusted Margin: Xerography, Art, and Activism in the Late Twentieth Century* offers a riveting study of the photocopy machine. Analyzing how it was as appealing for executives and bureaucrats as for artists and anarchists during the 1970s, 1980s, and 1990s, she notes the complicated cultural and epistemological changes wrought by this reproductive technology in the late age of print. As one writer for the *New Yorker* put it in 1967: "In a society that sociologists are forever characterizing as 'mass,' the notion of making one-of-a-kind things into many-of-a-kind things showed signs of becoming a real compulsion."[16]

According to Eichhorn, the repetitious monotony inherent in the photocopy was in fact linked to its subversive potential. While I would argue that photography shares much in common with the photocopy machine in this respect, there are distinctive shifts between the two mediums. "Only rarely are we unaware of the fact that we are looking at a photocopied text or image," writes Eichhorn: "Photocopies are marked by the machines that reproduce them."[17] Photography, by contrast, is most often seen as successful when it convinces viewers that they are directly seeing the real world, when they are unaware of the mechanics of their creation. Nevertheless, Eichhorn's second point also holds true for photography, especially in the analog moment of early conceptual art. Photographs are indeed marked by the machines that reproduce them, albeit often in ways that are not immediately perceivable. Perhaps Bochner's work with photocopies—which one imagines was a labor of loading and reloading paper and toner, locating and retrieving jammed paper—led him toward investigating the pixelation and warping of reproduced images, as well as the tension between perceptual illusion and the marks of a machine. In this way, we might imagine *Working Drawings* and its preoccupation with process and delay (and delayed process) as a mode of photographic thinking. This conceptual framework poses a useful model for understanding conceptual art, in terms of both its often-overlooked materiality and its complicated communicative capacity.

As "working drawings," or more precisely reproductions of working drawings, the documents presented by Bochner are layered with ambiguity, with authorship and originality seemingly beside the point. The works on view were ultimately not the thing themselves but "images of images of projects" in process that are references to, yet not entirely indexes of, the thing itself.[18] This paradox of referencing yet not convincingly indexing is another element of the photograph that Bochner continued to probe in his experiments with photography in the following years. Already in this early experimental exhibition, however, the physical demands of the installation (which find their match in Bochner's own plausibly physical engagement with the photocopy) visibly emphasize the importance of the space between the viewer and any comprehensive attempt to grasp the piece. Moving between plinths, leafing between pages, viewers experience gaps everywhere. This is anything but direct or demediatized communication. Suggestively, in its refusal of immediacy, *Working Drawings* leaves us with elusive iterations.

Foremost photocopies, the work is only ever a partial index, circumventing illusionism and any aspirations of "pure" presence of the original. Instead, following

Meyer's notion of the proliferating "second degree," by revoking modernist opticality, the very possibility of "a single point of view dissolves into endless views and reframings, further removals, and 'infinite myopia.'"[19] The realization that the object can no longer be seen with a confident eye, despite its proximity, demonstrates that the object in the modernist sense had vanished. It is thereby replaced with a postmodern object, which, in Craig Owens's poignant summation, fulfilled the criteria of the postmodernist work: "When the postmodernist work speaks of itself, it is no longer to proclaim its autonomy, its self-sufficiency, its transcendence; rather it is to narrate its own contingency, insufficiency, lack of transcendence."[20] Put another way, the self-reflexive stance of such work stands in as the trace of process without finality, the evidence of conditional absence, the mark of contingency. Just as the viewer experiencing the exhibition *Working Drawings* would have been inevitably worn down, the realization that vision itself relies on the body is made manifest. For how could one realistically stand, bent over these plinths, turning page after page of photocopied sheets, without the onset of both physical and intellectual fatigue? Caught between the enigmatic and even frustrating meanings of the assembled reproductions and the awkwardness of viewing them, the inextricable link between thought processes and the experience of inhabiting a body becomes unavoidable.

This emphasis on delay, as theme and method, often tinged with wry humor, appears repeatedly throughout Bochner's oeuvre. It is traceable, for example, in *Misunderstandings (A Theory of Photography),* his renowned *Measurement* series (1968–69), and even his ongoing paintings. Consider *Do I Have to Draw You a Picture?* (2013) as yet another instance that mocks the persistent desire for communicative understanding while vexing the possibility of aesthetic immediacy (Figure 1.4). The phrase is one of incredulity and frustration. It is the rhetorical question uttered when irritated by a decided lack of fluid communication. In terms of artistic content, it ridicules the primacy of painting through its own media, resorting to drawing as subject, once more removed, or remediatized. It is as if to say the punch line of the joke is the very idea that any representation could ever actually bring one closer to the thing being represented and, moreover, that all media are ontologically predisposed to relay and delay in tandem. In a retrospective account of conceptual art and its various mediums presented at the New Museum in New York in 2010, aptly titled *The Tedium and the Medium,* Bochner recounted how, for him, "the medium was never transparent, never something to be seen through, never a neutral delivery system. No matter how reduced the means, they always remained something material, something to be taken apart and put back together, something to be confronted." Through a similar logic, conceptualism's embrace of reproducible media in the name of immediacy paradoxically persists, riddled with stumbling blocks of delay. In terms of communication and transmission, deferred meaning and suspended satisfaction form the modus operandi of conceptual art production.

Analogies between art and information characterized the first era of conceptual art in the long 1960s. Moreover, conceptual art's affinity for demediatization, and its quest for objective, neutral, and immediate media, found its most compelling vehicle

Figure 1.4. Mel Bochner, *Do I Have to Draw You a Picture?,* 2013. Enamel and acrylic on paper, 22 × 28 inches. Courtesy of the artist.

in the incorrigible photograph. This relationship, and its push-pull dynamic, also set the stage for other media formats to follow. In this regard, David Joselit's recent essays "Conceptual Art 2.0" and the "Epistemology of the Search" reveal significant links between the logics of reproducibility, conceptualism, and aggregation that resonate with that earlier moment of photography's intertwinement with conceptual art.[21] Joselit accounts for contemporary art practices such as the work of Seth Price or Rachel Harrison as the descendants of 1960s and 1970s conceptual artists, who, despite their search for easy translation between states, inevitably run up against the realities of the aggregation of information. The culling of information is similarly foregrounded in these practices, and, as opposed to the production of original content, what matters above all are network connections across meanings. Processes of "*reframing, capturing, reiterating* and *documenting*," in Joselit's view, become focal; networks oust discrete objects.[22] In this light, we might return to Bochner's installation and see veritable "databases." Bochner's analog aggregates on plinths function akin to computer search engines. As a precursor, they impel the user's body to strain and hunch. Both contemporary databases and Bochner's version physically exert the user, lured in by the dizzying yet frequently banal information they generate and blankly present. This view suggests new ways to interpret early conceptual art's concern with systems, elusive objectivity, and measurement, in relation to more recent cultural phenomena such as the widespread preoccupation with data collection and self-quantification. Instead of demediatization, we have perpetual "remediatization." Additionally, from the vantage point of "Conceptual Art 2.0," though the circulation of paper may have dwindled, the questionable status of what is indeed "visible" remains.

Taking Shape

The work of LeWitt, Smithson, and Bochner in the late 1960s demonstrated a distinct break with minimalism as characterized by stalwarts such as Flavin, Andre, and above all, Judd. Though the work of these artists might, at least at the outset, still have shared many formal similarities, the serial systems that underscored minimalist practices became increasingly crucial to artists who gave primacy to the concept above all else. As Rothkopf has explained, "Whereas Judd used serial systems as a hidden means for generating objects, LeWitt inverted the emphasis so that the three dimensional work appeared to serve simply as a mechanism for describing those serial systems."[23] Bochner similarly sought to expose the serial secrets of minimal sculpture by drawing attention to the spaces *between* serial objects, and, as an effect, he realized the potential in photography to destabilize the art object while retaining a material focus. In this regard, as a way to hover between conceptual impetus and material life, the liminality of the photograph offered Bochner unforeseen possibilities.

Beyond the resistance to photography established by the art market and the line of criticism promoted by Clement Greenberg,[24] Bochner also found himself working against the anti-illusionistic claims of minimalist art. Judd wrote avidly as an advocate for nonrepresentational art, vehemently against illusionism. The photograph's inherent connection to the world of representation, and as a result to artifice at a remove from the real, posed a serious impasse for Judd and others. According to Judd, the only escape from the slippery slope of illusionism was to create art that existed as an object to be experienced physically in three dimensions without indexical reference. As Judd memorably proclaimed: "Three dimensions are real space. That gets rid of the problem of illusionism."[25] Against these streams of opposition, Bochner mobilized photography in a new way, opening up a space to radically reconsider the status of the image as a process in tandem with an investigation into the material limits of photography itself.

Significantly, as Bochner has explained, he "came of age during the apogee of photographic reportage," an era that promised liberation through the presentation of pictorial "facts" in popular magazines such as *Life* and *Look*.[26] Yet, of course, these "facts" were always characterized by a high degree of affect. As an influential counterpoint to such expressionistic images, Bochner was influenced by the vernacular images of Walker Evans (such as *Penny Picture Display, Savannah* [1936], which Bochner owned) (Figure 1.5). He also saw a similar model of unemotional, plainspoken pictures in the work of Ed Ruscha, who too was an admirer of Evans.

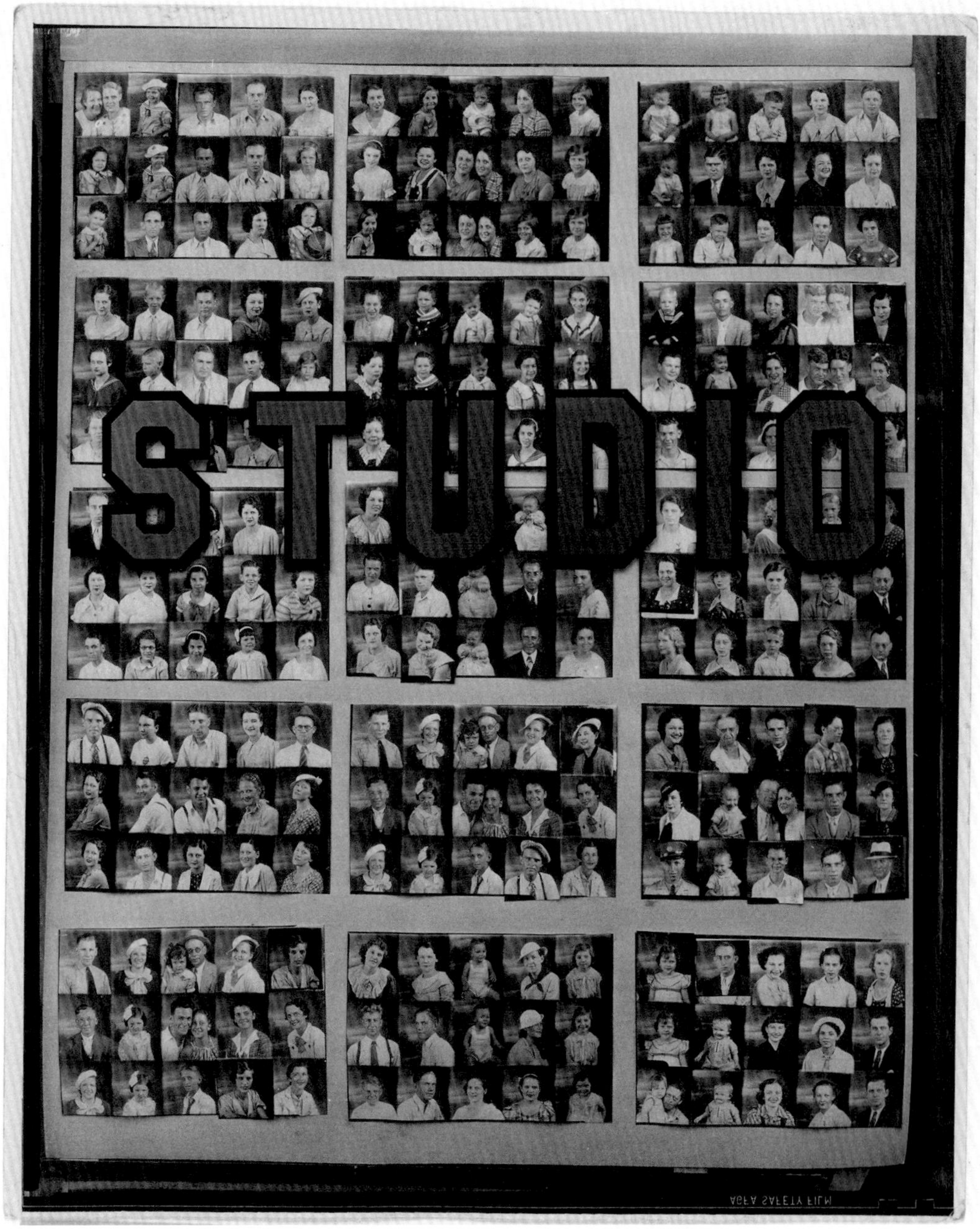

Figure 1.5. Walker Evans, *Penny Picture Display, Savannah,* 1936. Gelatin silver print, 24.7 × 19.3 cm (9¾ × 7⅝ inches). Ford Motor Company Collection, Gift of Ford Motor Company and John C. Waddell, 1987 (1987.1100.482). Copyright Walker Evans Archive, The Metropolitan Museum of Art. Image source: Art Resource, NY.

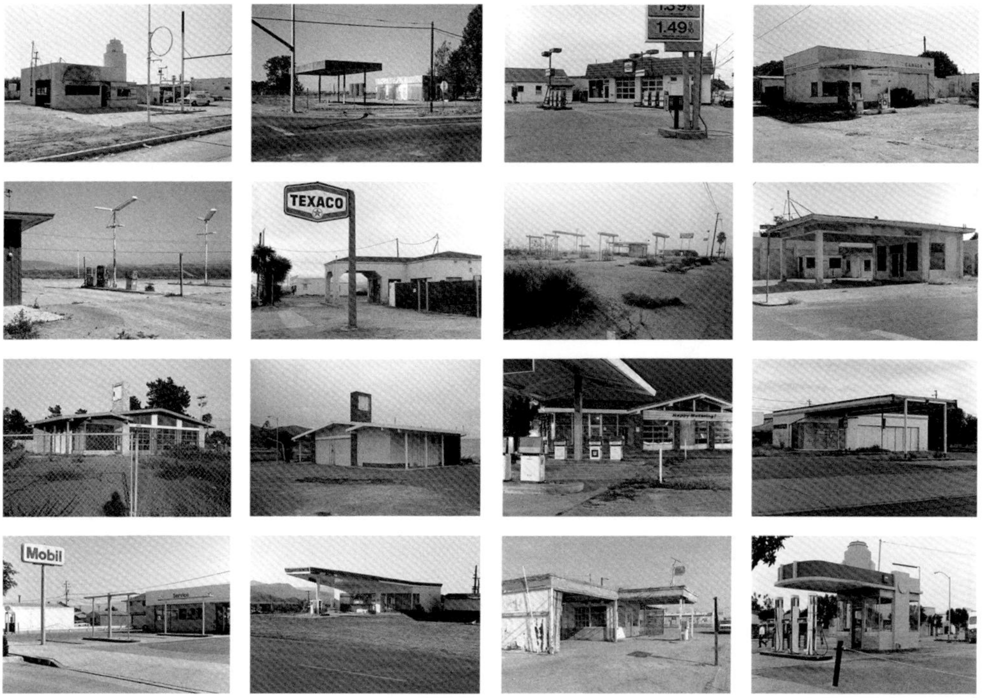

Figure 1.6. Edward Ruscha, *Twentysix Gasoline Stations,* 1963. Copyright Ed Ruscha. Courtesy of the artist and Gagosian Gallery.

Ruscha's nearly generic photographs avoided pictorial effect and emotional affect, and were shown as series, causing the overall sequence of each project to override the importance of any single image therein (Figure 1.6). Ruscha worked in the Duchampian/Warholian tradition, using the photograph, and often his subject matter, as a readymade object without apparent inflection. In these works, ordinary and familiar objects enact an intellectual challenge, including the question: "Is it art?" Ruscha himself claimed his banal photographs of gasoline stations and palm trees for example were not "arty" but closer to "technical data like industrial photography."[27] Adding to this objective look, Bochner decided to pursue his own photographs with as much restraint as possible to avoid the pitfalls of subjective composition. To accomplish this, he turned to the quintessential method of minimalist production: he hired a professional.[28]

Bochner commissioned Gretchen Lambert to shoot twelve unique stacks of blocks. Each seen from three fixed viewpoints, the changing configurations of these modular constructions form *36 Photographs and 12 Diagrams* (1966) (Figure 1.7). Much like Ruscha's proto-conceptual *Twentysix Gasoline Stations* (1962) or *Some Los Angeles Apartments* (1965), the factually inflected title divulges the linguistically predetermined premise of the piece. Additionally, despite the straightforward claims made by both text and image, a sense of unpredictable randomness undergirds the system. A similar logic operates in Bochner's case. The title references twelve cubic constructions arranged in vertical columns, accompanied by the original gridded drawings that preceded them as plans, positioned at the apex of each respective column. All this gives the impression of order. The twelve configurations are then represented by three respective photographs, each showing a distinct vantage. The chosen three vantages correspond to architectural categories describing three-dimensional form in space. These include the plan, a bird's-eye view of the structure; the elevation, the view perpendicular to the facade; and the perspective, taken above one corner in line with the diagonal axis. As standardized, measured, and pictorially uninflected as these photographs appear, they nevertheless fell short of Bochner's desire for literalism. Despite his use of minimalist tenets in his pursuit of the "objective," mediation by the medium of photography was unavoidable. Confounded, Bochner recalls his initial intention for these early photographs: "The thing is the thing and not a representation of the thing; there's no mediation at work."[29] Yet, rather than being unmediated and objective, the photographs in fact produced strange unintended shadows, and the linear structures curved slightly in reproduction, as an effect of the convexity of the camera's lens. In photography, Bochner had envisioned "a medium so completely illusionistic as to sidestep the problem of illusionism altogether."[30] Yet this fantasy of surpassing illusionism or mediation was bound to fail. For one thing, the shift in scale that the photographs effected on the blocks in Bochner's experiment was out of proportion with the original sculpture. The fact of its inevitable inexactitude, that it could never measure up to the dream of precision promised by the idea of indexicality, demonstrates how, despite Bochner's desire, the thing could never be the thing itself.

These photographs succeed at underscoring the serial attitude that unites the pictured forms. Each begins with a configuration of two-inch cubes. However, rather than emphasize a logic that is self-contained, the piece questions the absurdity of the predetermined system, highlighting instead the ways its premise fails.[31] Though one may be able to convincingly read the sequences horizontally across the rows, displayed in a grid, three simultaneous yet different views of each single object cause the initial object to effectively shift by degrees, becoming increasingly unrecognizable. The subject, rather than being relayed objectively, "unravel[s] with an almost cubist complexity."[32] Similar to Eadweard Muybridge's photographs of bodies in motion through serial photography, often presented with three correlating camera angles (which, not surprisingly, Bochner was very interested in), more photographs taken from more angles do not naturally generate a greater understanding of the figure depicted. Instead, one is confronted with the jarring disconnects between the images—gaps in the proposed logistical sequence.[33] One wonders at the distance that separates each instance. The simple cross structure in Bochner's series, for example, becomes almost entirely indecipherable from the elevation view. Despite their plain presentation, there is nothing straightforward about these standardized shots. Moreover, rather than move toward conceptual dematerialization, the emphasis on the object status of the photograph in relation to sculptural form

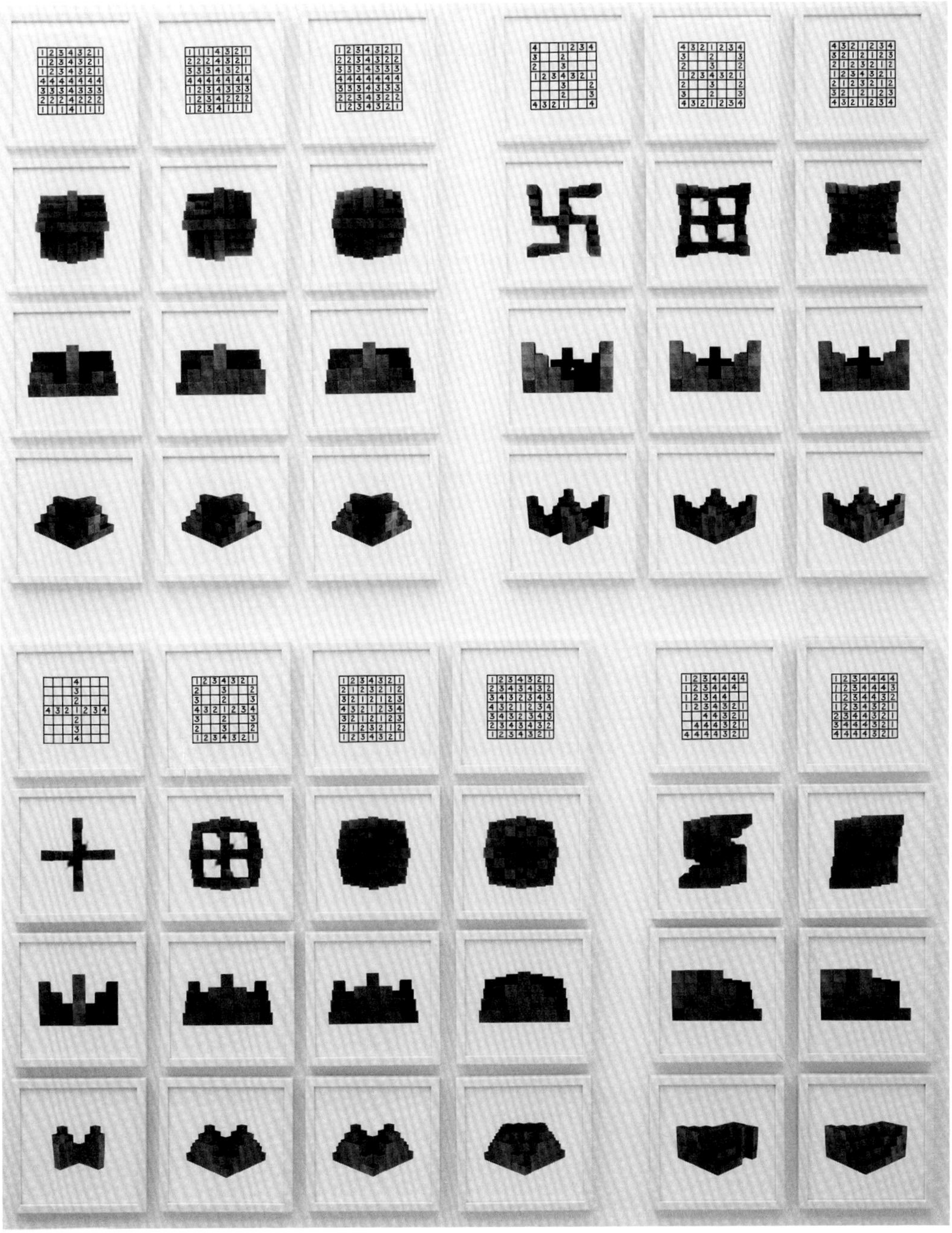

Figure 1.7. Mel Bochner, *36 Photographs and 12 Diagrams,* 1966. Documentary photograph, 10 × 8 inches. Courtesy of the artist.

becomes paramount. Jeffrey Weiss has similarly assessed the paradox of Bochner's *36 Photographs and 12 Diagrams,* explaining that "the object is repeatedly recuperated by being remade," and as such, "the proliferating object actually signifies an intensification of material means."[34]

The doubt Bochner's project casts on both the medium and the object became invaluable to the artist's later works, which further test the limits and possibilities of conceptual art through photographic conditions. For despite conceptual art's insistence on being associated with objective systems, whether deliberately or by chance, it was nonetheless forced to contend with and acknowledge the subjectivity and flaws of its own methods. As LeWitt proclaimed in his seminal 1967 article in *Artforum,* "Paragraphs on Conceptual Art": "Conceptual art is not necessarily logical. The logic of a piece or series of pieces is a device that is used at times only to be ruined."[35] In many cases, as I show with Bochner's work, the ruin exists as a shortfall of the system itself.

Photography's stubborn resistance to any predetermined conceptual idea encouraged Bochner to take measure of the structure of the photographic print itself, investigating it as a systematic entity, probing its physical and conceptual fragility. Somewhat ironically this gesture brought him narrowly close to contemporaneous developments in modernist painting, with a twist. This proximity to modernism, created by Bochner's investigation of the medium of photography, avoided modernism's demand for medium specificity or self-reflexivity. In fact, Bochner's experiments with photography further elucidate the contradictions embedded in both modernist and minimalist discourse by demystifying the medium of photography as vastly contingent and always unpredictable.

In late 1966 Bochner created *H-2* (1966–67), a work that addresses the sculptural tension inherent in the earlier series while magnifying the aforementioned issues further, concentrating increasingly on how photography affects the thing photographed while nevertheless being its own object (Figure 1.8). In *H-2,* a dark recessed square seems to hinge the work from its center, with a cross formation of escalating steps ascending from it. Surrounded by alternating cubes, like an Escher-staircase, subtle tonalities of shifting gray disorient the viewer. Four blank squares are poised at attention. Viewed from a distance, the blocks of the nearly four-foot-square structure imaged by *H-2* appear to move forward into the exhibition space, until one realizes that this is a trompe l'oeil. The sense of three dimensions suggested by this relief is an illusion, since the actual object presented is in fact completely flat. The image is a photograph of an aerial view from *36 Photographs and 12 Diagrams,* enlarged and mounted on Masonite. The effect of spatial depth was achieved by cutting the photograph's border to the edge of the structure depicted, before hanging the photograph at a slight distance from the wall. Bochner did not see this approach, which was both sculptural and photographic, as a threat to his interest in literalism and he had no qualms with compromising the autonomy of the medium.

The parallel, whether intended or not, between work such as Bochner's *H-2* and Frank Stella's contemporaneous shaped canvases is hard to miss and may be as re-

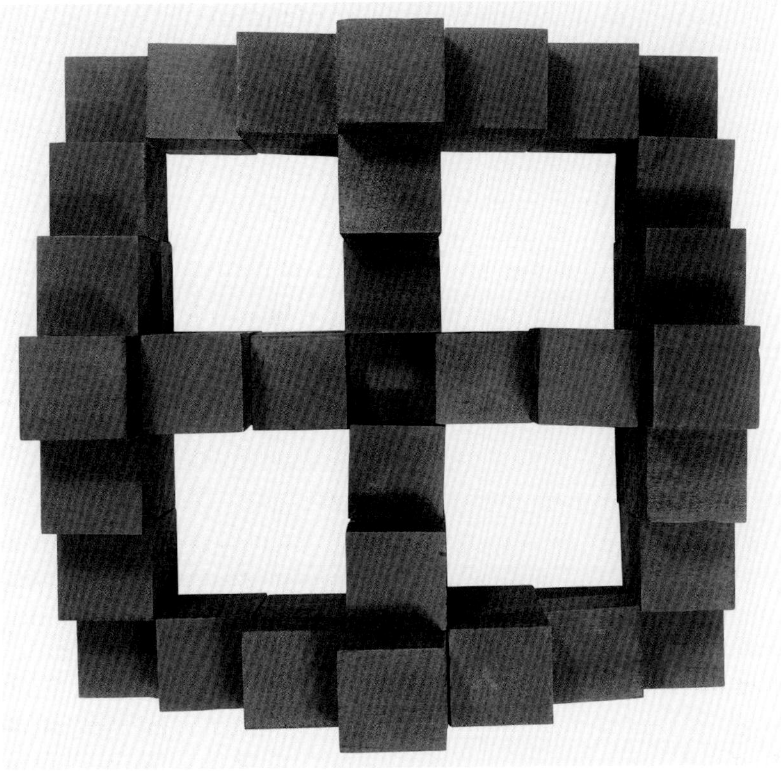

Figure 1.8. Mel Bochner, *H-2,* 1966–67. Silhouetted gelatin silver print mounted on Masonite, 45¼ × 45¼ inches. Courtesy of the artist.

vealing about Bochner's status as a conceptual and postminimalist artist as it is of Stella's "terminally ambivalent" position between modernist art and objecthood at this juncture.[36] In each case the picture surface is pushed away from the wall, giving it a deliberately sculptural appearance (Figure 1.9). Stella was of course not the only painter working in this mode, considering that "the shaped canvas was the dominant form of abstract painting in the 1960s."[37] However, among those artists anthologized in the mid-sixties by definitive exhibitions such as *The Shaped Canvas* (1964–65) and *Shape and Structure* (1965), he was certainly the most prominent.[38] Significantly, in addition to Stella's works shaped into notched rectangles and crosses, he also made canvases that similarly appeared as "cut-outs" that had their centers removed to reveal the wall beneath and their dependence on this structural support. "Although frequently described as a hybrid of painting and sculpture," writes Frances Colpitt of the shaped canvas, "[it] grew out of the issues of abstract painting and was evidence of the desire of painters to move into real space by rejecting behind-the-frame illusionism."[39] Bochner, by contrast, sought to move into real space by exposing the illusionism that nevertheless was suggested by the frame.

Though Bochner's work at this point formally resembled works such as Stella's *Carl Andre* (1963) (first exhibited as part of his *Portrait* series at Castelli Gallery in

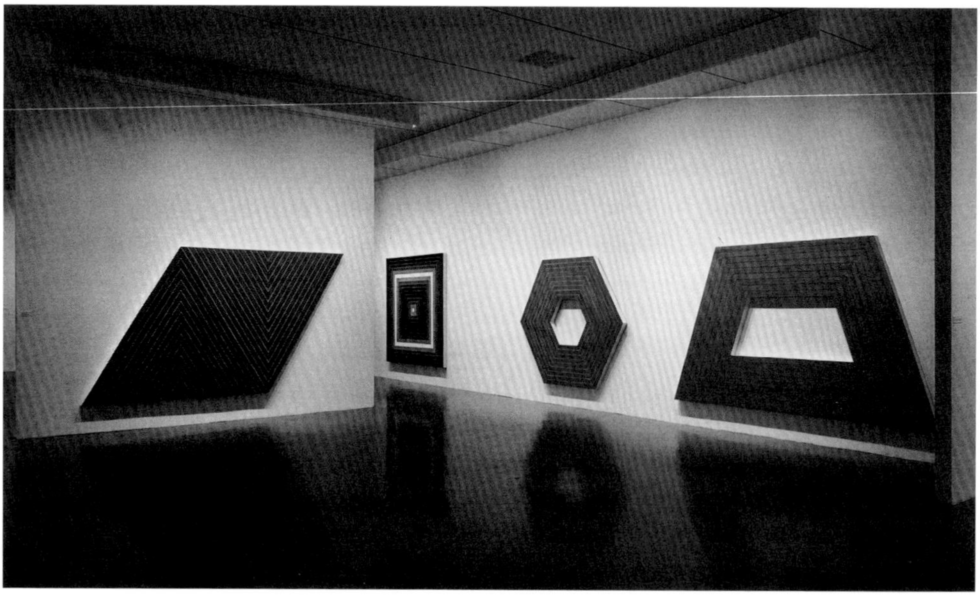

Figure 1.9. Frank Stella, installation view of the exhibition *Frank Stella,* The Museum of Modern Art, New York, March 24–June 2, 1970 (paintings); March 24–May 24, 1970 (drawings). Left to right: *Valparaiso Flesh and Green* (1963), *Cato Manor* (1963), *Sidney Guberman* (1963), and *Ileana Sonnabend* (1963). Photograph by James Mathews. Photograph from Digital Image. Copyright The Museum of Modern Art. Licensed by SCALA / Art Resource, NY. Copyright 2019 Frank Stella / Artists Rights Society (ARS), New York.

1964), they were each based in distinctly different, even opposing, methodologies and philosophies. Stella's striped painting derives its appearance from the shape of the frame, thereby reinforcing the support and the direction of its axis. This was the technique hailed by Michael Fried as "deductive structure" and, according to Fried, the ostensible route to modernist painting's pure and autonomous self-reflexivity, "generated by the framing edge."[40] Arguably, such "explanatory acrobatics"[41] were among Fried's controversial attempts to salvage Stella's work on the side of painting in opposition to sculpture.[42] Bochner inverted this approach by trimming the perimeter of the object to convene to the image, simultaneously violating the camera's rectangular viewing frame and undermining Fried's "deductive structure."[43] This project also illustrates Bochner's move away from focusing on seriality as means and ends, and his move toward a clearer investment in the photographic object as such.

In Bochner's work, choices such as hanging the work slightly away from the wall to appear more present are exactly the elements of the work that reveal its ruse, since the shadows in the photograph and the shadows cast by the photograph on the wall do not correspond. These are only convincing from the perspective of viewing the work straight on. At an angle, the illusion falls apart like a "stage-set façade that demands a particular viewpoint or stubbornly withholds its illusory rewards,"[44] explicitly pitting "the 'artificial' perspective frozen in the photograph against the changing 'natural' perspective of its viewing."[45] This perceptual discrepancy makes one aware of the photograph as a living object liable to unique, specific, and changing viewing conditions.

Under the Skin

"In the process of thinning the physical life of the concept," Carol Armstrong writes, "Bochner arrives at an awareness of the ultrathin thickness of the photograph."[46] Armstrong's eloquent and evocative words suggest that no matter how thin the material presence of the photograph might become, its conceptual thickness denies easy understanding. Armstrong's turn of phrase, and its emphasis on distilling the palpable form of the photograph, recall the viscerality of Bochner's *Surface Dis/Tension.* It also summons the boundary-bending capacities of photography, which Bochner explored at length in his experiments with photography throughout the late 1960s. Here I would like to turn to the ways in which Bochner addressed the dimensions of opacity and transparency in his investigations of photography's material and conceptual liminality, and how these qualities are bound together in a paradoxical state of "ultrathin thickness."

Bochner's act of rephotographing the disembodied image in *Surface Dis/Tension* further complicates viewers' ability to discern what they are looking at. Beginning with the abstract form of the grid, compounding it with the abstracting medium of photography, one is confronted with an object that appears to be three-dimensional, belying the smooth and flat illusion of the photograph. These interventions disrupt long-standing Renaissance pictorial ideals and minimalism's rigorous geometry while marking a transition to more fluid, material, subjective, and chance-oriented modes of art practice that ask the viewer to consider the uncontainability and uncontrollability of the piece or pieces. This is coincident with similar investigations by other artists, including Barry Le Va, Eva Hesse, Robert Morris, and Nauman, who also flouted minimalism's severity by creating soft, materially sensitive, and irregularly shaped sculpture that came to be grouped under the rubric of "Post-Minimalism" or "Anti-Form."[47]

Given its matrix structure, *Surface Dis/tension* embeds references that reach beyond the body. Indeed, the work strikingly recalls the history of early photography, or to be precise, the oldest photographic negative in existence, William Henry Fox Talbot's print image of a latticed window at Lacock Abbey, made in 1835 (Plate 2).[48] The reference to the window is implicit in Bochner's piece via its gridded structure and its test of transparence, and whether intended or not, can be read as a metacommentary on photography. Moreover, the paper negative of *The Oriel Window, South Gallery, Lacock Abbey* (1835) formally shares the bleed and the blur of Bochner's *Surface Dis/Tension* in ways that shed light on these respective works. The window in each case, both Bochner's and Talbot's, is conceptually see-through yet materially obscure, rigidly organized yet distended. These contradictory dimensions cannot be severed from one another. Here windows are layered as well as segmented. Their grids extend into space and are nevertheless hemmed in. Calling to mind the glass plates of early photography, we are redirected to thinking about glass panes. The hedges that creep into the lower frame of Talbot's window, with inevitable shadows lurking in the corner, echo the riveting rivulets of Bochner's formed photograph. Ghostly, otherworldly, and abstract, the "ultra-thin thickness" of Talbot's image is magnified retrospectively through viewing Bochner's.

A comparison with Talbot is particularly revealing for Bochner's project, since Talbot, as one of the many competing progenitors of the medium of photography, was the first to use the word *fix* in relation to photography.[49] Against this grain, Bochner steers toward the ultimate impossibility of photographic "fixity." Instead, in opposition to Talbot, Bochner actively worked to unfix photography, so to speak, removing it from its traditional supports (philosophical, perceptual, and physical) by literally taking the picture apart. Bochner's gestures expose the reality that Talbot's method of fixing was never totally successful, and not simply because it was eventually replaced by John Herschel's "washing out" process. "Fixed," as Geoffrey Batchen has insightfully made clear, is itself misleading, suggesting "only a momentary and untrustworthy stability."[50] Bochner challenges the questionable "art of fixing a shadow" as the basis of photography.

Among other reference points in Bochner's work is the artist's interest in Nauman's thematization of form and material in *Flour Arrangements* (1966), which Bochner encountered in the September 1967 issue of *Artforum* and in Nauman's solo show at Castelli Gallery in January 1968. Nauman's piece consisted of seven photographs featuring isolated mounds of white flour that Nauman reshuffled on his studio floor every day for a month. Though the larger implications of *Flour Arrangements* are discussed at length in the next chapter, for the moment it is worth noting the correspondence between Bochner and Nauman. Both artists began working with photography in 1966, and by 1970 both had abandoned it almost entirely. Other parallels appear between their practices. Bochner's *36 Photographs* and *Surface Dis/Tension* intimate affinities with Nauman's use of materials—the process is paramount in each. Both also exemplify the tricky tension between the frame of the image that seeks to contain and the contents that become increasingly unruly.

Not coincidentally, Bochner also shared Nauman's and Smithson's interest in early satellite photography and images of the surface of moon. Views of outer space, such as those transmitted to earth from the Lunar Orbiter on August 23, 1966, were conspicuously publicized at the time and informed the visual vocabulary of popular culture. The abstract documentary form of Nauman's *Composite Photo of Two Messes on the Studio Floor* (1967) alludes to lunar photography and could be productively compared with the grounds or small-scale topographic effect discussed earlier in Bochner's *Surface Dis/Tension*.[51] Each evidences an alien terrain that questions the bare notion of evidence itself. Moreover, Bochner and Nauman demonstrate a mutual interest in using the method and appearance of decomposition as a way to work against traditional notions of artistic composition. Consider, for example, the way each undoes expectations of artistry and representation. Bochner flays the epidermis of the image, disorienting normative perceptions of the photograph's surface and its material life, while Nauman documents disarrayed and unidentifiable messes on his studio floor, then assembles them as a composite, as though attempting to reconfigure the real. In even more expansive terms, both Bochner's and Nauman's oblique references to NASA's space program and the extraterrestrial images the program shared publicly bring to mind the ways such imagery inspired people in the late 1960s to think beyond one's self and in increasingly global terms surpassing the boundaries of the nation-state.

Beyond recognizing the scale of the earth in the scheme of the universe, other strategies for gaining perspective circulating in the late 1960s emerge in Bochner's photographic projects. In 1968 Bochner produced an offset lithograph of *Surface Dis/Tension* printed with an aptly named "rainbow roll" of colored ink (Plate 3). The soothing and hypnotic quality of the color gradations in this print, flowing softly from pink to green against the disorienting waves of the distorted perspective lines, subtly connotes ideas of psychedelic reverie. The allusion is worth pursuing, especially considering the abundance of contemporaneous psychedelia in surface design and popular culture. The twisted torsos of Bochner's vibrantly tie-dyed *Crumples* (1966–67), featuring crumpled photocopies of a perspectival grid that were then rephotographed, similarly lend themselves to this reading (Plate 4). Far from the appearance of intellectual distance that characterized much conceptual art, or the cold severity of most minimalism, psychedelic art employed a mind-bending mix of optical swirls and transitions intent on altering and expanding consciousness. Bochner's creation of these works in 1968 coincides with the publication of Timothy Leary's *Politics of Ecstasy,* a widely influential book that advocated for psychedelic revolution as a way to find freedom from limitations, both personal and societal. Given Bochner's disposition to manipulate the body of the photographic image, there seem to be connections to this mode of "expansion" beyond limits and its implicit desires. Something close to psychedelia recurs in Bochner's practice, which the artist has admitted offered "a way to slice into the culture backwards."[52] Circular vortexes and dynamic hues, for example, featuring mantra-like repetitions of words continue to appear throughout his *Thesaurus* paintings in the 2010s.

Add to this compulsion the fact that color and physicality became ever more central to Bochner's experiments with photography, as his images took on increasingly corporeal aspects. This inclination is most apparent in his early documents of two rapidly sketched grids on glass, one drawn in mineral oil, *Viscosity (Mineral Oil)* (1968), and one drawn in shaving cream, *Grid (Shaving Cream)* (1968), then photographed with his Polaroid camera (Figures 1.10, 1.11). As though vandalizing the classic trope of the window onto the world, Bochner's visceral liquid squirts and puffy pliable foam challenge the clean conventions of straight photography and documentary. Once more, as possible references to lattices on a window, these grids on glass deny the easy understanding of the picture as window. One can also read these works as mocking the modernist grid of meaning, especially given the ephemeral nature of these slippery substances. Certainly, the use of these ordinary household

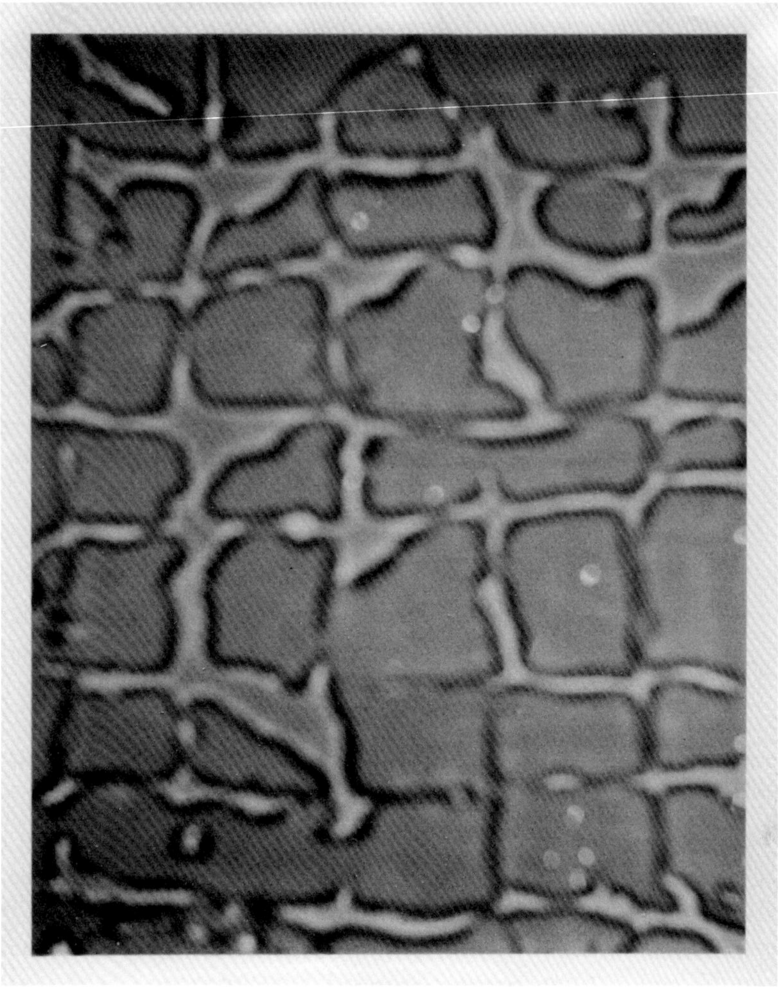

Figure 1.10. Mel Bochner, *Viscosity (Mineral Oil)*, 1968. Color Polaroid, 4¼ × 3⅜ inches. Courtesy of the artist.

products parodies the imagined purity of modernist materials. More than that, their position as body products insinuates fleshly boundaries—things applied to skin as lubricants and as barriers. Like the slightly abject quality of *Surface Dis/Tension*, the literal limits and interstices of photographic form are probed. Through tactility, Bochner repeatedly calls attention to the skin of the image. *Viscosity (Mineral Oil)* and *Grid (Shaving Cream)* produce a kind of glassy-eyed vision as one stares at them, suggesting yet another allusion to the trippy effects of substances and the influential context of late-sixties psychedelic culture.

Bochner's use of Polaroid instant film is also worth pausing on. Not simply an inexpensive apparatus, the Polaroid promised an immediacy that even Kodak with its famed "You Press the Button, and We Do the Rest!" adage could not deliver. Without the need to send one's film away for developing, Polaroid came to life before

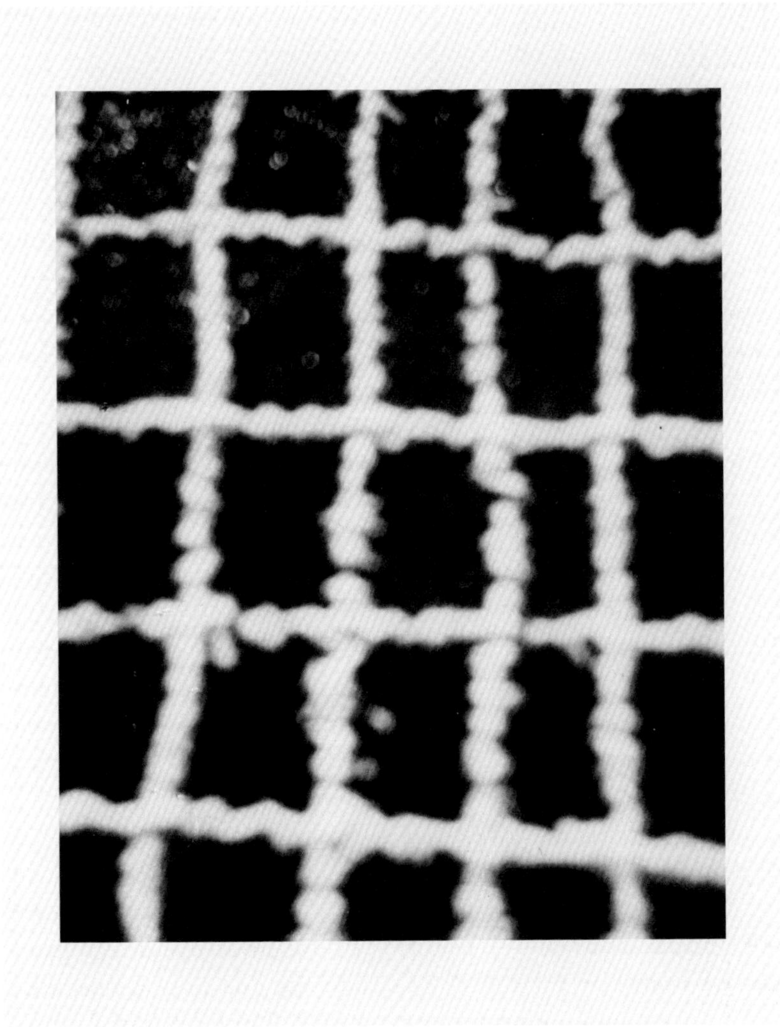

Figure 1.11. Mel Bochner, *Grid (Shaving Cream)*, 1968/2003. Color Polaroid, 4¼ × 3⅜ inches. Courtesy of the artist.

your eyes and could indeed be for your eyes only. In this regard, it allowed for more privacy and less patience. In a near analogy with *Surface Dis/Tension*, with a push of the shutter and a pull on the image, the Polaroid photograph revealed itself after shedding its skin. Through self-acting chemicals, it was as if the camera possessed its own agency. In *The Camera Does the Rest: How Polaroid Changed Photography* (2015), Peter Buse reminds us of the transformative power of Polaroid in the history of analog photography and the ways it shaped notions of immediacy and material presence. In a description that sounds uncannily conceptual, Edwin H. Land, the inventor of this peel-apart film with its somewhat salacious associations, described his ambitions for Polaroid in 1949: "The process must be concealed from—nonexistent for—the photographer, who by definition need think of the art in the *taking* and not in *making* photographs."[53] The register of Land's vision for this photographic technology echoes the logic of the use of photography by conceptual artists.

For its part, Polaroid possessed an inherent subversive potential that branding agents and advertisers recognized immediately. Notably, one of the most popular Polaroid cameras in use between 1965 and 1970 was named the Polaroid Swinger (following the Joy Cam). The name connoted not just the ideal of being groovy but also the sexual liberties of nonmonogamous open relationships. The jingle accompanying a 1965 television commercial featuring an exuberant Ali MacGraw covertly lays out this logic, as it melodically sings, "Meet the Swinger, the Polaroid Swinger! It's more than a camera, it's almost alive! It's only nineteen dollars and ninety-five! Swing it up, it says, Yes! Take the shot, count it down! Zip it off!" Though everyone in the ad is fully clothed, the illicit allusion adds to the camera's allure. Yet another televised advertisement shows a bikini-clad MacGraw moving slowly down a sandy beach as she swings the Polaroid camera back and forth with her strides. The first few seconds zoom in entirely on her body from the waist down. The availability and accessibility of Polaroid in economic, social, and technical terms bears mentioning as well. After all, it was pitched as a decidedly nonspecialist device that anyone could use. Tying Polaroid to the 1960s notion of "free love" and pervasive slogan "make love not war" gestures toward sharing and counterculture protest simultaneously. Finding a nuanced partner in a photographic technology, the free love of being a swinger inferred a challenge to violence, and to the repression and hypocrisies of polite society more broadly.

Bochner's next series continued to investigate the constant negotiation between surface and depth perception as a way to understand the substance and meaning of photography. Now moving further into the use of color, Bochner developed the *Transparent and Opaque* series (1968), featuring twelve silver-dye bleach prints (Plate 5). With funding from E.A.T. (Robert Rauschenberg and Billy Kluver's Experiments in Art and Technology), Bochner once again began by hiring a professional photographer.[54] This time, it was one who specialized in product photography, a choice that seems to indicate Bochner's desire to also engage with the photographic economy of advertising and, perhaps by extension, its business of seductive manipulation and truth bending. The photographer was asked to make the most beautiful pictures possible of smeared Vaseline and sprayed layers of shaving cream that Bochner had manually applied to glass. As the title suggests, each image in the series proves itself to be both: transparent and opaque. The clear yet viscid Vaseline and the thick frothy foam each reveal light as the critical agent in the photographic process, accentuated by the use of lurid colored lights. These tonal variations are visible throughout the series and test the sensitive limits of the surface while alluding to the centrality of the body in their sensual consistency. As I have acknowledged in the earlier discussion of baby oil and shaving cream, such products (in this case Vaseline and shaving cream) have domestic associations to bodily use. On the one hand, the attempt to make these substances "beautiful" is the stuff of practical jokes. On the other hand, the photographs produced are unquestionably formally impressive.

Hovering somewhere between psychedelia and disco, with their luster and pulsating tints, allusions to glistening jewel-like colors, such as crimson, amethyst, jade, and gold, dominate the transparent parts. Meanwhile, contaminating blood spatters are suggested through iodine against the opacity of swirling shaving cream. On the transparent plates, traces of Bochner's fingers streak the glass; on the opacity side, it is as if we were looking at the insides of a human body. In either case, these viscous bodies, somewhere between a solid and a liquid, imply sticky adhesion between forms and beings that returns to possibilities embedded in the inchoate and amorphous movement of psychedelic visual culture.[55] What we could call Bochner's latent but continuously resurfacing politics of psychedelia connects to the zeitgeist aspiration of the 1960s to produce altered states of bodily perception through technological and chemical means.

Notably, Yve-Alain Bois and Rosalind Krauss and Meyer Schapiro acknowledged these corporeal connotations and the way they ask base materialism to contend with the elision of matter, by including images from Bochner's *Transparent and Opaque* series in their 1996 exhibition, *L'Informe: Mode d'emploi (The Formless: Instructions for Use)* at the Centre Pompidou, Paris.[56] It is true that these works formally parody the heroism of abstract expressionism's "allover" compositions, but beyond parody, they enact something much more radical.[57] By accentuating the possibility of formlessness, they destabilize the organizing principle of form and the idea of form as an organizing principle. This was the curators' professed post-structural position in assembling *L'Informe* and exploring Georges Bataille's notion of "l'informe" (formlessness) as the curatorial conceit.

According to Bataille, form itself is filled with doubt and contingency. Bataille writes, "formless is not only an adjective . . . but a term serving to declassify the requirement that each thing have its own form. . . . Actually, for academics to be happy would require the universe to take shape. All of philosophy has no other goal. . . . On the other hand, to say that the universe resembles nothing and is nothing but formless is the same as saying that the universe is like a spider or a blob of spit."[58] Bochner's use of photography evokes the kinds of excessive bodily connections that Bataille alludes to. As I have shown with the photographic skin of *Surface Dis/Tension* and the visceral viscosity of the *Transparent and Opaque* series, many of Bochner's works call attention to their material realities and function akin to Bois and Krauss's understanding of formlessness by performing the work of "undermining concepts, of depriving them of their boundaries, [and of] the capacity to articulate the world."[59] Despite taking the "form" of the photograph, *Transparent and Opaque* nevertheless resists empirical understanding.

Bochner's choice of subject thus continues his repudiation of the formalist account of modernism, as well as the persistence of Leon Battista Alberti's metaphor of "transparency," which has been central to the history of Western art since Alberti compared the surface of a perspectivally constructed picture to a transparent pane of glass.[60] Modernist painting supposedly shifted away from this view of a "window unto the world" in order to emphasize painting as "a material sign—an opaque object."[61] Bochner's photographs demonstrate how neither paradigm is entirely sufficient and both rely heavily on cultural and technical assumptions. Bochner's 1966 review of the *Primary Structures* exhibition at the Jewish Museum outlines this view of art, describing all art as the root of artifice, as "unreal, constructed, invented, predetermined, intellectual, make-believe, contrived, useless."[62] Bochner's play on and with photography provocatively denies use-value and form as a value, by putting metaphors of painting in dialogue with the stubborn presumptions about pictures that had shaped photography since its inception. Investigating the underlying structure inevitably exposes the skeptical supports of both systems of representation.

Perhaps Bochner's ecstatic operation on the photograph's "ultrathin thickness" could further be understood in terms of Marcel Duchamp's invented category of the "infra-thin."[63] Notoriously undefinable, the infra-thin poses a kind of measure without definition that combines a consideration of an object's physicality with its conceptual structure and questions the relation between the two. Mentioned first in 1945, Duchamp described the liminal partition of the infra-thin as the "immeasurable difference or separation between things,"[64] stating that "the possible, implying the becoming—the passage from one to the other—takes place in the infra-thin."[65] In taking apart the photograph, Bochner draws attention to the interstitial nature of the medium as a space of becoming in literal and figural terms. Physically, the deceptive flatness of the photograph is opened beyond its apparent two-dimensional confines, revealing what could be described using Duchamp's language as "invisible and intangible, but otherwise manifestly present."[66] Among analogies used to further illustrate his point, Duchamp suggested the infra-thin was like "fire without smoke, the warmth of a seat which has just been left, reflection from a mirror or glass, watered silk, iridescents, the people who go through (subway gates) at the very last moment, velvet trousers their whistling sound is an infra-thin separation signaled."[67] Each of these imagistic and textured examples challenges the existential logic of the photographic index and the flat capture of reality suggested by documentary. For instead of pointing back to the original as a trace of the real, the fire does not have smoke, and the warmth of the vacant seat or even the reflection in the mirror is temporal, unstable, and vanishing. The index may exist, but it does not hold. After all, an infra-thin "measure without definition" is precisely the subject of Bochner's following body of work and the next series under consideration here: *Measurements* (1968–69).

A Labyrinth That Is a Straight Line

A black-and-white close-up of a faux-marbled linoleum floor extends before our eyes, plain in one sense and obscure in so many others. A dirtied door frame cuts into the upper right-hand corner. An impression of geometric rigidity is given, but compromised by further looking, when gaps and smears become apparent. Speckles and spills, shadows and ridges coat the image, and it is difficult to deduce if they are part of the scene or photographic faults. Then, most oddly, a small, nearly imperceptible **36"** emerges, three blocks up, running perpendicular to the picture plane. This is *Singer Lab Measurement (#2)* (1968) (Figure 1.12), one of a five-part series of photographs Bochner created while he was artist-in-residence at the Singer Laboratories in Denville, New Jersey (Figure 1.13). Bochner had the good fortune of being the first artist selected to participate in this collaborative program devised by E.A.T. and Singer. That same year, the Singer company had acquired Link aerospace, in a critical move to diversify away from the production of sewing machines and the craft of sewing toward the production of aerospace electronics and high-technology devices for commercial and military airlines. What they hoped to gain from Bochner is hard to say, but his "artistic" presence fed into a growing corporate ethos of the 1960s, which emphasized creativity as a core value in management theory.[68] In any case, this bizarre photograph clearly shares formal and conceptual commonalities with *Surface Dis/Tension,* proffering further evidence of Bochner's developing interest in unhinging representation.

Bochner's project at Singer was verifiably open-ended. He claims to have been inspired by his twice-weekly discussions with engineers and scientists at the research lab. In his own words: "Most of the conversations emphasized how to communicate experience and information, and communication always came around to quantification, and that's how I got the measurements."[69] The bizarreness of the resulting photographs bears an uncanny resemblance to crime scene photography, and one wonders how to stitch the pieces together. Collapsing the literal with the pictorial, there is a comic aspect to the graphic black Letraset numbers seen in each. A door frame appears to recur in at least three of the five photographs, but, given only partial perspectives, it is hard to be certain whether it is the same door or indeed a door at all. We have the visibly beat-up bottom corner in *Singer Lab Measurement (#4),* duct-taped shiftily, scuffed by anonymous, long-gone feet (Figure 1.14). *Singer Lab Measurement (#3)* seems to show the upper body of the door, swung away from the wall, yet not casting a shadow (Figure 1.15). Within another frame, *Singer Lab Measurement (#5),* we see a frayed and obscure black square rising from the lower left-hand side, **12"** marked between it and the molding against which one imagines is the ceiling (Figure 1.16). A partial cup of pencils alongside an aerosol spray can is depicted in *Singer Lab Measurement (#1),* marked this time by **10"**, perhaps located across from the door frame, but nevertheless a boundary of some sort. What meaning is to be made of these puzzling pictures? In one sense, it seems that the very act of making meaning, across the series and within individual photographs, is at stake.

The forensic tone of Bochner's stills can be understood in relation to larger thematizations of perception, ambiguity, and even potential criminality that were circulating contemporaneously. This is particularly evident in peculiar and popular photographs that were, at first glance, entirely unassuming yet purported to provide proof. Looking for truth between frames, and within frames, was a national obsession throughout the 1960s, in the wake of President John F. Kennedy's assassination, with Abraham Zapruder's haphazard 26.5-second Super 8 film of that fateful day

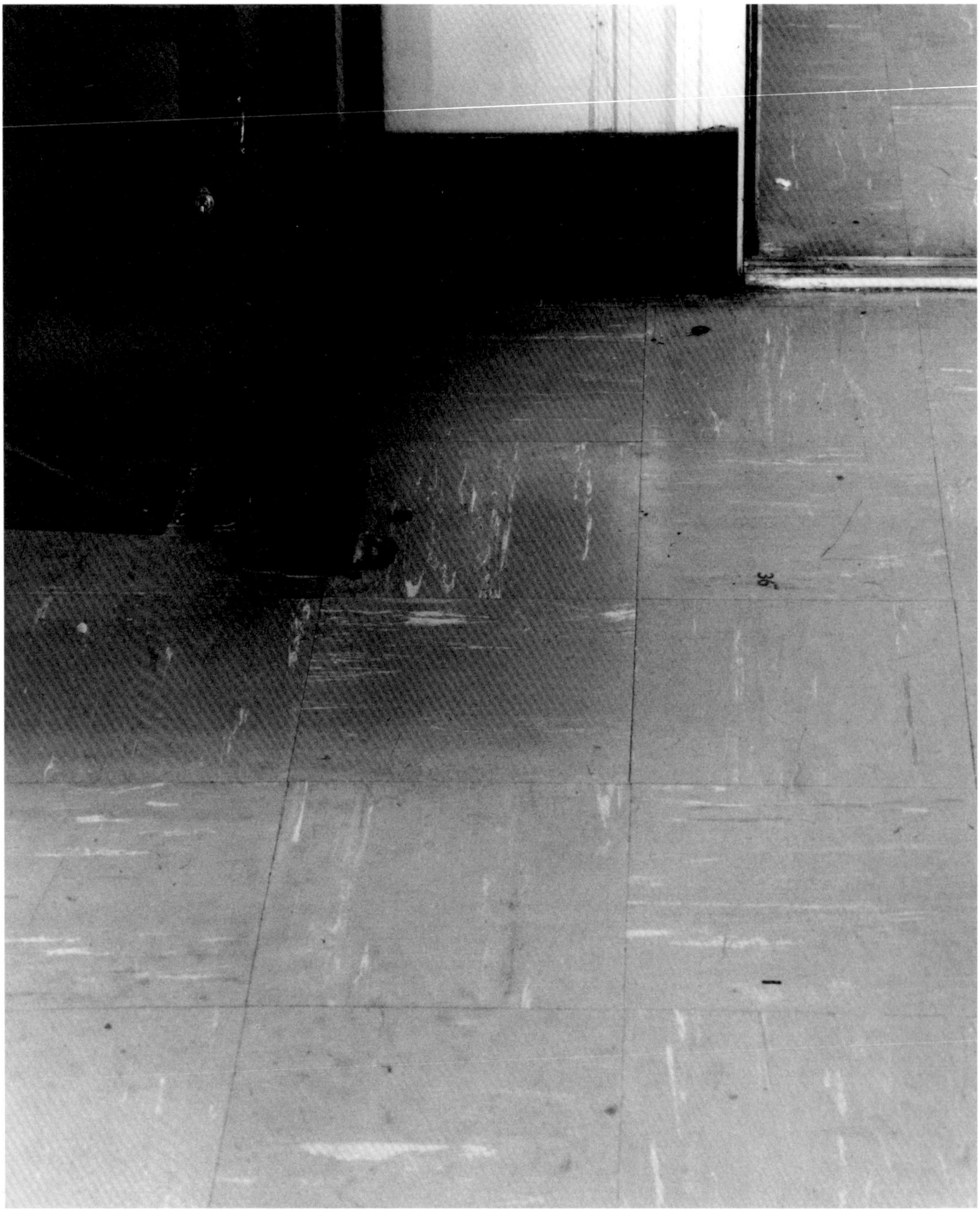

Figure 1.12. Mel Bochner, *Singer Lab Measurement (#2)*, 1968. Gelatin silver print, 10 × 8 inches. Courtesy of the artist.

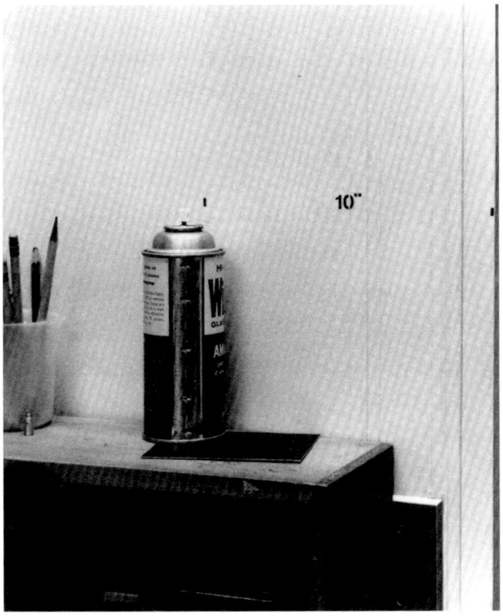

Figure 1.13. Mel Bochner, *Singer Lab Measurement (#1),* 1968. Gelatin silver print, 10 × 8 inches. Courtesy of the artist.

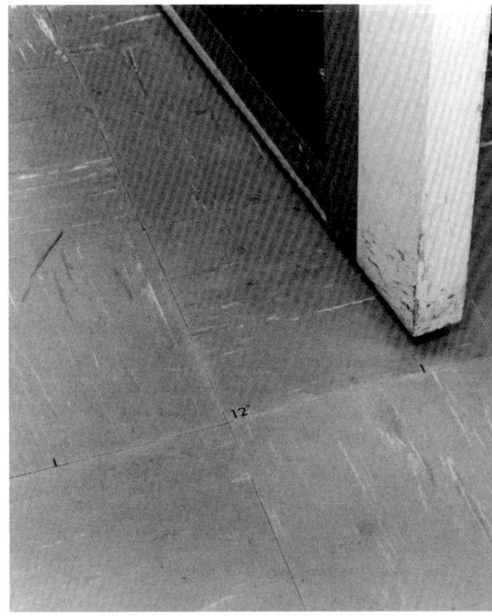

Figure 1.14. Mel Bochner, *Singer Lab Measurement (#4),* 1968. Gelatin silver print, 10 × 8 inches. Courtesy of the artist.

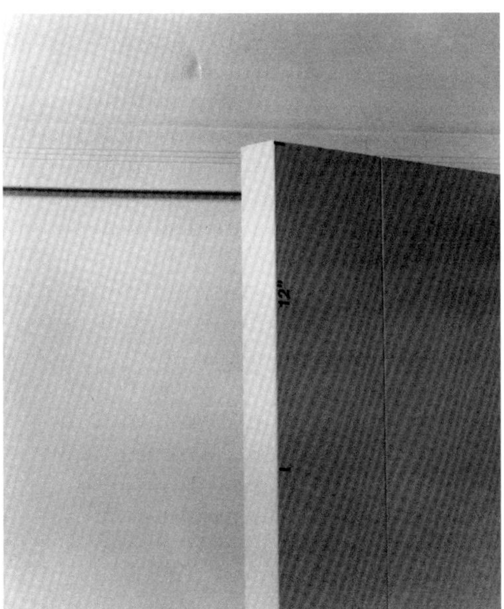

Figure 1.15. Mel Bochner, *Singer Lab Measurement (#3),* 1968. Gelatin silver print, 10 × 8 inches. Courtesy of the artist.

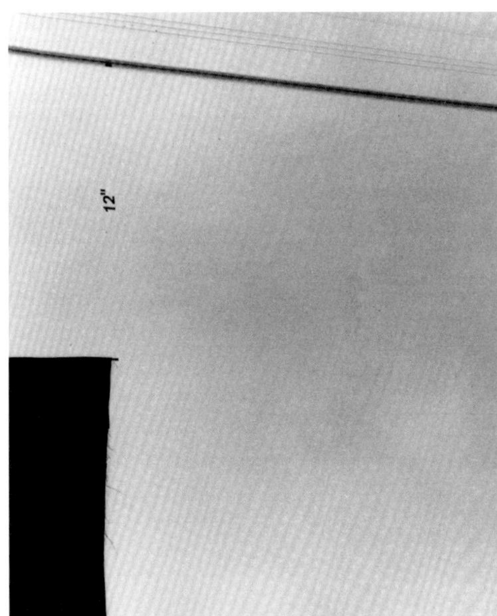

Figure 1.16. Mel Bochner, *Singer Lab Measurement (#5),* 1968. Gelatin silver print, 10 × 8 inches. Courtesy of the artist.

in Dallas, November 22, 1963, at the center of the mystery. Released to the public first as a series of photographic stills, the Zapruder documents fostered countless conspiracy theories. The complete moving sequence of images was censored for twelve years.[70] *Life* magazine ran 31 of the 486 frames in its November 29, 1963, issue but, at least initially, withheld frame no. 313 (Plate 6). This "decisive" grainy image, blurred further by the motion of the amateur cameraman and the speeding vehicle, is arguably the most dissected image in American history. Briefly obstructed from view by trees, Kennedy reemerges into the frame after being shot in the back. Swiftly the president is then shot in the head. Frame 313 famously shows this gruesome fatal moment. As the visual culture historian Marita Sturken has rightly argued, the Zapruder image has been read as a surrogate for Kennedy's absent corpse, which itself has been weighted with symbolically representing the nation at large.[71] Explaining the shifting registers of this traumatic instant, Sturken describes how this image of death on a sunny afternoon became "historicized as the moment when the country changed, when it went from being a nation of promise, good intentions, and youthful optimism to one of cynicism, violence, and pessimism." This stark shift, from Camelot to dark days, is compounded by the unresolved case of the assassination, marked partly by photographic contingency. "Far from revealing the 'truth' about a mysterious, unsolved crime," writes the art historian David Lubin, "it reveals instead the impossibility of knowing, of seeing beyond the frame, of getting to the bottom of one specific imbroglio or, more generally, the human capacity for violence, terror, and evil."[72] The evidence provided by the photographic documentation famously defies analysis while nevertheless compelling endless scrutiny.

On page 32H of that same issue of *Life,* a large-scale photograph, made a day after the assassination to re-create the scene, shows the view over and out of a shady window ledge (Figure 1.17). The attendant text explains: "From this grimy warehouse window ledge of the Texas School Book Depository, the assassin shot President Kennedy." Before a description of the precision of the sniper's aim, how measured his shot must have been, the reader is informed that in addition to "three spent cartridges and a beat-up sawed-off .30-caliber rifle of Italian make fitted with a four-power telescopic sight," detectives also found "an empty soft drink bottle, a crushed cigaret [*sic*] package and gnawed remnants of fried chicken in a greasy paper bag."[73] This descriptive passage sets the scene for the reader's imagination but does little to actually explain what took place. The photograph plays a similarly vacant role, more illustration than evidence. A black arrow indicating the position of Kennedy's car is overlaid on the image, pointing yes, but proving nothing. Akin to Talbot's window and Bochner's photographic play with windows, we have references, indexes, directions, yet we are left empty-handed. Even with the addition of a vector line (which appeared in numerous iterations of the Zapruder stills), the actual information relayed wavers. Was there a second gunman? Someone on the grassy knoll? The Zapruder images would be reprinted and circulated repeatedly throughout the decade. In the November 25, 1966, issue of *Life,* a magnified still would make

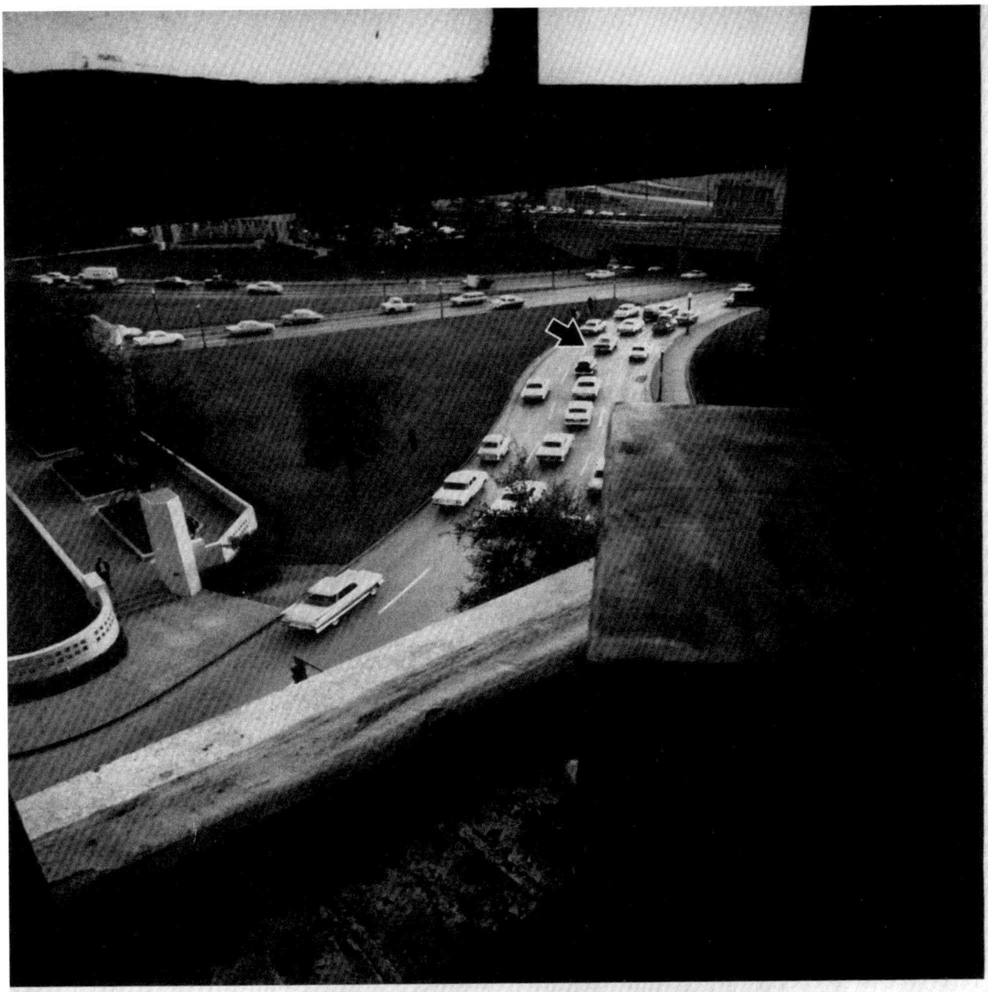

DEATH FOUND HIM FROM THIS WINDOW

From this grimy warehouse window ledge of the Texas School Book Depository, the assassin shot President Kennedy. Stacked book cartons, one of which still lies in right foreground, afforded him makeshift privacy, but he perilously risked exposure by any passerby. It is not yet known how long he waited, but police found an empty soft drink bottle, a crushed cigaret package and gnawed remnants of fried chicken in a greasy paper bag.

This photograph was made a day later to re-create the scene. The President's car had just turned left off Houston Street (where white ornamental fence curves at lower left) and onto Elm Street which funnels into the triple underpass. Slowed by cornering, the car was traveling only about 15 mph when it reached the point in the center lane indicated by an arrow. At that moment two loud, sharp reports were heard and then another.

Measured as sniper's work, the shooting was remarkably effective. The target was moving, 75 yards from the muzzle and about 60 feet lower than the assassin. And both the President and Governor John Connally were hit within seconds.

Under the window police found three spent cartridges and one unused. Then, hidden between two stacks of books, they found the weapon, a beat-up sawed-off .30-caliber rifle of Italian make fitted with a four-power telescopic sight.

On page 37: Story of the man held as assassin
On page 72D: The life of President Lyndon Johnson
On page 101: Warm memories of J.F.K.

32H

Figure 1.17. "Death Found Him from This Window," page 32H, *Life* magazine, November 29, 1963.

the cover with the tagline "A Matter of Reasonable Doubt." Within mass culture, the very notion of photographic evidence becomes ballistic in the 1960s.

On the subject of the Zapruder "evidence," Bochner recounts how "the mind boggled at so many contradictory versions of one six-second period."[74] In July 1967 Bochner published a pointed article titled "Consumer Testing *The Warren Report*: Kennedy's Assassination as TV Serial," in which he analyzed a four-part CBS television series moderated by Walter Cronkite on *The Warren Report*. Each segment revolved around a specific question. First, did Oswald kill Kennedy? Second, was Oswald the lone assassin? Third, was there a conspiracy? Fourth, should we trust *The Warren Report*? The way the sequence of questions foreclose on possible answers comes across as near parody. "Given the way in which the questions were framed on the first night, the 'answers' became self-evident," concluded Bochner.[75] The constructed fiction of the mini-series imitated police dramas, sounding like "a 'Perry Mason' cross-examination,"[76] and every attempt to measure the evidence led only to further degrees of doubt. Commenting specifically on the camera work, Bochner describes the way this CBS special presentation shared the look of cinema verité: "unusual angles predominated, cropped shots of figures, exaggerated zooms from the window to the street to the window, usually winding up nowhere in particular."[77]

Michelangelo Antonioni's *Blow-Up* (1966), the Italian director's first English-language film, poses a further pop-culture connection to Bochner's interest in photographic displacement and duplicity. At the center of "Swinging London," the protagonist is a photographer, notoriously "a man who looks but doesn't see," who inadvertently photographs a murder.[78] Or does he? During the most memorable sequence, we witness the unnamed photographer, solo in his darkroom. The camera cuts between photographs and the photographer's gaze, moving in closer and closer until we are immersed in blown-up pixels, confronted with what might be a gunman in the bushes and a body on the ground. Or not. Like Bochner's close-ups in the *Singer Lab* series, photographs in *Blow-Up* hint at intriguing cover-ups while remaining anticlimactic.

The obsession of the 1960s with scrutinizing obscure photographs, in an ultimately inconclusive search for meaning, weaves its way throughout Bochner's artistic experiments with the medium. The term *blow-up* in fact became the subtitle of yet another version of *Surface Dis/Tension* in 1969, which, by a paradoxical twist, is actually substantially smaller than Bochner's original from 1968. *Surface Dis/Tension: Blowup* subverts our expectations of size and of what might be gained by scaling an image up or down, calling attention to the volatility of the photograph (Figure 1.18).[79] In this instance Bochner's elusive sculptural image is an identical reproduction of the first version shrunk down to half its dimensions. Sitting on the floor, leaning precariously against the wall, this iteration involves a renewed recognition of the surface of the wall itself. Surrounding the photographic work is an outlined measurement, echoing the *Singer Lab* Letrasets, demarcating the size of the missing original *Surface Dis/Tension*.

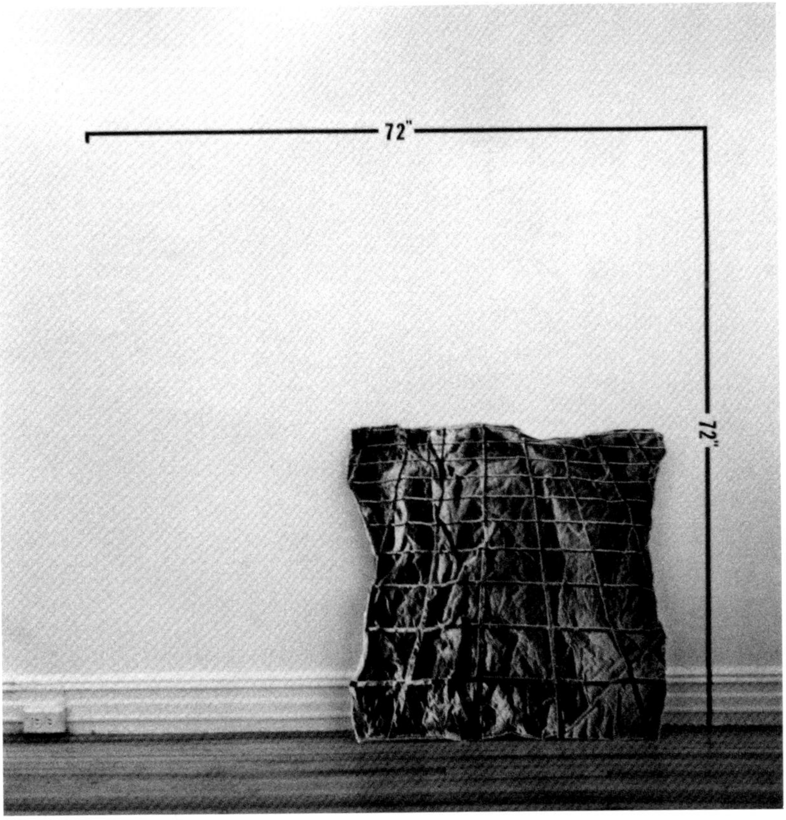

Figure 1.18. *Surface Dis/Tension: Blowup,* 1969. Gelatin silver print mounted on board, black tape and Letraset on wall, 73½ × 73½ inches. Courtesy of the artist.

Measurement preoccupied Bochner in tandem with photography during the final years of the 1960s. By 1969 Bochner had begun his most well-known installations, including *Measurement: Room* (1969) and the more ominous *Measurement: Shadow* (1969) (Figures 1.19 and 1.20). Thick strips of black run along plain-faced walls accompanied by notational numbers, reasonably giving the impression of architectural plans, forensic reports, and staged preparatory sets. Their purpose and meaning are indistinct, despite their simple presentation of objects and measurements. Courting yet another conceptual game between opacity and transparence, the artist began to consider these new measurements as works in themselves rather than as situations for photographs.[80] Notably, Bochner has commented on the connection retained between these installation works and the medium of photography, calling the distances marked on the wall, projections of the room's "negative" or blueprint onto the space in question.[81]

The ghostly aspect of the barren "measurements," floating eerily in the empty white space of the modern gallery, also recalls André Malraux's hypothetical situation described in his 1947 book *Le Musée imaginaire (The Museum without Walls),*

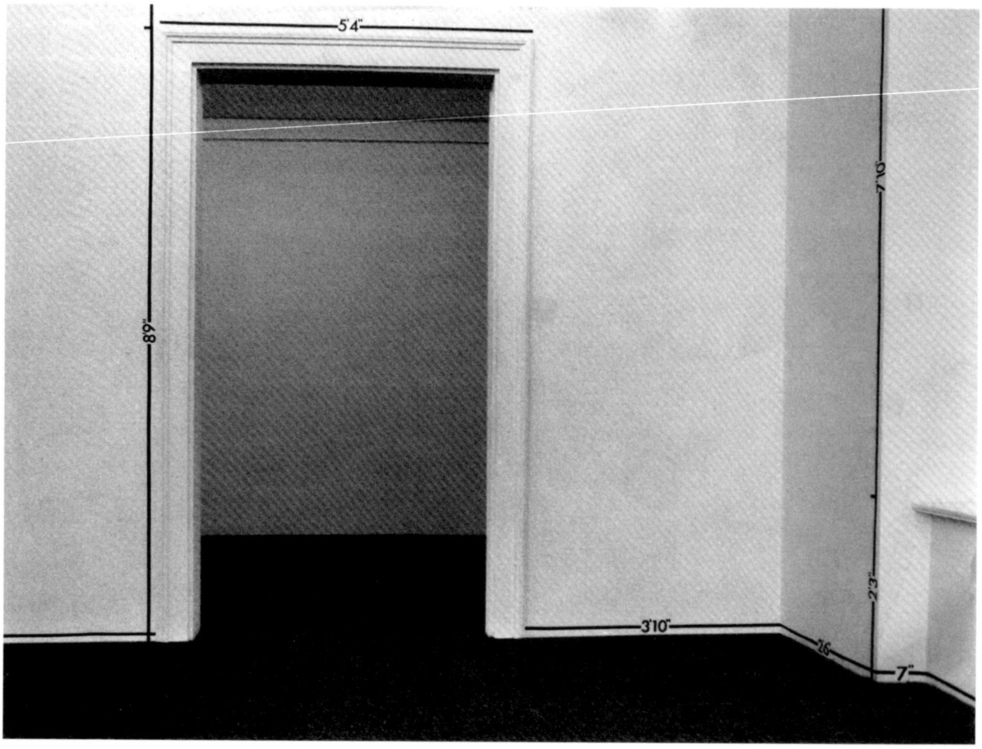

Figure 1.19. Mel Bochner, *Measurement: Room,* 1969. Tape and Letraset on wall. Courtesy of the artist.

in which the physical body of the museum would dissolve, to be replaced by photographs. Bochner's artwork seems to propose that even if Malraux's museum were possible, it would certainly still have walls, albeit conceptual ones, seeing as photography is always a medium as well as a support. Photography gives access at the same time that it inevitably sets up new boundaries. As Douglas Crimp has explained, "Photography not only secures the admittance of various objects, fragments of objects, details of objects to the museum; it is also the organizing device; it reduces the now even vaster heterogeneity to a single perfect similitude."[82] Bochner pursues the imperfection of this correlation by interrogating photography as an illusionistic medium. His initial aspirations for objectivity, coming out of minimalism, were frustrated repeatedly, and thus he began to deconstruct photography as a depictive, comprehensive, or self-sufficient medium, challenging its purported ontological ground. The use of the measurements parallels this destabilization. Moreover, the very idea of measurement can in fact be viewed as a conceptual work of art, particularly since any measurement is a feat of conceptualization. After all, as Bochner emphasized in his comments on the kinship between photographic framing and the act of measuring, measuring as a conceptual process certainly shares much in common with the process of photography.

Closing in on how measuring is an attempt to delimit the world while building on

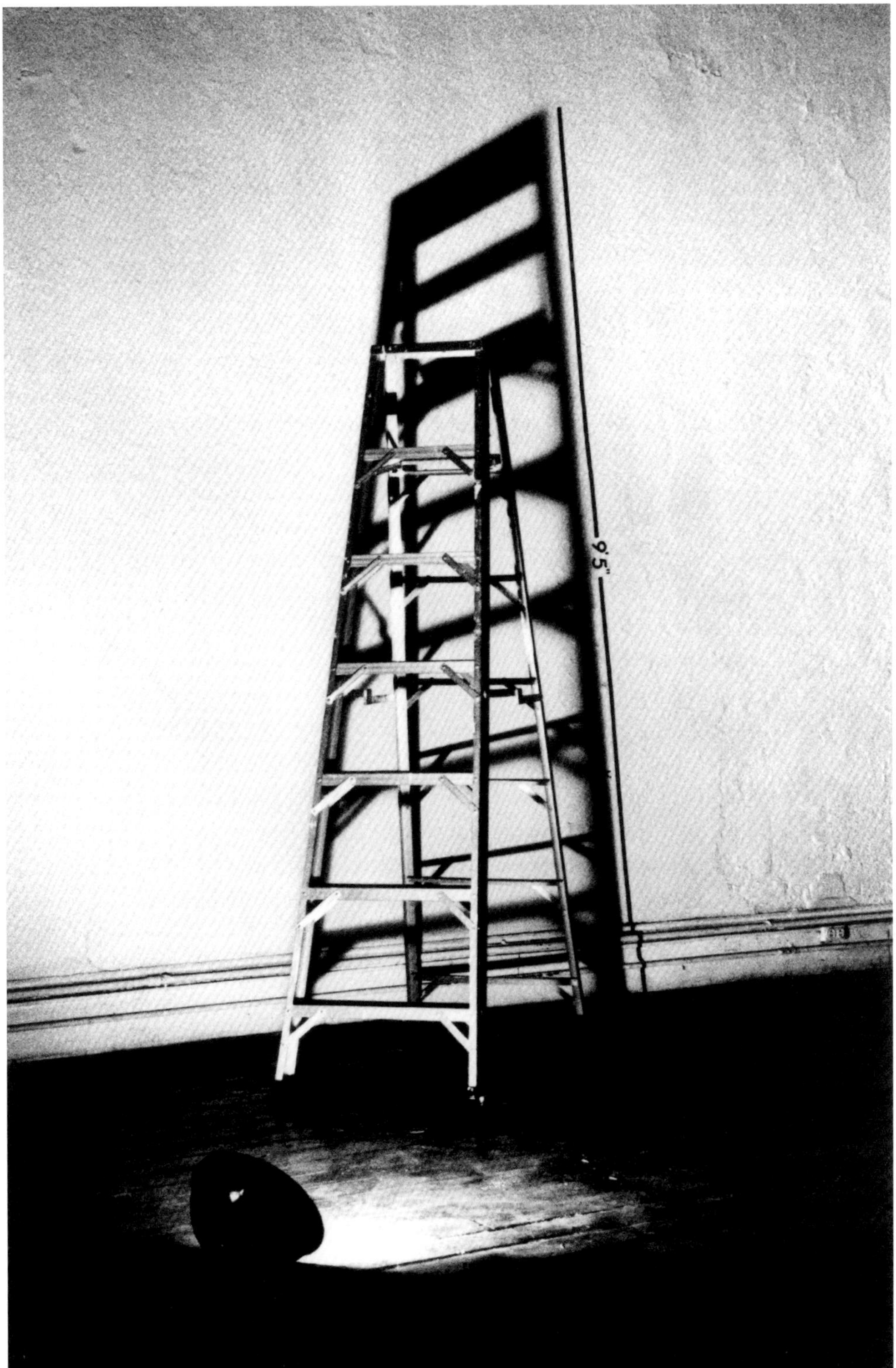

Figure 1.20. Mel Bochner, *Measurement: Shadow,* 1969. Ladder, lamp on floor, and vinyl on wall. Courtesy of the artist.

minimalism's approach to art as an epistemological inquiry, Bochner attempted to expose the inherent instability of measurements, in order to highlight the parameters that are too often taken for granted. Beyond problematizing photography in both material and representational senses, Bochner made the very idea of inches and feet strange. Though many of these projects were exhibited exclusively as "direct" experiential spaces, with no photographic mediation after 1969, it is significant to remember that the artist's initial foray into the measurements took the form of photographs, and, at least initially, they could be experienced only through images. In this way, we could say that a photographic logic underpins the *Measurements* series as a whole. Looking back to those initial inconspicuous black-and-white photographs, in which Bochner marked off various distances in small black Letraset numbers, the square linoleum tiles can be read as allusions once more to the modernist grid. The photographs also draw connections to the Renaissance construction of space, which Bochner had pried apart in previous photographic experiments. The ultimate significance of the spaces, the objects, or the measurements contained therein is never clearly deducible.

More than a conceptual redefinition of space and sculptural objects, Bochner's measurements implicate the photograph as measure of the world and as a way to glean experience. Perhaps more compellingly, the predictive sensibility of Bochner's demarcated measurement rooms also registers the increasing separation of lived reality from direct experience: "All this empty space can be unexpectedly uncomfortable, the tape wrapping around your sense of self like a searing curl of existential dread—a public-pool-size uncanny valley. There's a prophetic tinge in seeing the work now, as though Bochner's 1969 design anticipated the ubiquity of screens in our lives, and the fact that direct physical perception is not valued in the same way as it was, or at all."[83] Elaborating specifically on his understanding of the conceptual supports that account for standards of evaluating dimensions and for buttressing belief systems, Bochner explained:

> Its commonness of application renders it virtually invisible. Measurement is one of our means of believing that the world can be reduced to a function of human understanding. Yet, when forced to surrender its transparency, measurement reveals an essential nothing-ness. The yardstick does not say that the thing we are measuring is one yard long. Something must be added to the yardstick in order that it assert anything about the length of the object. This something is a purely mental act . . . an "assumption."[84]

The very notion of measurement here seems remarkably interchangeable with the photograph. In both instances, transparency contends with the ultimate opacity of the world.

On the other hand, Bochner's clever use of feet and inches points significantly back to the bodily nature of these measurements and of the perception/experience of space. Beyond referencing the often-unacknowledged perceptual baggage that ac-

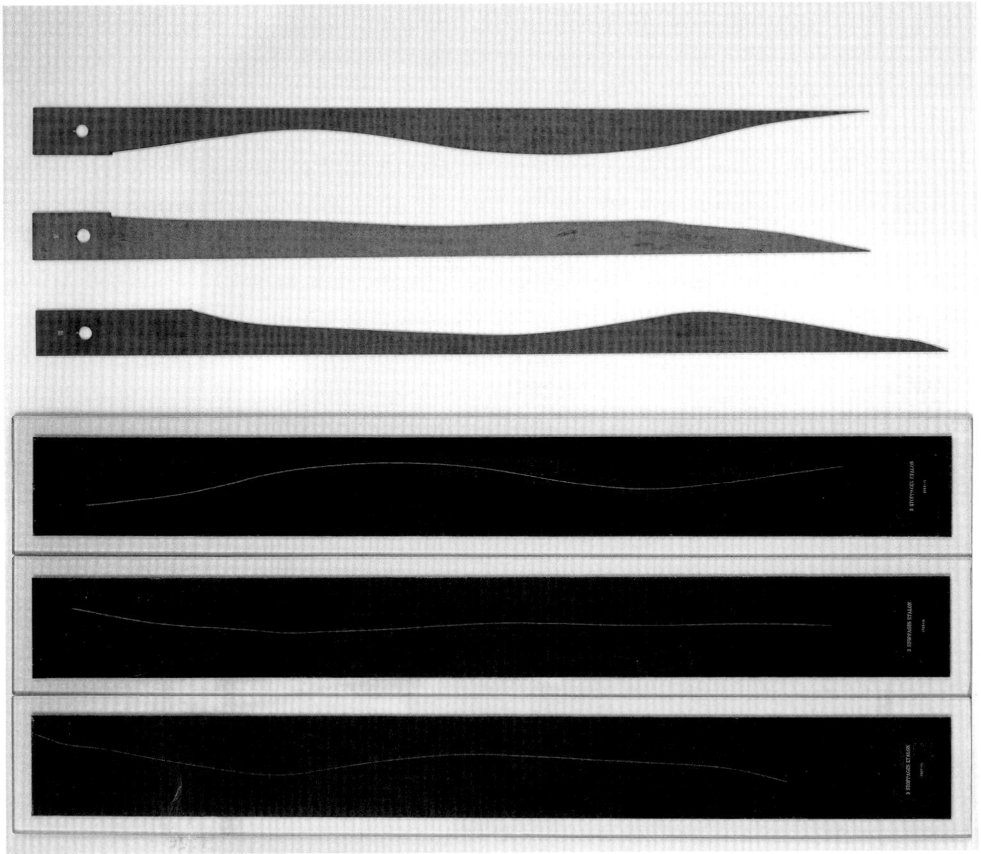

Figure 1.21. Marcel Duchamp, *Three Standard Stoppages,* 1913–14. Wood box 11⅛ × 50⅞ × 9 inches (28.2 × 129.2 × 22.7 cm), with three threads 39⅜ inches (100 cm), glued to three painted canvas strips 5¼ × 47¼ inches (13.3 × 120 cm), each mounted on a glass panel 7¼ × 49⅜ × ¼ inches (18.4 × 125.4 × 0.6 cm), three wood slats 2½ × 43 × ⅛ inches (6.2 × 109.2 × 0.2 cm), shaped along one edge to match the curves of the threads. Katherine S. Dreier Bequest. Copyright Artists Rights Society (ARS), New York / ADAGP, Paris / Estate of Marcel Duchamp. The Museum of Modern Art digital image copyright The Museum of Modern Art. Licensed by SCALA / Art Resource, NY.

companies all systems of human measurement, the foot and inch system specifically is tied to the proportions of the human body—despite the fact that those proportions are by no means universal. Noting a shift from index to implex in Bochner's work, Yve-Alain Bois contends that Bochner's experiments reveal how "all measurements are indices."[85] Bois's choice of words here is telling, since "indices" in French also signifies "clues," thereby suggesting traces marked by doubt rather than firm or conclusive answers.

The way Bochner's *Measurements* series questions the referential nature of measurement can be productively compared to Marcel Duchamp's *Three Standard Stoppages* (1913–14) (Figure 1.21). Both pieces are implicitly photographic, and *Three Standard Stoppages* (also known as *Canned Chance: Trois stoppages étalon*) is the most illustrative conceptual precedent of this conundrum of indices. Like Bochner's work, it demonstrates the artist's interest in mathematics as well as the concept of chance. Duchamp dropped three threads, each one meter long, from a height of one meter, and documented the results. Each fell in its own random shape and was then glued on Prussian blue canvas cut into three strips. These canvas strips were glued to three glass panels through which the threads are visible. Three wood slats were shaped along one side to match the curved paths taken by the threads. Together all these pieces were encased in a wooden box. This piece demonstrates the generative activity of creating a work as the expression of a procedure, which anticipates the core principles on which much conceptualism operates. Brought about by following a step-by-step set of rules, *Three Standard Stoppages,* like Bochner's *Measurements,* reveals the arbitrary nature of standards and measurements. The typically functional aspect of such measures is thrown into doubt. Instead, a meter, or any other quantifiable measurement for that matter, is revealed as culturally constructed and pliable. In effect, these projects also question the notion of the straight line, in that when it falls to chance, a meter no longer equals a meter. There is also an additional analogy to the photograph embedded in these glass plates, for "when Duchamp's pieces of string twisted themselves, 'as they pleased,' through time and space, they were stopped, frozen, by their impact with the pieces of canvas glued onto glass plates, just as the movement of the real world through time and space is stopped, frozen, by the exposure of glass photographic plates."[86] *Three Standard Stoppages* emblematizes photographic chance while denouncing the possibility of objective measurement.

Connections can also be made to the work of other conceptual artists who were grappling with the dubious standardization of the world, such as John Baldessari's *Measurement Series: Measuring a Chair with a Coffee Cup (Top-Bottoms)* (1975), in which the artist photographically documents his use of his coffee mug as a kind of viewfinder in sizing up his studio while he reclines in a chair behind the camera. The coffee cup as standard or measure seems about as arbitrary here as the concept of a meter. Baldessari's later *Three Metaphorical Measurements* (1980) humorously takes this point further by inscribing the walls of a room not with numerical measurements but with language in a manner that brings Lawrence Weiner to mind. For example, one wall reads "AS FAR AS FROM EAST TO WEST" and another, "AS HIGH AS HEAVEN AND AS DEEP AS HELL," using metaphoric expressions to map out the width and height of the space. Baldessari has explained that, as opposed to "specific measurement," he believes "idiomatic language is usually more evocative of what we really mean—more to the point than specific information. A person that is really cold does not say, 'it's 10 degrees below zero' but 'it's colder than hell!'"[87] The irony of Baldessari's example makes the idea of finding appropriate analogies in order to understand the world doubly abstract by describing hell, which is typically described as an inferno, as particularly cold.

One striking difference between Duchamp or Baldessari and Bochner is that Bochner retains the use of the regimented straight line. No curves or extrinsic language enter his measurement series. Or at least, so it seems. His apparently uninflected method is deceptive. As Bochner described in 1969, "I slowly came to realize that these measurements are so deeply imbedded in our experience that they regulate our perception, yet remain completely invisible."[88] Bochner tests this invisibility just as he had deconstructed objectivity and transparence in the earlier photo pieces.

Bochner's refusal to disclose the meaning of the physical marks in this series causes them to seem nearly absurd, being "robbed of the function they would usually perform."[89] The concept of a straight line itself is of course misleading. In a 1971 installation in Spoleto, Italy, Bochner inscribed with chalk across a stone floor: "THERE IS A LABYRINTH WHICH IS A STRAIGHT LINE . . ." JORGE LUIS BORGES. Positioned between two walls, and titled *Quotation Piece: "There is a labyrinth . . . ,"* this piece speaks not simply of the popularity of Borges in New York art circles in the late 1960s and early 1970s but to the importance of a basic skepticism regarding objectivity that increasingly became crucial to Bochner's conceptually labyrinthine work.

Similarly, each scene in the *Measurements* series, whether a photographic work or an installation, poses an a priori spatial concept (such as a particular measurement or perspective) in relation to the physical world it is expected to describe. Each is also burdened by the reality of its situation, which makes any one concept insufficient for understanding the world. Noticeably, there are small intervals between the actual architectural elements and the taped measures that mark the space. This observation reinforces "the impression that the room had been duplicated,"[90] in effect posing a meta-interrogation of the photographic process. The apparent disregard for the specific "ground" of the measurement makes them only all the more imprecise, which is compounded again when the scale shifts further by being photographically documented. Such projects point to how space is always perceived according to a set of culturally constructed standards and Bochner's stated intention to "change the work of art's function for the viewer," so that "art would go from being the record of someone else's perception to becoming the recognition of your own."[91]

The art historian and critic Robert Pincus-Witten described Bochner in 1971 as "an epistemological Conceptualist . . . engaged in the study of knowledge as its own end. He tends to make or do things for the kinds of information, knowledge or data, which the things or activities reveal. He tends to be a grammarian, a mathematician, a cartographer."[92] Pincus-Witten was right to note Bochner's distinctive epistemological questioning; however, it is important to also mention that this search for "information, knowledge or data" is a way to open more questions rather than be grounded in any definite answers. Whereas "Modernist theory led us to believe that these issues were all resolved," Bochner has explained that in his deconstructionist practice, "[he wanted] to show that there is no resolution, no firm ground. Everything that is given is immediately taken away."[93]

Beyond the way that the taped measurements in the room suggest the phenomenon of reproduction by doubling the frame of the space, there is another crucial link between the measurements and the photograph, which, though it is accentuated by the fact of having the rooms or spaces photographically documented, remains true even when there is no attendant photograph. I am referring to the ways in which the photographs and measurements are able to serve as implicit, if not explicit, tools of institutional critique. Photographs and museums, particularly in the sixties, were considered containers of art rather than art themselves.[94] Art practices such as Bochner's, or Michael Asher's or Nauman's for that matter, reveal the suspension of disbelief that underpins these viewpoints.

By taking measure of the space of the gallery or museum, Bochner in effect measured the supports that prop "up the ideology of the autonomous art object."[95] Like the photograph, the measurements seem to "picture" any given space without apparent discrimination, yet, via their seemingly invisible framing capacity, the measurements are also able to make visible the constructed dimensions that had previously seemed inevitable.[96] The medium of photography, like the space of the museum, adds something magical to what it records or frames. Both photography and the museum also share the metaphoric if not literal function of preserving time and conserving their contents.[97]

As Luke Skrebowski eloquently outlines, "Taping up the gallery space has the effect of taping it off, making us acutely aware of its presence, as if at the scene of a crime."[98] Skrebowski's observation brings to mind Walter Benjamin's description of Eugène Atget's photographs of deserted Parisian streets. This connection is not haphazard, since both examples emphasize the "exhibition value" of photography and the use of the photograph as evidence. According to Benjamin, "With Atget, photographs become standard evidence for historical occurrences and acquire a hidden political significance."[99] With Bochner, the gallery is revealed as supporting canonical art forms and entrenched ways of seeing that similarly hold implicit political meaning. Moreover, this suggestion of the crime scene as an exhibit of evidence returns to the preceding discussion of the ambivalent status of photography as evidence at this juncture.

The suspicious rupture between subjective perception and objective measurement can never be fully mended. The first two photographs from the *Measurement* series bring this challenge of self-doubt to bear on "actual" photographs of the artist. In *Actual Size (Face)* and *Actual Size (Hand)* (both 1968), the first shows Bochner's face, the other his hand, each positioned next to a vertical line that has been traced on the wall as an indication of his measurements (Figures 1.22, 1.23). In both gelatin silver prints, Bochner's body appears alongside this thin black line, featuring a segmented section that reads **12"**. Oddly, the numerical inclusion of a distinct measurement actually makes the image and the figure of the artist only more abstract as an empirical entity, since it remains difficult to judge precisely where the demarcated twelve inches intersect Bochner's body. The image of the hand could be read as even more misleading, since the absence of the artist's face also calls into question the identity of the "actual" body to which this hand belongs. These images were intended to be printed at a ratio of 1:1, so that the **12"** mark in the image occupies

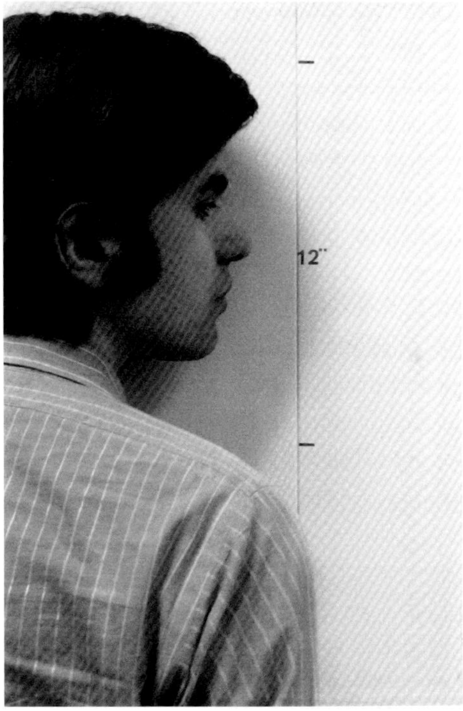

Figure 1.22. Mel Bochner, *Actual Size (Face)*, 1968. Gelatin silver print, 22 × 14¼ inches. Courtesy of the artist.

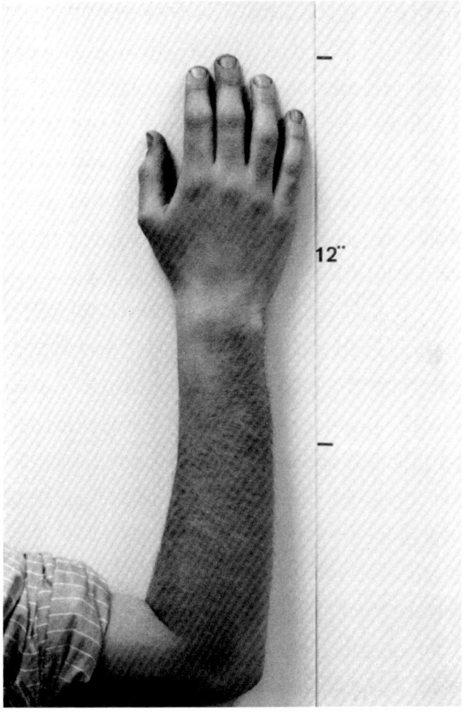

Figure 1.23. Mel Bochner, *Actual Size (Hand)*, 1968. Gelatin silver print, 22 × 14¼ inches. Courtesy of the artist.

exactly twelve inches on the paper. Doing so does not make the images more real; rather, it reveals the unwieldy incompleteness of this circular logic.[100] At any size, the photograph will never be the thing itself. This somewhat ironic emphasis on the actual recurs in the photographic work of many conceptual artists, for example, in Joseph Kosuth's *One and Three Chairs* (1965) and in Nauman's *Composite Photo of Two Messes on the Studio Floor* (1967). Though the motive in each of these cases differs, the impulse shares something in common—namely, pushing the limits of photography's presumed privileged access to objective reality. A further precedent can be found in the work of Robert Rauschenberg a decade earlier, who described his plan "to walk across the United States and photograph it foot by foot in actual size." This ambitious piece was never realized. Rauschenberg confessed: "I figured that in twenty years I would be in jail in Ashland for trespassing if I followed through with that idea."[101] The artist's sense that there would be something transgressive in attempting to tie a photograph so closely to the actual has echoes as well. Notably, turning back to Bochner's profile prints, these images too are loaded with implied criminality. If anything, *Actual Size (Face)* and *Actual Size (Hand)* return convincingly to the scene of a crime, in that their structure alludes to categorical photography and, more specifically, to mugshots. Like the attempted rationalization of police photography by Alphonse Bertillon in nineteenth-century France, an essential irrationality is instead exposed. "Contrary to the commonplace understanding of the 'mugshot' as the very exemplar of a powerful, artless, and wholly denotative visual empiricism," argued Allan Sekula, "these early instrumental uses of photographic realism were systematized on the basis of an acute recognition of the inadequacies and limitations of ordinary visual empiricism."[102] Bochner's project similarly confounds expectations of appearance and understanding, exemplifying the artist's accurate awareness of the fundamental and highly contingent inadequacy of human perception and photographic vision at every turn.

In the end, Bochner's photographic puzzle is left at loose ends. The realization of this "vicious circle," as Bochner has called it, obliged him to announce: "That, for me, was the end of photography."[103] Deducing what photography was *not*, rather than gaining any certainty as to what photography is, Bochner understood that the medium of photography, despite its indexical claims to comprehension, was and would always be a test of the immeasurable flux between reality, representation, and perception.

Misunderstandings

Arguments against autonomy are essential tactics of conceptual art practice. Aided and abetted by photography, conceptual art's critique of stable authorship takes on multiple dimensions, many of which are consciously contradictory. Bochner's *Misunderstandings (A Theory of Photography)* is a conceptual piece that deliberately calls attention to photography's distinctive characteristics while encouraging a game of mistaken identities (Figure 1.24). It is composed of a manila envelope containing one reproduced photograph and nine photographs of index cards, each with a quote from a famous author handwritten on it. Each quote is presented as a "theory of photography," as a way, as Roland Barthes would say, "to learn at all costs what Photography was 'in itself.'"[104] Beyond the fact that the index-card format is reminiscent of notes for studying, the collection is presented in an envelope that may also be read as a reference to Barthes's calling the photograph a "transparent envelope,"[105] despite the opacity of the information contained therein. Yet another connotation, in both form and theme, is the popular detective board game Clue, which asks players to determine who murdered the game's victim, the punningly named "Mr. Boddy." The solution to the crime remains hidden in a small manila envelope at the center of the board, itself organized as though it were an architectural plan, while players move from room to room, taking turns asking one another for clues.

An eclectic grouping of suspects is involved in Bochner's version, including Marcel Duchamp, Émile Zola, Ludwig Wittgenstein, Taine, Mao Tse-tung, Marcel Proust, James J. Gibson, Maurice Merleau-Ponty, and the *Encyclopedia Britannica*. Each one is subsumed paradoxically by Bochner's own asserted "authorship," evidenced by the fact of his purposely handwritten transcriptions, and stylistically by his quick, apparently haphazard penmanship to inscribe their quotations. His use of handwriting, as opposed to the typewritten statements that typify most conceptual art of this era, suggests his desire to emphasize the inevitably subjective as-

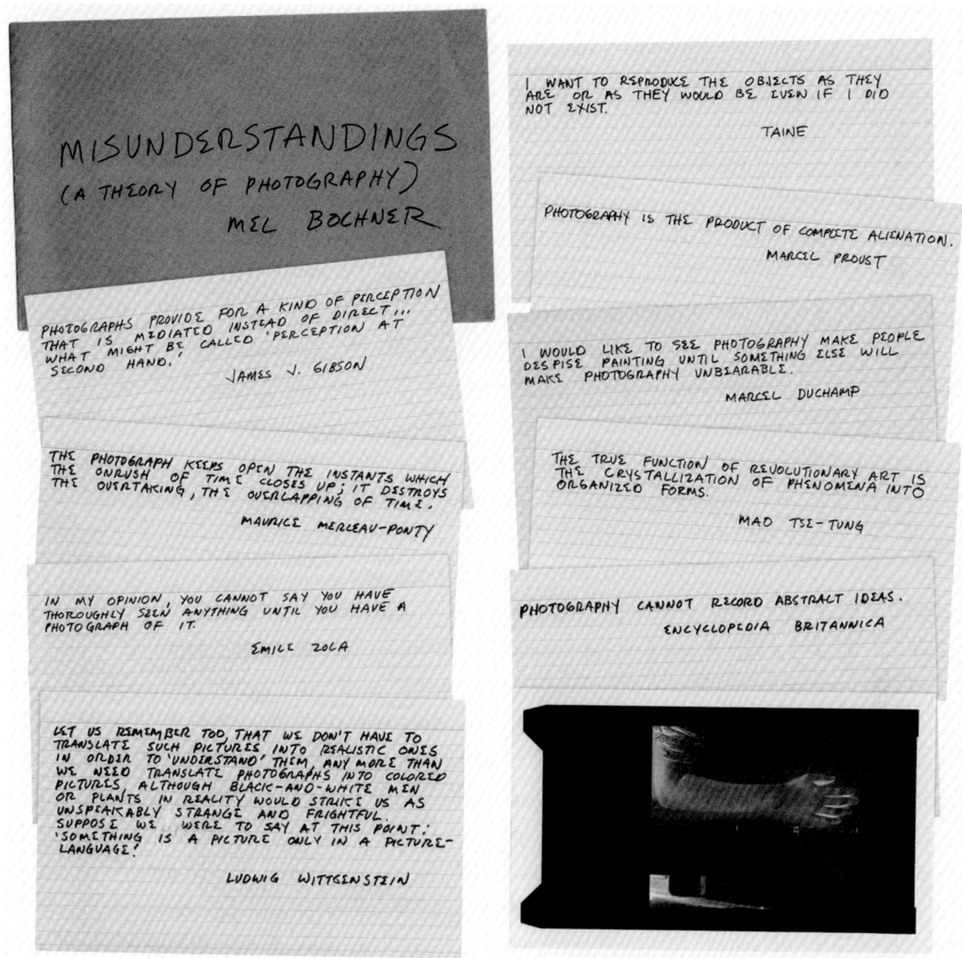

Figure 1.24. Mel Bochner, *Misunderstandings (A Theory of Photography)*, 1970. Photo offset on ten index cards, manila envelope, 5 × 8 inches each. Courtesy of the artist.

pects of purportedly objective theories. This casualness is itself misleading. As an ironic gesture, the hand of the artist thus underscores and complicates the logic and readability of the overall piece, seeming to say that not only is any theory of photography subjective, but it is always entwined in multiple subjectivities.

Originally compiled by Bochner for an article appropriately titled "Dead Ends and Vicious Circles" (1969), the quotations themselves have many layers of provenance. They were initially offered to and rejected by both *Artforum* and *Art in America* in the late spring of 1969. In Bochner's words:

> I submitted it to *Artforum* but Philip Leader said "we're not a goddamn photography magazine, this is an art magazine, don't give me anything on photography, we don't do photography!" Then I sent it to *Art in America* and they were not interested either, but suggested that I send it to a photography magazine! Like

> *Popular Photography*! Well I knew that no photography magazine could possibly be interested in this, so I put it in a drawer and forgot about it.[106]

Bochner's *Misunderstandings (A Theory of Photography)* became the artist's farewell to photography as such, for though on occasion he would make individual photographs after 1969, fewer than five exist. The *Misunderstandings* collection, enclosed in a standard manila envelope, albeit without a seal,[107] finally saw the light of day under the auspices of Marian Goodman's Multiples Gallery as part of *Artists and Photographs*. This box set included contributions by Christo, Jan Dibbets, Tom Gormley, Dan Graham, Huebler, Allan Kaprow, Michael Kirby, Kosuth, LeWitt, Richard Long, Robert Morris, Nauman, Dennis Oppenheim, Rauschenberg, Ruscha, Smithson, Bernar Venet, and Andy Warhol, and a text by Lawrence Alloway.

Each quotation in Bochner's piece is inscribed on an index card, which has been reproduced photographically and is equivalent in size to all the rest, as well as to the only "actual" photograph contained: an image of Bochner's own arm and hand. This formal and measured equivalence between the frame of the cards may be taken as a proposal that all the claims are equal, and by extension that each author's authority on the subject is equal. It can also be read as a formal wink back at Bochner's early interest in minimalism's systemic organization. Difficulties arise immediately, however, as one considers the disparities. For example, the fact that the grand authority and conventional wisdom of the *Encyclopedia Britannica* is ultimately the most anonymous and unknowable of all the contributors, and that individuals such as Duchamp founded entire careers on their ability to be duplicitous by keeping their identities and intentions in flux. As Skrebowski has insightfully noted, it is not by chance that Bochner chose the *Encyclopedia Britannica,* since to check the veracity of the citation, "the scholar would have to take up the labyrinthine challenge of working through the entire back history of the Britannica from the date of first entry on photography. This is so extensive that even the British Library does not hold the complete set of all relevant editions."[108] Raising parallels with *Working Drawings, Theory of Photography* highlights once again how a statement that seems straightforward can become a labyrinth.

Fundamentally, Bochner's *Theory of Photography* intentionally courts confusion. Rather than provide clear insight into the ontology of photography, for example, it frustrates one's ability to "know" photography at all. One is presented with myriad false identities, some more persuasive than others, yet all are cloaked by a peculiar shadow of a doubt that questions the ultimate truth-value of photography and any theoretical or conceptual measure of the medium. While Émile Zola claims, "In my opinion, you cannot say you have thoroughly seen anything until you have a photograph of it," the viewer/reader of *Misunderstandings* is paradoxically challenged by the cryptic legibility of the photographs presented.

In the age of the internet, decisive clarity on the sources and veracity of Bochner's quotes remains elusive. If one searches for the *Britannica* quote, thousands of pages come up reiterating the statement. None of them are officially the *Encyclopedia*

Britannica, however, and in fact, most cite Bochner citing *Britannica,* as though the repetition of the utterance itself makes it true. Similarly, a search for the Duchamp quote returns only results attributed to Bochner, suggesting that Bochner indeed took notes from Duchamp's cagey maneuvers. The Zola quote is indeed from the man himself, but it bears mentioning that Zola suffered from a diagnosed case of myopia, so what he did or did not "thoroughly" see is ultimately questionable.

Duchamp and the *Encyclopedia Britannica* share, despite their admittedly differing definitions of photography's meaning, the assertion that truth is a social construct, created by popular agreements on how the world can be legitimately organized, classified, and by extension understood. While *Encyclopedia Britannica* articulates "common-sense" definitions in order to give wider authority to them, Duchamp's practice highlights the internal contradictions in the notion of "common sense" and challenges the authority that claims to substantiate it. Thus these two "theories" could be read as an argument against each other. Each nevertheless exposes the subjective element intrinsic to human measures of truth. Importantly, Bochner has admitted that three of the nine quotations are fake, invented by himself, and he has never disclosed which are which.[109] Perhaps it does not matter. As Bochner has explained in a description that draws striking parallels to the earlier exploration of the index in the *Measurement* series: "The 'groundlessness' of the quotations became the equivalent of the 'groundlessness' of photography itself, focusing attention on the artificiality of any framing device."[110] What is crucial for this project is the knowledge that the "theories" can never entirely be trusted, all frames are subject to falsehoods, and their inevitable "groundlessness" leads to a vertigo-like dizzying doubt. The quotation, like the photograph, always exists at a remove from the original utterance and is thus always subject to being confused or altered in translation. Both exist in a space from which the referent is absent. The space between the statements in *Misunderstandings* and their sources is recursively suspect, since they are then presented as photographs, adding a further level of indexical remove to what each purports to represent.

Among the quotations that compose *Misunderstandings,* one in particular seems to have been especially prescient for Bochner, since it is the only one among them that was singled out and reproduced as the subject of an individual photographic print. This is the text attributed to *Encyclopedia Britannica* that reads "Photography cannot record abstract ideas." *Photography Cannot Record Abstract Ideas* (1969) was also issued as an individual work, and, ironically, both versions of this quotation give the lie to themselves, by being records of an abstract idea. Like Duchamp's quotation "I would like to see photography make people despise painting until something else will make photography unbearable,"[111] which evokes the cliché that one representational art will simply replace another, this quote challenges the limits of photography's representational abilities. The photograph may act as a stand-in literally and figuratively, but what are the boundaries of this make-believe?

Ideological and political investments are further implicated by Bochner's piece with the inclusion of definitions of photography by figures such as Mao, while theoretical commitments and varying contextual approaches are also thrown into the mix, namely, through contributions from Wittgenstein, Merleau-Ponty, and Taine (who one imagines is Hippolyte Taine). Whose statement is to be taken as true, or valuable? Or, for that matter, real? Should Mao's belief that "the true function of revolutionary art is the crystallization of phenomena into organized forms" be more or less weighted than Proust's idea that "photography is the product of complete alienation"?

The only image included with this set of photographed quotes further accentuates the viewer's frustrating inability to firmly grasp any ultimate meaning of photography, and with that, the tacit analogy between understanding and touch is brought to the fore. The image is a negative of that earlier work by Bochner titled *Actual Size (Hand),* which, as previously mentioned, consisted of a photograph of the artist's own forearm and hand printed to the exact size of his real arm and hand, a choice that seems to insist on the photograph's duty to record and reproduce real measurement. Recall, *Actual Size (Hand)* was originally accompanied by another measurement piece that further implicated the corporeality of the artist: *Actual Size (Face). Actual Size (Hand)* is reduced here to the index-card size, confounding its original claim to factual size from yet another angle and playing again on the literal and rhetorical failure of the index. This photograph's claim to either truth or reality is additionally subverted by the fact that this particular copy is presented as an inversion, as a negative rather than a positive print.

To make matters more questionable, one realizes that this photograph appears to be from a Polaroid—a camera that does not produce negatives. Paradoxically, the look of the negative masks the fact that it is indeed a positive print. In a move that cleverly reverses the logic of Talbot's two-step negative/positive print system, Bochner's visual riddle denies one's ability to take anything for granted. The very idea of an original, which is always put into question by the photograph,[112] becomes even more complicated here. This puzzle precedes digital photography and is revealed as an intrinsic issue to analog processes. Contrary to Alloway's argument in *Artists and Photographs* that "the fact that photographs are multiple originals, not unique originals, as well as one's sense of them as evidence rather than as source objects, should protect their authenticity ultimately,"[113] Bochner's photographic intervention points to the oxymoron that is a "multiple original." This, to raise the specter of Talbot once more, was in essence the criticism and praise of his photographic process. Talbot's calotype had been dismissed as being unreliable until the realization of the benefits of reproducibility allowed it to surpass the daguerreotype in popularity.

This series of conundrums involving the confusing conceptual interchange between duplicity and originality should not be surprising, considering that Bochner announced his intentions at the outset by titling the work *Misunderstandings (A Theory of Photography).* The same conceit (or perhaps more aptly deceit) is doubled (or tripled, or quadrupled . . . etc.) by the quotes on the cards, for, as mentioned, three of the nine quotes were falsified by Bochner: "I added three fake quotes, which I invented (and have never revealed which are which)."[114] Their purportedly "original" source does not exist. Nearly forty years later, Bochner still will not reveal which ones are fake and which ones are real. Finally, according to Bochner, the "truth" is beside the point. Bochner denounces the very search for a true definition of photography as meaningful by stating: "What mattered . . . was not photography *per se,* but thinking about photography and how we use it."[115] This emphasis on thinking deliberately runs counter to Greenbergian criticism, and against what Bochner has summed up as Greenberg's desire for the Kantian moment of aesthetic revelation: "[Greenberg] said he didn't want to think in front of an artwork."[116] It is also suggestive of Sekula's discussion about how the "meaning" of a photograph is always a result of cultural definition, depending "on some external matrix of conditions and presuppositions for its readability,"[117] always presenting only "the *possibility* of meaning."[118]

Ultimately, the sense of tremendous arbitrariness with regard to photographic meaning should be read with and against the context of not only the intellectual but also the political and social investigations of the time. The widespread backlash against the American military intervention in Vietnam, the unresolvability of the Zapruder stills, the dramatic and enigmatic documentation of the Space Race, and the leftist political suspicion of all "official" information, photographic or otherwise, after 1960 in the United States, for example, form a crucial backdrop to the artistic resistance to viewing photography as truth or knowledge, or even as a "clear" image. As Susan Sontag explained in the early 1970s, "Photography implies that we know about the world if we accept it as the camera records it. But this is the opposite of understanding, which starts from *not* accepting the world as it looks."[119] Bochner's work with photography in the late sixties is but the beginning of these conceptual explorations, which reveal insistently that the unpredictable contingency, which Greenberg and later John Szarkowski identified as the central weakness of photography as a modernist medium, is in fact the very attribute that earned photography a key role in contemporary art in ways that continue to be relevant today.[120] Despite the *Encyclopedia Britannica*'s admonition (or was it Bochner's charade?) that "photography cannot record abstract ideas," it remains apparent that the idea of photography (let alone the subject matter depicted) is always slightly out of reach, continuously intangible, and characterized by an often-repressed yet critically persistent doubt. In other words, the very idea of photography is, at base, conceptual and abstract, notwithstanding the onslaught of opposing claims about its indexical, and by extension ontological, security.

Two
Pressing the Point
Bruce Nauman Performs with and against the Frame

Palm atop the back of a hand, interlaced fingers press against a mirrored surface. Amid this web of refracted flesh, thumbs multiply, wrists contort, and appendages seem to pull and push simultaneously. Bathed in a dull green light, visible smears appear on the glass. Perhaps these too are traces of touch. A taciturn photograph calls attention to this relay of hands. The gestural melee is difficult to disentangle. Bruce Nauman's *Finger Touch with Mirrors* (1966–67/1970), from the series *Eleven Color Photographs,* can be seen as a meta-reference to photography (Plates 7–17). In it, limits of the real and representation are pressed literally and figuratively at the same time that conclusive meaning evades the viewer's grasp. Though the artist's hands are figured as pivotal, the role of dexterity and manual labor nevertheless remains ambivalent. Constrained by the photograph's frame, seen against a sequence of mirrors, these tense hands suggest the slippage between the real and representation that has arguably become the true circumstance of contemporary times.

Known for demanding his audience's concentration, sometimes blatantly in pieces such as *Please, Pay Attention Please* (1973) or *Pay Attention Mother Fuckers* (1973), Nauman persistently cultivates evasiveness in both form and content. Pay attention to what, precisely? The unresolved yet adamant invective in *Pay Attention Mother Fuckers* is printed in reverse in black, with one word per line, each separated by a thick black stroke, and then, as though redacted, some of the letters are overwritten to the extent that they obscure the legibility of the text. As in *Finger Touch with Mirrors,* the dictate to pay attention seems pressing, but not necessarily pointed. Nevertheless, the gesture of pointing repeatedly appears in Nauman's artwork, with fingers floating, flexing, and fumbling all over the place. Hands recur as motif and material throughout, yet their gestures remain hard to read and difficult to assess, particularly when photography enters the equation.

While photography has easily been accepted as the recorder, providing the documentary proof of an event, what are the resistances to, and potentials of, considering photography as a participant in what it records? In other words, thinking of photography as not simply a supplement that breaks the event into static segments but an intrinsic aspect of the piece itself. Such a perspective reaffirms the camera's logic as essentially theatrical, thereby complicating photography's grounding force as evidence. Thinking deliberately against the grain of modernist critics such as Michael Fried who were averse to either literalism or theatricality in art, Nauman engaged photography as a way to accentuate analytically, conceptually, and aesthetically the theatrical dimension of the work of art, thereby making literal situations not only self-reflexive but also representationally subversive.[1] Though recognized foremost for his pioneering work in sculpture and video, close reading of Nauman's photographs from the late 1960s discloses unexpected contributions to the experimental framework of performance art in relation to the dynamics of photographic recording, as well as the performative contribution that photography grants to conceptualism. The sociopolitical climate of the late-sixties United States poses a pivotal moment, in which the trace, often interpreted as an index, is taken to task. On the one hand, this reckoning disavows the dominant discourses of conceptual art and photography as dematerialization, and, on the other hand, it challenges any interpretation of photography as legible fact. Though conceptualism was very much concerned with self-reflexivity, it was not associated with medium specificity in the ways heralded by modernism. Rather, Nauman's evocation of bodily experience under the rubric of conceptualism ultimately complicates the notion of the dematerialization of the work of art, insisting, by contrast, on conceptualism's and photography's shared interest in corporeality and equivocal temporalities.

Beginning with an account of the contextual terrain of photography in the late 1960s, especially notions of credibility, the present chapter considers the ways in which Nauman provoked a rethinking of photographic proof at the outset while pressing for a larger reconsideration of traditional definitions of conceptual art. In the preceding chapter, through Bochner's photographic experiments, I delved into the malleable material limits of photography in conceptual art. In Nauman's work with photography I explore the performative dimension. These approaches, the material and the performative, are in many ways inextricable and mutually reinforcing. Performativity, as I understand it in relation to Nauman's work, is concerned with prodding physical, theatrical, and communicative limits. The artist's early use of photography opens onto a complex nexus of photography, sculpture, and performance that consciously binds these concerns together, and which propels the conceptual scope of Nauman's prolific practice.

Between the Art and the Act of Photography

At a time when fine art photographic discourse found itself mired in a conservative emphasis on artistic biography and narrative content, the anxiety of leading photographic curators such as John Szarkowski at the Museum of Modern Art, New York, and Nathan Lyons at George Eastman House, Rochester, was palpable. Arguably the two most important institutional curators of photography in the United States in the late 1960s, they each wrangled with the difficulties of deciphering and articulating a clear position on "the art of photography," especially as it concerns the ways photographs construct meaning. This ambiguity was partly a result of grappling with the legacies of high formalist theories of the 1950s, which stressed photography's seemingly inevitable equivalence with transparency. In 1946 Clement Greenberg explained this popular assessment as follows: "Photography is the most transparent of the art mediums devised or discovered by man. It is probably for this reason that it proves so difficult to make the photograph transcend its almost inevitable function as document, and act as a work of art as well."[2] For Greenberg, photographs were foremost documents, and a document could not be art. By contrast, for most conceptual artists, positing all photographs as documents was a way to call attention to the mendacity that is inextricably linked to the medium. Photography's inability to transcend its connection to ordinary life was envisioned as a radical potential. Moreover, by positioning documents as art, conceptual artists revealed the often-overlooked yet operative banality of art itself. Like strategies of the historic avant-gardes, artists using photography under conceptual art disavowed autonomous artistic purpose in order to insist on the photograph's integral and contingent basis in the praxis of everyday life.

Two significant exhibition catalogs were published in 1966, sharing an interest in establishing photography as a meaningful art, yet approaching from opposing logic. The curatorial essays for Szarkowski's *The Photographer's Eye* and Lyons's *Contemporary Photography: Towards a Social Landscape* exemplify the negotiation between a modernist view of photography as antithetical to art and a desire to critically locate the contemporary status of photographic work as art.[3] Szarkowski's text focused on "photography as a self-referential autonomous art," highlighting the singular photograph, while Lyons's underscored the inextricable "relationship between photography and external 'reality.'"[4] Lyons was intrigued by the possibilities of reading photographs in sequence or series, and argued that constructed or staged images were as crucial to the medium's unique possibilities as the instantaneity of perception and selection that Szarkowski emphasized. While Szarkowski saw the photograph's precision and its capacity to capture the "actualities" of human experience as its key virtues, Lyons was interested in multilayered meanings and abstract "inner realities."[5] The respective views of these era-defining curators are indicative of the late-sixties institutional struggle to situate and communicate photographic meaning while striving to understand the conditions of the world in which they lived.

Nauman's early photographic work wrestles with the perceptual problems inherent in the photograph in ways that seem to combine the approaches of Lyons and Szarkowski. Using the connective logic of series and sequence, yet tempered by emphatically framed moments, Nauman blurs the boundaries between the actualities of the outer world and evocative inner realities. In the germane year of 1966, after completing his MFA at the University of California, Davis, Nauman began to stage color photographs that were received initially as daring by virtue of their "artless and perfunctory nature."[6] Nauman's purported "unthinking" or mechanical facade functioned as a way to insolently engage with the limits of art practice and discourse. Denying the exclusive autonomy of art and authorship while teasing out its implications and working in opposition to the prevailing "fine-print" aesthetic, Nauman chose to work with photography in some measure precisely because it could still be identified with nonart functions. There was something attractive about the unavoidably "in-between" medium. Bearing an uneasy relationship to an increasingly mechanized culture, Nauman's photographs and their performed "perfunctory nature" can partly be read as an interrogation of the mechanics of contemporary culture through the canny medium of mechanical reproduction.

Series such as *Studies for Holograms* (1968–69) demonstrate these tensions. Involving the artist's own body as material on which, and with which, to act, these screen-printed duotones, photomechanically reproduced from infrared photographs, using radiation and heat rather than light, depict the artist's face contorted physically and distorted representationally.[7] An analogy between the mechanical control of the camera and the mechanical control of the body underscores these pieces. And yet, meaning is neither entirely expressive nor decisive. In fact, as other viewers have noted, "Without the eyes, facial flesh is reduced to matter, and emotional connections become more ambiguous."[8] In the context of intense political and social upheaval in the United States (including a crescendo of resistance and civil disobedience in connection with the civil rights movement, rising throughout the sixties and culminating in 1968, as well as rising violence in protest of the war in Vietnam), these images must be seen as more than childish insolence. Though their content may initially be perceived as apolitical, in their emphasis on discomfort and deformed information, these photographs arguably perform a reaction to and against their time. In this way, these photographs can be understood as questioning the possibility of protest in art and the public realm more broadly. Their claustrophobic sequence of performed disfigurements can also read as an ambivalent inquiry into the confusing registers of attention, affect, and even apathy.

Ambivalence in contemporary art of the late 1960s has frequently been received as a mode of aesthetic withdrawal. As a one-liner, it leaves the viewer at a kind of dead end for its own sake. A more poignant approach, and one I think fits Nauman's efforts, is to take ambivalence seriously, as a subject and as a strategy, and to see such gestures as a mode of engagement with the social and political context of its emergence. More than neutral play, the jarring plasticity of Nauman's manipulated face in this series suggests connections to protest culture and to forced interrogation or torture in ways that resonate with the larger tumult of its time. According to Tony Godfrey, a central underlying debate of not simply conceptual art but also the constitution of society in the late sixties was the public's growing distrust of politicians and the media. Godfrey's description of the flexible and camouflage uses of language during the Vietnam War era shed light on how artists struggled with the possibility of forming a speech act at this time. A seemingly endless proliferation of euphemisms emerges from this nexus. For example, military concepts were frequently dubbed with confusing aliases, in order to confound meaning and simultaneously make the ideas themselves more publicly digestible, at least insofar as they sounded solid and certain, in their attempts to preempt doubt or insecurity. Terms such as *acute environmental reaction,* which really meant *shell shock, ballgame* as a reference to a military operation, so-called *friendly fire,* which resulted in death, or *credibility disaster,* which translated into "being found out," typified this confusing time when the order to kill could be presented as "terminate with extreme prejudice" or "collateral damage." All these concepts baffled one's ability to ever be fully "in the know" yet provided a sense of officiousness, a degree of reassurance. As Robert Slifkin has expressed it, the conflicting realities of this moment reveal "a world where referential certitude, subjective sentiment, and immediate and universal communication were deemed increasingly problematic if not impossible."[9] Linguistic and visual conceptual strategies were conflated by artists such as Nauman to probe the rampant and irrepressible doubt that ultimately underpinned the sociopolitical system itself.

Godfrey elaborates further: "According to news broadcasts, it seemed that the war was being waged by acronyms (NVA, DMZ, ARVN, MACV, PX—mystificatory names by which the North Vietnamese Army, Demilitarized Zone and such like were invariably referred to), but in reality it was being fought, on the American side, by teenagers (the average soldier was aged nineteen), uncertain why they were there and, in many cases, high on drugs."[10] Acknowledging the manipulative power of words further underscores how language can indeed function as a weapon and how it possesses the capacity to be deployed both on the side of questioning authority and in the service of reifying authorial certainty. Images are inseparable from language as representation. This barbed dualism would become invaluable source material for Nauman's later works, including his *Eleven Color Photographs* series. In one parodic image from this series, plainly titled *Eating My Words,* we see a young, pale Nauman, dressed in a red gingham button-down shirt to match the tablecloth, concentratingly spreading a gory, crimson jam on sallow white bread cut to spell "O-R-D-S" across his plate. One imagines he has already consumed the "W." The allusion is above all unappetizing, and, as the title reinforces, the work suggests an acknowledgment of being wrong, of regret, of needing to go back to revise claims already made.

Like other scenes in *Eleven Color Photographs,* the image pivots on the visual and verbal instability of language while relying specifically on photographic documentation. Seeing Nauman spread bloody-looking preserves over his sickly bleached bread is, on the one hand, completely innocuous. Read from another angle, however, in the complex context of its production, this unemotional reckoning of an individual with implicitly violent/violated words takes on amplified meaning. More intrinsically, one could argue that photography's connection to war and conflict imprints all photographs. As Eduardo Cadava, a photography historian and theorist, has explained, just as there is no war that does not depend on technologies of representation, the war machine is in every way a photographic machine.[11] By extension, the crisis in photographic and linguistic representation in the late sixties linked directly to the experience of large-scale traumatic events that were circulated to and experienced by the public through photography and television.[12]

This moment of unrelenting social crises and intense human self-consciousness was partly orchestrated by the infiltration of photographic media into all aspects of life—public and private, at home and abroad—leaving unclear which artistic direction was relevant to the experience of contemporary life. Referring specifically to the turn toward conceptual art in the late 1960s, the philosopher and art theorist Peter Osborne characterizes the proliferation and omnipresence of photographic visual culture as the moment at which contemporary art emerges. Photographic culture's integration into nearly all aspects of everyday life, according to Osborne, situates "the photographic" as the ultimate and thereafter inescapable crisis of the real and of contemporaneity.[13] Always both confirming and denying reality, photography comes to define the split-entity (or split-identity) of contemporary subjectivity. Nauman's early use of photography exemplifies this dynamic. As a work of conceptual and contemporary art, Nauman's animated contribution to the Museum of Modern Art's *Information* exhibition (1970), titled *Grimaces* (1969), visibly mocks not only the cliché photographic imperative to smile but demonstrates a painful inability to do so (Figure 2.1). In fact, duplicates of Nauman's *Studies for Holograms,* the reticent character of these images derides the very idea of self-expression in an art context as well as in a broader public framework. Moreover, it suggestively engages with the growing anti-authoritarian thrust of broader culture while conveying a sense of entrapment, indeed, a frustrating lack of agency. There is a tension between the way in which these images look like the artist is trying to force himself to speak versus the possibility that the hands imaged are not his own but belong instead to an external interrogator.

This riddled muteness manifests itself as a result of the confines of the photograph as a visual medium rather than an auditory one, and alternately by the way the hands in the photographs ply at the artist's mouth. Speaking on the body and its correlation to emotions, Nauman has explained: "The idea of making faces had to do with thinking of the body as something you can manipulate. I had done some performance pieces—vigorous pieces dealing with standing, leaning, bending—and as they were performed, some of them seemed to carry large emotional impact."[14]

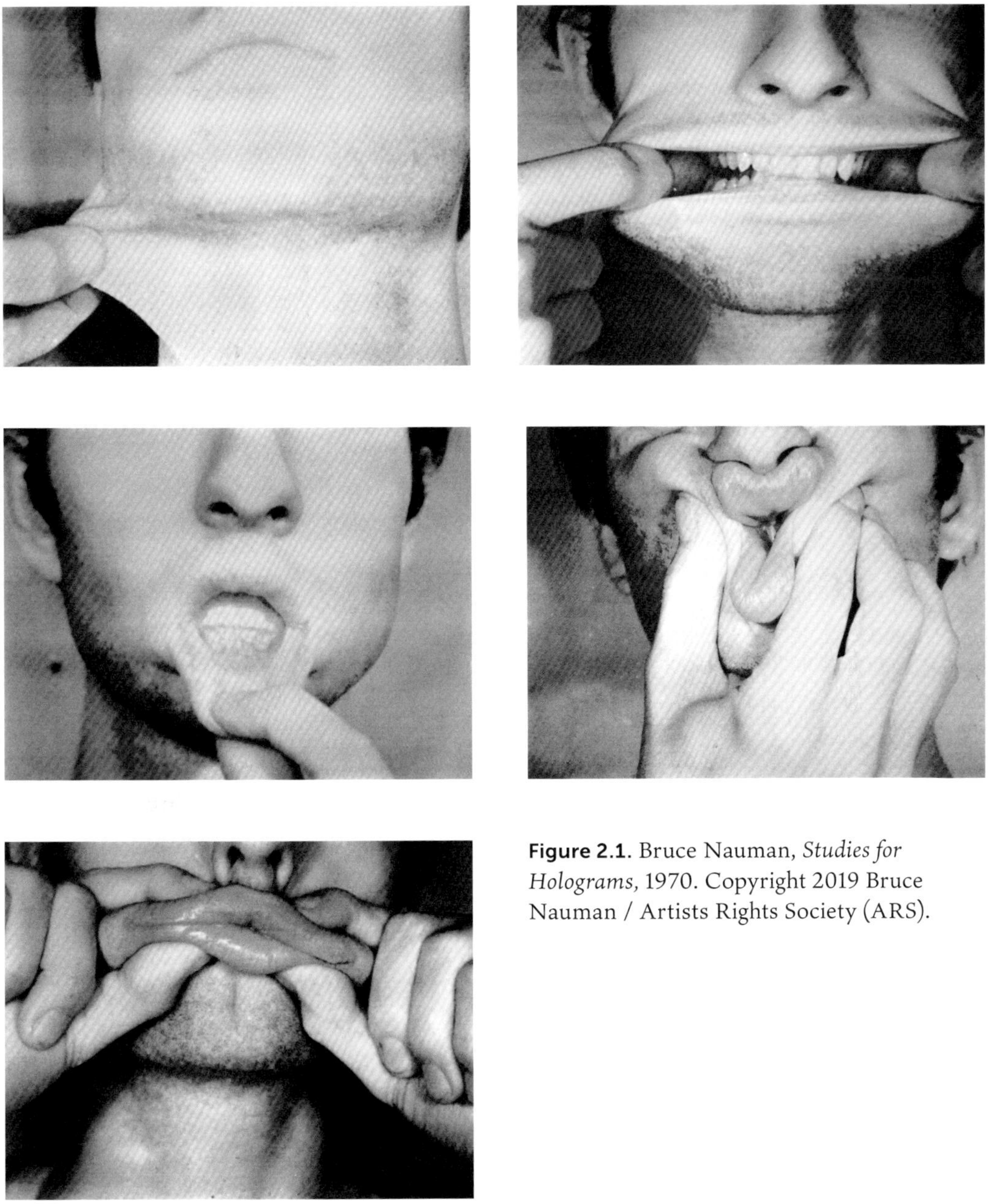

Figure 2.1. Bruce Nauman, *Studies for Holograms,* 1970. Copyright 2019 Bruce Nauman / Artists Rights Society (ARS).

The photographic prints from *Grimaces* are cropped intentionally below the artist's eyes, focusing attention exclusively on the lips and neck and their sequential distortions as Nauman fools around with his visage. Including pinched and pulled lips, bared teeth, squeezed cheeks, and strained neck, these images appear simultaneously banal and mischievous, even intimidating. They are further complicated by being reproduced in large format, at a scale larger-than-life and in a shade of nauseating yellow, which accentuates a disturbing undertone, spreading the sensation of unease to the viewer. Speaking to the volatility of language and self-expression at the end of the 1960s, these apprehensive pictures strike a pose between tenacity and tenuousness, confounding comprehension while nevertheless pressing for attention.

Nauman was of course not alone in performatively testing the boundaries of the self, subjectivity, and speech acts through photographic form. Ana Mendieta's *Untitled (Glass on Body Imprints)* (1972) offers a complex and compelling touchstone of a synthesized performance for and with the camera, bearing a disquieting resemblance to Nauman's *Grimaces* (Figure 2.2).[15] In a work that was first recorded as thirty-six color slides, Mendieta forcibly pressed a piece of glass against her naked body—her face, torso, breasts, back, pubis, and buttocks. Each compressed body fragment then formed the focus of a single image. From these, thirteen headshots were selected and printed as black-and-white photographs.[16] Whereas the hostility inherent in Nauman's work remains to some extent beneath the surface, open to inference, in Mendieta's work, violence manifests as overtly aggressive. The glass is more or less visible in varying frames, its border moving up and down Mendieta's face as it harshly squashes and smothers her features, deforming them in a grotesque sequence. Though the artist's fingers are seen holding the glass, the viewer's unease remains unmitigated.[17] In some images the exaggerated effect on her mouth, her tongue smeared across the glass, seems to mock male fantasies of puckered lips on offer, while in others it deflates racial stereotypes connected to Mendieta's identity as a Cuban American woman of color by virtue of calling overt attention to them.[18] Sexual violence and domestic abuse reappear in other works by Mendieta during 1972 and 1973 (sometimes via allusion and other times by means that are irrefutably explicit). Examples include visceral photographic works such as *Untitled (Facial Cosmetic Variations)* (1972), *Untitled (Self-Portrait with Blood)* (1973), *Untitled (Rape Scene)* (1973), and films such as *Sweating Blood* (1973). Seeing Nauman's and Mendieta's contortions side by side calls to mind the unequal weight of history on different bodies, and thus different subject positions. Indeed, the direct gut reaction provoked by Mendieta's loaded conceptual combination of performance and photographic recording accentuates the "in-between" equivocation that dominates Nauman's approach. In Nauman one might comfortably conclude that he is clowning around, whereas in Mendieta's series, such respite is nowhere to be found. Instead, a harrowing sense of threat from outside the frame drags the viewer's own complicity in for questioning. This is all the more powerful, since it coincides with the very same moment that we are also situated as witnesses.

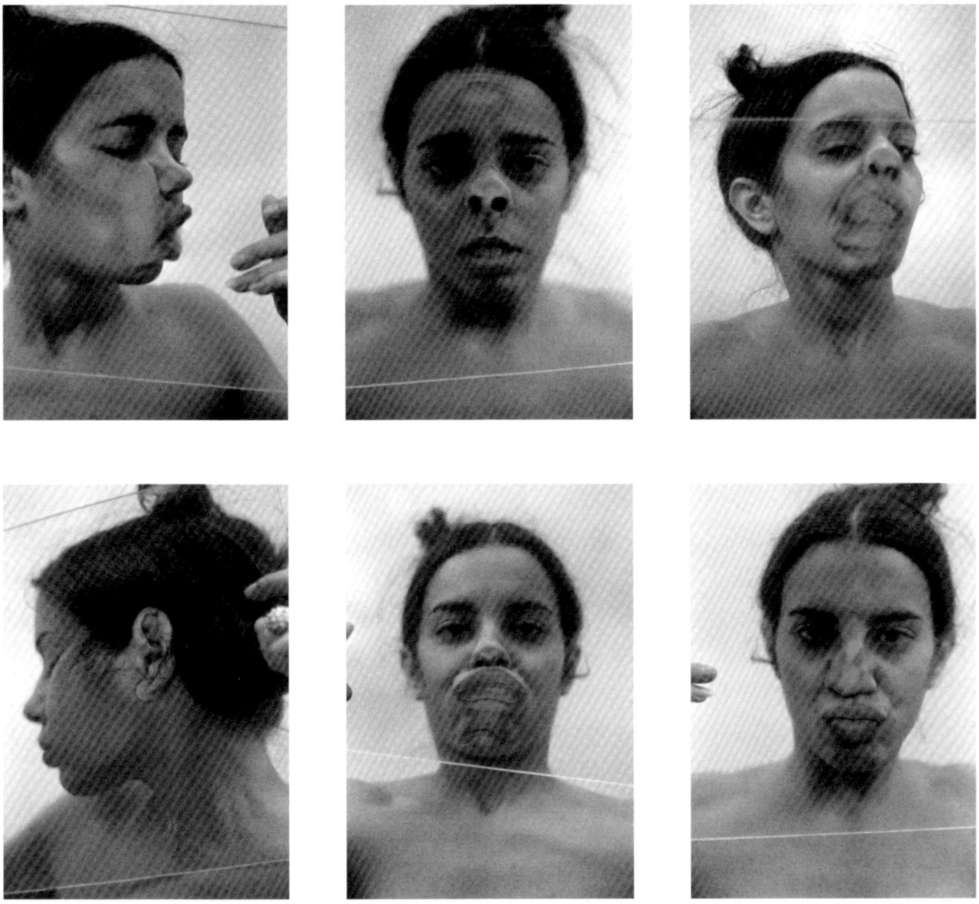

Figure 2.2. Ana Mendieta, *Untitled (Glass on Body Imprints)*, 1972. Copyright the Estate of Ana Mendieta Collection, LLC. Courtesy Galerie Lelong & Co.

Eleven Color Photographs

Photography's ambivalent relationship to reality imparts a revealing conceptual framework for understanding Nauman's broader artistic practice. As Eva Ehninger has articulated, though the photographic medium insinuates a direct connection to the world it records, and thus to reality, the photograph should also be "seen as a medial surface, multiplied a thousand times over, thereby interacting with a diversity of technological and social contexts to the point of signaling the loss of an ineluctable reality."[19] Arguing for the inseparable interplay between the body and technology, Ehninger takes Nauman's work as an influential model for artists such as Ed Atkins and the artist duo Lizzie Fitch–Ryan Trecartin, who performatively investigate the possibilities of contemporary subject positions (while demythologizing the idea of the autonomous subject), often using analogies between the surface and fragmentation of the body and the surface and fragmentation of the image. The loss of the real that is instantiated by photography and signaled by Ehninger indeed traces back to the medium's early days. The inevitable anxiety of the photographic takes on particular resonance in the discourse and art of the 1960s, when, as Roland Barthes characterized it in his 1963 essay "The Rhetoric of the Image," "the real unreality of the photograph" masks constructed meaning under the appearance of a given reality.[20]

The images that compose Nauman's portfolio *Eleven Color Photographs* (1966–67/1970) cooperatively set the stage for Nauman's larger investigations of "real unreality" by overtly exemplifying the interrelation between language, physical behavior, communication, and photographic confines. Influenced by seeing a retrospective of Man Ray's work at the Los Angeles County Museum of Art in 1966,[21] the photographs were actually taken by Jack Fulton at the direction of Nauman. Nevertheless, they remain squarely Nauman's artwork. This fact adds yet another complication to the issue of authorship in relation to this series and to art as a practice in general.[22] Released by the Leo Castelli Gallery in New York in 1970, these photographs have been called "a quasi-document of the artist in his studio."[23] The insistent liminality of *Eleven Color Photographs,* and the inability of critics to assign a single identity to the photos themselves, reiterate the idea that Nauman transposed the enigmatic logic of wordplay onto the image. Driving the point further, this series resists being read as a whole at the same time that it necessitates being understood as such. Semantics play a crucial role here, with the larger sequence functioning in the mode of a discursive network. By using puns, palindromes, anagrams, repetition, and linguistic as well as visual strategies, Nauman shifted meanings and underscored the syntactical dependence of his practice. In each photograph, and across the images as a series, normative or standard meaning is repeatedly put into doubt. The decision to use color photography, for example, evokes associations with vernacular and commercial forms of photography, further challenging their status as art.[24]

Two of the *Eleven Color Photographs* look uncannily similar: *Coffee Thrown Away Because It Was Too Cold* (1966–67/1970) and *Coffee Spilled Because the Cup Was Too Hot* (1966–67/1970). Seeing them as "quasi-documents" reinforces the photographs' liminal position between the artifact of evidence and playful artistic experimentation: one photograph presented as the result of accident and the other the result of choice. The titles of these two images, similar to the others included in the series, act as the textual explication of the physical act performed, telling viewers explicitly what they are looking at. Allowing the title to dictate the sense of the image in this way provides what Janet Kraynak has eloquently described as a "performance structure" to the work, in which linguistic signs become tools to create a situation.[25] The act of creation becomes contingent on the title, viewed as a statement. The condition of performance implied by this contingency is multifaceted, as it also summons a paradoxical link to duration and hinges on the possibility of change through time, despite its dependence on the still image.

One of the means by which the viewer may engage this performance is by either accepting or denying the photographic proof presented. For example, should one concede that it is what it says it is, because it says it is? Extending the logic of nominalism in this way is crucial, since it echoes an emphatic reliance on the ways the performative has also been used to describe the reception of the Duchampian readymade as a declarative statement.[26] In both cases, Nauman and Duchamp, it is finally in the reception that the proposition for the work is fulfilled. The individual titles read as conceptual statements, or veritable "event scores" as in the work of John Cage, echoing popular models of language in conceptual art, characterized by the terse works of artists such as Lawrence Weiner and Sol LeWitt.[27] And yet this reliance on the titles as axiomatic simultaneously throws into question the content of the image, particularly in the example of Nauman's coffee photos, as we view the two cups of coffee, one supposedly spilled and the other thrown away, alongside each other.

Without keying the photograph to its respective title, how can the viewer judge which coffee was too hot and which one was too cold? Which was spilled and which was thrown? Credibly, does each image conclude with the same result? Does the narrative matter? What do these photographs actually tell us? Do we simply take the artist's word for it? The blurry double exposure in *Coffee Thrown Away Because It Was Too Cold* suggests an extended temporality that might lead one to think the coffee has been out too long, overexposed in fact, becoming tepid over time. But upon reflection, it is even stranger than that. What at first appears to be a tabletop seems to have a handle. Are we looking at a cup of coffee and its saucer atop another giant cup of coffee? Though the images in this series have been repeatedly taken at face value by critics and art historians, hardly given an iota of analysis beyond noting that they are "photographs of [Nauman] enacting simple, tasklike exercises in his studio,"[28] closer looking reveals these are much more nebulous and hallucinogenic.

Coffee Spilled Because the Cup Was Too Hot engages with an exaggerated spectrum of color, and the resolution of the image, in contrast to the "cold coffee," is sharp and vibrant. Hues of blue, yellow, gold, orange, and green gradate dramatically across the surface, closing in on the rivulet of spilled russet coffee. The photograph itself appears hot. But this is all a matter of deduction and, more important, attention. The inability to concretely distinguish between the event of these two images, except via the statement of the title, can also be read as a play on the arbitrary distinction between chance and purposefulness. It might also be received as a derisive nod to high modernism, and Jackson Pollock's grandiose claim to control and mastery in his drip paintings. Nauman responds with spill photographs. The reality that both of Nauman's *Coffee* photos reveal nothing about the state of the coffee contained—photography not being capable of testifying to temperature—compels us to ask what kind of proof these images actually possess. In effect, as Lawrence Sillars has suggested, these two photographs undermine "the words' capacity to convey finite meaning."[29] Nominalism is posited here as an operative structure that is simultaneously undermined. The words both matter and are beside the point. Subtly, these images contradict the meaning imposed by the textual reference and, in so doing, open up a space for further deliberation, leaving the viewer in a space of doubt.

And what is with all the coffee? Coffee as a motif recurs with nearly obsessive regularity throughout Nauman's long career, for example, in the balancing act that is the lithograph series *Caffeine Dreams* (1987) or the two-monitor video *Coffee Spilled and Balloon Dog* (1993).[30] In his often-quoted autobiographical account, Nauman narrates the story of graduating from art school in the sixties and finding himself with a lot of time on his hands. Alone in his San Francisco studio day after day, he says that "it was difficult to think of things to do everyday."[31] The veracity of Nauman's story is debatable. We are told only what he wants to tell us, and as such, much of the mythology surrounding Nauman and his practice is based on the artist's selective account. Nauman continues by recounting how he began to use what he was in fact doing in the studio as his work—in other words, routine and banal activities such as walking around the studio and drinking coffee became the subject matter and even the enactment of his artwork. Using creative blockage to his advantage, his paralysis became his parameters. Nauman states, "My conclusion was that I was an artist and I was in the studio, then whatever it was I was doing in the studio must be art. . . . At this point art became more of an activity and less of a product."[32] By the same token, coffee became less of a product and more of an activity. It is likely no coincidence that coffee enters the scene, since it is a substance long used to focus attention, renew energy, and promote the idea of working more efficiently. Once more, however, Nauman foils the association in the act. He complicates the connotative power of coffee by the perceived simplicity of his practice, or his apparent lack of work.

Over and over, Nauman's own words encourage viewers to read his work as easy. Describing his turn to photography at this moment, for example, Nauman seemed to look for the path of least resistance: "Somehow I think, I may be mistaken, I had the idea that I could just take a picture, and I wouldn't have to think about how to draw it or something. Of course, when you take a picture, you have to think about how to take a picture, but in another sense I knew enough about painting to know that it would be a whole lot of work and I didn't really know enough about photography to get involved in trying to make a really interesting or original photograph."[33] Despite Nauman's dismissive tone about the status of photography, his photographs nevertheless incline toward evidence and even surveillance in ways that should be taken seriously. What might it mean for Nauman to photographically document his ordinary activities, however slight or seemingly innocuous they may be?

Retaining evidence of his working process through the photograph, Nauman both revealed and questioned the nature of making art, exposing the systems of belief that buttress the idea of art itself, including the mythically charged idea of the artist's studio as the place where "magic happens." In this way, Nauman unworks the space of art. As though disavowing the manual work of the artist, in *Self-Portrait as Fountain* Nauman throws his hands up in the air for the camera. On the one hand, the gesture seems to read "there's nothing up my sleeve." On the other hand, he resembles a person under arrest, posed at surrender. All this is further complicated by the action of spitting water, which, while an ostensibly playful and disorderly act, creates a strangely graceful arc when performed for the camera by Nauman. The contentious artlessness of Nauman's photographs performs the avant-garde strategy of dialectically questioning the role of "work" in art. Seen as an off-the-cuff "slight" of hand rather than, or in combination with, a sleight of hand, Nauman's photographs are offered not exactly as the results of work or skill in the traditional sense but, and somewhat paradoxically, as the dexterous documentation of idleness and uncertainty.

The wider implication of evidence here opens up yet more questions, especially about the stability of the concept of art viewed through and as the photograph. As if the medium were unobtrusive and transparent, Nauman claims to have chosen to work with photography because of its effortlessness. Though the photograph is ontologically linked to "self-evidence," it is not evidentiary in the ways one might conventionally expect. Ultimately, though the photographic image may be fixed, its meaning and by correlation its possible "proof" and temporality are not stable. In *Eleven Color Photographs* the reception of time and event apprehended by photography depends very much on which narrative one chooses to believe.

Nauman's imperfect coffees become a metaphor for failed evidence and the failed work of art. These works reveal how the contingency of such failure might also allow its success. Earlier works, such as *Failing to Levitate in the Studio* (1966), which I turn to shortly, offer similarly performative paradigms for "working" through failure. Nauman's admitted admiration of the philosopher Ludwig Wittgenstein provides insight here. Nauman described how Wittgenstein "would not throw away the failed argument, but would include it in his book."[34] The coffee, then, like the failed argument, though seemingly "thrown away," is retained for its process.

Throughout Nauman's *Eleven Color Photographs,* language and its relation to the visual content of the image behave like actors orchestrated cleverly by the artist/director. Mischievous punning at once unifies and destabilizes the structural relationship between title and object, undermining the use value and intelligibility of language. The titles are dictates as well as jokes. Almost transformatively, the titles challenge the viewer's subservience. They subtly expose how bound we are by language to understanding the functional limits of the world. Drawing on the titular logic of yet another photograph from this series, Nauman's work also demonstrates how this dependence on language is futile, or in other words, how it is "bound to fail."

The photograph *Bound to Fail* depicts the roped torso of the artist from behind, wearing an oversized orange sweater. But one wonders if we as viewers are the ones being roped in. We have no way to confirm the identity of the Houdini-esque artist in the image. The garish orange seems to be a parody of restraint, read against the sense that the figure pictured is somehow being assailed. The color is also a play on conviction, since, in another elliptical twist, this series coincides with the adoption of bright orange uniforms as the marker for high-security prisoners in the federal penitentiary system. A contemporaneous piece, *Henry Moore Bound to Fail* (1967), a cast sculpture based on Nauman's body that mimics the rear view pictured in *Bound to Fail,* displaces and aligns Nauman's own supposed failure with the weight of moored modernist sculpture. Unhinged by the photograph, Henry Moore's authority is lassoed to Nauman in an ongoing series of double binds, linking tradition and innovation, presence and absence, and weighted meaning with floating signifiers.

Nauman has described his desire to push and prod the "functional edges" of language, explaining that when words appear the most self-evidently sufficient, they are most susceptible to breakdown. In this way, for Nauman, the most ordinary aspects of language become interesting: "When these functional edges are explored . . . other areas of your mind make you aware of language potential." Drawing connections between Barthes's exploration of the pleasures derived by language "when what is known rubs up against what is unknown," to his own interests, Nauman concludes: "I think the point where language starts to break down as a useful tool for communication is the edge where poetry or art occurs."[35] This investigation into the usefulness or potential uselessness of language (or work/worklessness of language) correlates in Nauman to an investigation of the use value versus the useless value of the art object.

Like language, photography has all too frequently been taken as a given, assigned a fixed function of transparency and self-evidence—as proof. Here the proposal is that nothing can be taken for granted, and both structural and deconstructive analyses are as requisite for an understanding of photography as they are for the complexities of language. Not allowing for any givens instead turns the focus to what can only be understood unstably as variables. Visibly, humor is one of the many mechanisms in Nauman's artwork through which this variability operates. Consider, for example, *Drill Team,* a row of five auger bits of varying heights and incrementally growing widths that are partially drilled into a block of wood. *Drill Team* contains militaristic undertones, denoting, for example, routine precision performances by a formation of soldiers. From this perspective, the auger bits read as soldiers standing at attention. From another angle, as with *Bound to Fail,* the image suggests torture and interrogation, and also the unreliability of information received through such means.

In Nauman's only explicit evocation of war, *Raw War* (1970), the artist hung three neon light letters, spelling W-A-R, on the wall. These are programmed to flash in a sequence from left to right, calling attention to the palindrome contained therein: RAW–WAR. The piece builds on a drawing from 1968, Nauman's first word image print, in which WAR is written obliquely, receding in space as a way to dramatize the embedded word RAW, which echoes in reverse behind the crimson letters. Created at the height of the war in Vietnam, Nauman inscribed the following on the drawing: "sign to hang when there is war on." The suggestion that war could be turned on or off, as rhythmically as the red letters that flash sequentially before going dark in the neon work, analogizes the conflict in Vietnam as not only the first televised war but the first seen in vivid color. As with the use of color in the larger series of *Eleven Color Photographs,* this aspect seems crucial for Nauman. Moreover, each of these works speaks to the complacency of turning off or of tuning out in the face of such raw, visceral horror. Nevertheless, as *RAW–WAR* makes clear when the bloodshot letters continue to pulse, "WAR" flashes up again with chronic (albeit repressed) insistence. Beneath the neon sign, exposed and unwieldy wires hang down, linking up with the transformer apparatus and resembling the outlines of theater drapery. At once subtle and glaring, Nauman's piece performatively displays its own seams as a work of art while calling attention to the mechanical underpinnings of both art and war.

Nauman's photographs perform acrobatics similar to his neon signs / word games that repurpose words for altered meanings (which could themselves be read as photography in that they literally write with light). Moreover, Nauman's photographs, like his neon sign works, continue his larger investigation into language's ability to broker meaning between public and private spheres. Viewing these photographs alongside Nauman's neon word sculptures and their material reference to the ubiquity of advertising as a form of social communication and identification impels further considerations of Nauman's engagement with the social construction of language and its visual translation. One of his earliest neon pieces was *Sweet, Suite, Substitute* (1968), in which the word *SUITE* flashes alternatively as a superimposition over the same letters in the word *SUBSTITUTE,* with the word *SWEET* layered in the center. Each word is a primary color, and each is lit for five seconds. The title is a reference to the 1940 Jelly Roll Morton song "Sweet Substitute," and its suggestion of settling for a secondary support or replacement instead of the original alludes to a further photographic dynamic. Additionally, this textual neon reveals the interdependent construction of meaning created by the allusion and collusion between words and their physical manifestation. This neon can be read as a kind of *photo-graphy,* then, as the writing of light, which alternates between being a substitute and a material manifestation of language.[36]

The photograph *Waxing Hot* literally shows the artist's hand waxing the sculptural letters *HOT* with a product intended for a hot rod, not coincidentally a classic American car with a reputation for high "performance." Visually similar to *Raw War* with its capitalized red letters, the piece rests on a rhetorical pivot by questioning the literalness of language. The expression of waxing hot derives from the Latin word for sincerity *(sine cera)* meaning "without wax." For Nauman, "waxing hot" reads as the opposite of sincerity, instead suggesting disingenuous appearances. Beyond the surface of linguistic play, this piece also makes sculptural references to artifice and artistic process, connoting the traditional wax cast technique of filling a statue's cracks with wax that would melt on a hot day, leaving what was referred to as an "honest" sculpture, rather than a ruse. Gesturing toward this tension between duplicitous process and truthful representation mimics the tension inherent to the photograph, as a duplication process and as unstable evidence. The photograph gives an appearance of continuous and contained reality, even while it is suspended, partial, and fragmented. Aligned with the layering logic of the linguistic puns presented, the functional edges of both the photograph and language are pressed by such works. Or, perhaps more aptly, the functional edges are pulled, as in photographs such as *Untitled (Potholder),* from the *Eleven Color Photographs* series, which depicts hands enmeshed in the weave of a knit textile. The hands' dexterity is tested while the artist's hands are tied. The binding intimated by this knit implies another reference to craft that also recursively returns the viewer to the knit sweater in *Bound to Fail.* Forgoing the possibility of finite meaning, Nauman's photographs cannot be immobilized, despite their still capture within the frame of the photograph or even the staged scenes proposed by the images themselves.

The title of the photograph *Feet of Clay* (1966–67/1970) plays on yet another outdated verbal expression that denotes (or stands in for) a weakness or hidden flaw in the character of a greatly admired or respected person.[37] Viewed in the complicated context of the late sixties, these muddied feet and their tragic futility also call to mind Larry Burrows's vivid color photographs of everyday realities of combat in Vietnam. Wounded and mud-encrusted soldiers feature prominently in Burrows's iconic coverage of the war, for example, in his series of pictures from the battle on Hill 484 in 1966. The war photographer's images echo an overwhelming theme of senselessness, confusion, and failure that, however obliquely, find an unsettling resonance in Nauman's photographs.

In Nauman's art practice, the metaphoric reference embedded in *Feet of Clay* functions as a statement that disavows the artist as both genius and source of authority. Slightly larger than all the other uniform prints in *Eleven Color Photographs,* Nauman's vision of himself with or as "feet of clay" can be read as mocking his artistic authority, even anticipating his idolization as source material for a future generation of artists and art historians. On this point Pamela Lee has written a provocative piece titled "Pater Nauman," a review that discusses Nauman as a model for subsequent generations in terms of the development of the "slacker artist."[38] Lee elaborates how "Nauman's persona as 'impotent father' reverses these terms: rather than failing to idealize, it seems to idealize failure." This allows failure to become a banal trope as seen in work by artists such as Karen Kilimnik, Cary Leibowitz (a.k.a. Candy Ass), and Sean Landers, among other contemporary practitioners.[39] Noting "a proliferation of categories around powerlessness as a wide-ranging cultural phenomenon," Lee marks what is visible in such works by Nauman: the ways in which failure—particularly failure situated in the body—becomes the deliberate antithesis of the expressionist artist's virility in the fifties and eighties.[40] Nauman's extensive use of punning can also be seen in this regard, with punning being a quintessentially "lame" slacker word game. Color brings a visual pun to bear in this photograph. Washed in eerie contrasts of red and green light, the image suggests the confusion of signals—stop or go. *Feet of Clay* trades on this rhetorical stance and can be viewed alongside a wide array of statements within conceptual art: abandon aesthetic authority, emphatically deny uniqueness and originality, and proclaim their ease of reproducibility as a way to renounce artistic control.

Rather than assert self-determination, Nauman's suggestion of self-defeat strategically allows the viewer the power to decide. The very notion of the self-determination of individuals, objects, and language is opened to questioning. Nauman thus recalls

Mikhail Bakhtin's conception of the "utterance," in which spoken words immediately become part of a dialogic relationship whose "meaning is determined not at the moment it is spoken but at the point when it is received."[41] Similarly, Nauman's photographs-as-utterances adhere to Lawrence Weiner's 1969 dictum on conceptual art: "The decision as to condition rests with the receiver upon the occasion of receivership." In this way the viewer's position as the receiver is paramount, particularly in the face of the artist/author's lack of final control and unlimited fallibility.

Nauman consciously reiterates his performance as the beleaguered artist, locating himself and the work of art in the position of failure from the outset, at the mercy of the utterance and the occasion of the receivership. His immobility is made literal in photos such as *Feet of Clay*. Of course, this is also the source of the work's success. As Anne Wagner has insightfully observed, "behind each of Nauman's apparent failings stands a shadow antithesis, a bygone practice of sculpture that the artist has coolly trumped."[42] Washed in a warm yet somewhat menacing light, a pair of anonymous human feet, with each toe distinctly outlined, appears modeled in clay. In fact the feet of the artist's wife, this particular photograph is slightly larger than the other ten photographs in this series. Its prominence reinforces Nauman's repeated reference to dated modes of traditional art, such as the sculptural techniques alluded to throughout *Eleven Color Photographs*,[43] and raises yet another aspect of his admitted helplessness—not knowing what to do next. Acknowledging failure as his starting point,[44] Nauman claims that "I was just sort of tied in a knot and couldn't get anything out."[45] His comment gains further ironic momentum in view of his photograph *Bound to Fail* (1966–67/1970). The multivalent semantics of being "bound" suggest the inevitable propulsion of destiny—being beyond one's control—while also contending with an implied restraint or set of restrictions that precede and preclude the artist's desires.[46] This aspect of being bound can be tied back to Man Ray's influence on Nauman. *Bound to Fail* acts similarly as a visual riddle, and moreover, in this way Nauman's photography rhymes with the surrealist artist's famed photo of his sculpture the *Enigma of Isidore Ducasse* (1920). Man Ray's black-and-white image mysteriously depicts thick cloth lashed with rope, concealing unknown objects beneath that are taken as a reference to the Comte de Lautréamont's irrational evocation of a chance encounter on a dissection table of a sewing machine and an umbrella. Nauman praised Man Ray's "unreasonableness" and specifically his "lack of tied-upness" in a 1972 interview with Jane Livingston.[47] Like Man Ray, Nauman untethers meaning by combining unpredictable objects, unwieldy metaphors, and ordinary situations. The finagled fingers featured in *Untitled (Potholder)* further reinforce this reading. Acting out colloquialisms such as "waxing hot," "feet of clay," or "bound to fail" marks the constraints put on the artist even as he demonstrates his wily ways by combining sculptural form, linguistic content, and photographic staging.[48]

Continuously evoking wisecracks by staging verbal puns that denote weakness, error, and lack of competence refers back to the artist's limits but also to the traditions of art making. That Nauman chooses to use photography, or let someone else take photographs that he claims as his own, can be compared with his return to the use of and reliance on sculptural casts and molds as well as his ambivalent denial and simultaneous claim to artistic mastery. "His revisionist conception of sculptural practice," observes Roxana Marcoci, "became methodologically contingent on the photographic lens."[49] Nauman's prescient desire to transcend sculpture's definition as "shapes to look at" marks him as an important inaugurator of conceptual art.[50] Other contemporaneous examples of Nauman's prevalent use of simple casts and molds that also pivot on the idea of absence rather than presence include *A Cast of Space under My Chair* (1965), *Wax Impressions of the Knees of Five Famous Artists* (1966),[51] *Device for a Left Armpit* (1967), and *Hand to Mouth* (1967),[52] among others. Wagner has further outlined these sculptural aids as "traditional tokens of sculptural de-skilling."[53] This deliberate sculptural deskilling parallels the larger deployment of "amateurism" through photography in conceptual art, and deskilling as avant-garde resistance, providing yet another instance in which the art is in the gesture, rather than the gestural.

When asked if his artwork, and *Raw War* in particular, bore any relation to the war then raging in Vietnam, Nauman replied, "Well, certainly there are political feelings present in them. But nothing more specific than that."[54] Certainly present yet lacking specificity sums up one of the central contradictions of both Nauman's conceptual art and the dubious status of the photograph. In a recent characterization, Nicolas Guagnini, whose own practice has been undoubtedly spurred by Nauman's example, refers to Nauman provocatively as "an overachiever of neutrality." The irony is rife, and yes, as with the blandness connoted by the white bread on which Nauman spreads his rubicund and routine jam in *Eating My Words*, the artist's work might be read in line with his critical reception in the 1990s: complacent and impotent in relation to the sociopolitical realities of the world at large.[55] I argue, however, that Nauman is possibly both more radical and more normative than acknowledged by existing scholarship. Indeed, when considered within and against the parameters of photography at the dawn of the 1970s, the conditions of the medium and the anxiety of his time seep in, evoking pervasive possibilities for rereading what has largely been taken as a given.

Messes among Us

Despite its tidy boxlike format, the medium of photography consists of ontological disarray. Responding to this contradictory clutter, a number of conceptual works confront photography's claim to verisimilitude. Employing the ironic gesture of producing life-size replicas of an object, and exaggerating the very idea of the 1:1 ratio as a "real" equivalence with reality, for example, have been used as a way to underscore representation's dubious character. My earlier discussion of Mel Bochner's *Actual Size (Hand)* (1968) in chapter 1 as well as my ensuing discussion of John Baldessari's *California Map Project* in chapter 4 relate here. Each instance exposes impossibility within the photograph. Despite the desire for the "real" that is so often encouraged

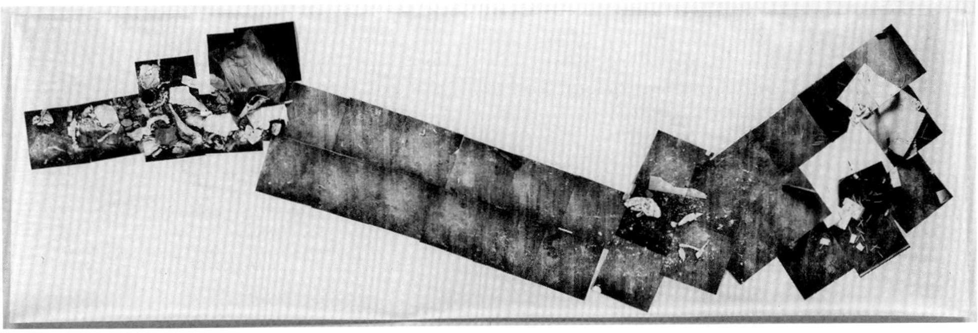

Figure 2.3. Bruce Nauman, *Composite Photo of Two Messes on the Studio Floor,* 1967. Gelatin silver prints, 40½ × 123 inches (102.9 × 312.4 cm). The Museum of Modern Art, New York. Gift of Philip Johnson. Copyright 2019 Bruce Nauman / Artists Rights Society (ARS). Digital image copyright The Museum of Modern Art/Licensed by SCALA/Art Resource, New York.

by the seductive belief in the potential capacity of photography's indexical function, every photograph is also a testament to an unavoidable lack of control. Nauman's *Composite Photo of Two Messes on the Studio Floor* (1967) provides a compelling case in point and an illustration of how the boundaries of literalism were explored through conceptual photography at this juncture (Figure 2.3).[56] A rephotographed montage measuring 40.5 by 123 inches, *Composite Photo of Two Messes on the Studio Floor* is a sprawling black-and-white photograph that reproduces an area of the floor of the artist's studio, featuring piles of debris joined by a strip of relatively clean floorboards.[57] The plain banality of subject matter, often a signature of Nauman's practice, is ironically the most striking aspect of the work, at least initially.

Pictured at this scale, Nauman's composite poignantly complicates not only photography's claim to represent but moreover the possibility of reading its mode of representation as a direct stand-in for the thing photographed.[58] Despite the scale, the "whole picture" leaves gaps in the information. First, we see the seams in the composite, as the edges of the numerous individual pictures are clearly visible. In this way, *Composite Photo of Two Messes* functions analogically, as an unruly constellation that figures the realities of life in this period, "filled with gaps, not only between words and things but generations and missiles."[59] As a straightforward document of artistic work, it is evidently a failure.[60] Despite the starkness of the title and the contents, the information contained is inevitably frustrating—a mess. The empiricism of "two messes" is thwarted further by the actual experience of looking. Where does one mess end and another begin? What constitutes a mess in the first place? Additionally, though the photographs that form this composite are themselves technically unremarkable—focused, evenly lit, clearly controlled[61]—they nevertheless recompose the decomposition that is their subject matter in an opposite way. One that is random, disjointed, and discontinuous.

As an accumulation of debris, this detritus appears as the excess of studio production.[62] However, in becoming the subject of the photograph as a work of art, the disarray on the studio floor is cast as much more than a leftover mess. In fact, it takes

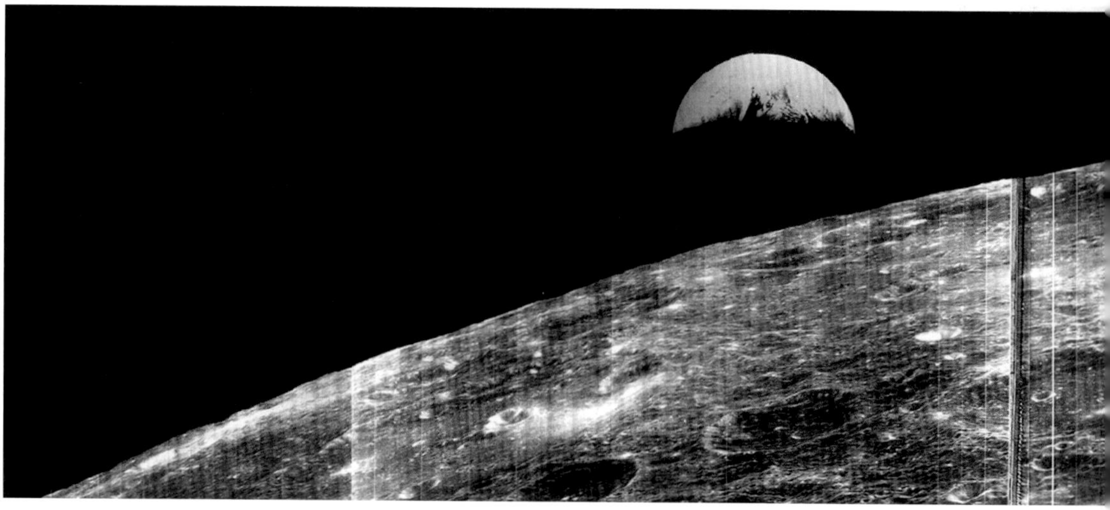

on a kind of coherence. Through a photograph on any scale, these messes would take on a sense of monumentality. In this case, by being reproduced in life-size versions, their imagined import is amplified. David Whitney heralded *Composite Photo of Two Messes* in a catalog text accompanying Nauman's first solo exhibition at the Leo Castelli Gallery, in New York in January 1969: "A long rambling composition, it is a direct statement on how the artist lives, works and thinks. Unlike Jasper John's [*sic*] painted bronze of a Savarin can with brushes, a statement about how the artist works, it is a documentary photograph of what is there."[63] It is striking that even in the context of the exhibition space, Whitney chooses to describe these photographs as documentary rather than art photography. One way to understand such categorization is as a perceived condition of the photograph itself. The seeming insignificance of the messes are monumentalized and transposed through selection and magnification, making the contents appear to be evidence of a strange uncharted territory.

These images have been compared in their montage format to early satellite images of outer space. Inspired by space exploration, "by the earliest moon shots, which were all composite photographs," this association draws attention to the alien presence that photography can endow its subjects with.[64] Through photography, an ordinary scene can become not simply compelling but extraterrestrial. In this way, *Composite Photo of Two Messes* engages viewers' fantasies as projected onto the abstraction that is the photographic image. *Composite Photo of Two Messes* poignantly coincides with other groundbreaking and culturally reorienting images. These include close-ups of the moon's dusty surface captured by the NASA lunar orbiter in 1966 (Figure 2.4), a precedent to the vivid 1968 photographs taken by the Apollo 8 mission.[65]

Brassaï and Salvador Dalí's *Sculptures involontaires (Involuntary Sculptures)* (1933), which features close-up photographs of quotidian bits of detritus, such as old bread, little twists of paper, a scrap of molded soap, and a rolled-up, wilted bus ticket, finds an echo in Nauman's *Composite Photo of Two Messes* (Figure 2.5). These typically discarded objects were forgotten about or unconsciously fumbled with before being

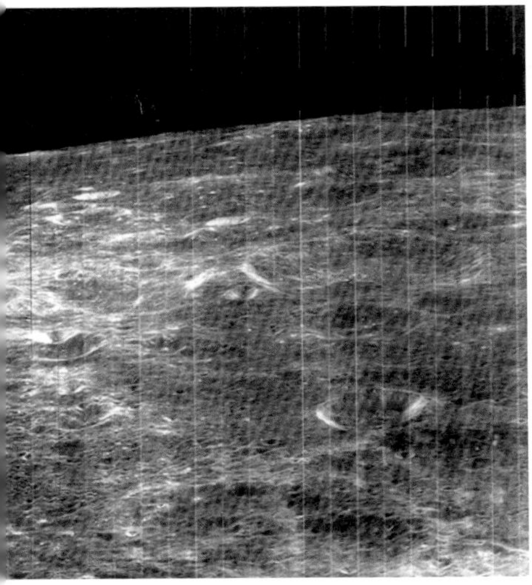

Figure 2.4. NASA lunar orbiter view of earth from the moon, August 23, 1966. Courtesy of NSSDCA/NASA.

found and photographed. And it is in the act of being photographed that they are elevated from throwaway entities to surreal and even somewhat mythical status. Playing on the pliability of materiality, representation, and recognition, one of the involuntary sculptures presents a smear of toothpaste, magnified and made strange in ways that connect directly to the discussion of Bochner's viscous close-ups in the previous chapter. Like the surrealist photographs by Brassaï and Dalí, Nauman's images focus on the excess of everyday minutiae, performing a parody of the traditions of monumental sculpture and highlighting the ways material is transformed by virtue of being photographed. Arguably, in this way, photography as medium takes on the sculptural capacity of elevating the ordinary. Even the most banal materials become photogenic points of interest. Another parallel between *Sculptures involontaires* and *Composite Photo of Two Messes* involves the shared emphasis on somehow being involuntary. Both works pivot on the notion of idle hands and unconscious shapes yet are nevertheless a result of artistic choice. This commonality signals an inherent tension between what can and cannot be controlled. It also suggests a more complex notion of resistance that implicates the artist's agency, pointing to what the artist is willing to control or not control. Nauman's work, read as involuntary sculpture, reiterates the artist's implicit and explicit disavowal of artistic "work."[66] It is simultaneously presented as a work of art and a declaration of aesthetic indifference. Both *Sculptures involontaires* and *Composite Photo of Two Messes* deliberately evoke defamiliarization techniques central to the early avant-garde. Nauman's concept-driven assignments at the San Francisco Art Institute in the mid-1960s form yet another bridge between the two artworks, particularly the instance in which he instructed his students to "make something in their pockets."[67]

Yet another Dada–surrealist piece that Nauman's work shows an affinity with is Man Ray's collaborative photograph of Duchamp's New York studio, *Dust Breeding (Duchamp's Large Glass with Dust Notes)* from 1920, a document of *The Large Glass* (1915–23) after it had collected a year's worth of dust on the floor of Duchamp's

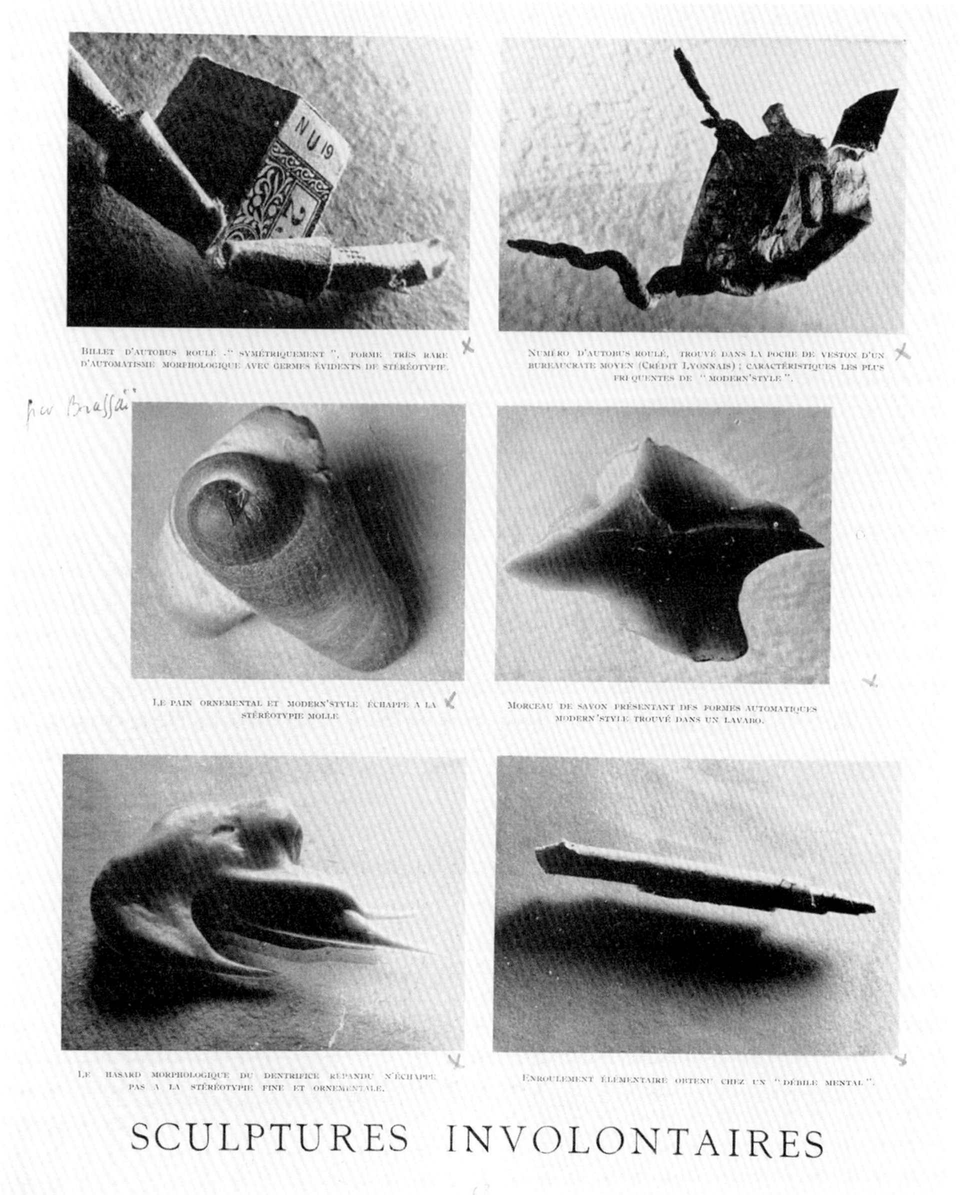

Figure 2.5. Brassaï and Salvador Dalí, *Sculptures involontaires (Involuntary Sculptures),* 1933. Copyright The Metropolitan Museum of Art. Image source: Art Resource, NY. Copyright Estate Brassaï; copyright RMN–Grand Palais / Art Resource, NY.

studio (Figure 2.6).[68] Man Ray's photograph served as a point of reference held for conceptual artists and was even included in MoMA's *Information* exhibition in 1970. Like Nauman's images, Man Ray's ambiguous document depicts artistic work in the studio as passive accumulation. Doing nothing is, of course, precisely the way to breed dust or messes. In this way, traditional ideas about artistic creativity and production are inverted. The use of photography to capture and transpose art is not

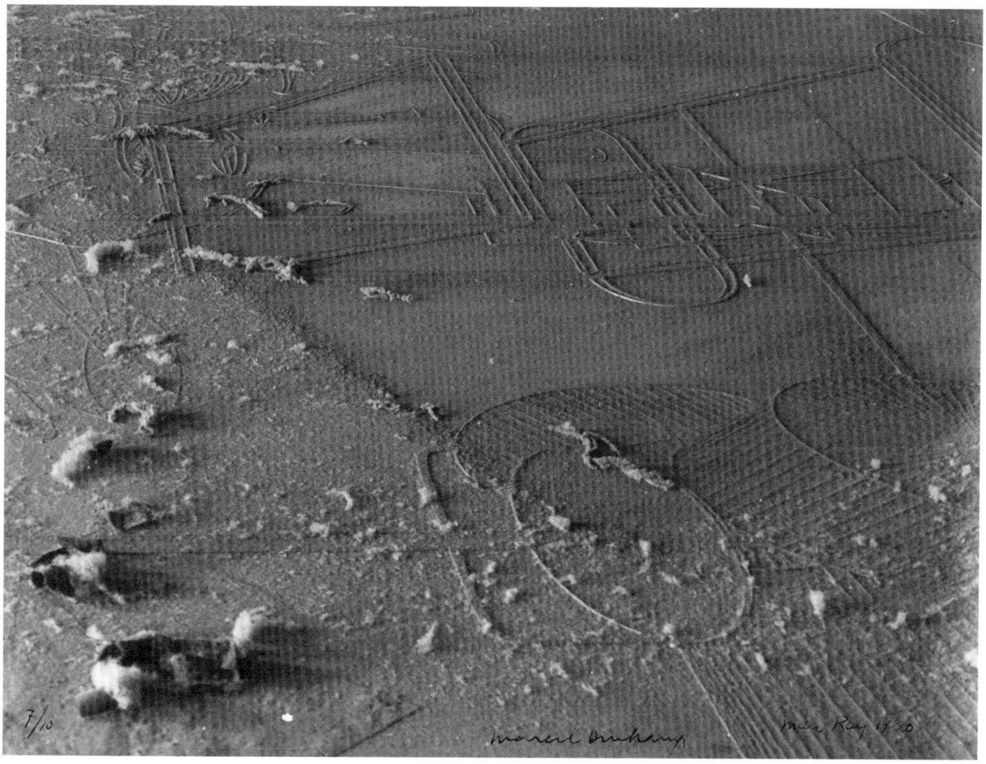

Figure 2.6. Man Ray, *Dust Breeding (Duchamp's Large Glass with Dust Notes),* 1920. Copyright Association Marcel Duchamp / ADAGP, Paris / Artists Rights Society (ARS), New York 2019; copyright Man Ray 2015 Trust / Artists Rights Society (ARS), New York / ADAGP, Paris.

haphazard, and it can be read further as an implicit comment on the medium itself. It underscores the view that to take a picture is to do nothing. Dust and messes are inevitable aspects of everyday life, which can cause a sense of futility in the struggle to contain or exorcise them. Such debris are traces of life, indices of a lack of action—a description that shares characteristics with the photographic index. Moreover, dust is said to consist mostly of human skin, returning the reality of dust, messes, the photograph, and the work of art to considerations of the physical body.

These particular photographs by Nauman resemble Victor Burgin's *Photopath* of the same year (1967), included in the London version of Harald Szeemann's landmark conceptual art exhibition, *When Attitude Becomes Form: Works—Concepts—Processes—Situations—Information* of 1969 (Figure 2.7). Burgin reproduced a linear section of the gallery floor in black-and-white photographs, developed proportionally to the size of the floor photographed, to be displayed on top of the same gallery floor depicted in the images, precisely in the order in which they were derived. According to Burgin's predetermined instructions, *Photopath* consisted of "a path along a floor, of propositions 1 × 20 units, photographed. Photographs printed to the actual size of objects and prints stapled to the floor so that the images are perfectly congruent with their objects."[69] In contrast, Nauman's life-size floor photomontage

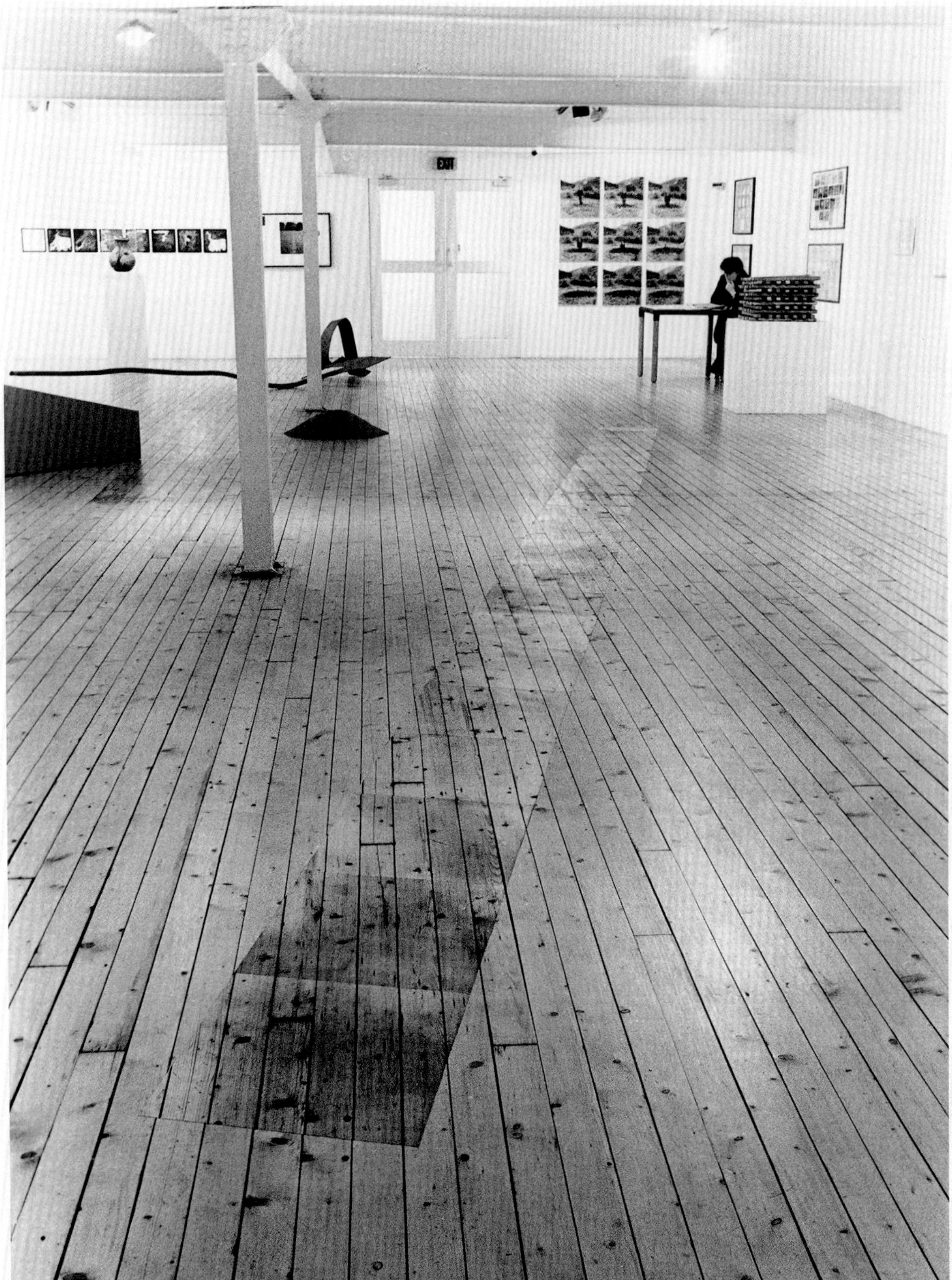

Figure 2.7. Victor Burgin, *Photopath,* 1967–69. Installation view. Courtesy of the artist and Cristin Tierney Gallery, New York.

was intended to be exhibited hanging on any wall, displacing the horizontal reality of the floor for the vertical space of display. Nauman's piece is emphatically not site-specific in the ways that Burgin's is. Despite this difference of orientation and situation, however, both Burgin's and Nauman's projects in this instance reflect a shared interest in Wittgenstein's *Philosophical Investigations* (1953), in particular the author's discussion of how one can simultaneously look at something and think about it.[70] A common interpretation of pieces such as Nauman's *Composite Photo of Two Messes*, in view of structuralist works such a Burgin's, sees them as "tightly contained self-referential units, in which the title provides the conceptual framework for the eponymous photograph,"[71] without asking the consequent question of what exactly that "framework" signifies. To end one's reading there, without explicitly addressing the specific contents of Nauman's image and their significance, is an overly neat and insufficient reading that neglects the ironic and fundamental inclusion of the messes for what they actually are: messes.

The starkness of Burgin's structuralist piece and his search for "perfect congruence" provide a productive character foil in this regard. Nauman's act of photographing the messes alters their essential temperament, changing them from unruly to contained and essentially clean, manageable, and movable. He never hides the superficiality of this containment, however. The tension between the clean photographic product and its messy contents throws the photograph into relief as ultimately imbalanced and imperfect, becoming by extension a proposition about the disorderly ontology of the photographic real. In contrast to André Bazin's statements on the ontology of the photographic image as grounded in its objective character, for example, Nauman points to the disarray and its inevitable subjective manipulations. Bazin based his theory partly on the nuance implied by the term and the function of the "lens," which in French is called an *objectif*. Nauman's translation of terms here denies the credibility that Bazin claimed was the nature of photography in the name of inherent "objectivity."[72]

Consisting of a select set of seven photographs featuring random piles of a common white baking staple in varying configurations across the artist's studio floor, *Flour Arrangements* (1966) offers a revealing precedent for *Composite Photo of Two Messes* (Figure 2.8). This piece was recorded over time, as Nauman committed to making one ephemeral flour sculpture each day for over a month. Identified as one of the "first true process sculptures" by Benjamin Buchloh, *Flour Arrangements* provides yet another example of the artist's recurring interest in authenticating ostensibly banal and seemingly pointless incidents, a thread throughout Nauman's oeuvre that has consistently proved as deceptive as it is disarming.[73] In fact, it is somewhat ironic that Buchloh chooses the word *true* to express the weight of Nauman's piece. Indeed, the misrepresentation of truth and/or misperception of truth compels much of Nauman's practice. Even when he admits in a 1980 interview that he was "interested in the idea of lying, or not telling the truth,"[74] the inclusion of the thorny word *idea* complicates the "lying." *Flour Arrangements* and *Composite Photo of Two Messes* suggest a similar call to attention about meaning. The pun of using flour instead

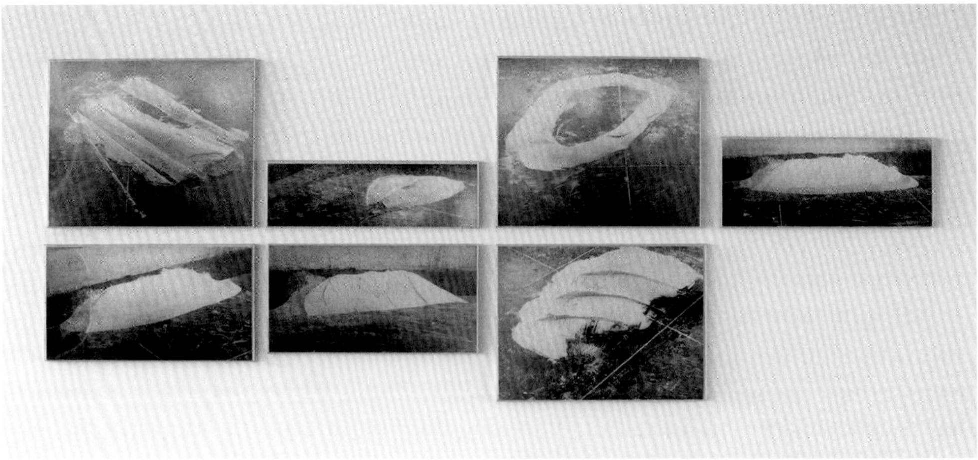

Figure 2.8. *Flour Arrangements,* 1966. Seven color photographs, dimensions variable. Raussmuller Collection, Basel. Copyright 2019 Bruce Nauman / Artists Rights Society (ARS). Courtesy of Sperone Westwater, New York.

of flowers furthers a critique of traditional art, disavowing the pursuit of beautiful subjects and organized compositions as well as nature and still-life paintings dating back to the seventeenth century.[75] Given the cultural currency of "flower power" in the late sixties, the piece adds the seeing Nauman not quite as a pacifist but more aptly a passive-ist. Shot in black and white, the piles of flour resemble ashes, raising a morbid specter of cremation, reinforced by the photograph's memorial-like capacity. This funereal quality despondently suggests a grave occasion on which one might need to make flower arrangements. The unruly status of language again functions as a retort against facile meaning, and, as the pun is visualized, the secondary homonym becomes its primary meaning. In this way, the inversion of meaning parallels the way in which the abstraction that is a photograph becomes "real," or credible. Nauman returns to such gestures repeatedly, evoking a game of mimetic representation that defies idealized reflection or containment, and whose disordered implications I continue to investigate throughout the present chapter.

Language–Performance–Photography

Nauman's prolific practices assert themselves as uncontainable by language, photography, or conventional linear thinking. They press against the boundaries of language and logic in the tradition of Wittgenstein, who famously asserted that "the meaning of a word is its use."[76] In every instance, Nauman's work threatens to literally and figuratively spill over borderlines of medium and subject matter, as well as physical, temporal, and conceptual delineations. Emphasizing Nauman's interest in word games and language structures, many scholars and art critics have commented extensively on his unconventional displacement of meaning and his inversion of self-reference in particular works.[77] However, the medium of photography is nearly absent as a frame of reference in the existing scholarship.[78] The kinship between photographic effects and Nauman's concern with the mind's accumulated apperception of reality is striking. Though I would not claim that photography has been Nauman's central medium, I contend that photographic thinking underscores and sets the stage for his overall corpus of production, and that series such as *Eleven Color Photographs* are propositions about a central epistemological shift in art practice of the late 1960s. In fundamental ways, they challenge not simply the logic of referential language but also the logic of referential pictures.

One key way in which photographs effect this challenge is through a play on and with time. Accenting the essential discontinuities inherent in lived time, Nauman's photographs exemplify the spatial immediacy conjoined with temporal anteriority that Barthes described as the illogical essence of photography.[79] Barthes's "message without a code" is contingent on both the "here-now" and the "there-then," inevitably proposing multiple ways in which one's understanding of what has happened might be unhinged. By such means, photography challenges linear thinking as a stable basis for understanding the world. Like Friedrich Nietzsche's claim that thinking is always untimely, photographs are never what they seem, yet, somewhat paradoxically, they instigate and often become the supplement for the very conception of the real.

This ponderous disjuncture troubles both mass media imagery and art practice. As mentioned earlier, perhaps the most perceptive theorization of the photograph's role as a supplement and a substitute for reality comes from Robert Smithson. His nonsite projects depended on photographs to exhibit his works that were located too far outside the traditional gallery circuit to be accessible to most viewers. Smithson understood that the photographs inevitably and effectively change the piece, and that they rely on a tacit suspension of disbelief. He noted in 1969 that, through photographs, "people have the experience but miss the meaning."[80] According to Smithson, photographs would enigmatically allow people to believe that they grasp the site, but without visiting the actual site they would never "be confronted with the intangibility of something that appears to be very tangible."[81] Such an ambivalent dialectic between experience and meaning proves central to Nauman's use of photography as well.

Nauman's photographs contradict the theoretical division posited specifically by the discourse of sixties art history, which attempted to separate the models of "performance" and "language" as simultaneously emergent yet competing artistic paradigms.[82] The photographic documents Nauman created between 1966 and 1970 complicate the desire to divide the corporeal from the cerebral and experience from ideas. He also speculates about the ways that notions such as the "real" and "authenticity" were being overhauled in relation to photography.

Throughout the late 1960s and early 1970s, conceptual art incorporated an assessment of language and its discursive and institutional frameworks in relation to the status of the art object in order to question the underlying conditions of aesthetic experience. It also included performance practices, which introduced connections to the body and were thus suggestive of the social construction of subjectivity more broadly. Nevertheless, from an art historical standpoint the contemporaneous discourse surrounding these works predominantly tends to emphasize a distinction between performance art in opposition to the dominant conceptual art paradigm of language, as if there were a "rational" and pure version of conceptual art in direct contradiction to any consideration of the adulterated, and perhaps by extension "irrational," physical body.

In retrospect, Buchloh, whose foundational account of conceptual art has remained authoritative in the field of art history,[83] has reviewed the relationship between the "linguistic paradigm" and performance in art history of the sixties, observing that "the opposition is upheld between a victorious paradigm of conceptualism, which represses, excludes, denigrates all other practices—which at that moment are of performance, of the body."[84] The privileging of language in this popular version of art history risks further disembodying the subject in conceptual art and bringing it much closer to particular strains of modernist painting and modes of abstraction that sought to maintain art as an autonomous enclave. The other hazard of this formulation is that it bypasses the particularities of so many artistic practices in this moment and maligns the work of artists who deliberately wanted to collapse the divide between performance and concept. Consider for a moment the wildly varied artworks of not simply Nauman but also Vito Acconci, Chris Burden, Ana Mendieta, Adrian Piper, Martha Rosler, Carolee Schneeman, and Dennis Oppenheim, among others. In their own respective ways, each of these artists sought to conduct a critique, from within a broadly conceptual framework, of the positivist claims made for rationality in conceptual art that denied its "burden of physicality."[85] More immediately, the separation of performance from language under this commonly accepted aegis ignores the ways that the language of rationality can also have intimately physical effects.[86] Recall that it was in rebellion against the bourgeois denial of the physical body that the Dadaists turned to performance. Similarly, many conceptual artists sought to investigate the body as a manifestation of simultaneity rather than the refinement of one sense in isolation, and conceived of the photograph as embodied rather than embalmed.

Acknowledging the mocking contempt played out in the "bureaucratese" of much conceptual art is yet another indication of indignation about the refusal of the erratic body in the "aesthetics of administration." These playful acts function also as a denial against any singular philosophy of art, conceptualism, or life, articulated by the rhetoric of absolutism evident in writers/artists such as Joseph Kosuth who overlooked the provocative potential of even the most banal tautologies. By contrast, the work of conceptual artists such as Nauman renounces any ability to ground the subject in hermetic conceptual reason. He leaves the subject purposefully with an undecidable and often frustrating status, in the position of doubt. There is no master reading of these works, as any reading is fraught with the implicit awareness that subjectivity within either the institutional frame of art or the wider public sphere consists of "a complex ambivalence toward the uncertain determinations of subjectivity."[87] This failure to articulate and identify resulted in the propagation of doubt, in dialogue with a pervasive sense of conceptual, social, and, by extension, political uncertainty.

Suspended between Gravity and Levity

On October 21, 1967, more than one hundred thousand antiwar activists flooded Washington, D.C., to protest the United States' escalating military involvement in Vietnam. That particular Saturday, the Pentagon rather than the Capitol formed the focal point, since, as Jerry Rubin, one of the organizers, put it, the Defense Department was the *real* seat of power. Photographs from this day have since become inspirational documents of nonviolent resistance, showing moving acts such as protesters putting flowers in the barrels of military police guns. Perhaps the most memorable gesture, however, focused on another sort of movement, namely, the engrossing effort to levitate the Pentagon. According to *Time* magazine, Abbie Hoffman and Allen Ginsberg "asked for a permit to levitate the Pentagon 300 feet off the ground, explaining that by chanting ancient Aramaic exorcism rites while standing in a circle around the building, they could get it to rise into the air, turn orange and vibrate until all evil emissions had fled. The war would end forthwith." Albeit absurd, the conceptual mind over matter attempt is replete with lasting meaning. As with conceptual art's emphasis on thinking rather than isolated considerations of form, concentration and attention in this instance can be seen as a deliberate challenge to "unthinking" positions, including those that made the continuing violence in Vietnam possible. In many ways, the rhetorical imperatives of the antiwar movements parallel the logic of conceptual art. The call to "Think!," for example, was emblematic of both antiwar protests and conceptual art, rallying for a shift away from "passive contemplation to arenas of active questioning."[88]

Although they were unable to actually levitate the Pentagon, protesters nevertheless received a permit to perform the act, an official bureaucratic recognition of their sincere intent and effort, and an acknowledgment of their cause. Though they failed, their creative action in the face of a vicious, incongruous reality continues to resonate and to suggest the potential political power of humor and determination. Ahead of this specific manifestation, the experiential ethos of such a protest performance—its desire to levitate and its attempt to do so despite its likely failure—already formed the crux of Nauman's artistic practice.

The now-iconic photograph, *Failing to Levitate in the Studio* (1966), presents a double-exposed grainy black-and-white image of Nauman's attempt to defy gravity through his concentrated effort to hover above his studio floor (Figure 2.9).[89] We see the artist lying rigid, at attention, suspended between two metal folding chairs overlaid with an image of the chair pulled out from under him, legs splayed on the scrap-laden floor of his studio, his body limp and slumped to the ground, with his neck in what looks to be a painful collision with the edge of the other seat. We have a document of the attempt at a transcendent feat and both its metaphysical and its viscerally physical failure. Failure itself is staged and systematically documented.

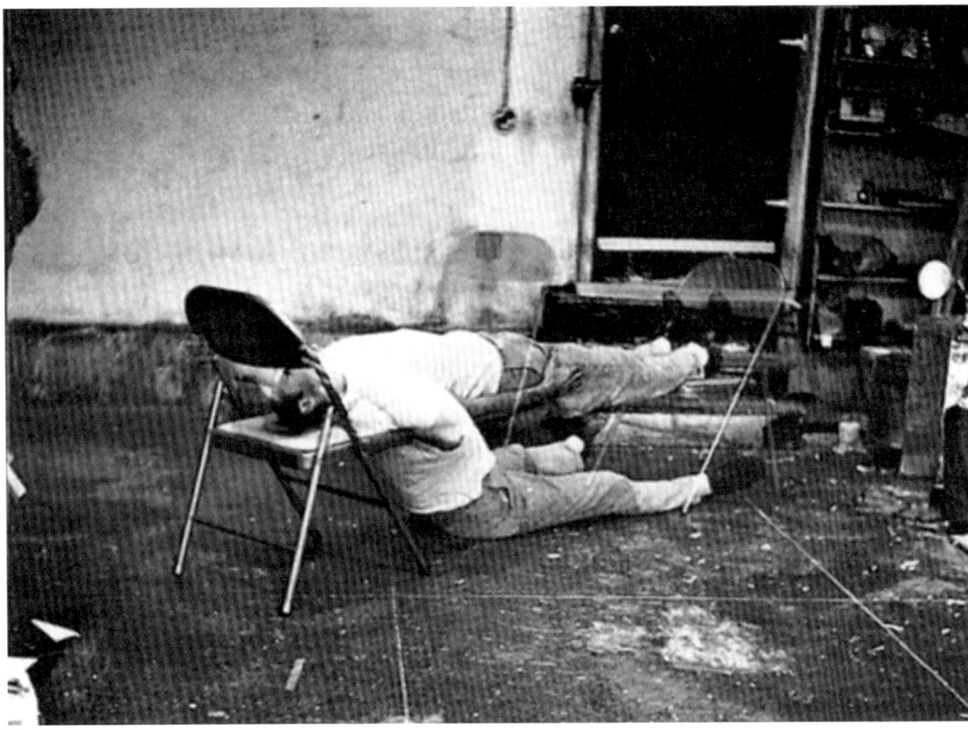

Figure 2.9. Bruce Nauman, *Failing to Levitate in the Studio,* 1966. Copyright 2019 Bruce Nauman / Artists Rights Society (ARS). Courtesy of Sperone Westwater, New York.

The awareness that Nauman is also famous for the nautilus-shaped neon work *The True Artist Helps the World by Revealing Mystical Truths* (1967), which he installed in the storefront of his San Francisco studio, and the fact that he continued throughout his career to set himself a variety of odd if not impossible tasks,[90] raises the question of Nauman's sincerity. Is he being truthful? In an interview with Brenda Richardson in 1982, the artist disclosed that the statement was indeed a kind of paradox, simultaneously "true and not true at the same time."[91] Extending this logic, is *Failing to Levitate* simply a performative conceit? Not according to Nauman. He claims he did not fail to levitate for lack of effort, explaining: "I was working on the exercise in the studio for a while and wanted to make a tape of it, a record, to see if you could see what was happening. When I did the things, they made me tired and I felt good when I finished, but they were not relaxing; they took a lot of energy and concentration and paying attention."[92] Nevertheless, the predictable failure and photo-document show the futility of his efforts.

Failing to Levitate in the Studio encapsulates Nauman's conceptually heuristic sensibility. Like Robert Morris's *Box with the Sound of Its Own Making* (1961) or *Card File* (1962) and other process-oriented conceptual works of the period, this image describes its own making. Not simply because the title directly explains the contents, but because the object's status as a work of art hinges on the process.

Nauman's *Failing to Levitate* piece is pushed further than Morris's propositions by turning this equation against itself. More than the idea of the repetition of futile process that dominated much conceptual art, such as Acconci's *Step Piece* (1970) or Robert Barry's *Inert Gas Series* (1969), *Failing to Levitate* documents the failure to accomplish the thing proposed. It literally depicts a trial and error process, with the title functioning as a punch line based on a witty double entendre, describing simultaneously exactly what is present in the photograph and what will never be.

Like the concentrated meditation that does not lead to Zen, the artist remains grounded, and his process in the studio is exposed. There seem to be no secrets here, no mystic truths, no confidential techniques mythologically hidden by the sacred space of the artist's studio. Instead, there is only the realization that Nauman's art represents the failure of transcendentalism and demythologizes the magic of the artist's work. The process does not exceed the limits of experience, but is contained by it, as we are confronted with the limits of the knowable world. It is imaginable that Nauman emphasizes the impact of gravity for this reason. Gravity is one of the more constant reminders that we are never entirely in control of our own world and are always under pressure from an ultimately unknowable elsewhere. Like many of Nauman's later projects, such as the video *Elke Allowing the Floor to Rise Up over Her, Face Up* (1973) or *Tony Sinking into the Floor, Face Up, and Face Down* (1973),[93] the recurring twinned themes of failure and mind over matter demonstrate a persistent affinity with Samuel Beckett and how "the will to depict the impossible [feeds] on the futility of the very goal."[94] Nauman's interrogation of his bodily identity was partly the result of being extremely influenced by formative readings of Beckett along with Gestalt psychology and phenomenology. Nauman's work has often been compared to that of the dramatist and founder of the Theatre of the Absurd, who similarly captured a sense of life's maddening disjunctures and humorous continuums in plays such as *Waiting for Godot* (1953).[95]

Failure, self-deprecation, and uselessness—these concepts are central to Nauman's practice and can often be as humorous as they are disparaging. One aspect of the humor is derived from how such pieces play on the gravity of the situation or lack thereof. After all, these are not really death-defying feats, unlike the artistic performances of some of his contemporaries such as Burden or Bas Jan Ader, or their precursor Yves Klein. They are not even situations where the stakes seem particularly high. By contrast, they seem mundane, banal, and ordinary. Yet the degree of effort Nauman exerts on film and in recounting the details draws attention to the disconnection between effort and product, as well as the dialectic between gravity and levity.

In the late 1960s, gravity also formed the punch line of a common slogan during the war in Vietnam, frequently scrawled on the walls of bathroom stalls and etched on the obverse side of soldiers' Zippo lighters: "There Is No Gravity. The World Sucks" (Figure 2.10). Given the undeniably high mortal stakes for combat soldiers amid a war whose meaning seemed contradictory at best, and wrongheaded,

Figure 2.10. Will Kuberski, *Vietnam Zippos at a Barcelona Flea Market,* 2011. Courtesy of the artist.

misguided, and nefarious at worst, the popularity of this timely existential saying makes sense. Nauman's refusal to accept gravity as a necessary given may therefore be imagined as a willful engagement with the difficult truths of the Vietnam War era and the contemporaneous and pervasive feeling of helplessness. Gravity, in Nauman's piece, refers not just to the force that the earth exerts on animate bodies and inanimate objects alike, but also to the degree of seriousness with which his own seemingly inconsequential task is undertaken. The human fallibility exposed by this dynamic creates the comedic effect. The artist's impotence, his inability to levitate, is propped photographically against his stiff horizontal body. The transcendental myth of the artist is replaced by an anxious conflict between what is and is not possible. Like the playwright Beckett, who evoked the painful yet plain drama of existence, whose evocation of laughter was often caught up in a loop of tragic paralysis, or Buster Keaton, whose comedic gestures were dominated by Sisyphean traps, Bruce Nauman makes one laugh from a place of suspended discomfort.

The comedic fallout of the piece is directly connected to a long lineage of slapstick and pratfalls. The conjunction of the documentary photograph's "official" delivery of information with the absurdity of the information contained produces a deadpan twist. The discontinuous image marks the fundamentally disruptive potential of a seemingly naive act and reveals a poignant connection between Nauman and Duchamp. In both cases, the question of where the art resides is linked tacitly to the question of where labor is visible. In the same way that the readymade was a rebuke to aesthetics in its apparent lack of the manual skill expected of art, Nauman's *Failing to Levitate* shows no "real work," despite being documented in a chronophotographic style. Each work (Nauman's *Failing* and Duchamp's unassisted readymades) is a product of intellectual labor rather than physical. This shift is crucial to understanding the radical interventions these pieces set in motion.

The role of intellectual labor is among the dominant themes of much Duchampian scholarship; however, it is typically formulated as a witty joke at the expense of handcraft, rather than an assessment of the radical implications of art unassisted by artistry.[96] While this reading rings true, one does well to consider the possibility that Duchamp's gesture, and by extension Nauman's, goes beyond a simple gag. The unassisted readymades might resist sensuous rewards or palpable artistic labor, but does art not consist of more than pleasure and skilled labor? The refusal to deliver the goods demanded by bourgeois culture is one aspect of its unruly avant-garde potential. Reading these gestures simply as dead-pan mockeries, without considering their wider reflection on the role of labor in connection to artistic skill, deprives the work of the deeper critique such a hoax mediates. The readymades, far from being clever one-liners, are actually sites of conflict and anxiety, both nuanced and overt.[97] What are the other potentials of this humor?

Henri Bergson was one of the rare philosophers to deal with the phenomenon of comedy at length and proposed a conceptual matrix with which to understand it. Bergson explained that "rigidity is the comic, and laughter its corrective."[98] In other words, according to Bergson, "laughter is a purgative response to the threat of rigidity."[99] Examples of this dynamic are plainly visible in the humor of Charlie Chaplin, but also extend to the art world through gestures like Duchamp's and Nauman's. Duchamp's claim to indifference overthrows an entire tradition of art on its head and begins a new episteme. We laugh at the extremes of the dialectic: the concentrated dignity that strives to control gravity and the slip that undermines dignified concentration.[100] Nauman's exaggerated inert rigidity in *Failing to Levitate* is thus at odds with the reality of his imperfect living-self when he falls on the floor. In trying to go beyond his natural limits, the artist bamboozles himself. As John Roberts explains in his analysis of the deskilling of art after the readymade, "This gap between desired outcome and actual outcome generates a comedic-effect that is central to Duchamp's reflections on artistic skill: misjudgments of labor undertaken."[101] The disproportion between the result and the labor undertaken to achieve it forms one of the disjunctures Bergson describes as comedy.

Humor arises from the fallout between desire and actuality, between art and reality. Nauman's collapse to the ground in *Failing to Levitate,* despite his concentrated efforts, is funny because of the absurdist exchange between work and failure, particularly since the failure pictured is then transposed into a work of art that seems effortless. Nauman combines the worker who tirelessly persists at a repetitive job that never ends in the desired result with individuals who, with complete indifference to their lack of skills, carelessly pass off their questionable work as artful. The rub is that where one looks for effort, it will not be found; each is a trick in the act of judgment. If these works are given the benefit of the doubt, a space opens up to rethink the object and reanimate it conceptually. This is one way to consider the unremarkable/remarkable capacity of conceptual art, and certainly the ways the unassisted readymade performs a nearly perfect transformation of productive labor into artistic labor. What appears effortless becomes effortful. Duchamp's importance lies in his eradication of the assumed distinction between skill and deskilling in art. By extension, the subterfuge of Nauman's artwork, following this line of inquiry, is not the dissolution of meaning but the act of exposing how contradictions can be indeed be performed and made visible in ways that ultimately evade categorical distinction. Nauman's artwork throws the concepts of art and work into dialectical tension with each other. Rigid aspects of mind and body, system and perspective, are exposed as fallible and pliable.

Following in the footsteps of Nauman, a great many artists have taken up this antiheroic gesture, including Mike Kelley, Erwin Wurm, Tom Friedman, and Lucy Gunning, falling into the "readymade frame" as obviously as slipping on a misplaced banana peel. Peter Fischli and David Weiss's *Équilibres* photo series (1984–87) (subtitled "Equilibrium is best shortly before it gives way") features precariously balanced objects amid random studio debris and manifests as a cross between *Failing to Levitate* and *Eleven Color Photographs. Failing to Levitate* can also be seen in a more historic light, viewed as a kind of motion study and an ironic attempt to uncover the best way to do work.[102] Resembling a chronophotographic image in the tradition of Étienne-Jules Marey and later Frank Gilbreth and Lillian Gilbreth, *Failing to Levitate* displays action over the span of time but within a single frame by containing both the before and the after shots simultaneously. Both Marey's developments and the Gilbreths' photo studies were used to buttress Frederick Winslow Taylor's famous studies of the labor process at the end of the nineteenth century and mark how entwined photography was with fundamental changes in modern society. Taylor's studies also revealed how photography could be used as both a tool for, or a critique of, the deskilling of productive labor that is at the very heart of Karl Marx's *Capital.* According to Marx, there is a systematic tendency in capitalism to produce work that is repetitive and unsatisfying. In volume 1 of *Capital,* he outlines how the development of the early manufacturing system is accompanied by the simplification and interchangeability of jobs among workers.[103] Photography was a central component of this shift. As proponents of Taylor's "scientific method" and the mechanized era of factory work, both Marey and the Gilbreths documented workers and used visual analysis to decipher the best way for a worker to perform tasks with the least amount of exertion and the most output of productivity.[104] These motion studies were more focused on how a task was done and how best to eliminate unneeded, fatiguing steps in any process. The labor of the worker in such chronophotographic images is continuously stripped of its autonomy and sensuous form as a means to aspirational, if unrealistic, ends.

On the other hand, these photographs were ostensibly taken as measures of work and efficiency, and in order to harness the power and ability of the machine to formulate a new kind of individual. Similar to the Gilbreths' photographs, in Nauman's *Failing to Levitate* we see a process that ultimately brings about a sense of alienation and psychological anxiety. But, rather than the economy of factory work, it is the economy of information and ideas. Notably, the social condition of alienation has been cited by Nauman as one of the central motivations of his practice: "My work comes out of being frustrated about the human condition. And about how people refuse to understand other people."[105] Based on this logic, perhaps Nauman's *Failing to Levitate* can be seen as a refutation of alienation by declining to be either efficient or straightforward. Paradoxically, Nauman's failure is his success.

The ironies of the effortful effortlessness pictured in this image may also be related to the popularity of the teachings of Maharishi Mahesh Yogi in California during the 1960s.[106] The Maharishi was the guru of Transcendental Meditation, a program for the mind that was supposed to be spontaneous and easy, intended to make the conscious mind aware of its infinite potential. Maharishi insisted on restful states and rejected the principle of hard work. The rhetoric and the principle sound remarkably akin to slacker ideology, including the idea that anyone could do it without preparation. In contrast with the Maharishi's principles, rest never comes easy for Nauman. As Lane Relyea has insightfully described, "Even when Nauman does invoke mental activity directly, as when he attempts to levitate his body or has a friend try to sink into the floor, those activities seem as much physical as conceptual, instances of the mind concentrating so hard it clenches into a fist."[107]

Despite Nauman's programmatic positioning of failure, his work is an achievement. The photographic double exposure *Failing to Levitate* provides an overlap of Nauman's self—he is represented twice in a single frame—so while the magic trick of levitating has failed, the artist succeeds in doubling himself in space (another credibly impossible feat), compressed in a seemingly singular time, through the power of photography. Linking inner experience with external appearances, the levitation experiment becomes a metaphoric success, despite its physical failure. The futility of Nauman's goal is fueled by the will to capture the impossible, resulting finally in an irresolvable state of suspension.

Performance Proof

As I have shown throughout this chapter, deciphering the visual signs and signifiers bound up in Nauman's photographs (however ironically effortless the artist's own professed input/output may be) returns inquiry to the photographic image and to an investigation of the varied role it has played in the exploration of authenticity and art through performance. Counter to Fried's defense of the aesthetically coherent, "wholly manifest,"[108] and self-sufficient art object, the objecthood of the photograph cannot be separated from its simultaneous specificity and confusion of space and time. Defying Fried's desire, the photograph is never entirely timeless or entirely removable from individual experience.

Self-Portrait as Fountain (1966–67/1970) endures as one of Nauman's most frequently reproduced pieces, and the most widely recognized of the *Eleven Color Photographs* series.[109] This image inevitably is read as an evocation of Duchamp's *Fountain* (1917), and while there are certainly other resonances at play, the connection bears further analysis. Nauman's reenactment of Duchamp's *Fountain* in the photograph *Self-Portrait as Fountain* functions not simply as a wink to Duchampian avant-garde tactics but also as a bold reformulation of Duchamp's questions through the body of the artist.[110] The formal allusion to Duchamp's earlier work might seem tenuous, since Nauman's features the artist in the act of spouting water, whereas Duchamp's fountain is not in service. Nevertheless, the conceptual bonds between the two pieces are striking. In Nauman's work, the body is put in the place of the readymade object. If photography is the medium, the other conduit is the body. Their mutually contingent relationship in the construction and understanding of the real is integral to the piece and has emphatic importance, considering performance art's popular dependence on photography for visible evidence and historical record.

From one angle, riffing on the photograph's ambivalent authenticity, especially as concerns the substitution of the photo for the "original" art object, Duchamp's *Fountain* sets the stage for Nauman. The only visual proof of the original fountain's existence takes the form of a photograph (snapped by Alfred Stieglitz at his 291 gallery), marking a turning point in art practice, exhibition, and reception. The fact that *Fountain* as an art object is as much imagined as it is revered by virtue of being photographed demonstrates yet another complication incited by the notion of readymade-process. Reading Duchamp's gesture as primarily performative opens up a conversation about play and contingency. It also sets his project and Nauman's apart from conceptual artists such as Joseph Kosuth, who wanted to read the readymade solely as an analytic proposition, tautologically occluding its experiential open-endedness.[111] Performance art in the late sixties developed alongside a critical dialogue about authenticity as expression based in the body and in a unique set of circumstances. It also insisted on performance as a nonreproducible, nonmarketable art form.[112] In resisting closure, performance art in the late sixties thus returns to the crux of Duchamp's readymade provocation. The tension between performance as real and authentic versus staged and ephemeral reiterates many of Duchamp's questions about the art object, truth, nominalism, and value, particularly as both cases (that of R. Mutt and Nauman) remain contingent on the reception of the photograph.

Nauman's derisive performance as water nymph throws both the body and photography into limbo. He evokes corporeal necessities and contingencies. Seeing Nauman figured in place of the *Fountain,* or urinal, suggests that Nauman's water expulsion here might also be read as the artist confrontationally relieving himself in the direction of the viewer. Nauman's mocking tone in *Self-Portrait as Fountain* further registers as an exposure of photography's performative status in the sixties—photography began representing an extension of the body as the legitimate site of experience and knowledge. It also posits a conceptual oscillation between the subject as object and back again while emphasizing how the photograph convincingly

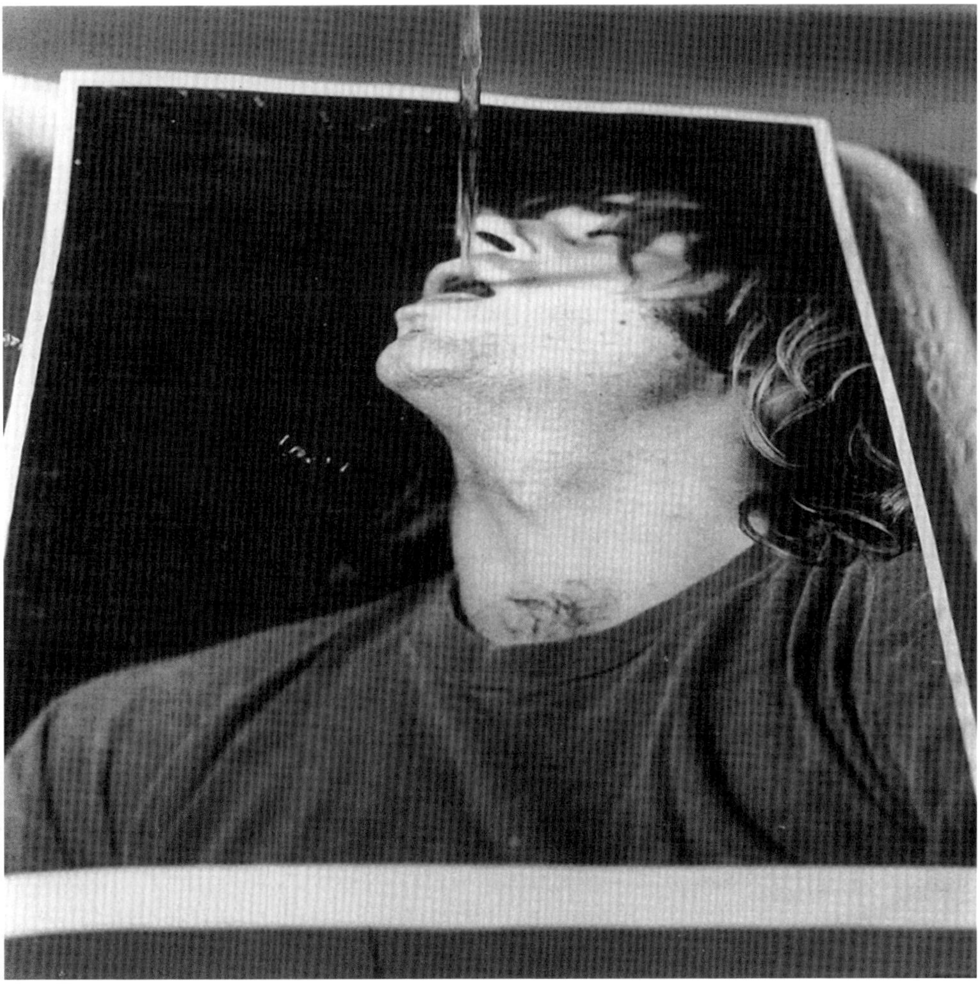

Figure 2.11. William Wegman, *Photo under Water,* 1971. Copyright 2019 William Wegman. Courtesy of the artist and Sperone Westwater, New York.

shared the same nonobject space as performance partly because it was perceived as more real than other mediums.[113] Many other artists were inspired by the possibilities of ontological resistance flowing through the photograph. William Wegman, for example, who had connections to Nauman at the University of Wisconsin and later played basketball with him in Southern California, admired Nauman's practice and, with full cognizance of Nauman's *Self-Portrait as a Fountain* (1966) and *The Artist as a Fountain* (1966–67), staged *Photo under Faucet* (1971) and *Photo under Water* (1971) (Figure 2.11). Rather than spewing water like Nauman, in this "picture of a picture of him performing,"[114] the photograph shows Wegman in the developing process, hovering above a photo bath, water streaming toward his imaged mouth, jointly commenting on the creation of photographs and identity itself.

As with Nauman's *Self-Portrait as Fountain,* these photographs function as a combined riposte to and an echo of Duchamp's inert sculpture. Nauman is static only through the power of photography, which documents him in the irreverent act of spitting water at the viewer. Or, perhaps a connotation, as suggested earlier, of "that other stream emanating from farther down the body."[115] This gesture can be read as a deliberate degradation of ideas of high culture in conjunction with elevating notions of low nature—it reformulates art in conjunction with the baseness of the body. The urgency of urination combines with the myth of spontaneous artistic creation. Playing on this dialectic of the urinal in *Fountain,* Nauman extends Duchamp's linguistic game, further exposing how the gesture of *Fountain* alters the terms of traditional subjectivity and receptivity in art.

Testing the boundaries of the real, literally and figuratively, remains integral in works such as *Finger Touch with Mirrors* (1966–67/1970) and *Finger Touch No. I* (1966–67/1970) as I discussed at the outset of this chapter. Both photographs comment on the process of art as metamorphosis and vanity through implicit reference to Ovid's Narcissus. These images are incongruous and intertextual, setting an oscillation of meanings in motion that contradict the ability to read these statements (either photographic or linguistic) as indexical. Symmetry is suggested, but frustrated.

The index in these images is represented literally—as a trace of a trace, tracing the trace—we see the artist's fingers pointing and touching their limits. Recalling that Narcissus became entranced by his reflection in a pool of water, not realizing he was looking at himself, exposes yet another aspect of the mythologizing function of photography as well as its psychoanalytic dimension. Contemplating himself and unable to apprehend the stranger reflected in the pool (like the artist here, and by implication like the viewer), Narcissus was positioned in a kind of self-imposed closed-circuit. Here Nauman is effectively Narcissus. This photographic example also provides a productive link to thinking about Nauman's move to video at this time in the late sixties. These images illustrate "the double effect of performance-for-the-monitor" that Krauss identifies as the narcissistic quality of video.[116] Though Krauss reads this recurrent reflexivity in contemporary art (in works by Acconci, Nancy Holt, and Lynda Benglis, for example) as an extension of modernist consciousness doubling back on itself, we would do well to consider Narcissus's or Nauman's position as alienated artist in this piece and characterized "as the unchanging condition of a perpetual frustration."[117] The fact that the proposition is left without resolution is crucial. When Narcissus reached out to touch the image before him, he was transformed into a flower forever fixed in place. Dexterity, deception, and delusion are all put into play in these two photographs by Nauman—which, though formally not exact, do share the effects of semblance and yoking the viewer into this sequence of mirrors.

Nauman's photographs "act out."[118] Moreover, their disaffirmations act on the viewer. Like Wittgenstein, Nauman finds the investigation more important than its conclusion. Within this ethos open-ended inquiry, the unfixed ontologies of both performance and photography are ultimately cast under suspicion. At once an illustration and an embodiment of ideas, we see how unlocatable the referents of performance and photography are. By blurring the disciplinary borders, Nauman's work constructs a situation in which one might imagine performance through photography and contemplate the performance of photography. It proposes that one might be forever sorting through the variable histories of gesture and meaning, particularly in relation to the status of the photograph as art object. Photography's precarious entry into the pantheon of artistic mediums in the late sixties, a time of great uncertainty, is but one more testimony to the possibility that, as opposed to being a stable index of the real, photography is inherently a form of disruption as well as a paradoxical litmus test of unpredictability.

Three
Everyone Who Is Anyone
Douglas Huebler and the Social Capacity of Photography

A blurry photograph of a bustling city intersection, streets slick with rain, crowds on the move. Signs abound, yet direction regarding where to look remains unintelligible. Marquees announcing films, shops selling shoes, massages, and everything in between, dot the background. The tail end of a car is caught as it exits the frame. People of all walks of life freeze in time, some with umbrellas, some without, some looking languid, others rushed, yet all are equally hazy so that it is impossible to identify any clear subject in this image. A glaring neon sign hanging overhead boldly spells DONT WALK.[1] Many pedestrians ignore the sign and cross anyway, against oncoming traffic. A typewritten statement provided by Douglas Huebler states that this indistinct image and a contact proof print constitute the form of the artwork titled *1/Variable Piece #70: 1971* (Figure 3.1). The note continues:

> In November, 1971 a number of photographs were made in New York City to document various aspects of "everyone alive"; from those one was selected to represent: AT LEAST ONE PERSON WHO MAY NOW BE DEAD

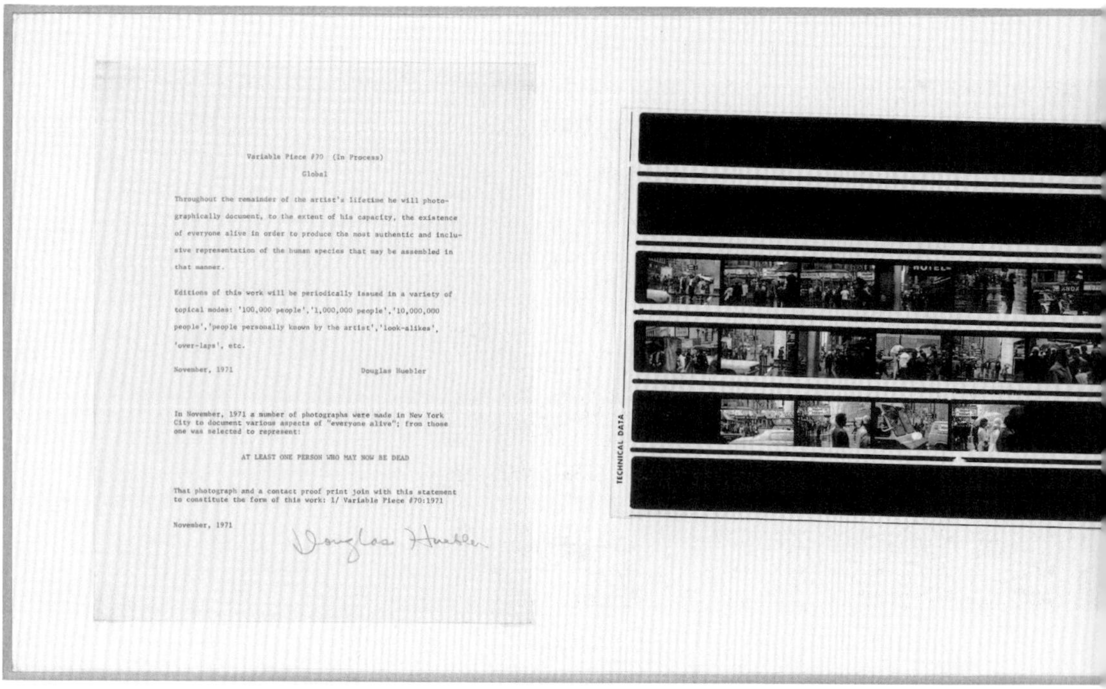

Figure 3.1. Douglas Huebler, *1/Variable Piece #70: 1971 (In Process) Global,* 1971. Copyright 2019 Estate of Douglas Huebler / Artists Rights Society (ARS), New York. Courtesy of Darcy Huebler / Artist Rights Society (ARS), New York and Paula Cooper Gallery, New York.

This is in fact the first work included in Huebler's renowned, expansive, and ultimately impossible project "to photographically document the existence of everyone alive." Begun in 1971, composed of innumerable photographic documents, and concluded with the artist's death in 1997, *Variable Piece #70: 1971 (In Process) Global* looms large in the history of conceptual art. The project's reliance on invariably inconsequential photographic images is notable and revealing. It was not simply about the devaluation of the visual or of the art object in the early seventies, but more profoundly about the compression of attention spans, the confusing heterogeneity of an unstable world, and the critical role that photography played in these vicissitudes. Certainly, it is no coincidence that of the potentially millions of photographs taken by Huebler, the first three that he isolated as individual pieces for *Variable Piece #70* all depict urban junctures filled with ordinary commotion, pedestrian in every sense of the word. These are social spaces replete with alienation. And at each juncture, unidentifiable people traverse the street against glowing words that unambiguously tell them not to. The caption for the second *Variable Piece #70* reads: AT LEAST ONE PERSON THE ARTIST MAY POSSIBLY KNOW, while the third *Variable Piece #70* states: AT LEAST ONE PERSON WHO APPEARS TO EXPERIENCE THE EXISTENCE OF THE ARTIST (Figure 3.2). These captions confound more than they clarify. Conclusions are naught, but there are nevertheless commonalities. Uncertain what to make of these scenarios, one wonders if a clue in fact lies in the roving glances of the indi-

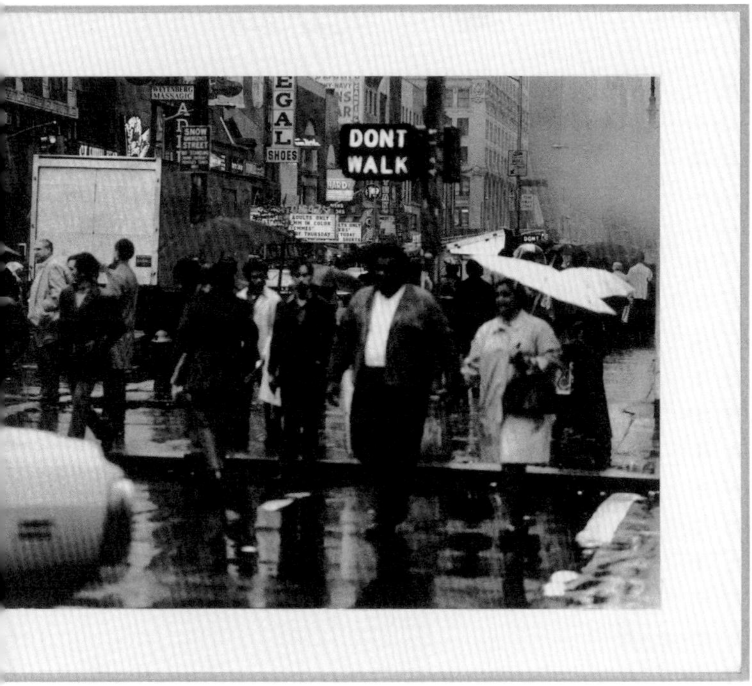

viduals who vigilantly look both ways and indeed cross despite official injunctions against doing so.

"The plethoric use of photography in the domain of art introduces an enormous confusion," explained Huebler in 1973. "It blurs the tracks and returns the problem to a level I had not previously located."[2] For Huebler, the surprising disorientation offered by photography opened a way to "liberat[e] things that are present in the world from the weight and the pressure of their specificity."[3] Akin to Mel Bochner, with a background in abstract expressionist painting and minimalist sculpture, the lessons learned from these approaches greatly influenced the artwork that followed.[4] Rather than present photographs in isolation, Huebler developed unique installations of multiple photographs often involving maps and text, in order to explore social environments. He also probed the affective interchange between time, location, and subject as related to the idea of art, documentary photography, the traditions of portraiture, and cataloging systems. Each of these facets of exploration poses infinite questions rather than claim finite resolutions. Perhaps more so than any other artist of the late sixties, Huebler engages in a practice that models the deliberate suspension of belief enacted through photography under conceptual art.

Like many conceptual artists committed to challenging the established tenets of art practice, Huebler conceived of the photograph as a readymade. Emphasizing "taking" as opposed to "making," Huebler's photographs presented appropriations rather than

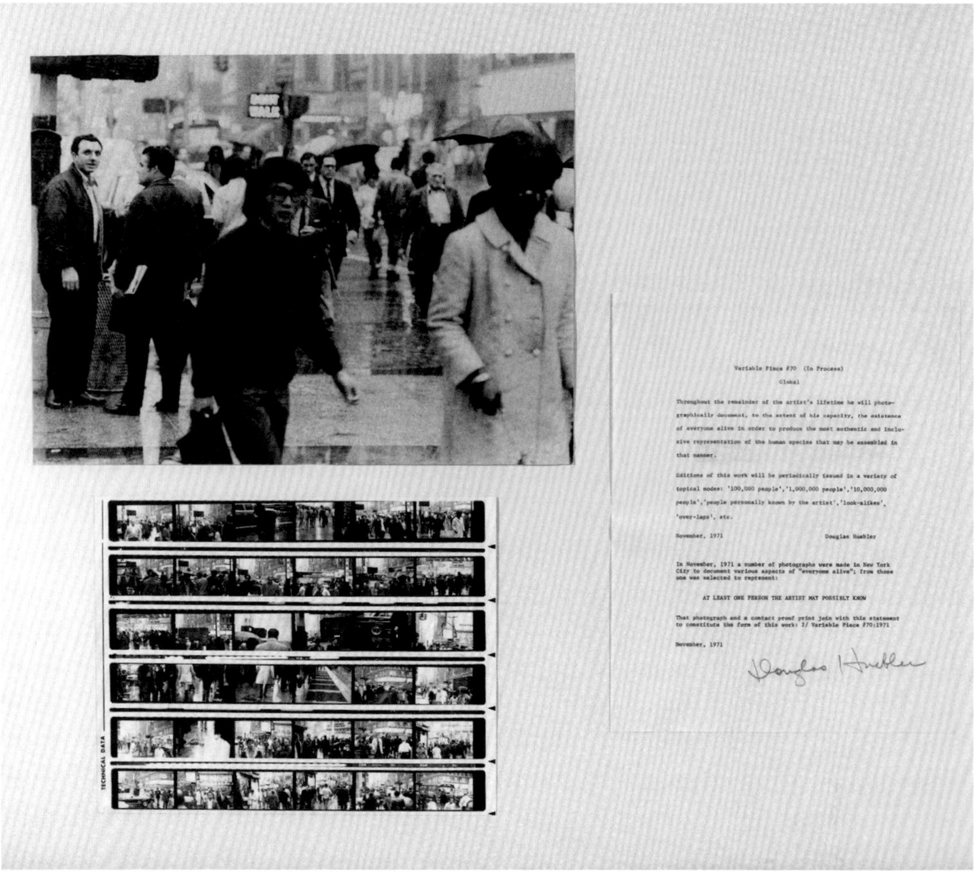

Figure 3.2. Douglas Huebler, *2/Variable Piece #70: 1971 (In Process) Global,* 1971. Copyright 2019 Estate of Douglas Huebler / Artists Rights Society (ARS), New York. Courtesy of Darcy Huebler / Artist Rights Society (ARS), New York and Paula Cooper Gallery, New York.

the virtuosity of craft as dependent on skill. Through their play on and with photography, Huebler's projects self-consciously highlight the tension between the proposed ideological liberation and simultaneous foreclosure inherent to photography's power as an economic and social agent. Put another way, the agency of the photograph itself is under investigation. Huebler's 1969 declaration "I use the camera as a 'dumb' copying device that only serves to document whatever phenomena appears before it through the conditions set by a system" highlights one of the central internal contradictions of Huebler's practice;[5] namely, that he at once disavows technological determination as a modus operandi and rescinds his own control as artistic producer. As a result, the question remains: who or what "makes" the art? As I contend in this chapter, from Huebler's point of view the answer seems to be anyone and, therefore, possibly, everyone. Or, put another way, everyone who is anyone. I explore this dynamic and how Huebler used photography to suggest broad social inclusiveness and irreducible specificity at once, bringing attention to the wider waning of attention in the face of the tenacity of images. Ultimately, anonymous individuals (in the positions of both subjects and viewers) are implicated in the meaning of Huebler's work, in ways that call on their agency. Looking back on his work over a decade later, Huebler admitted the unforeseen social dimensions discovered through the use of photography as art:

> Actually, the photographs were a complete surprise to me. . . . I found I was giving myself permission to photograph people. I began recognizing myself as a social being, recognizing the camera as a social instrument, in that I could use it as a form of social mediation. . . . For me, the issue of the social capacity of art, the quality that it may have to mediate, is something that I think is the most important thing that art may do at this point.

In every instance, Huebler's artwork reveals idiosyncrasies of the political, social, and aesthetic systems in which photography and its subjects were, and continue to be, enmeshed.

At Least One

In 1966 the now-legendary *Primary Structures* exhibition at the Jewish Museum in New York set the stage for the critical reception of minimalist art for decades to come. On the occasion of his exhibition, Kynaston McShine praised Huebler's sculptural work as a key example of "standardized blandness and ubiquitous impersonality."[6] Arguably, McShine's assessment acknowledged only one dimension of Huebler's practice. It is indeed true that Huebler himself said that he wanted "to make an image [without a] privileged position."[7] However, I demonstrate that the perceived denial of personality, the emptying out of either the image or the art object, functions in Huebler's art practice as a proposition to reaffirm uniqueness and difference despite the serial logic presented. Working against privileged positions does not foreclose the possibilities of personality.

Repetition and resemblance, literally and figuratively, formed the building blocks of minimalism. Such systematic organizing principles carried over into conceptual art. Yet, as opposed to Donald Judd's "one-thing-after-another,"[8] Huebler's move from objects to photographs, from blank form to portraiture, signals his deep investment in the irrepressible humanity of human systems. Even with reference to his neutral-toned Formica sculptures, Huebler expressed his desire to reductively "move the form from volume towards flatness (or illusion)" while envisioning "formica [as] a skin that relieves the object of its 'history.'"[9] This description of his minimalist sculpture sounds remarkably akin to photography: cut out of its historical continuum, "a skin" that is both flat and illusionistic. I have shown clear connections to skin in Bochner's work, as well as the visceral and often-unexpected ways photography called attention back to the body and to the contingent subjectivity of

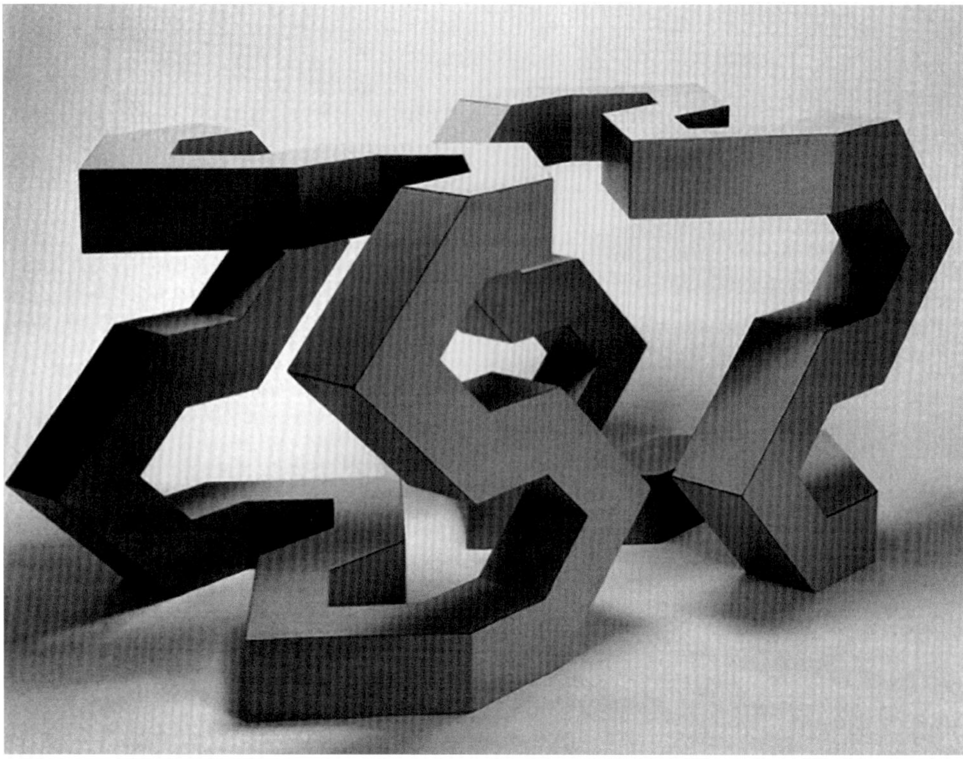

Figure 3.3. Douglas Huebler, *Truro Series #3,* 1966. Copyright 2019 Estate of Douglas Huebler / Artists Rights Society (ARS), New York. Courtesy of Darcy Huebler / Artist Rights Society (ARS), New York and Paula Cooper Gallery, New York.

embodied vision. Huebler's artwork extends this relation still further. If one considers Huebler's *Truro Series #3* (1966), perhaps the analogy is clearer (Figure 3.3). At first glance, it appears that we are looking at a pair of identical forms on the floor. It is as though we have a set of twin figures within a single sculpture. Yet this suggestion of sameness and mutual identification is not entirely accurate. By less than an inch, one of the two objects is imperceptibly smaller than the other. Upon closer inspection and final measurement, the perceived uniformity falls apart with the realization that they are ultimately not exact. Even though this difference was the result of execution rather than artistic intention, it nevertheless points toward outcomes inevitably beyond the artist's control. Additionally, it summons how the viewer's cognitive sensitivity and visual acuity crucially contribute to the making of meaning in Huebler's art.

Propositions featuring deliberate misrecognitions and irreconcilable differences compose the central dynamic of Huebler's practice. Turning away from minimalist sculpture in the late sixties, in 1969 he famously stated: "The world is full of objects, more or less interesting; I do not wish to add any more." His resolve not to participate in art as defined by object making in the traditional sense opens his practice to focusing on effects, and photography is the medium by which this change is manifest. Despite Huebler's acknowledgment of the fullness of the world, it is precisely this moment that bookends his most prolific period of artistic production. After all, it is only two years later in 1971 that he announces his intention to "photographically document . . . the existence of everyone alive." How can these two statements be reconciled? Renouncing object making in the traditional sense sets the stage for his turn to photography, especially portraiture. Huebler's photographic portraits speak to the impossibility of coherently mapping either the individual subject or the collective whole. Huebler's ambition mimics the very logic of the photograph, insofar as photographic portraiture par excellence represents the desire to preserve life from its inevitable passing while serving as the reminder of death in every living photograph. The double that emerges from the photographic act is always also severed: the spitting image is always also a splitting image. Huebler's declared dialectic divulges the internal opposition that sets his practice in motion, epitomizing the dilemma of the unique subject in a world that is ever-increasingly indifferent, systematized, and globalized (Figure 3.4).

In describing *Variable Piece #70,* a full announcement of the project is often left out.

> Variable Piece #70 (In Process) Global "Throughout the remainder of the artist's lifetime he will photographically document, to the extent of his capacity, the existence of everyone alive in order to produce the most authentic and inclusive representation of the human species that may be assembled in that manner.
>
> Editions of this work will be periodically issued in a variety of topical modes: '100,000 people,' '1,000,000 people,' '10,000,000 people,' 'people known by the artist,' 'look-alikes,' 'over-laps,' etc."
>
> November 1971—Douglas Huebler

The statement notes "to the extent of his capacity" as the limit of this enterprise. Huebler admits the human (and thus fallible and mortal) boundary to the project's completion, namely, the limit of living experience. Huebler explained, "For one thing people are dying and being born faster than any one person could click the shutter of a camera." *Everyone Alive* (as it has come to be known) thus depends not simply on the artist's mortality but also his capacity "to produce the most authentic and inclusive representation of the human species that may be assembled in that manner." Add to this, the ever-changing composition of *Everyone.* It should come as no surprise, then, as we saw with the morbid caption for the first *Variable Piece #70,* AT LEAST ONE PERSON WHO MAY NOW BE DEAD, death is necessarily embedded at the outset. Documenting "everyone alive" is indeed an enigmatic endeavor; for how would this pseudo-ethnographic experiment ever be verified? And what could the photograph possibly prove in the end? The suspension of the photograph, with its ontology as a liminal space outside the normal continuum of time yet also as a persistent reminder of the presence of absence—described by Roland Barthes and others—as the medium's existential ethos, only further amplifies the contingency of being "alive."[10] Huebler's acute awareness of this strange temporality is marked

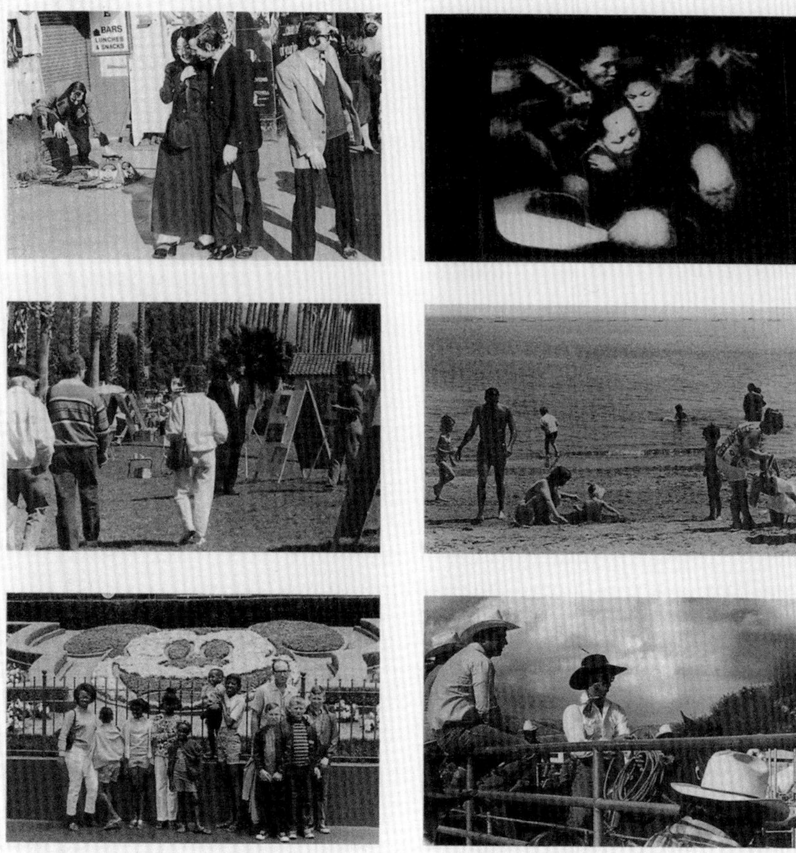

Figure 3.4. Douglas Huebler, *Variable Piece #70: 1971 (In Process) Global,* 1971. Copyright 2019 Estate of Douglas Huebler / Artists Rights Society (ARS), New York. Courtesy of Darcy Huebler / Artist Rights Society (ARS), New York and Paula Cooper Gallery, New York.

by a number of his subcategorical inclusions such as *25/Variable Piece #70* (1972), "AT LEAST ONE PERSON WHO, FOR AN INSTANT AT LEAST, BECAME MORE THAN NORMALLY CONSCIOUS OF HIS EXISTENCE," a statement accompanied by a photograph showing a young man who seems to look straight into the camera (Figure 3.5). Nevertheless, the doubling of the qualifier "at least" only serves to magnify the fractional representation offered by the photograph, at the very same moment that being aware or "conscious" is brought to the fore as similarly partial.

The success of *Everyone Alive* as a project is partly predicated on its indefinite status and its openness to doubt. From the beginning the title was "In Process," leaving this purportedly humanist endeavor to be read as a quixotically antihumanist gesture due to its grand impossibility at the outset and decidedly open-ended incompletion. Several curators and critics have emphasized Huebler's conception of this ultimate collection of photographic documentation as "an ironic yet calculated twist to the futility of scientific rigor."[11] I would like to argue the point further, noting how Huebler's dubious control of this "In Process" project is precisely the formula to enact the dialectic between control and chance that productively provides for the benefit of doubt. This epistemological break has become increasingly necessary in a world bent on claiming certainty even when its opposite stares back at us. The fact that Huebler served as a part of the U.S. Marine Air group, stationed on an island in the Pacific during World War II, certainly affected his point of view. He was in charge of reading aerial reconnaissance photographs, and his experience with this form of surveillance, information collection, and analysis provides a nearly absurd instrumental logic for his distrust of the photograph as substantive evidence. Living in a moment flooded with images ranging from advertising's promise of eternal bliss through consumption to massacres in Vietnam, Huebler documented, collected, and in some cases appropriated thousands of photographs. Compiled together, they provide excessive and often contradictory information about our world. Any attempt to order the meanings contained therein is bound to fail, yet—and this I contend is crucial—the attempt to scrutinize in order to make sense remains significant.

Among the photographic portraits Huebler included in *Variable Piece #70,* numerous works are labeled explicitly by the artist, yet they nevertheless remain uncanny. His series of "look-alikes" is one striking case, presented comically as if race and gender can be subsumed by sartorial choices. The nonidentical status between any two corresponding images is what becomes most obvious. Reflecting on his project and its operative models, Huebler explained: "I work for the general and discover the specific, but of course it's only an example of the specific against the general."[12] Ultimately, as much as a leveling out is enacted through the photographic frame, it is also the exposure of difference within those parameters that occurs, making apparent the inimitability of the subject that cannot be assimilated.

His further grouping of photos from the *Everyone Alive* project into increasingly obscure categories of resemblance surely implies a joke about art historical attribution as much as the relativity and accumulative meaning involved in "reading"

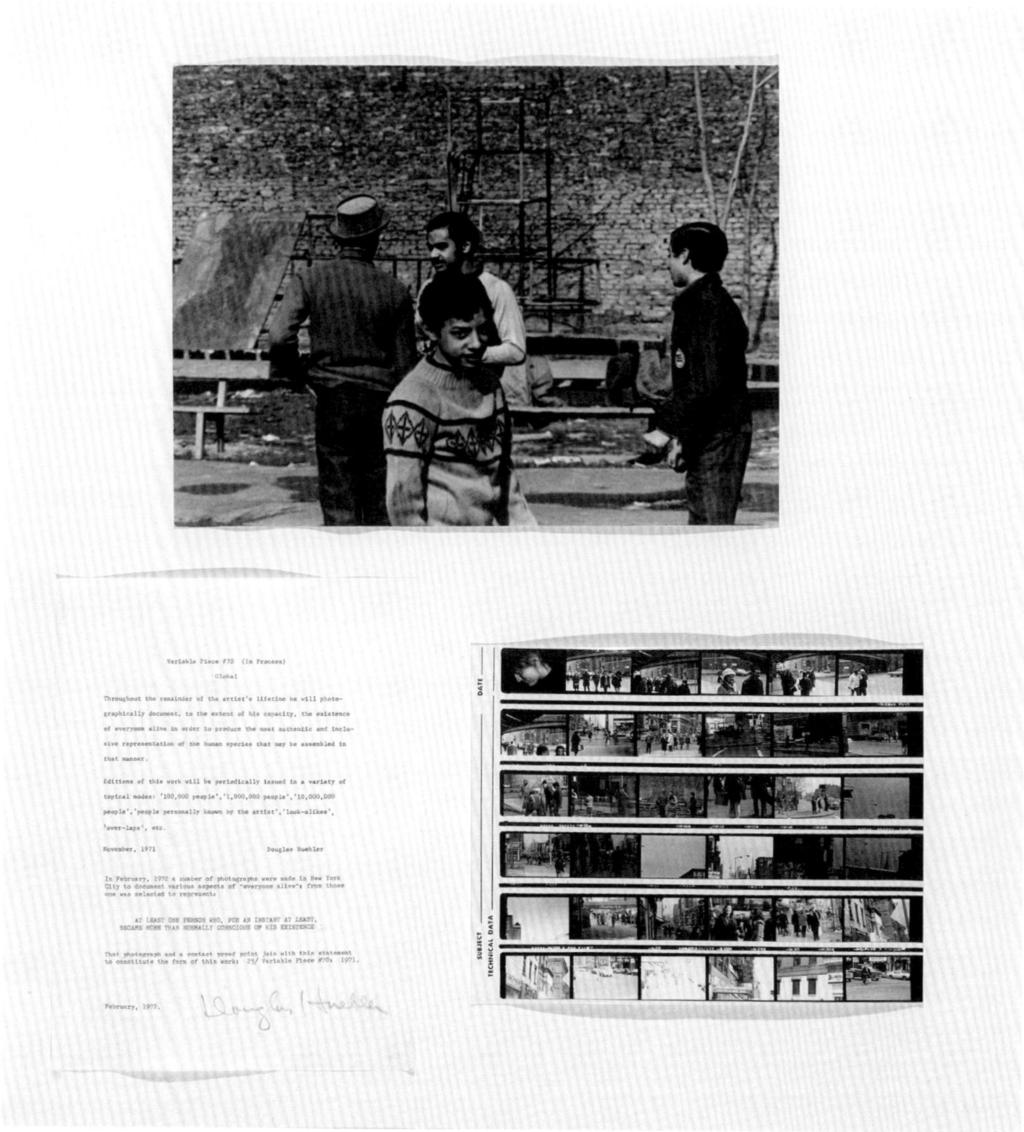

Figure 3.5. Douglas Huebler, *25/Variable Piece #70: 1971 (In Process) Global,* 1972. FNAC 2015-0265. Yvon Lambert donation to the French state / Centre national des arts plastiques (National Centre for Visual Arts). Long-term loan at the Collection Lambert, Avignon (France). Copyright 2019 Estate of Douglas Huebler / Artists Rights Society (ARS), New York, ADAGP, Paris / CNAP. Courtesy of Darcy Huebler / Artist Rights Society (ARS), New York and Paula Cooper Gallery, New York.

pictures. Consider, for example, the many-layered triptych that is *633/Variable Piece #70: 1971 (In Process) Global* (1978) (Figure 3.6). The centerpiece reads:

> "Fifteen one-inch portraits produced for the "everyone alive" project have been further enlarged to characterize:
>
> AT LEAST THREE PEOPLE ALIVE IN THE 20TH CENTURY WHOM THE 17TH-CENTURY ARTIST, ARTEMISIA GENTILESCHI, VERY LIKELY WOULD CHOOSE AS MODELS FOR HER REPRESENTATION OF A 6TH-CENTURY B.C. EVENT . . . IF SHE WERE ALIVE TO PAINT IT TODAY
>
> A photographic reproduction of Gentileschi's Judith Beheading Holofernes appears next to the photographs of possible models. They have been arranged so that the choice for the Maidservant may be found in Row A, Holofernes in Row B, and Judith in Row C. More than fifty photographs join this statement to constitute the form of this piece."

The fifteen enlarged portraits appear painted, with color tinting applied over the photographs. The "models" offer many options for this hypothetical proposal, which imagines Gentileschi sourcing her painting from twentieth-century photographs. Perhaps most conspicuous is the realization that the feat of fictional exchange between time periods, from the sixth century B.C.E. to the seventeenth century to 1978, is made possible thorough photography. This exchange between anonymous people, envisioned as characters, brings social valences into play. And though Huebler identifies in which row the Maidservant, Judith, and Holofernes can be found, he once again implies categorical confusion. Notice how some of the figures represented look remarkably similar, despite their stated gender, for example. Almost without intending to, one begins see the androgeneity of each person (not just "look-alikes" but also "over-laps," to use Huebler's suggestive subcategories from his original *Variable Piece #70* statement). Deciphering characters, whether masculine, feminine, or otherwise, depends on our own contingent judgments. In a separate frame, Huebler included a small reproduction of Gentileschi's legendary baroque painting depicting the climax of this biblical drama. With this reference, obstinate debates over the dynamism and the restrictive clichés of virtue and violence involving female sexuality as a veil for more masculine associations of aggression are brought to bear on Huebler's piece. An oscillation between sameness and difference, homogeneity and heterogeneity, moves across these images and throughout *Variable Piece #70* as a whole. Moreover, the specificity of individual selections and propositions necessitates mining, searching, and thinking through many layers of connotative power. Looking back to *Variable #70,* endless inferences continue to pose litmus tests for our present moment and its place within the ever-changing push and pull of historical meaning.

Perhaps most curious of all is Huebler's decision to include another panel from September 1978 as an additional component part of *633/Variable Piece #70,* a choice that seems to introduce even more disconnections than the other two. Accompanied

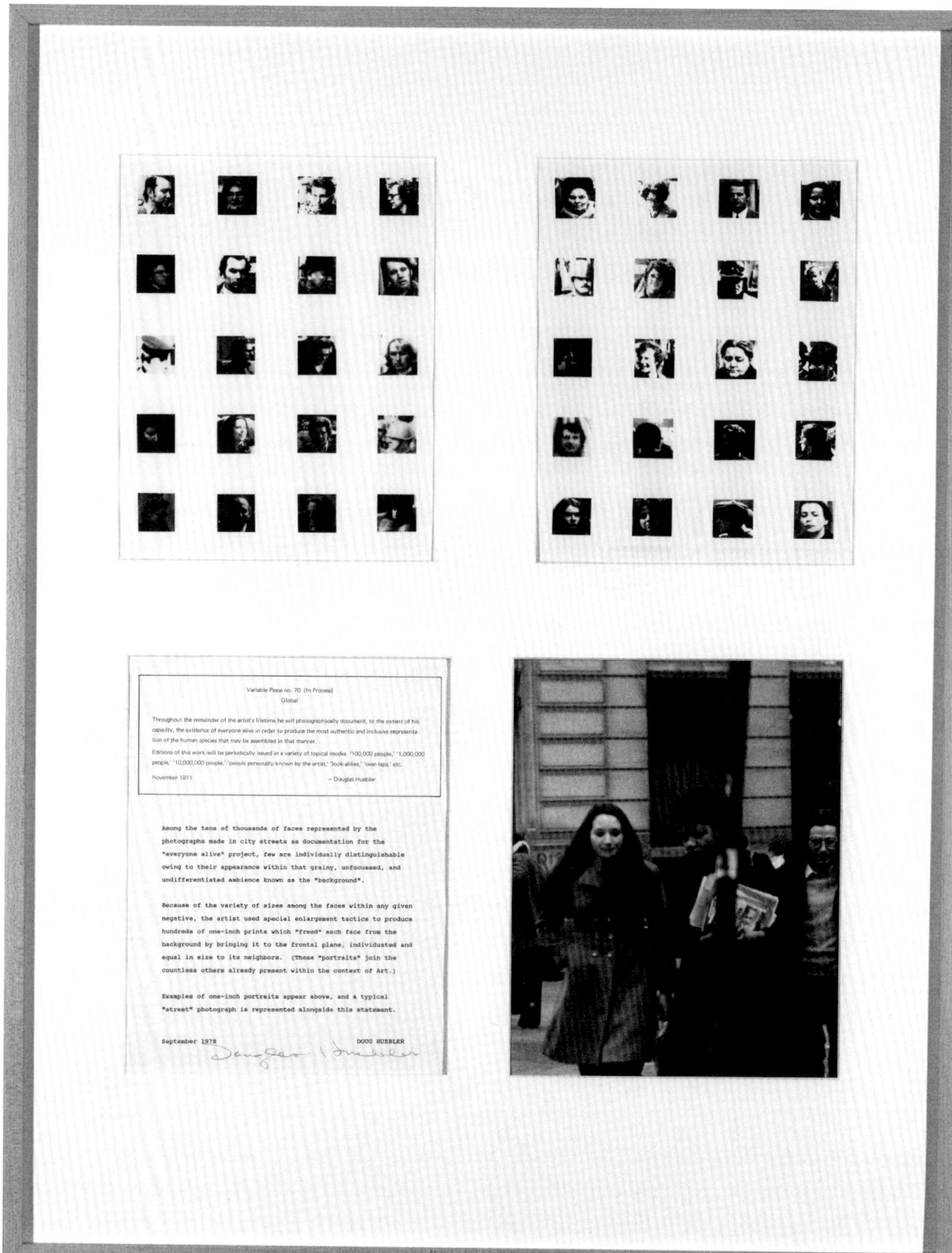

Figure 3.6. Douglas Huebler, *633/Variable Piece #70: 1971 (In Process) Global,* 1978. J. Paul Getty Museum, Los Angeles. Copyright 2019 Estate of Douglas Huebler / Artists Rights Society (ARS), New York. Courtesy of J. Paul Getty Museum, Los Angeles, Darcy Huebler / Artist Rights Society (ARS), New York and Paula Cooper Gallery, New York.

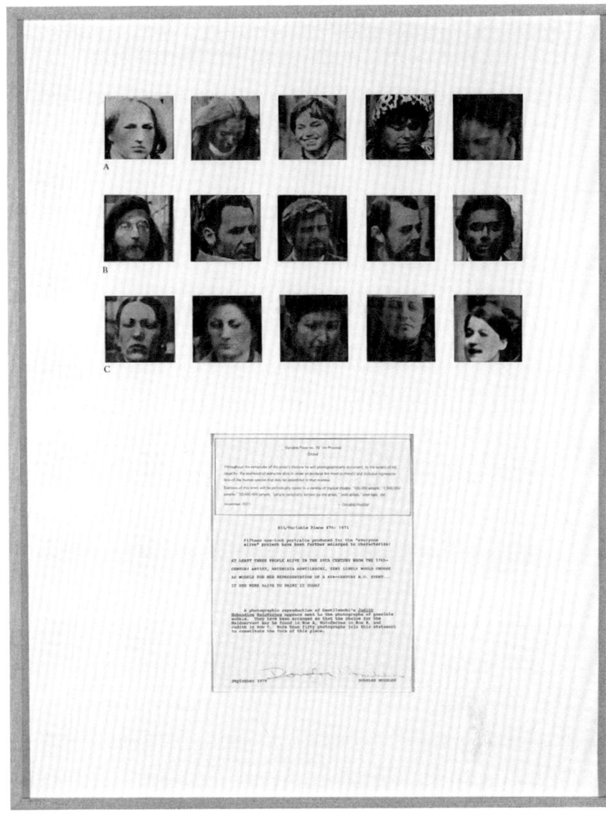
A
B
C
Fifteen one-inch portraits produced for the "everyone alive" project have been further enlarged to characterize:
AT LEAST THREE PEOPLE ALIVE IN THE 20TH CENTURY WHOM THE 17TH-CENTURY ARTIST, ARTEMISIA GENTILESCHI, VERY LIKELY WOULD CHOOSE AS MODELS FOR HER REPRESENTATION OF A 4TH-CENTURY B.C. EVENT... IF SHE WERE ALIVE TO PAINT IT TODAY
A photographic reproduction of Gentileschi's Judith Beheading Holofernes appears next to the photographs of possible models. They have been arranged so that the choice for the Maidservant may be found in Row A, Holofernes in Row B, and Judith in Row C. More than fifty photographs join this statement to constitute the form of this piece.
September 1974
DOUGLAS HUEBLER

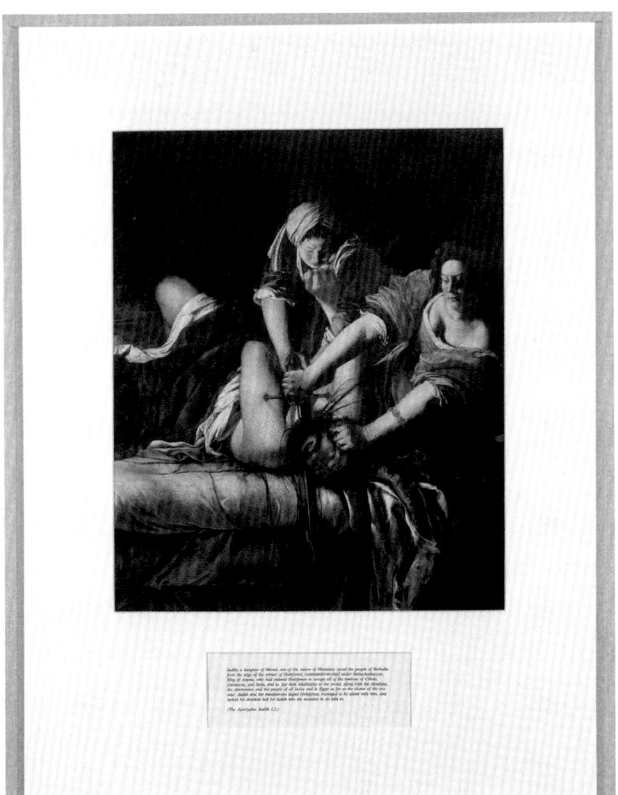

by an awkward, seemingly haphazard photograph of two young women walking toward the camera deep in conversation, the face of a man in glasses visible over their shoulders, we are given the following information:

> Among the tens of thousands of faces represented by the photographs made in city streets as documentation for the "everyone alive" project, few are individually distinguishable owing to their appearance within that grainy, unfocused, and undifferentiated ambience known as the "background."
>
> Because of the variety of sizes among the faces within any given negative, the artist used special enlargement tactics to produce hundreds of one-inch prints which "freed" each face from the background by bringing it to the frontal plane, individuated and equal in size to its neighbors. (These "portraits" join the countless others already present within the context of Art.)
>
> Examples of one-inch portraits appear above, and a typical "street" photograph is represented alongside this statement.

Above this text and image, a gridded series of cubed faces appear, row on row. What might it mean to claim that these faces are "freed"? Huebler's strange description of the "background" is also intriguing, with its "grainy, unfocused, and undifferentiated ambience," especially since so many of his photographs appear intentionally out of focus and undifferentiated.

Huebler's archival impulse to photograph everyone alive is of course not without precedent. The project recalls idealistic but also dystopic parables such as Gaston Bachelard's bureaucrat who dreams of a file cabinet large enough to store the world's entire knowledge.[13] Not by chance, the fantasy of documenting and by extension collecting "everyone" seems to be at the very heart of the photographic impulse. Theorists such as Allan Sekula have argued that photographic desire has always been intimately related to the drive for comprehensive possession and mastery.[14] Moreover, the ingenuous equation between photographs and knowledge is precisely the mania that so often occludes reflexive questioning. Given the photograph's illusionistic capacity—its appearance as whole and self-contained, for example—it is never enough to read photography on its own terms, within its frame. Instead, it is necessary to take each photograph to task as conjugated within the parameters of a larger discourse, within the structure of deeply embedded and even unconscious ideological positions, as a result of polyvalent forces and constructs.

Huebler imagined his photographs as a counterpoint to the conception of photography as a means for comprehensive knowledge, even despite (or perhaps heightened by) the artist's all-encompassing premise:

> Having entered the socio-political arena . . . it soon followed that I developed the "Everyone Alive" project as a logical form through which to forward the examination of the natural/cultural dialectic that was of primary interest to

> me. The obvious impossibility of its declared program turns its photographic representations into free-floating signs attached to the equally readymade terms of culturally fabricated aphorisms and sayings. As in all my work this project is meant to put the question to its audience about how willing it is—and anyone else—to accept arbitrarily constructed relationships between language and appearances.[15]

In drawing awareness to the persistent desire for, yet irreconcilable discrepancy between, pictures and truth, or documents and knowledge, Huebler makes visible the degree to which he infuses his projects with whimsy and doubt. He makes apparent, through humor and irony, the futility of such projects. At the same time, he presents the potential their failure offers as a productive way to affirm the heterogeneity and unknowability of life. Despite being described as the result of "forensic reports prepared by a Buddhist monk in collaboration with the Marx Brothers,"[16] Huebler's antipositivist project could not be more serious. The gravity of *Everyone Alive* becomes apparent when considering the increasingly insidious relationship between people and the camera, in which subjects are so often presented as "knowable" objects and social relations are understood as things. This reification marks a specific form of alienation, which the photograph seems to support at first glance. As I continue to argue, however, particularly in reference to Huebler's and Barthes's thinking on photography, the subject can never be entirely fixed or knowable.

598/Variable Piece #70 (1975) further demonstrates Huebler's resistance to the pull of universal humanism and reiterates his attention to the "background," which in this case is called a "grainy continuum" (Figure 3.7). The attendant statement reads:

> As of this date, tens of thousands of people have been photographed, in America, Europe and Israel, for the "everyone alive" project: most often photographed in the streets, few appear strongly individualized and most appear as indeterminate and undifferentiated phenomena situated somewhere within that grainy continuum normally described as the "background." From [these] photographs . . . 160 faces have been individuated through a series of darkroom procedures, each having been transformed into a discrete portrait. Selected from these 160 faces, nine have been again enlarged to characterize an aspect of "everyone alive": AT LEAST ONE PERSON WHO WOULD HEAR NO EVIL.

Huebler complicates the legibility of photographic representation against totalizing assumptions and totalizing image systems. Magnifying these portraits truthfully does little to distinguish them. Their pixelated quality remains difficult to decipher. Moreover, why choose these nine portraits, in particular? While the artist seems to strive for resemblance and association in some photographs, he works against it in others.

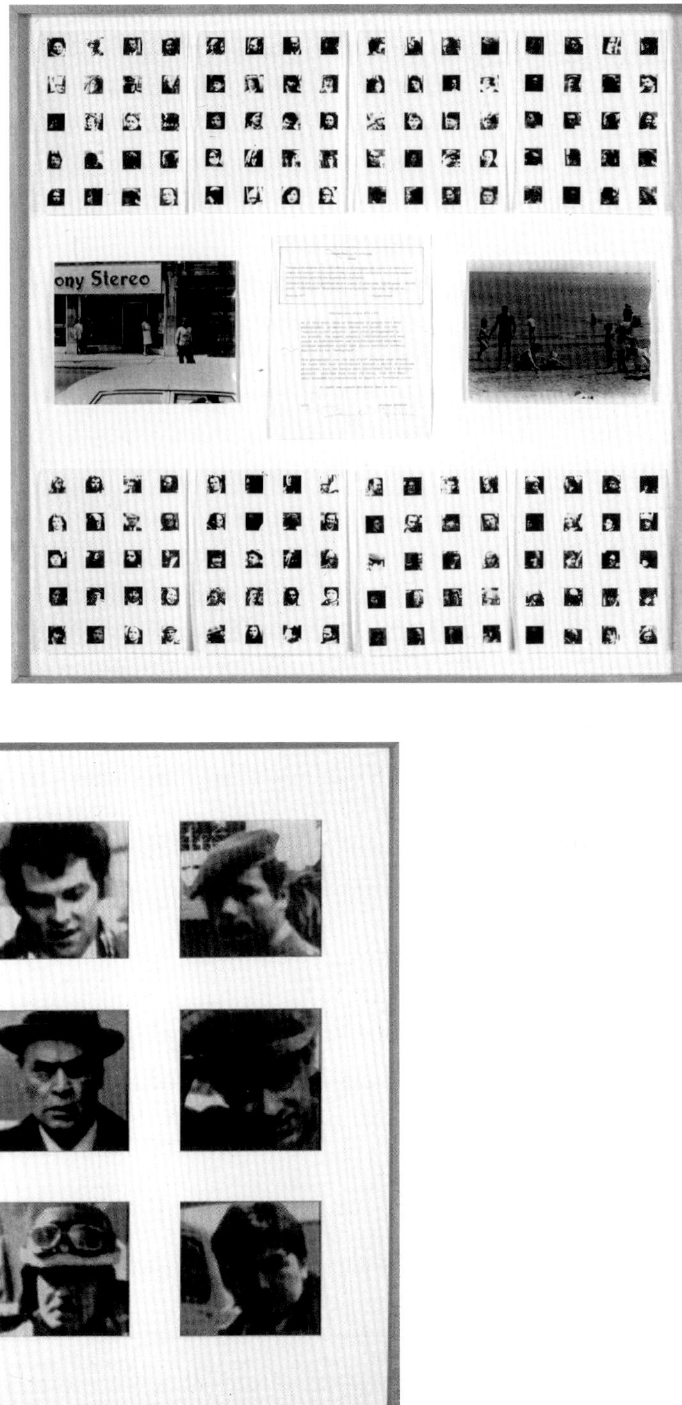

Figure 3.7. Douglas Huebler, *598/Variable Piece #70: 1971 (In Process) Global,* 1975. Copyright 2019 Estate of Douglas Huebler / Artists Rights Society (ARS), New York. Courtesy of Darcy Huebler / Artist Rights Society (ARS), New York and Paula Cooper Gallery, New York.

In his perceptive reading of Huebler's use of photography, Joshua Shannon remarks how, by "constantly promising detailed views into the hidden meaningfulness of things, Huebler kept instead giving his viewers elaborate proof of the world's disordered quality, its failure to obey our wishes to signify."[17] This tension between the claims made by Huebler's factual-seeming statements and the ambiguity of the photographs presented advances and retreats repeatedly over the course of *Variable Piece #70*. Looking specifically at the nine faces enlarged to characterize "AT LEAST ONE PERSON WHO WOULD HEAR NO EVIL," Shannon observes that in this case we exclusively have not only nine white men but all are scowling, their eyes shaded, most making sideways glances. From these furtive looks, reminiscent of spies or undercover agents, I believe we might find cues once more for gauging our own ways of looking.

Returning to that "grainy continuum normally described as the background," it becomes increasingly apparent that nearly every photograph put forward by Huebler to substantiate *Everyone Alive* can be characterized foremost by its overwhelming lack of focal clarity. Indeed, there seems to be nothing but background. On the one hand, these extensively pixelated images might be understood as showing the conditions of dematerialization "in process." It is as if the image were disintegrating before our eyes. On the other hand, at this very same moment, the moment of its threatened disappearance, of its fading into complete background, we are made precisely aware of the image's living materiality, its confusing evocation of meaning through signs, and, by extension, its sociability. The historical account of conceptual art has too often emphasized the dematerialization of the art object as a way to work against the fetishization of the visual as a commodity. However, in many respects, as in the example of Huebler, the use of photography in conceptual art acknowledges the morphing and enduring power of images, even if those images remain suspended in the guise of "dematerialization."

In her provocative essay "In Defense of the Poor Image" (2009), the artist and theorist Hito Steyerl describes the prevalent low resolution of contemporary images as copies in motion. Though Steyerl is preoccupied with the phenomenon of digital images and their compression, her insights point back to conceptual art in the late sixties in ways that Huebler's analog artwork seems to anticipate. Describing the blurry life of a JPEG, for example, Steyerl calls the poor image "a ghost of an image, a preview, a thumbnail, an errant idea, an itinerant image." "It often defies patrimony, national culture, or indeed copyright" as it is dragged around the globe.[18] It is by virtue of their incessant transmission, always on the go, that their deterioration inheres to their acceleration. "This flattening-out of visual content—the concept in becoming of the images," as Steyerl explains, "positions them within a general informational turn, within economies of knowledge that tear images and their captions out of context into the swirl of permanent capitalist deterritorialization." The fleeting faces captured by Huebler for *Everyone Alive* stand as metonyms of this shift, forming the background of a world in which sustained attention is itself increasingly transitory, even as the velocity of image sharing expands.

We Two

81/Variable Piece #70, made in 1973, offers another conceptual cross between the aesthetics of administration and the administration of absurdity (Plate 18). Focused on a photograph of a group of marching German soldiers, Huebler attempts to individuate twenty-four of them by creating painted portraits, imagining and then imaging their heads without helmets. The statement assigned to the image is "AT LEAST ONE PERSON WHO HAS EVERYTHING TO GAIN AND NOTHING TO LOSE." As opposed to the photographic regime noted by Susan Sontag in the 1970s, wherein "to collect photographs is to collect the world,"[19] Huebler's mass archive possesses the countereffect of divesting the social system that produces the sameness of things of its facade, challenging its constructed image of conformity and control. Huebler's world as such expands, contracts, and disperses through the medium of photography. The subject is reinvested with its own disposition within the system, rather than emptied out in the Warholian sense.

Early photoconceptualism was partly a result of the hybrid between the photograph and travel. As an effect of what Marshall McLuhan called "the photograph creating a world of accelerated transience,"[20] many photoconceptualists investigated the desire to comprehensively represent the world. The photograph seemed to promise the abolition of time and space—according to McLuhan's analysis of the Museum of Modern Art's *The Family of Man* exhibition and catalog (1955). McLuhan writes that "the logic of the photograph politically speaking is to wipe out national frontiers and cultural barriers regardless of any particular point of view."[21] It is revealing to compare *The Family of Man,* that earlier definitive exhibition of photography organized by Edward Steichen, involving 503 photographs from sixty-eight countries, with Huebler's *Variable Piece #70: 1971 (In Process) Global* (Figure 3.8).

Huebler's aspiration for democratic representation as a photo-project runs counter to the monolithic vision of the "photo-globe" posited by *The Family of Man,* which toured the world for a decade after its opening in New York.[22] Its particular ideological attempt to attain and contain completeness defies the positivist belief that history can be explained if an exhaustive account is accumulated. The title itself, "the family of man," elides the plurality of "family" within the singularity of "man." Described critically as a "mass-cultural phenomenon whereby very real social and political anxieties are initially conjured up, only to be quickly transformed and furnished with positive (imaginary) resolutions,"[23] scholars have insightfully pointed to the risks that liberal humanism runs as it seeks not only to map and reify the shape of the globe but also to "sentimentalize photography as utopian myth,"[24] universalizing meaning by understanding photography as a vehicle for global domination.

Allan Sekula's 1981 essay "The Traffic in Photographs" famously confronted what he saw in *The Family of Man* as "an aestheticized job of global accounting, a careful Cold War effort to bring about the ideological alignment of the neo-colonial peripheries with the imperial centre."[25] This "humanist Trojan horse"[26] sought to reconcile

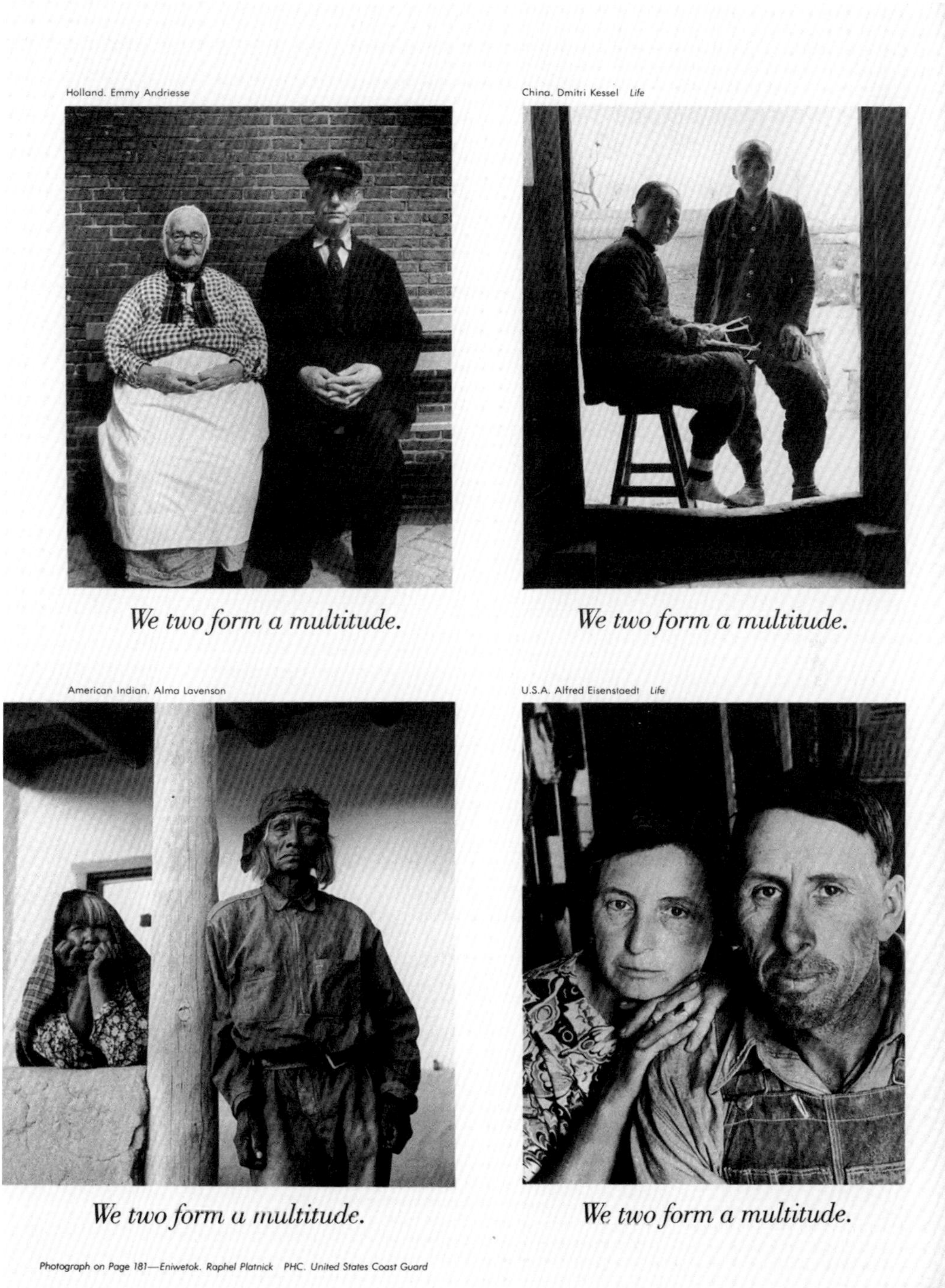
Holland. Emmy Andriesse

We two form a multitude.

China. Dmitri Kessel *Life*

We two form a multitude.

American Indian. Alma Lavenson

We two form a multitude.

U.S.A. Alfred Eisenstaedt *Life*

We two form a multitude.

Photograph on Page 181—Eniwetok. Raphel Platnick PHC. United States Coast Guard

Figure 3.8 Page 182 from exhibition catalog for *The Family of Man* (MoMA Exh. #569, January 24–May 8, 1955), by Edward Steichen. The Museum of Modern Art, New York, New York. Digital image copyright the Museum of Modern Art. Licensed by SCALA / Art Resource, NY.

difference by reducing people to what Steichen conceived as the most basic common denominators of humanity, namely, that we all are born and all die, all experience emotions ranging from happiness to sadness, and all are part of "families." The details of these experiences were not important for Steichen's "mirror of the essential oneness of mankind throughout the world,"[27] yet arguably, the details of such experiences, no matter how idiosyncratic or seemingly insignificant, are precisely what preoccupies Huebler's "global" photo-archive.

Recognition was a crucial concept for Steichen.[28] Within *The Family of Man,* the beholder was asked to identify with all the photographs in the exhibition. In an effort to expand the exhibition's reach, Steichen was adamant that the photographs included were concerned with a general, "basic human consciousness rather than social consciousness."[29] Images with the captions such as "I too will be old" or "I am just like everybody else in the world because I also have a mother," or "We two form a multitude" invited the viewer to "feel the pleasure of self-discovery in any and all contexts,"[30] overlooking the junctures inherent in the "contradictory certainty" of not just being in the picture but being in every picture.[31] Many of the installation photographs taken by Steichen at *The Family of Man* exhibition give a sense of his immersive impulse and his utopian desire to blur the distinctions between subject positions while disregarding the realities of social and cultural difference.

Huebler's project, by contrast, did not propose to function as a mirror in this way. Instead, his photographic works construct an interrogatory mode of viewing the idiosyncrasies of the everyday crowd, in which the beholder's identity is dissembled even as one searches for the linchpin within the ordinariness of Huebler's many laissez-faire street photographs. One could say that while Steichen's exhibition emphasized acquisition and containment, Huebler's *Variable* piece emphasized inquisition and proliferation.

Captions and subtitles were essential to both projects. However, whereas Steichen's captions were intended to ground and unify the images presented, Huebler's conceptual statements seem to have the opposite effect. Equations in Huebler's practice resist conclusion. Two do not become one. If "we two form a multitude" in Huebler, it is a multitude with loose ends. Such a multitude is more in line with the thinking of Antonio Negri and Michael Hardt: a multitude that acknowledges discrepancy and the inclusion of unequal and sometimes conflicting elements.[32] Either by chance or by design, Steichen selected nine individual portraits to be magnified and hung toward the close of his installation (Figure 3.9). For Steichen, these nine (three women, three children, three men) were stand-ins for all humanity, the personification of his "photo-global rhetoric," emblematizing the claim that "we are all alike." Huebler's decision to magnify nine portraits for *598/Variable Piece #70* echoes Steichen with a twist, reversing the platitudes of "we" in favor of a search for a counterhegemonic discourse.

A given photograph from *Variable Piece #70,* for example, could be placed alongside the descriptive caption "at least one person who reminds the artist of someone he knows" or "at least one person who always has the last word." At least . . . but

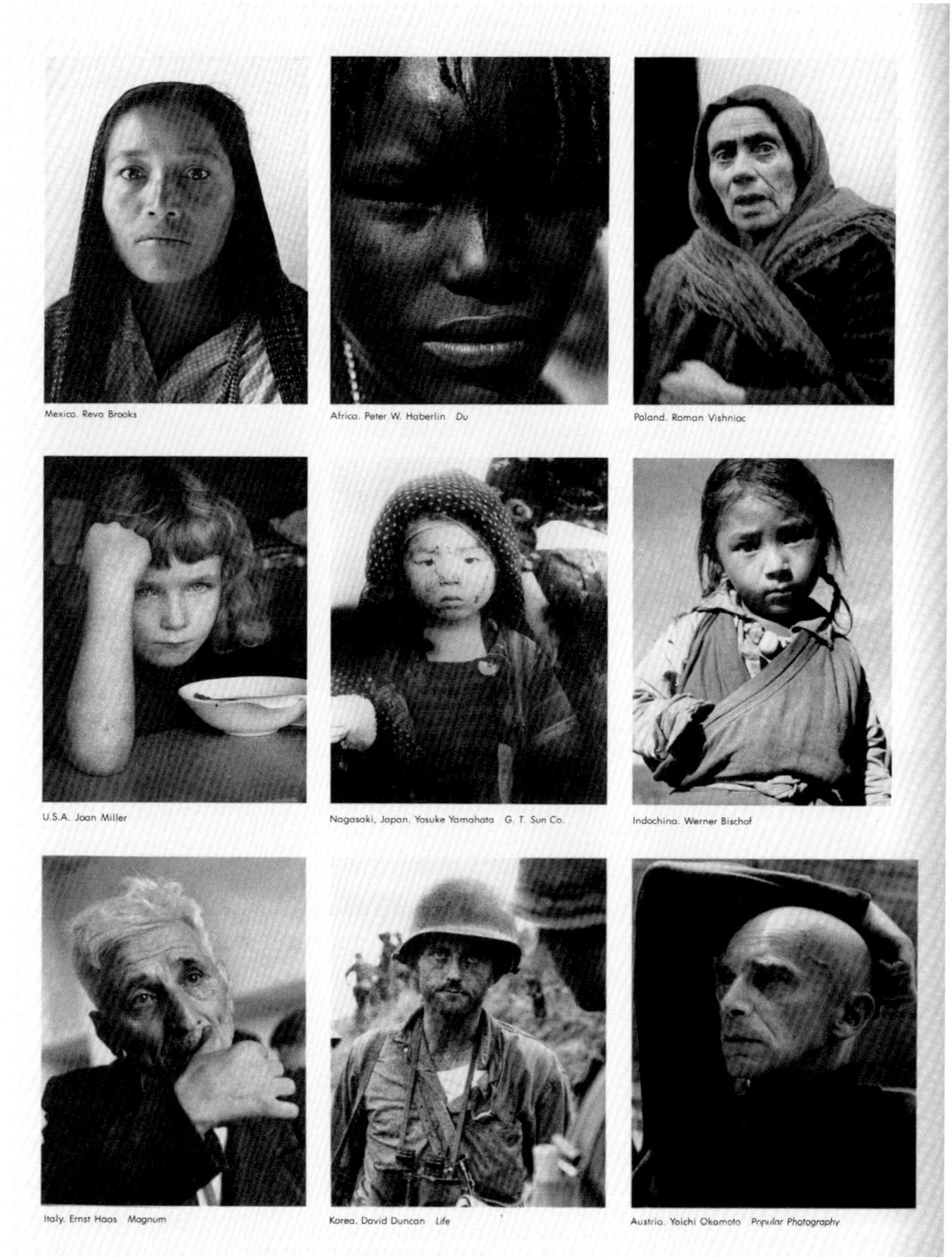

Figure 3.9 Page 178 from exhibition catalog for *The Family of Man* (MoMA Exh. #569, January 24–May 8, 1955), by Edward Steichen. The Museum of Modern Art, New York, New York. Digital image copyright the Museum of Modern Art. Licensed by SCALA / Art Resource, NY.

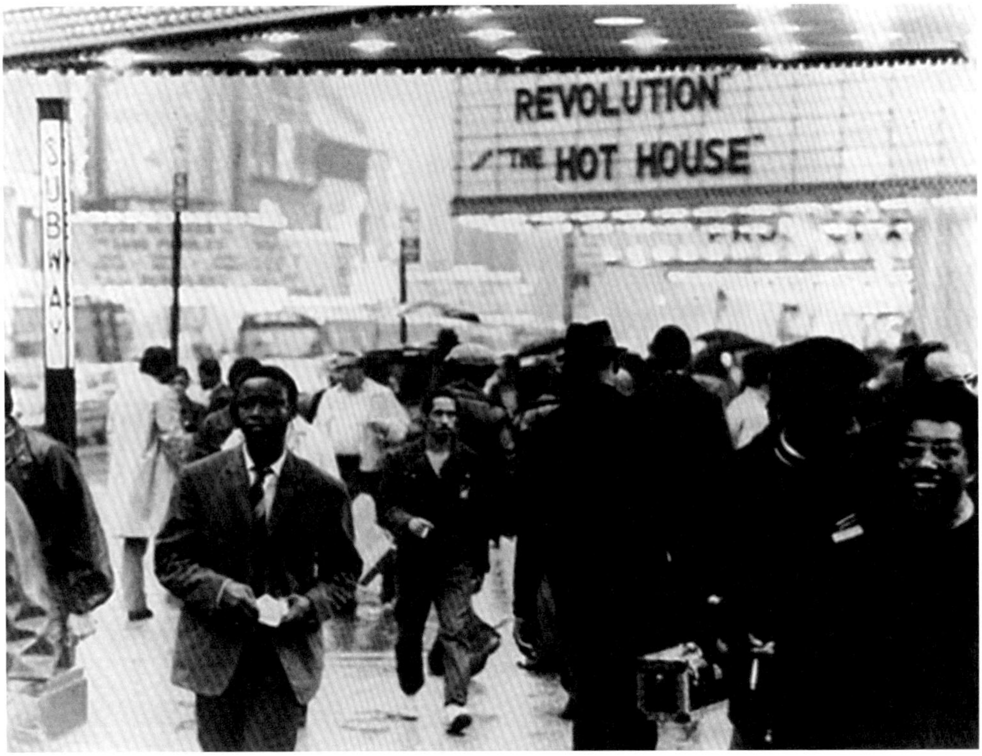

Figure 3.10. Douglas Huebler, *19/Variable Piece #70: 1971 (In Process) Global,* 1971. Copyright 2019 Estate of Douglas Huebler / Artists Rights Society (ARS), New York. Courtesy of Darcy Huebler / Artist Rights Society (ARS), New York and Paula Cooper Gallery, New York.

possibly more? The statement itself is definitively indefinite. The viewer is then given the challenge and the agency of guessing to whom the statement applies. The aesthetics of indifference are used in Huebler's work as a way to challenge dominant aesthetics and preconceived assumptions. "Who" the subject is, and one's own relation to the subject in the social, is constantly called into question.

Consider *19/Variable Piece #70.* In November 1977 a number of photographs were made in New York City to document various aspects of everyone alive (Figure 3.10). From those images, one was selected to represent AT LEAST ONE PERSON WHO MIGHT FEEL PLEASED TO HAVE BEEN MADE THE SUBJECT OF ART. The attendant photograph is yet another poor picture of a street scene. Pedestrians swarm the intersection in front of a movie theater's marquee. Who amid this crowd does the caption identify? Is our attention drawn to the man in the suit and tie, or the man in denim holding a cigarette, or the laughing woman with glasses in the right-hand corner, or someone whose back is to us? The unexceptional photograph does not seem to mark anyone more or less than anyone else, yet we are told that there is a specific quality to look for . . . maybe. After all, the text does say "might." The caption and its related grainy photograph give an impression of a seemingly trivial subject. Whereas observers of *The Family of Man* had "the feeling of having stepped into the Grand Canyon or the Carlsbad Caverns or something equally monumental,"[33] Huebler's photo-archive displays the world through what is unremarkable. This is partly the source of what I identify as Huebler's radical political drive. Being propelled into a position of uncertainty, against the comforts of liberal humanist values, gives momentum to a politics that can take nothing for granted and must acknowledge the discrepancies that resist sentimental anchoring and homogenization.

The evocation of being "represented," the recurring formula of *Variable Piece #70,* suggests that indiscriminate representation as such mattered to Huebler; each case poses the possibility that "at least one person feels represented."[34] This emphasis raises the condition of visibility made possible through photography as a means of political engagement, and thereby intersects productively with the theorization of political life put forward by writers such as Hannah Arendt. Though, according to Arendt, being recognized visibly by others is not political in itself, being political nevertheless is contingent on emerging *into* visibility.[35] Her book *The Human Condition,* published in 1958 while Arendt resided in New York, grows partly out of the tumult of the postwar civil rights era in the United States, in the midst of societal moves toward "becoming a *shared world* for all its citizens rather than a space where people simply live side by side."[36] Huebler's artistic practice, from his minimalist sculpture to his ambitious *Everyone Alive* endeavor, contains echoes of Arendt's definition of the world, envisioned as "the common meeting ground of all, those who are present [and] have different locations in it, and the location of one can no more coincide with the location of another than the location of two objects."[37] Furthermore, in Arendt's words, the world "opens up *differently* to every man,"[38] and thus contains the possibility of multiple viewpoints, multiple positions.

Huebler's account challenges the "truth" of photography by drawing attention to the aesthetic, intellectual, and emotional desires projected onto the photograph, as well as onto our connections with others, or lack thereof. In this way, his photographs ask us to consider how our reality is indeed shaped by interactions with others, and often instigated by and performed through images, acknowledging also the increasingly public visibility of *every* person, whether one is aware of it or not. The artist's self-conscious application of categories only further reveals photography's simultaneous omnipresence and arbitrary, if not absurd, incapacity to frame the subject, by referring in varying degrees to lived experience. As Ulrich Baer has poignantly described in his analysis of Arendt's writings on the relation between photography and public life in the 1960s, with a focus on photography of the civil rights era, "The camera marks the *elsewhere* from which people are seen, and which nobody, white or black, can fully assume. Photography carves out a viewpoint for the future, as the instance of the world that is never available to anyone in the present and from which everyone is incessantly being watched."[39] In other words, photography is everywhere, capturing everyone, at the very same time that it is unlocatable and impossible for any single individual to fully occupy. Similarly, as opposed to a project of rationalizing difference, Huebler's posits the irrational factors that logic cannot account for. His photographs and their related statements play on the identification process, producing laughter and frustration when one discovers that the aphorism proposed (such as "represented above is at least one person who knows that life is unfair" or "at least one person who had to be coaxed into having his picture taken") requires a negotiation of meaning that questions one's own identity and judgment far more than providing a fixed understanding of the subjects in the image. Importantly, not all of Huebler's works under the parameters of the *Variable Piece #70* project are lighthearted. *DM1 Variable Piece #70, 1972* (1978), for example, includes rephotographed photographs from the 1940s that Huebler found in the concentration camp museum at Dachau, showing a group of emaciated prisoners marching in file. Seemingly flip in some instances, and deadly serious in others, questions about the subjugation of the people pictured recurs throughout *Variable Piece #70.*

Clichés, repetitions, and resemblances are pushed to their limits, and meaning is perpetually multiplied in Huebler's work. His anti-aesthetic images mock the expressive qualities of contemporaneous photographers of the New York School such as Diane Arbus and William Klein.[40] In contrast to Arbus, for example, Huebler attributes the strange and the striking partly to a subject's apparent ordinariness, or to appropriate McShine's description of Huebler's early sculpture, to their appearance of "standardized blandness." Yet, like Arbus, Huebler's projects share an interest in how sameness persistently mutates into difference, leading to what Carol Armstrong has eloquently described in Arbus's work as "an infinite, unhierarchical number of irreducible differences," both on "the levels of biology and photography."[41] Seen in this way, Huebler's portraits also poke fun at systems-based categorical photography, along with its claims to objectivity, as in Bernd Becher and Hilla Becher's *Typologies* series. In Huebler's case, neither objectivity nor subjectivity ever entirely triumphs. Like the larger premise of the *Everyone Alive* project, each piece is underpinned by a profoundly antipositivist bent: more information can sometimes mean less knowledge rather than confirming the presumed positivist equivalence between accumulation and understanding. Such portraits function in Benjamin Buchloh's analysis as a way to "concretize the egalitarian aspirations of the late 1960s (the moment when Andy Warhol predicted that in the future everybody would be famous for fifteen minutes) and the reradicalization of the antihierarchical and the antimonumental potential of the photograph."[42] I return to the importance of Warhol's forecast later in this chapter, but for the moment I would like to reinforce how Huebler's photographic portraiture moves beyond the reading of any single photograph and instead enacts an affective logic by evoking a conversation between series and sequence, uniqueness and difference, suggesting that any individual photograph is both part and parcel of a larger undefined whole.

Using photography as a means akin to Michel Foucault's understanding of the relativity of language as a system of representation, Huebler puts to the test what Foucault called "the heart of the affirmative discourse on which resemblance rests."[43] In revealing "the constitutive illiteracy of the physiognomic face," Huebler allows for subjective uniqueness and affirming the irrepressible affect of any and all individual subjects, even within a standardized system.[44] Challenging the legibility of the physiognomic subject, Huebler repeatedly exposes the vulnerability of people in front of the camera, unfastening the very idea that meaning can be decisive. The one-thing-after-another sequential logic of serial and systems-based art coming out of minimalism is deliberately confused by Huebler, highlighting the succession of temporal disjunctures that necessarily inhabit all photographs.

When Sol LeWitt articulated his view of serial difference in 1966, he seemed to inadvertently sum up the dynamic operating in Huebler's practice. LeWitt stated that "the differences between the parts are the subject of the composition."[45] How is the meaning of serial difference affected specifically, when the subject at stake, the subject of difference, is a person or multiple people? This may be the most striking implication of the shift from minimalist practices in the late 1960s to conceptual ones: Robert Morris's "blank form"[46] and Judd's "specific objects" were no longer understood as sufficient in the critique of modernist orthodoxies, let alone the socio-political context of the late sixties. The move from the object games of minimalism to the subject games of conceptual art therefore signaled an increasingly direct engagement with the "illusionism" of representation rather than an oblique critique of it, as well as an increasingly prescient engagement with the complex realities of lived human experience.

Ludwig Wittgenstein's concept of the self as a source of agency and knowledge that is constituted publicly through shared language provides an additional argument for further understanding the work of conceptual artists such as Huebler. It denies the isolation of the self and the work of art in favor of recognizing their respective sociability, or how each "[takes] place in language as well as image, and thus in a shared, public domain."[47] Photography, like a universal language that no one can speak, repeatedly proves resilient to transparent readings. When employed as Huebler's palimpsest, photography becomes even more opaque. As Roland Barthes remarked, "The 'I' which approaches the text is already a plurality of other texts," meaning that subjectivity itself is a "fake plenitude." Barthes goes on to say that the I is composed of codes, so that ultimately, "subjectivity has the generality of stereotypes."[48] Thereby caught within a bind of uniqueness and stereotype, facility and obscurity, as well as the paradoxical exchanges between the positions of subject and object, photoconceptualism intervenes in the conventions of "art photography" through its deliberate use of amateur or snapshot techniques. It also simultaneously raises the bar of theoretical inquiry by insistently grappling with the paradigm of the text through the work itself. Riffing on what has been noted as photography's "uncanny ability to exceed, erode, and unfix . . . static visual certainties,"[49] Huebler's ethics of decentering performs a continual unsettling of hierarchical social relations. His antagonism toward modernist values of purity, autonomy, originality, uniqueness, and authorship evidence his avant-garde resistance to aesthetic standards and his complete disinterest in an evolutionary model of the photographic medium. Despite, and partly because, each work is made up of photographs joined with a statement, the work is never "wholly manifest"—thereby working against the criteria Michael Fried insisted on for modernist art and turning the modernist reverence for "presentness" against itself.[50] As one attempts to reconstruct the narrative, the contradictions internal to the notion of autonomy are revealed.

The life and death stakes of recognizing one's interdependence with others in the social and political world were crucial during the Vietnam War era. As I have shown in the work of other conceptual artists, including Dennis Oppenheim and Bruce Nauman, though the violence and ethical turmoil of war were often relegated to the blurry background, they were nevertheless there. Huebler's use of portraiture, particularly in *Variable Piece #70,* poses one of the more explicit acknowledgments of the deep associations between the destabilization of meaning enacted through photography and the social and political turbulence of the time. Militarization and death recur as a theme in Huebler's artwork, and one imagines that the artist's armed service during World War II had a formative effect on his conception of art, both its necessity and frivolity. Beyond looking for correlations in the sphere of art, striking parallels to Huebler's project can be found in the poignant portraits included in *Life* magazine's monumental thirteen-page spread, in the June 27, 1969, issue. Grouped under the banner "The Faces of the American Dead in Vietnam; One Week's Toll," *Life* collected and printed small black-and-white portraits of 242 U.S. servicemen listed as killed between May 28 and June 3 of that year (Figures 3.11, 3.12). Calling it "a record and a tribute," the publication notes that this is an average number killed for "any seven-day period during this stage of the war." Beneath each portrait the man's full name, age, and hometown are inscribed. No birth date listed, only the sad number of years, nearly exclusively between eighteen and twenty-four. They are not presented in alphabetical order, and so, looking for logic, it is conceivable that they are organized by the chronology of their death. Though many soldiers are pictured in uniform, the photographs themselves are anything but. Individual differences emerge, smiles or locked jaws, tilts of the head or rigid composure, whether they stare out at the viewer or off to the side: these and many other details emerge the more one looks. The youthfulness of the faces wrenches the heart: how to make sense of this loss of life? Huebler's project seems to echo the challenge put forward by "One Week's Dead,"[51] insofar as it asks not simply how we make sense of photographs and their constitutive meaning but, moreover, how loaded are pictures of people to begin with. These questions are amplified by the normalization of conflict in Vietnam within everyday life in the United States at this juncture. This photo-essay had a memorable impact. Unwilling draftees reported for training with copies of "One Week's Dead" and My Lai massacre coverage as supporting evidence of their disdain for the war and the U.S. military.[52] Imagine seeing these faces row after row in the comforts of one's home in 1969. The anonymous individuals become less so, and more familiar. Perhaps one resembles someone you know. This series of photographs is not simply about identifying the dead but also, and perhaps above all, the ethical need to identify *with* the dead.

"More than we must know *how many,*" explains *Life,* "we must know *who.*" The

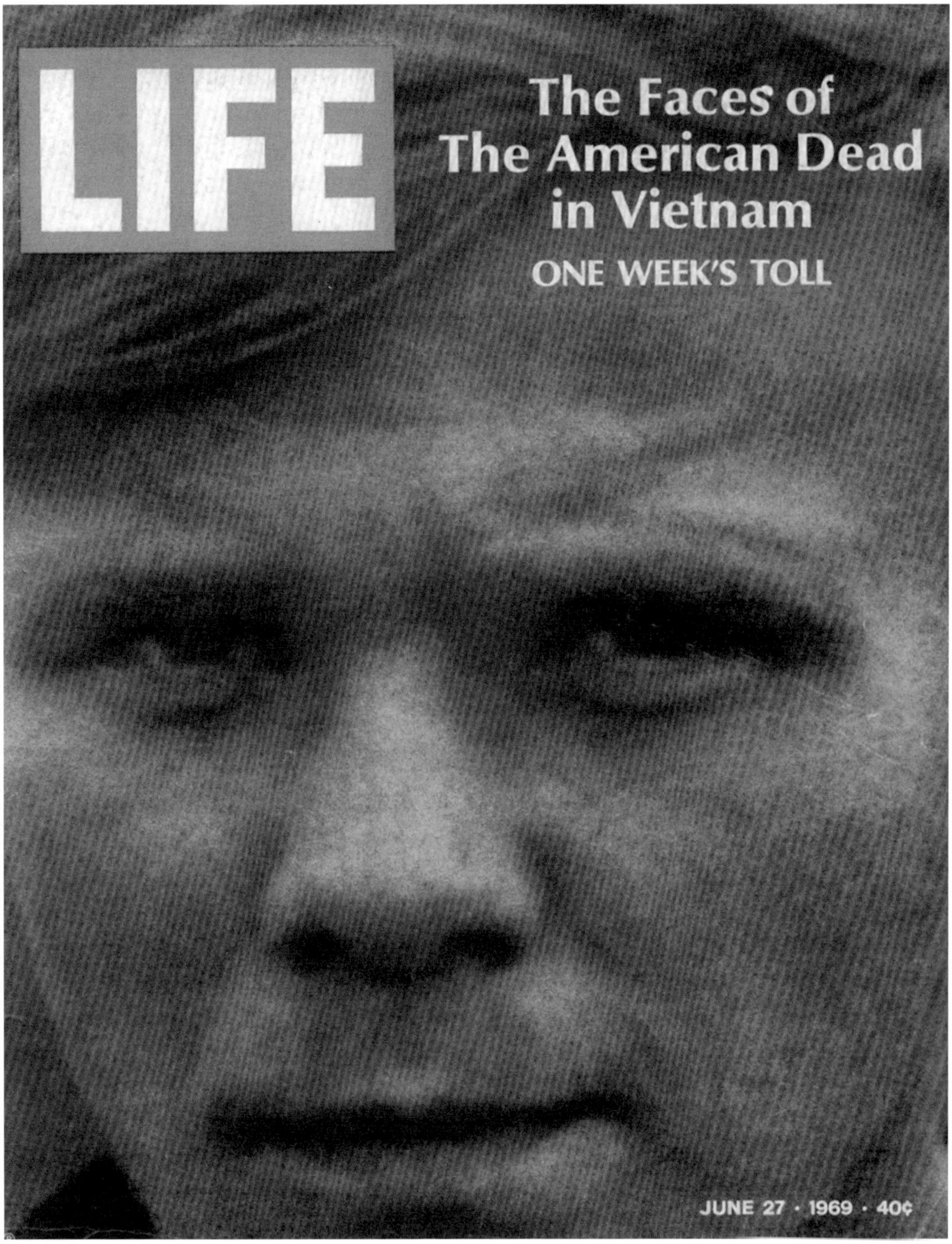

Figure 3.11. Cover, *LIFE* magazine, June 27, 1969. Copyright 1969 TI Gotham Inc. All rights reserved. Reprinted/translated from *LIFE* and published with permission of TI Gotham Inc. Reproduction in any manner in any language in whole or in part without written permission is prohibited.

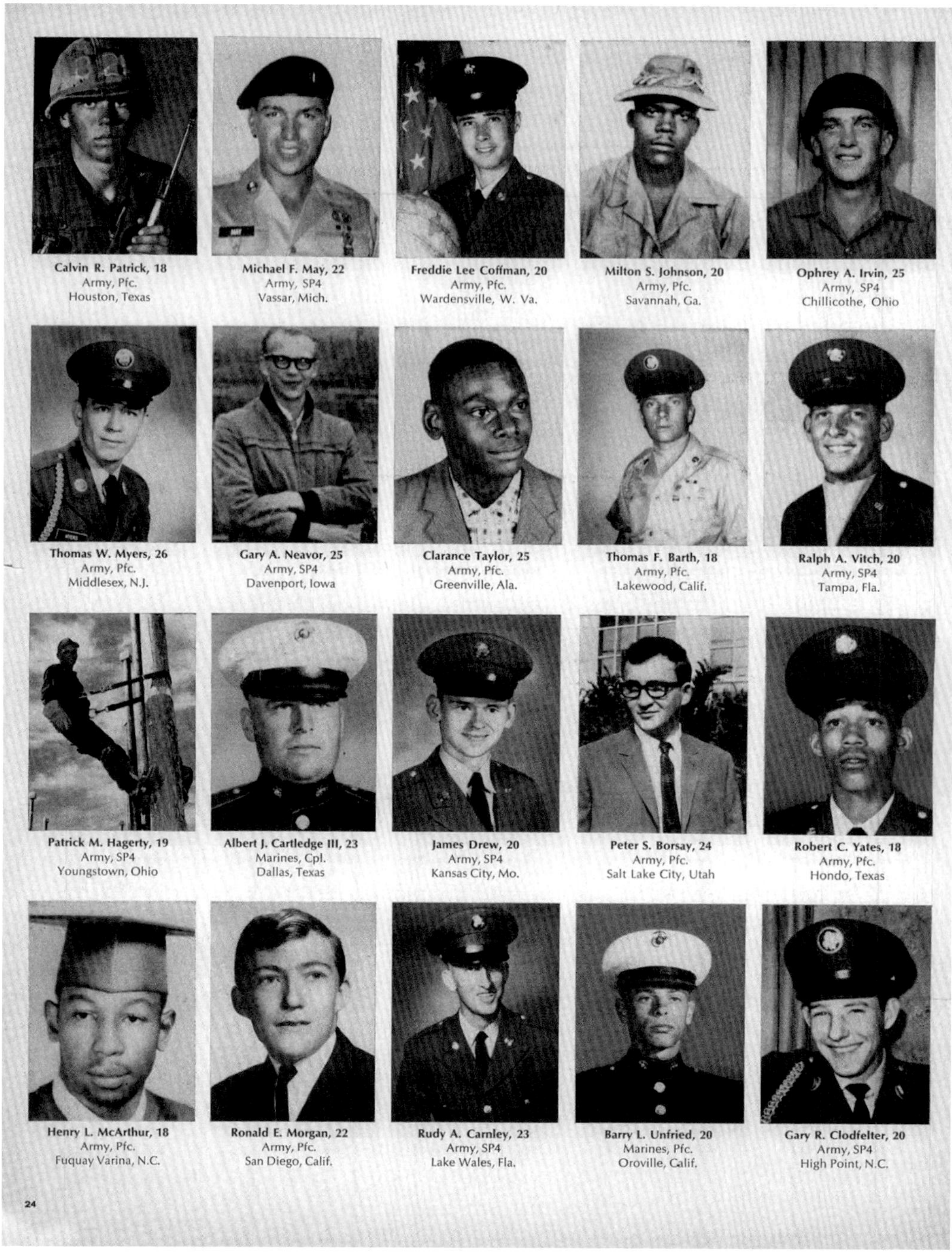

Calvin R. Patrick, 18
Army, Pfc.
Houston, Texas

Michael F. May, 22
Army, SP4
Vassar, Mich.

Freddie Lee Coffman, 20
Army, Pfc.
Wardensville, W. Va.

Milton S. Johnson, 20
Army, Pfc.
Savannah, Ga.

Ophrey A. Irvin, 25
Army, SP4
Chillicothe, Ohio

Thomas W. Myers, 26
Army, Pfc.
Middlesex, N.J.

Gary A. Neavor, 25
Army, SP4
Davenport, Iowa

Clarance Taylor, 25
Army, Pfc.
Greenville, Ala.

Thomas F. Barth, 18
Army, Pfc.
Lakewood, Calif.

Ralph A. Vitch, 20
Army, SP4
Tampa, Fla.

Patrick M. Hagerty, 19
Army, SP4
Youngstown, Ohio

Albert J. Cartledge III, 23
Marines, Cpl.
Dallas, Texas

James Drew, 20
Army, SP4
Kansas City, Mo.

Peter S. Borsay, 24
Army, Pfc.
Salt Lake City, Utah

Robert C. Yates, 18
Army, Pfc.
Hondo, Texas

Henry L. McArthur, 18
Army, Pfc.
Fuquay Varina, N.C.

Ronald E. Morgan, 22
Army, Pfc.
San Diego, Calif.

Rudy A. Carnley, 23
Army, SP4
Lake Wales, Fla.

Barry L. Unfried, 20
Marines, Pfc.
Oroville, Calif.

Gary R. Clodfelter, 20
Army, SP4
High Point, N.C.

24

Figure 3.12. "Vietnam: One Week's Dead," *LIFE* magazine, page 24, June 27, 1969. Copyright 1969 TI Gotham Inc. All rights reserved. Reprinted/translated from *LIFE* and published with permission of TI Gotham Inc. Reproduction in any manner in any language in whole or in part without written permission is prohibited.

reader is not informed of how each of these individuals was killed. Instead, we have only *Life*'s reiteration of the hollow words of the official announcement of their deaths: "in connection with the conflict in Vietnam." The brief accompanying editorial adds that "in a time when the numbers of Americans killed in this war—36,000—though far less than the Vietnamese losses, have exceeded the dead in the Korean War, when the nation continues week after week to be numbed by a three-digit statistic which is translated to direct anguish in hundreds of homes all over the country, we must pause to look at the faces." Despite the seeming lack of focus in Huebler's *Everyone Alive,* I contend that a similar reflective pause is enacted. Recall that *Everyone Alive* begins with AT LEAST ONE PERSON WHO MAY NOW BE DEAD.

There are other parallels. Following the photo-spread of "The Faces of the American Dead," a largely anecdote-driven page is included.[53] Filled with ordinary yet moving details, its tone and delivery come remarkably close to Huebler's captions. "One Pfc. from the 101st Airborne was killed on his 21st birthday. . . . One boy had customized his 13-year-old car and planned to buy a ranch. . . . One had been sending his pay home to contribute to his brother's college expenses." These descriptive particulars bring specificity to bear on the individuals pictured in the portraits while also emphasizing their relatability and what we might have in common with them. Furthermore, it signals the way these young men stand in for something much more complex and difficult to articulate. As the editorial continues: "To study even the smallest portion of them, even without reference to their names, is to glimpse the scope of a much broader tragedy." In one sense we have returned to the "humanity" of *The Family of Man,* yet, in another profound sense, we have splintered off in a much more Huebler-esque direction, in the attempt to "free" these faces from that continuum commonly referred to as the background. Revealingly, a magnified version of a single man's face, selected from among "One Week's Dead," is featured on the cover of this issue of *Life,* blurrily blown up to the imposing scale of just over ten by thirteen inches. A poor image to be sure; the resolution on this photograph seems even lower than numerous others that could just as easily have been selected from the collection. With eyes centered and enlarged, the young man glares back at the reader, triggering an intimate reckoning. There is no apparent rationale for why this soldier was chosen over any other. We find the original portrait buried in the rows with the others between the pages and learn that he is "William C. Gearing Jr., 20" from Rochester, New York. These coordinates nevertheless leave us empty-handed, suggesting that, at least in one sense, the recognition of failure is crucial to understanding this photographic project and, I would venture, to Huebler's.

The artist Mike Kelley, once a student of Huebler's at CalArts, described *Variable Piece #70* as "impossibly democratic."[54] This comment conspicuously marks the contradictory and utopian ambitions of the project, including its subversive critique of liberal humanist photographic traditions. The unobtainable aspiration to photographically document "everyone alive" exerts a leveling power on the world at large. Yet, in practice, it purposefully comes up against the resistant and unwieldy limits of its own conditions, and the further proliferation of systems that structure the viewer's reality. As opposed to using the photographic frame as a way to anchor the subjects pictured, or even interpellate one's subjective encounter with the images, Huebler's artistic practice ardently conceives of a world that, somewhat paradoxically, is perpetually unconstrained, unfixed. Instead, as Huebler himself described, his conceptual models suggest that "everyone in the world is free to conceive of all imaginable models in order to exist in a world where we are merely *contingent*."[55]

Significantly, the affective logic of this work depends not on the subject matter's rationality but on distinctions among images and the noise discovered in the process of viewing. Huebler's photographic portraits are ultimately more about inquisitiveness as opposed to acquisition. His quixotic archive poses an important epistemological break in "thinking photography."[56] It is a gesture that returns to the fallible and finite contingencies of corporeality, as well as to a reconsideration of the conceptual categories that at once cleave us together and tear us apart.

Categorical Refusal

For conceptual artists of the late sixties and early seventies, the German artists Bernd Becher and Hilla Becher offered an important model. The Bechers collaborated on a complicated international search to document vanishing industrial terrain from the 1950s until Bernd's death in 2007. The duo compiled an extensive photographic archive of "anonymous sculpture." Strikingly different from "popular, romanticized Modernist views of early twentieth-century industrialization that transformed banal industrial sites into gleaming futuristic visions, typified by Charles Sheeler's photographs of the Ford Motor plant in Dearborn, Michigan, in 1927,"[57] the Bechers devoted themselves to recording straightforward "typologies" of disappearing industrial architecture such as blast furnaces, water towers, lime kilns, and cooling towers. Each structure was marked increasingly by its supposed uselessness, despite its historical connection to labor and productivity. In these individual portraits of industrial architecture, the images famously bear no trace of emotion and are rather standardized shots of archetypal structures. Michael Fried, among others, has rightly compared the resolute frontality of the Bechers' photographs to the anterior pose of a subject directly facing the camera.[58] Despite this emphasis on the face—or facade—as a subject, many art historians have argued for the "draining of subjective content" they believe is enacted by a perceived flatness in the Bechers' photographs.[59] Gordon Hughes, for example, persuasively describes the recurrent face-forward quality of the Bechers' oeuvre as "devoid of subjective depth and physiognomic resonance."[60] This line of thought is reinforced by the fact that the Bechers' images are nearly exclusively displayed in grids, which, while enabling comparison between equivalence and difference, also suggests a formalist aesthetic preoccupied with objectivity and self-containment. In contrast to this view, I believe it is the trace of the face as an anamorphic evocation that gives force to these series. Moreover, the systematic organization enforced by the grid is, in effect, the method by which the personalities of the industrial architecture pictured are given a vital,

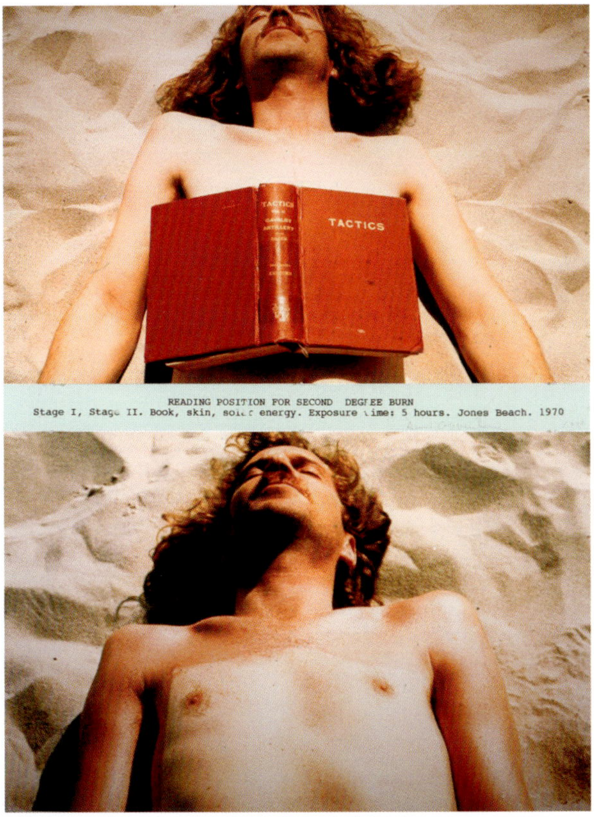

Plate 1. Dennis Oppenheim, *Reading Position for Second Degree Burn*, 1970. *Stage I and Stage II. Book, skin, solar energy. Exposure time: 5 hours. Jones Beach, New York*. Color photography, text. Courtesy of Dennis Oppenheim Estate.

Plate 2. William Henry Fox Talbot, *The Oriel Window, South Gallery, Lacock Abbey*, 1835. Paper negative; sheet 8.5 × 11.6 cm (3⅜ × 4 9⁄16 inches), irregularly trimmed. The Rubel Collection, Purchase, Ann Tenenbaum and Thomas H. Lee and Anonymous Gifts, 1997. Collection of the Metropolitan Museum of Art, New York.

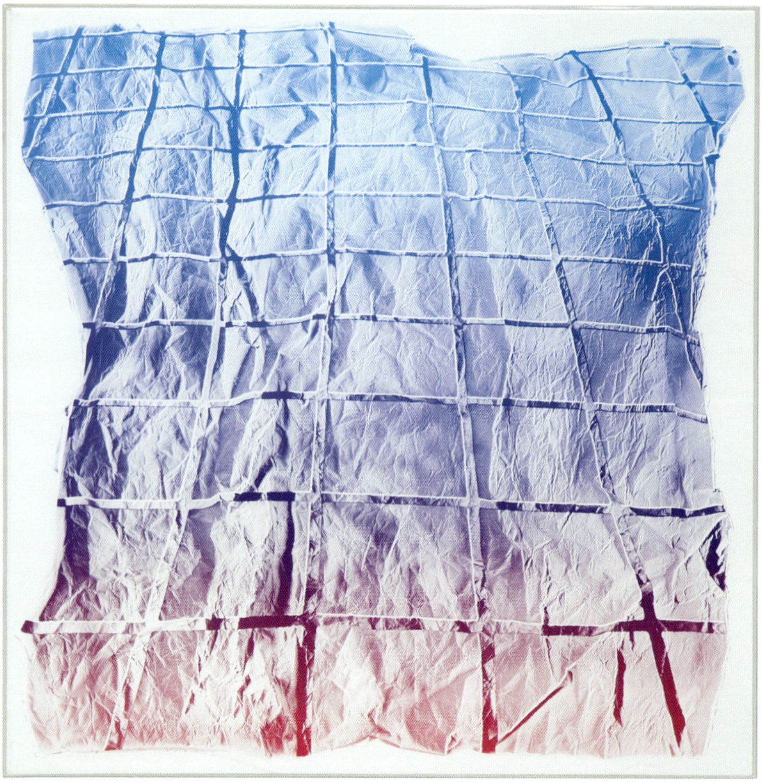

Plate 3. Mel Bochner, *Surface Dis/Tension: Offset* (RB), 1968. Offset lithograph, 18.75 × 18 inches. Courtesy of the artist.

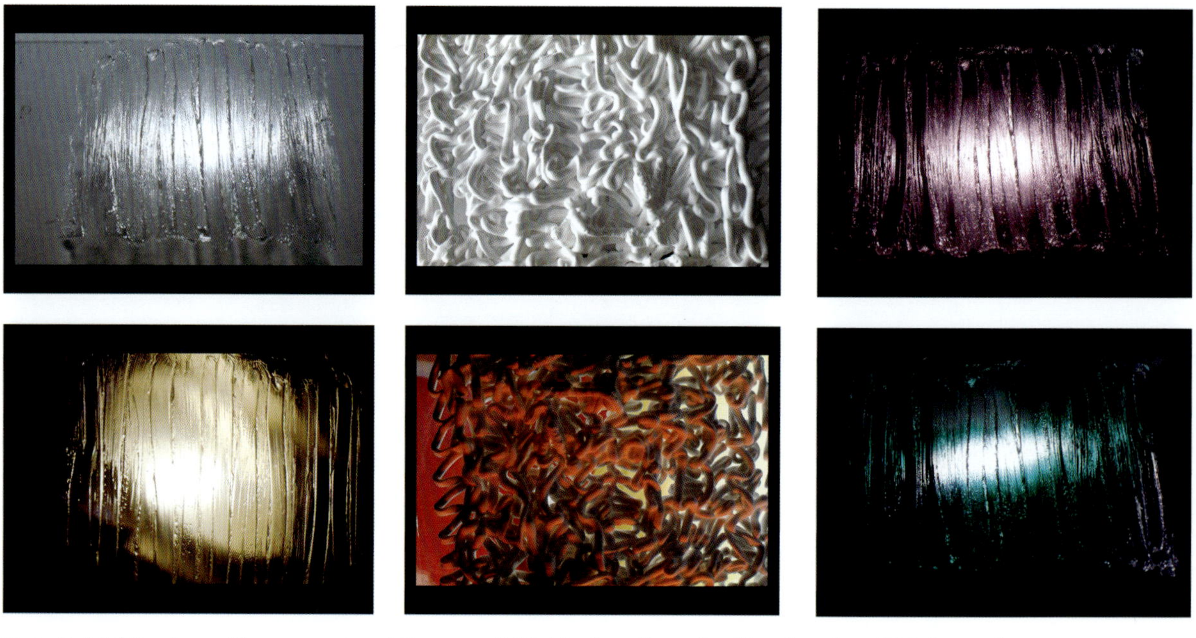

Plate 5. Mel Bochner, *Transparent and Opaque*, 1968. Twelve silver dye bleach prints (Ilfachrome), 16 × 20 inches. Courtesy of the artist.

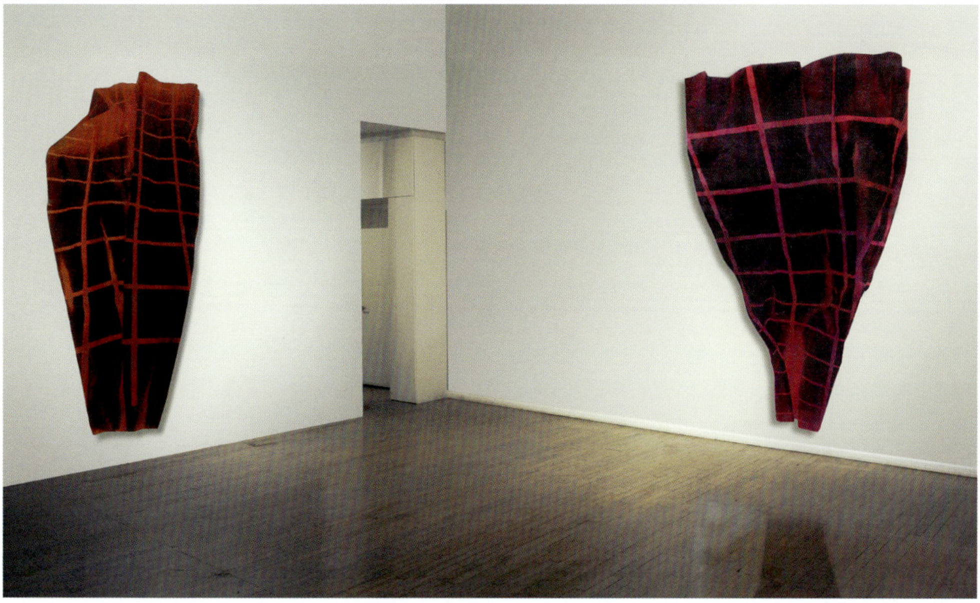

Plate 4. Mel Bochner, *Color Crumple #3, Color Crumple #2,* 1967 (remade 2011). Silhouetted c-print mounted on aluminum, 96 × 46 inches and 96 × 54 inches. Installation in Peter Freeman Gallery, 2011. Courtesy of the artist.

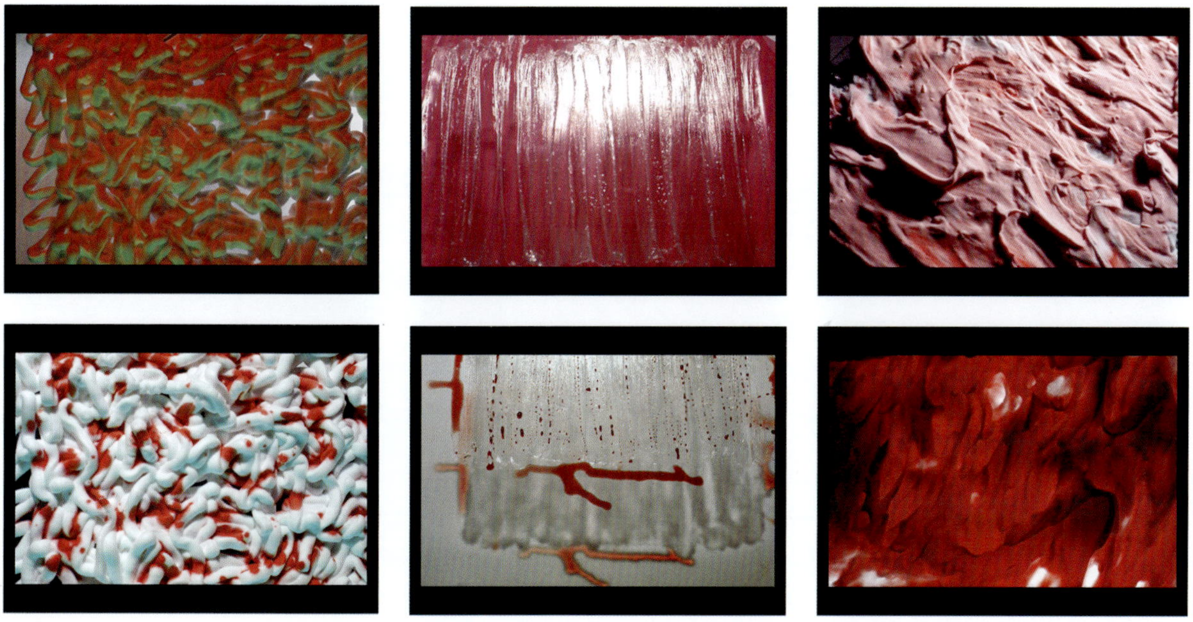

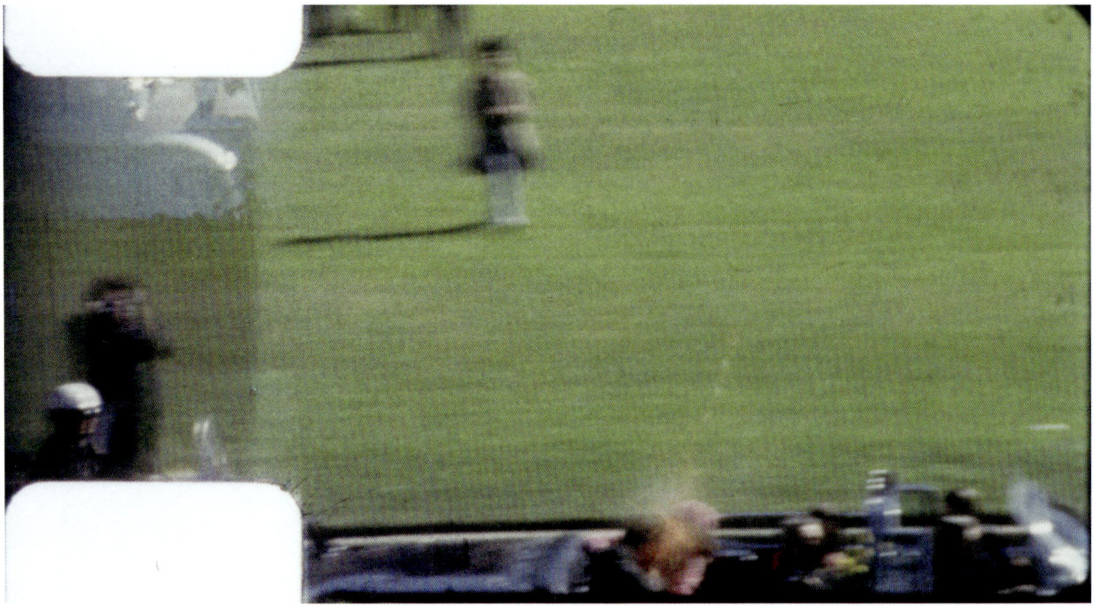

Plate 6. Abraham Zapruder, Frame no. 313, Zapruder Film, 1963. Copyright 1967 (renewed 1995). The Sixth Floor Museum at Dealey Plaza.

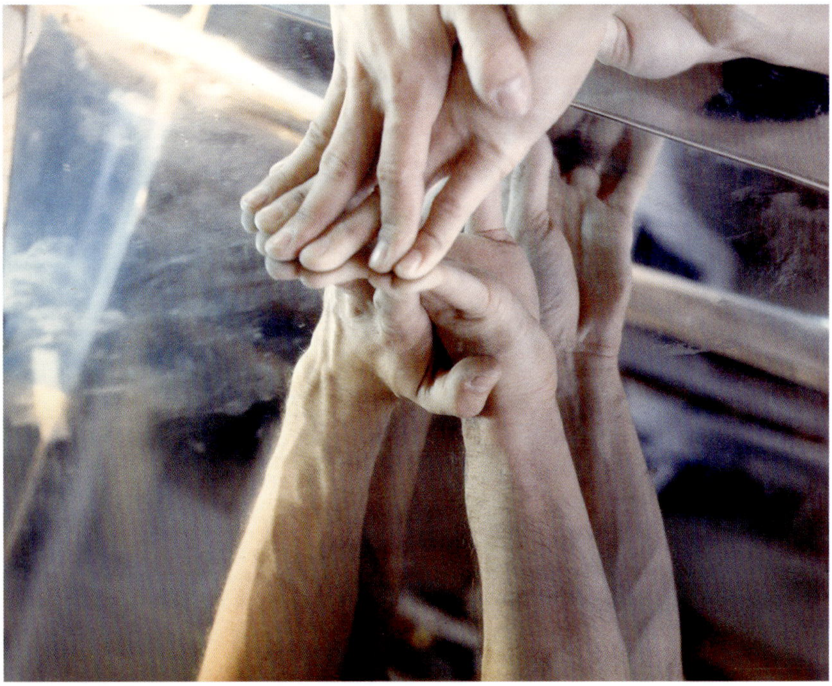

Plate 7. Bruce Nauman, *Finger Touch with Mirrors,* from *Eleven Color Photographs,* 1966–67/1970. Copyright 2020 Bruce Nauman / Artists Rights Society (ARS). Courtesy of Sperone Westwater, New York.

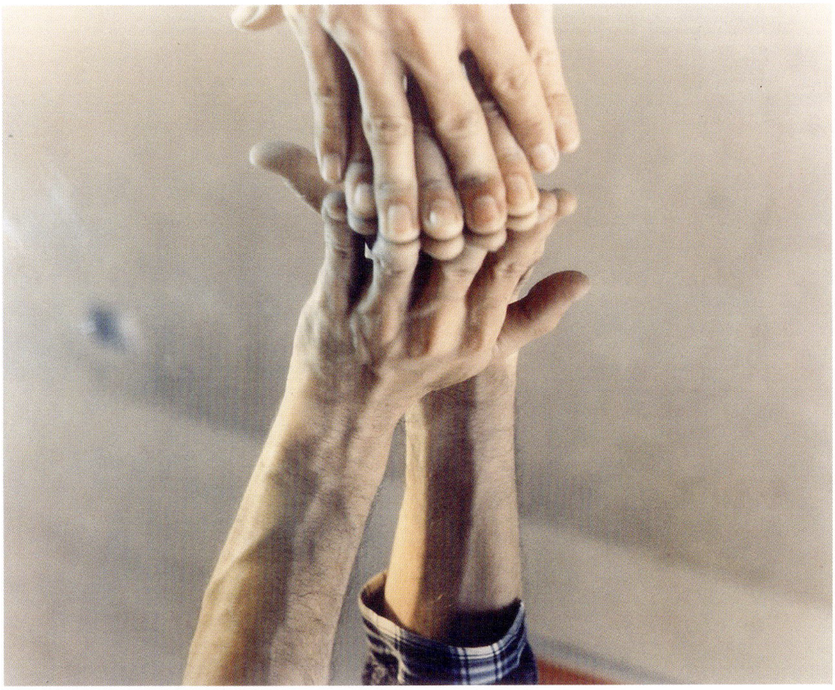

Plate 8. Bruce Nauman, *Finger Touch No. 1,* from *Eleven Color Photographs,* 1966–67/1970. Copyright 2020 Bruce Nauman / Artists Rights Society (ARS). Courtesy of Sperone Westwater, New York.

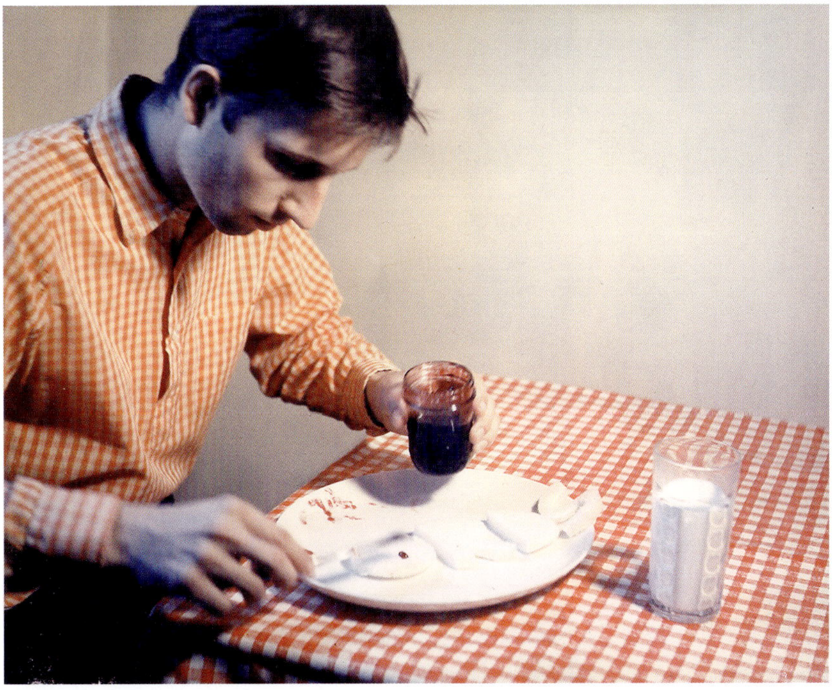

Plate 9. Bruce Nauman, *Eating My Words,* from *Eleven Color Photographs,* 1966–67/1970. Copyright 2020 Bruce Nauman / Artists Rights Society (ARS). Courtesy of Sperone Westwater, New York.

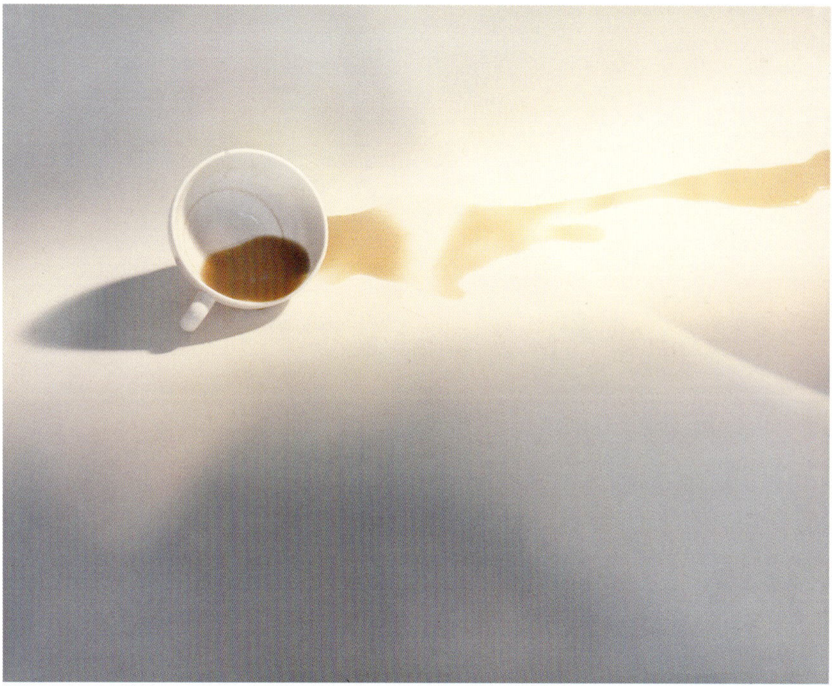

Plate 10. Bruce Nauman, *Coffee Thrown Away Because It Was Too Cold,* from *Eleven Color Photographs,* 1966–67/1970. Copyright 2020 Bruce Nauman / Artists Rights Society (ARS). Courtesy of Sperone Westwater, New York.

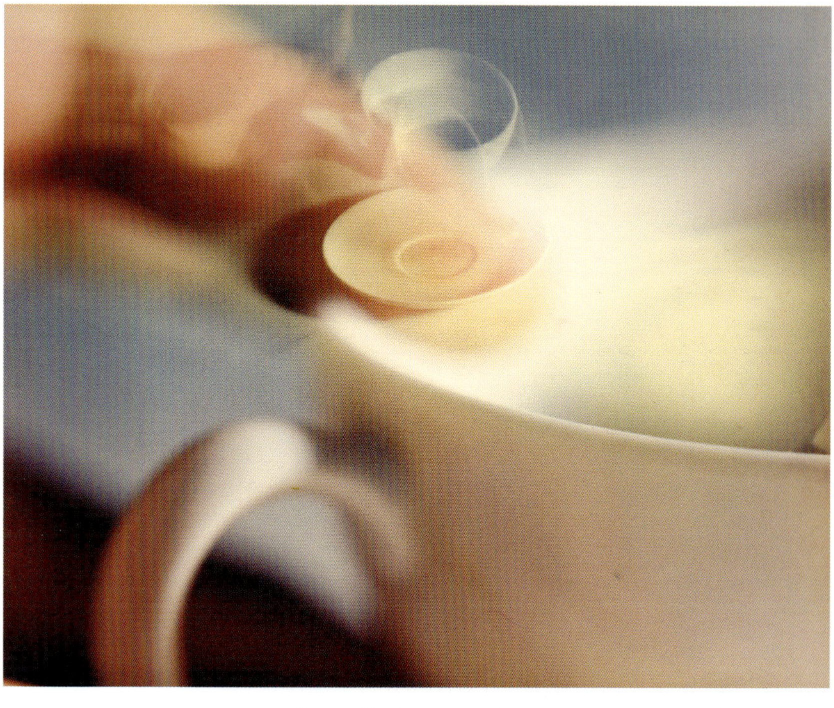

Plate 11. Bruce Nauman, *Coffee Spilled Because the Cup Was Too Hot,* from *Eleven Color Photographs,* 1966–67/1970. Copyright 2020 Bruce Nauman / Artists Rights Society (ARS). Courtesy of Sperone Westwater, New York.

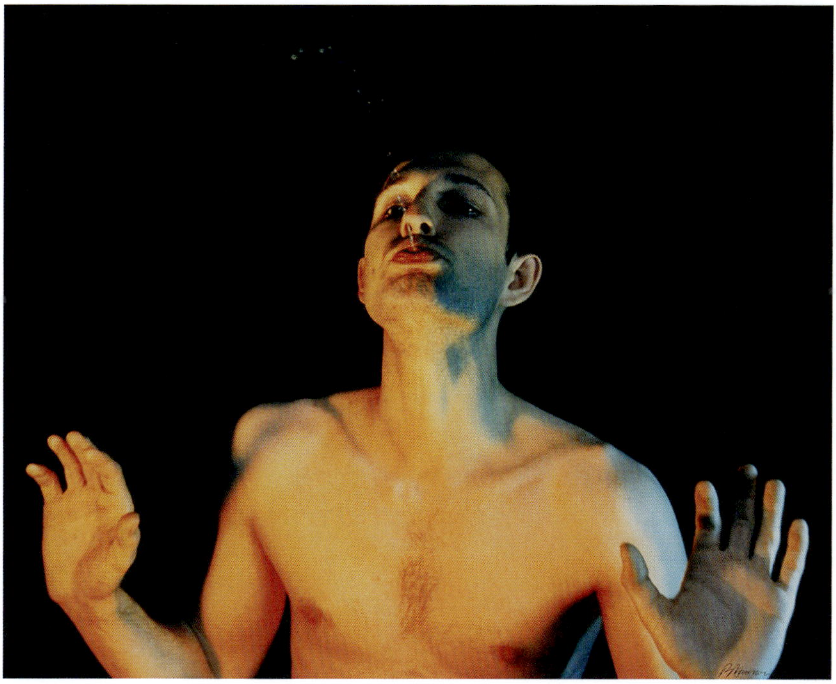

Plate 12. Bruce Nauman, *Self-Portrait as a Fountain,* from *Eleven Color Photographs,* 1966–67/1970. Copyright 2020 Bruce Nauman / Artists Rights Society (ARS). Courtesy of Sperone Westwater, New York.

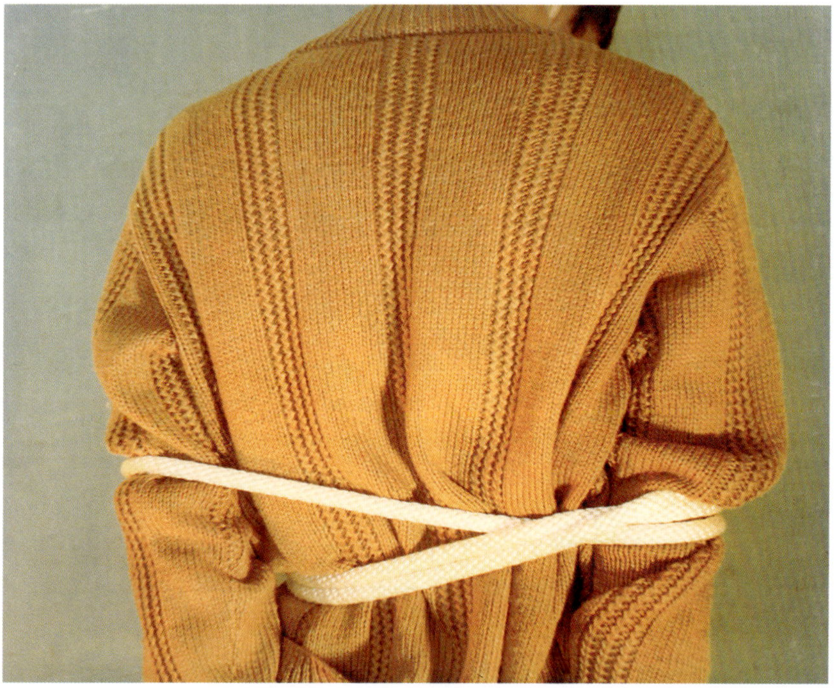

Plate 13. Bruce Nauman, *Bound to Fail,* from *Eleven Color Photographs,* 1966–67/1970. Copyright 2020 Bruce Nauman / Artists Rights Society (ARS). Courtesy of Sperone Westwater, New York.

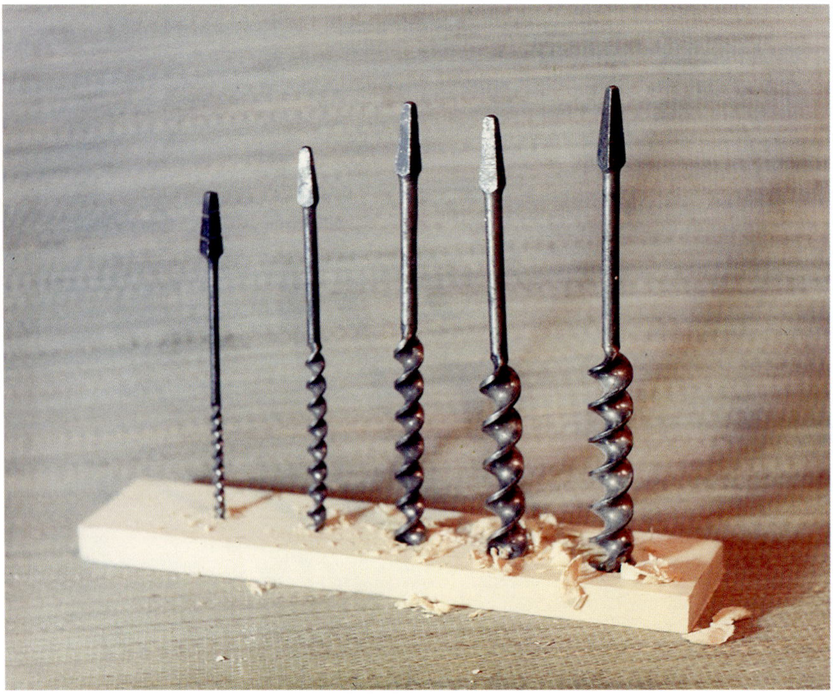

Plate 14. Bruce Nauman, *Drill Team,* from *Eleven Color Photographs,* 1966–67/1970. Copyright 2020 Bruce Nauman / Artists Rights Society (ARS). Courtesy of Sperone Westwater, New York.

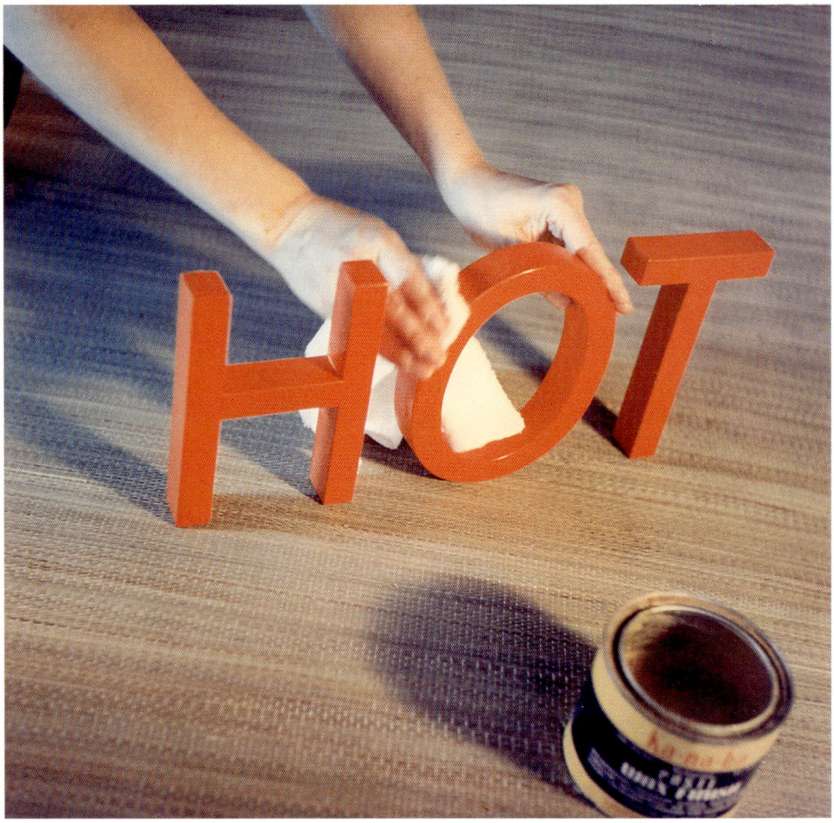

Plate 15. Bruce Nauman, *Waxing Hot,* from *Eleven Color Photographs,* 1966–67/1970. Copyright 2020 Bruce Nauman / Artists Rights Society (ARS). Courtesy of Sperone Westwater, New York.

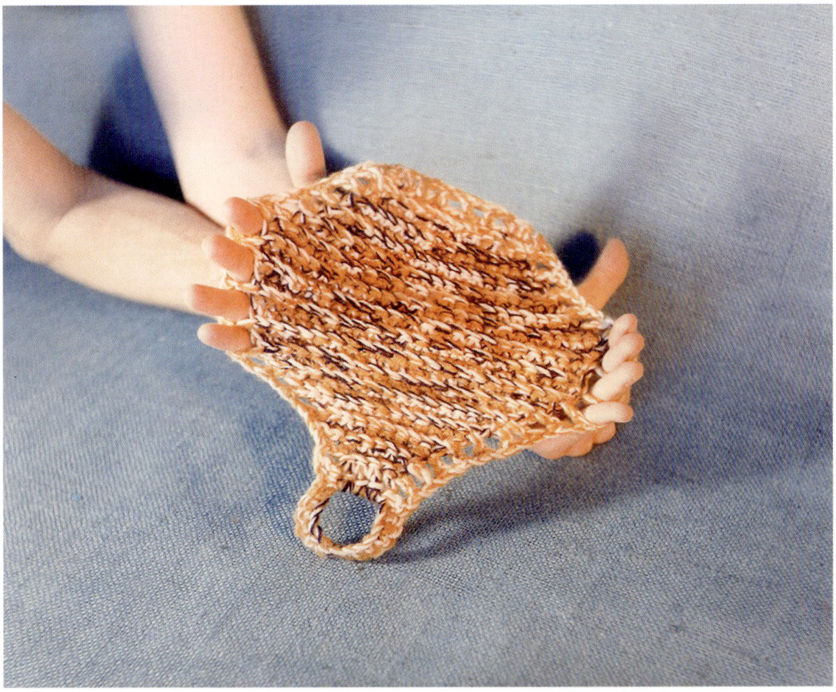

Plate 16. Bruce Nauman, *Untitled (Potholder),* from *Eleven Color Photographs,* 1966–67/1970. Copyright 2020 Bruce Nauman / Artists Rights Society (ARS). Courtesy of Sperone Westwater, New York.

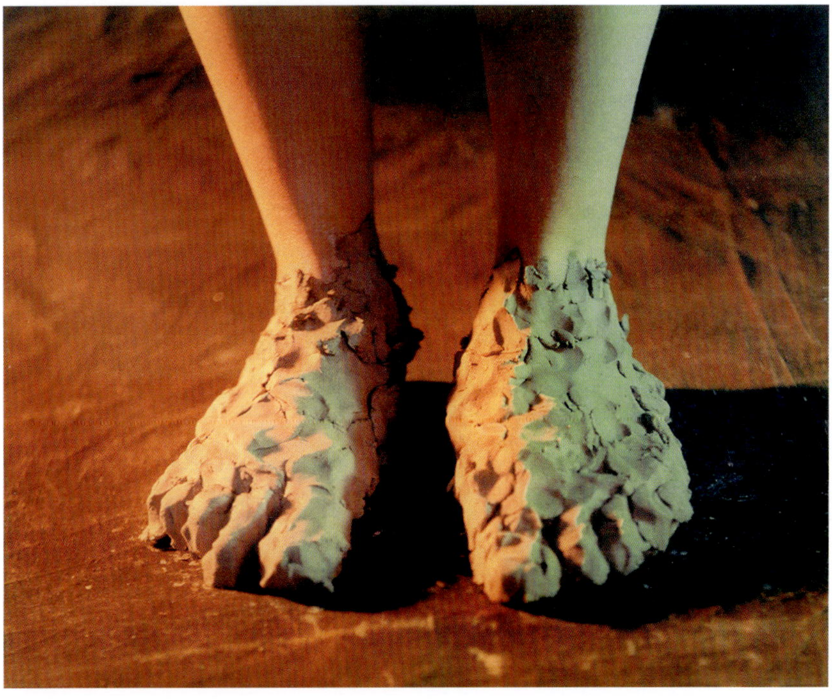

Plate 17. Bruce Nauman, *Feet of Clay,* from *Eleven Color Photographs,* 1966–67/1970. Copyright 2020 Bruce Nauman / Artists Rights Society (ARS). Courtesy of Sperone Westwater, New York.

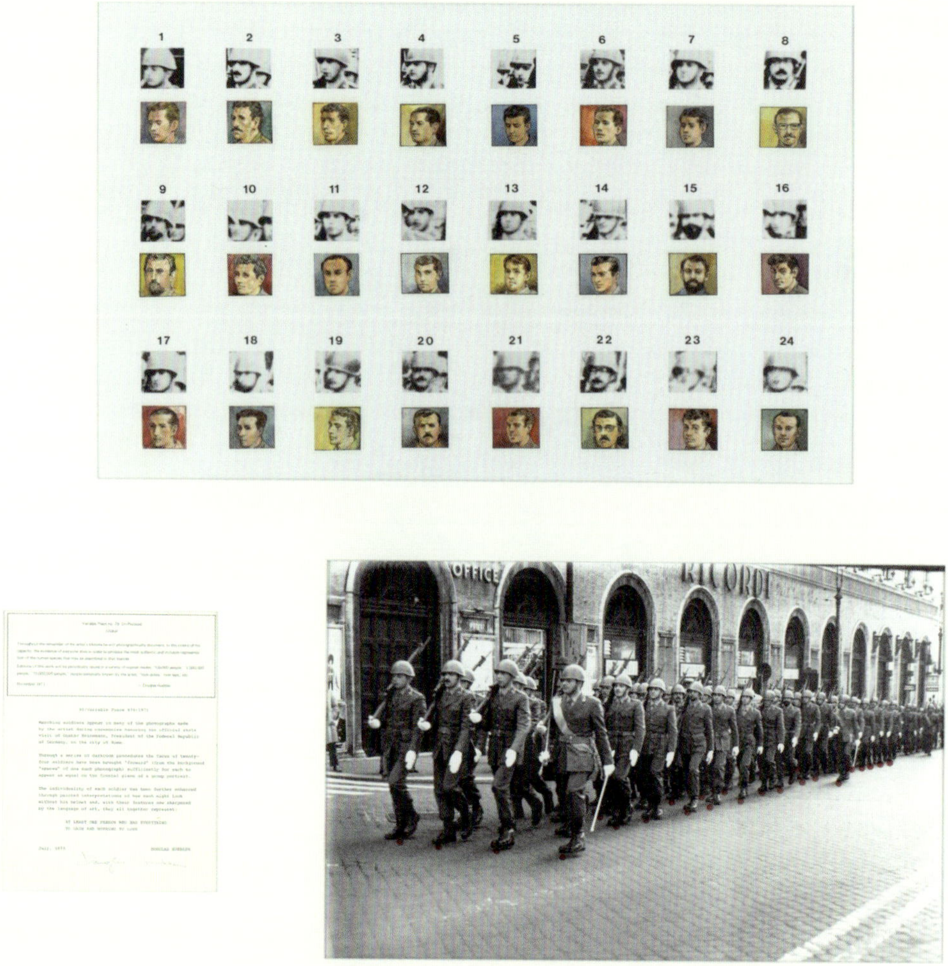

Plate 18. Douglas Huebler, *81/Variable Piece #70: 1971 (In Process) Global,* 1973. Copyright 2019 Estate of Douglas Huebler / Artists Rights Society (ARS), New York. Courtesy of Darcy Huebler / Artist Rights Society (ARS), New York and Paula Cooper Gallery, New York.

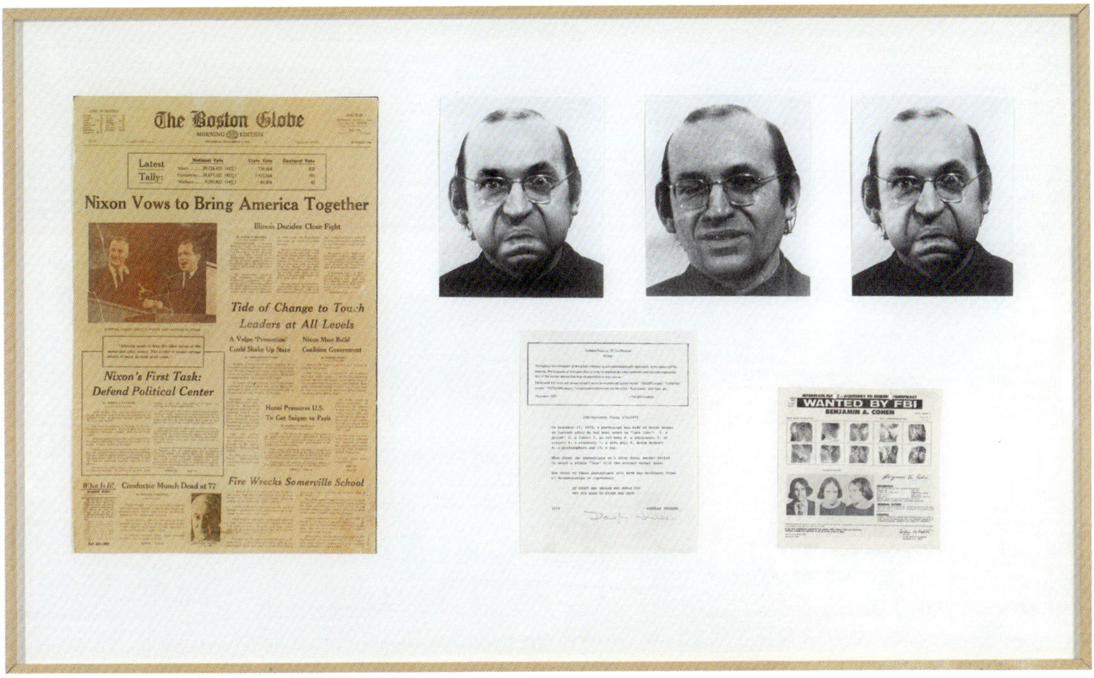

Plate 19. Douglas Huebler, *330/Variable Piece #70: 1971 (In Process) Global*, 1974. Gelatin silver prints, chromogenic print, typewriter ink on paper and offset lithograph on board, overall (sight): 32 × 52 inches (81.3 × 132.1 cm). Whitney Museum of American Art, New York; purchase, with funds from the Photography Committee, the Robert Mapplethorpe Foundation, Joanne Leonhardt Cassullo, Jodi and Michael Moreno, Renee Preisler Barasch, Elizabeth Fensterstock, Elizabeth Kabler, and Michèle Gerber Klein and partial gift of Dana Huebler Hinrichs, Darcy Huebler, and Dorne Huebler 2014.259. Digital image copyright Whitney Museum of American Art. Licensed by SCALA / Art Resource, NY. Copyright 2019 Estate of Douglas Huebler / Artists Rights Society (ARS), New York. Courtesy of Darcy Huebler / Artist Rights Society (ARS), New York.

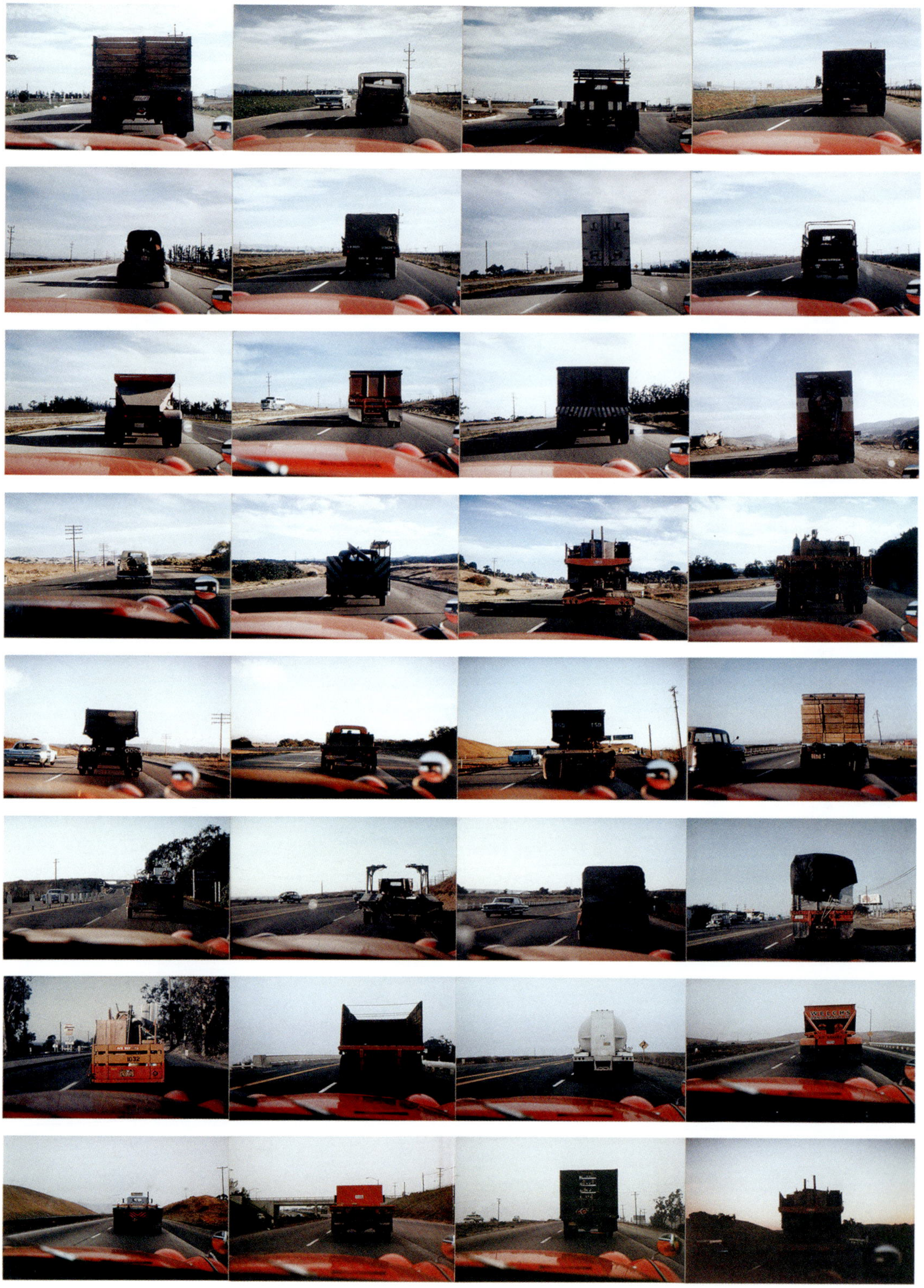

Plate 20. John Baldessari, *The Backs of All the Trucks Passed While Driving from Los Angeles to Santa Barbara, Calif., Sunday 20 Jan. 63*, 1963. Thirty-two color photographs, overall dimensions 60 × 42½ inches (152.4 × 108 cm). Courtesy of the Estate of John Baldessari and Marian Goodman Gallery.

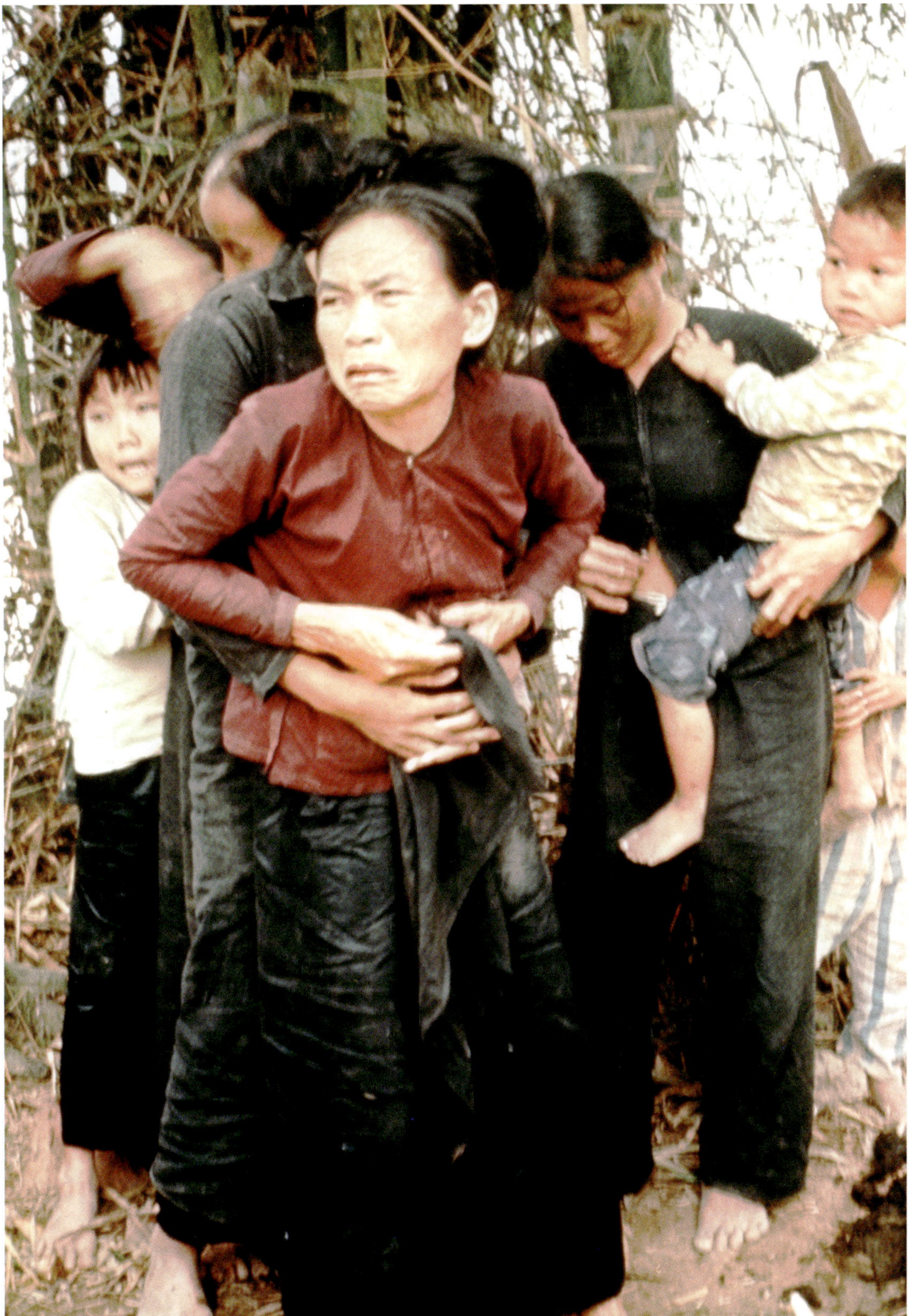

Plate 21. Ronald L. Haeberle, Group of civilian women and children before being killed in the My Lai massacre, March 16, 1968. According to court testimony, they were killed seconds after this photograph was taken. Life Images Collection / Getty Images.

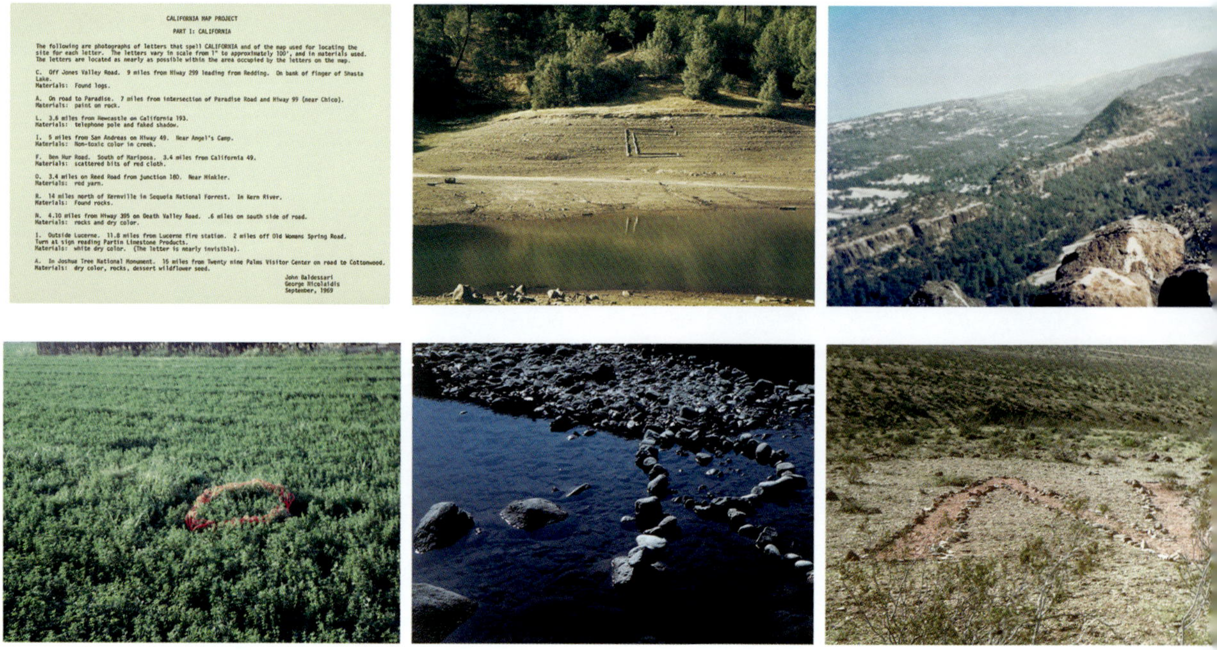

CALIFORNIA MAP PROJECT

PART I: CALIFORNIA

The following are photographs of letters that spell CALIFORNIA and of the map used for locating the site for each letter. The letters vary in scale from 1" to approximately 100', and in materials used. The letters are located as nearly as possible within the area occupied by the letters on the map.

C. Off Jones Valley Road. 9 miles from Hiway 299 leading from Redding. On bank of finger of Shasta Lake.
Materials: Found logs.

A. On road to Paradise. 7 miles from intersection of Paradise Road and Hiway 99 (near Chico).
Materials: paint on rock.

L. 3.6 miles from Newcastle on California 193.
Materials: telephone pole and faked shadow.

I. 5 miles from San Andreas on Hiway 49. Near Angel's Camp.
Materials: Non-toxic color in creek.

F. Ben Hur Road. South of Mariposa. 3.4 miles from California 49.
Materials: scattered bits of red cloth.

O. 3.4 miles on Reed Road from junction 180. Near Minkler.
Materials: red yarn.

R. 14 miles north of Kernville in Sequoia National Forrest. In Kern River.
Materials: Found rocks.

N. 4.10 miles from Hiway 395 on Death Valley Road. .6 miles on south side of road.
Materials: rocks and dry color.

I. Outside Lucerne. 11.8 miles from Lucerne fire station. 2 miles off Old Womans Spring Road. Turn at sign reading Partin Limestone Products.
Materials: white dry color. (The letter is nearly invisible).

A. In Joshua Tree National Monument. 15 miles from Twenty nine Palms Visitor Center on road to Cottonwood.
Materials: dry color, rocks, dessert wildflower seed.

John Baldessari
George Nicolaidis
September, 1969

Plate 22. John Baldessari, *California Map Project, Part 1: California,* 1969. Eleven color photographs and one typewritten text on paper. Photographs 8 × 10 inches (20.3 × 25.4 cm); text 8½ × 11 inches (21.6 × 27.9 cm). Courtesy of the Estate of John Baldessari and Marian Goodman Gallery.

Plate 23. John Baldessari, *Aligning: Balls (Version B)* (detail), 1972. Forty-one color photographs and graphite on wall. Photographs each 3½ × 5 inches (8.9 × 12.7 cm), overall dimensions variable (depending on wall length). Courtesy of the Estate of John Baldessari and Marian Goodman Gallery.

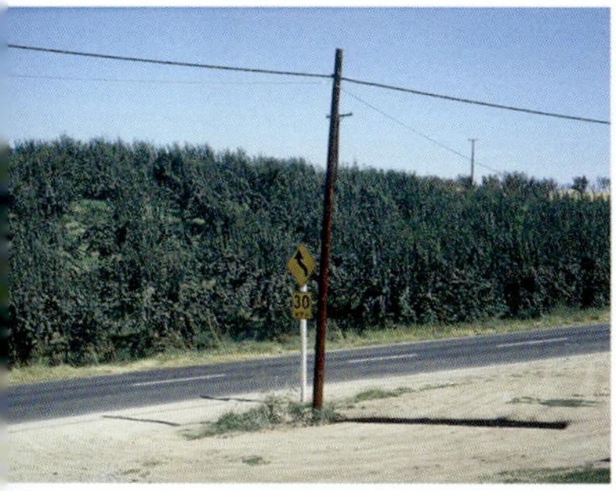

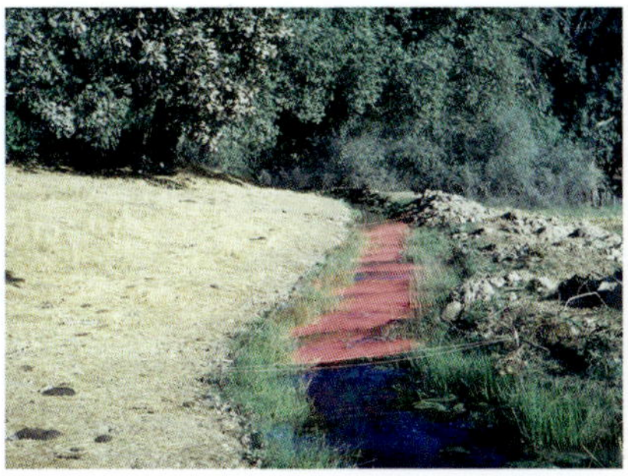

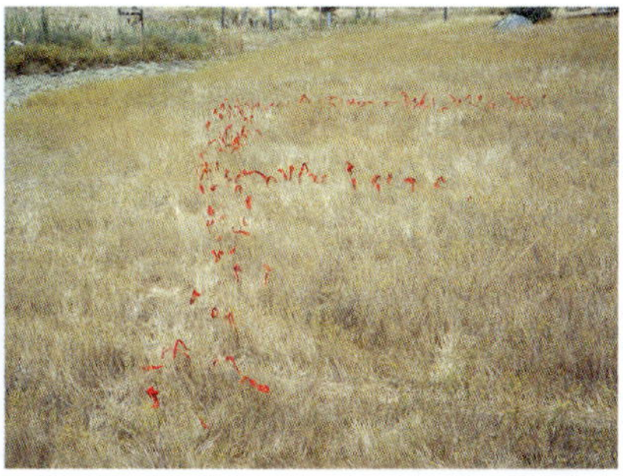

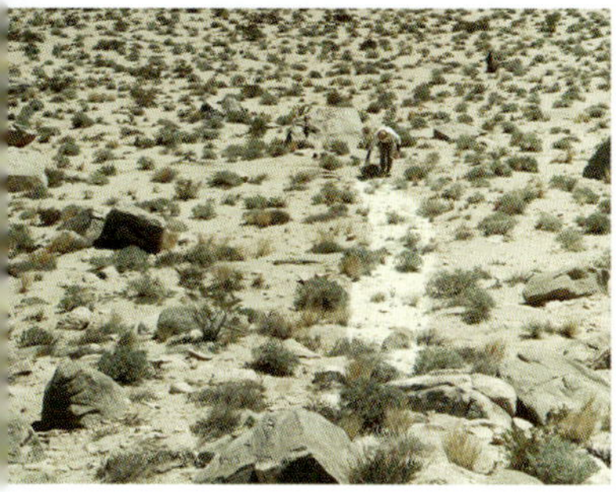

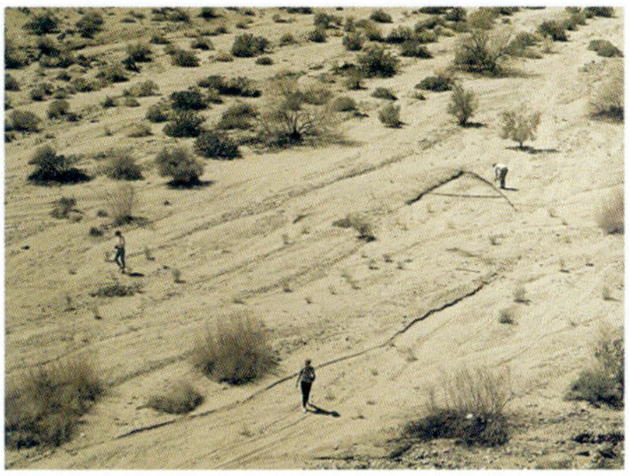

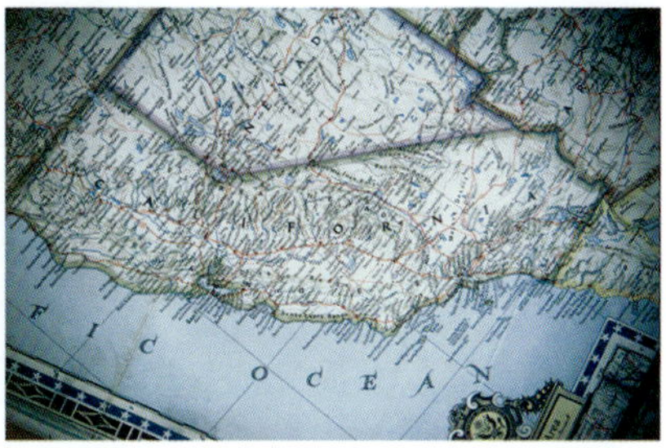
FIC OCEAN

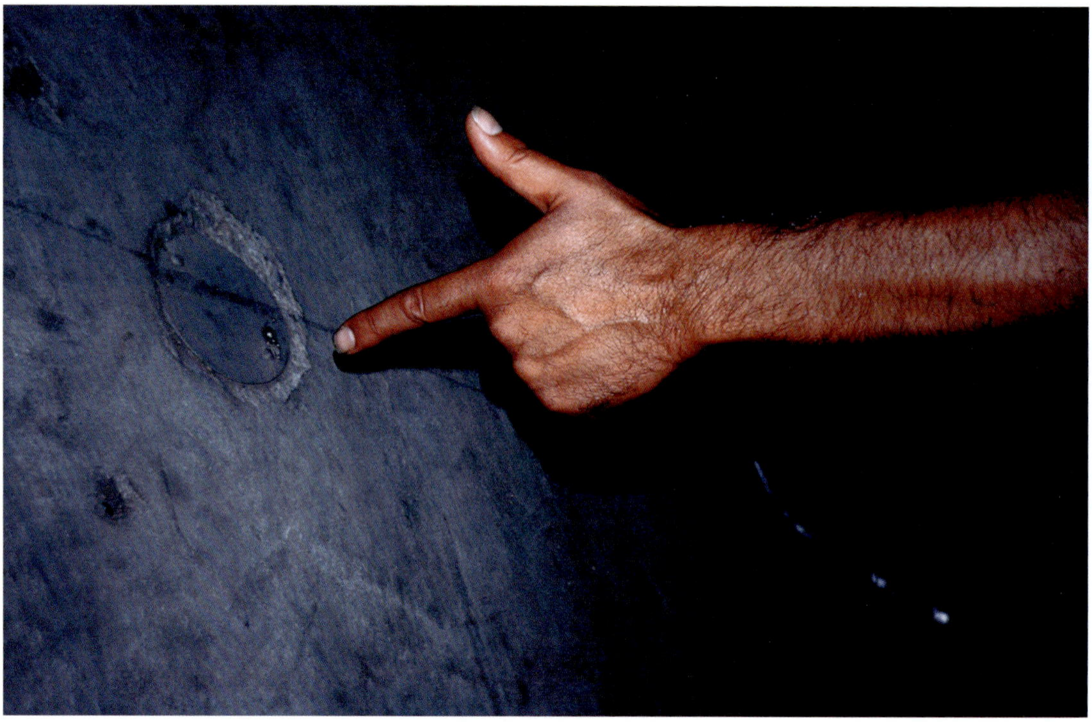

Plate 24. John Baldessari, *Pointing: Circle,* 1999 (photographed in 1969). Color photograph on board, 28¾ × 42½ inches (73 × 108 cm). Courtesy of the Estate of John Baldessari and Marian Goodman Gallery.

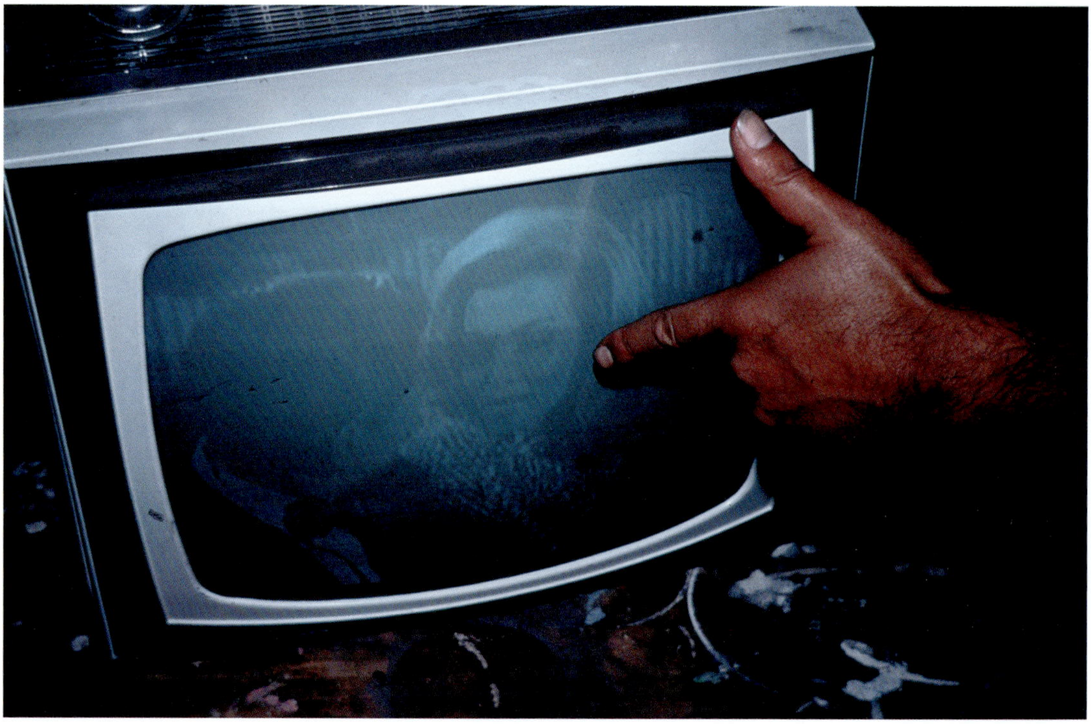

Plate 25. John Baldessari, *Pointing: T.V. Set,* 1999 (photographed in 1969). Color photograph on board, 28¾ × 42½ inches (73 × 108 cm). Courtesy of the Estate of John Baldessari and Marian Goodman Gallery.

breathing presence. It is in this way that the Bechers' subjects exceed the confines of their function as industry and live on through photography. A consideration of the Bechers' photographic work in this regard reveals important interventions within Huebler's use of photographic portraiture.

Rather than close down the possibility of subjective readings, the grid somewhat paradoxically exposes the need to address subjective content and the grid's own insufficiency. It also reveals the ways in which this structural formation implies the possibility of life outside the frame. As I have shown with the extensive *Everyone Alive* project, Huebler shared the Bechers' interest in the ongoing photographic archive and, like the Bechers, frequently displayed his photographs in a grid pattern. I argue, however, that Huebler's use of the grid and his turn to portraiture as a mode are not exclusively gestures in the name of modernist aesthetics, as so many critics have claimed. Rather, read as potential counterpoints, Huebler and the Bechers expose the preconceived "objectivity" of the grid as a strategy for mapping the contradictions of their subjects. The grid formation's proposal of nonhierarchical order, founded on its modular, mathematical, and repetitive structure, allows exponentially for infinite possibilities of difference rather than finite conclusions. Upon closer scrutiny, the rationale of the self-contained grid reveals itself as illusory.

A closer look at the theorization of the grid as the emblematic structure of modernist visual art sheds light on the conundrum at hand. In the touchstone essay "Grids" of 1979, Rosalind Krauss described the assertive gravitational pull of this formal construction:

> Surfacing in pre-War cubist painting and subsequently becoming ever more stringent and manifest, the grid announces, among other things, modern art's will to silence, its hostility to literature, to narrative, to discourse. As such, the grid has done its job with striking efficiency. The barrier it has lowered between the arts of vision and those of language has been almost totally successful in walling the visual arts into a realm of exclusive visuality and defending them against the intrusion of speech. The arts, of course, have paid dearly for this success, because the fortress they constructed on the foundation of the grid has increasingly become a ghetto.[61]

Krauss goes on to argue that, in addition to the enclosure provided by this systematic structure, the grid acts as a kind of self-proclaimed signature of the essential "modernity of modern art" in two ways: the spatial and the temporal. Regarding the spatial, she writes: "The grid states the autonomy of the realm of art. Flattened, geometricized, ordered, it is antinatural, antimimetic, antireal."[62] In the flatness of the grid, Krauss asserts, the dimensions of real objects are "crowded out" and replaced by the "lateral spread of a single surface."[63] Though Krauss does not discuss photography explicitly in this essay, I believe the display of photographs in a grid distinctly (albeit somewhat paradoxically) challenges the modernist sensibility she identifies. The photograph's persistent connection to lived experience and to multiple temporalities, as well as its inherent mimetic drive, confounds the presumed reductive order of the grid. The subject of the photograph, particularly when that subject is posed as a portrait, returns artistic inquiry to the cacophony that exceeds the grid's imagined parameters. This point is crucial for unpacking the radical shift proposed by artists using photography as conceptual art in the late sixties. Photography allowed a move away from high modernism, but additionally, and more poignantly, it provided an avenue to understand how photography as medium uncannily unfastened binaries of perception and categorical systems at this juncture.

In his oft-cited essay "'Marks of Indifference': Aspects of Photography in, or as, Conceptual Art" (1995), the photographer and art historian Jeff Wall contends that photography occupied conceptual artists as a way for photography to realize itself as a modernist art.[64] For Wall (and others in his footsteps), the evocation of the grid as an organizational format for many photoconceptual artists, including Sol LeWitt and Jan Dibbets, is but one way that he sees this manifest. More significantly, and this concerns the work of Huebler, Wall asserted that the seemingly arbitrary parameters of the "project" involving "systems of documentation" were ultimately exactly that: arbitrary.

Wall claims, with explicit reference to Huebler, that "the more the assignment is emptied of what could normatively [be] considered to be compelling social subject matter, the more visible it is simply as an instance of structure, an order, and the more clearly it can be experienced as a model of relationships between writing and photography. By emptying subject matter from his practice of photography, Huebler recapitulates important aspects of the development of modernist painting." Huebler's artworks, in Wall's view, are models of modernist abstract art in that their preoccupation is, in effect, nothing more and nothing less than the idea of art.

Building on this logic, Wall makes a somewhat surprising connection, and introduces the early twentieth-century Dutch de Stijl painter Piet Mondrian as Huebler's aesthetic kin. With a sweeping jump through history, Wall envisions both Mondrian and Huebler as artists who moved away from representation to "only a residual depictive value" and eventually to abstraction as a way to escape subjectivity and investigate the limits of the medium itself. In other words, Wall challenges his readers to think of art not as concerned with questions of representation per se but as a phenomenon engaged with its own internal structural relations, with the end goal of negating any specific subject. The link to Mondrian may at first seem a stretch, especially since Huebler's use of photography ties him directly to representational and figurative art in a manner that contrasts starkly with Mondrian's vision of paint. Nevertheless, there are persuasive aspects to Wall's argument, particularly if one ignores the actual content of Huebler's photographs, which Wall himself hastily dismisses, choosing to assign the pictures a subordinate value to the "program" or attendant statements, since the photographs appear aesthetically amateurish, and according to Wall, they decree only that "there is nothing of significance to depict."[65] The lack of significance that Wall notes in Huebler's photographic portraits reveals and reinforces his own entrenched ideological position. How can the sea of faces that are indeed depicted in Huebler's photographs be simply "nothing of significance"? Huebler's self-professed conception of his work was founded on his belief "in the capacity of the simple to be as worthy as the grand,"[66] and with that, such works are invested with the desire to look beyond the surface of the image as an image for its own sake.

Wall's refusal to take seriously the contingent and unstable role of the subject in the social as a provocation within Huebler's practice exemplifies his hermetic ideas about conceptual art. Reinstating his argument with unabated fervor two decades later, Wall describes Huebler's use of photography as a "passenger on the reductivist ride."[67] Huebler would have firmly disagreed with this interpretation of his work. In the early 1970s, in response to being asked whether he believed an artist could indeed "abstract" himself and his work from the "real" world, Huebler adamantly proclaimed: "I do not at all intend to situate myself [or my work] outside of society!"[68] Later, wrestling with the deliberate ambiguity of his practice, Huebler echoed Nauman's imperative that people "pay attention," by positioning himself in telling opposition to yet another abstract painter, saying,

> That *is* what I consider to be my social desire, my social responsibility. . . . I'm not interested in being easily seen. I know my work would be a lot more successful if I had stripped away an awful lot and made it as clear as [Kenneth] Noland's stripes. I want more out of my work for myself than that. I would like to accomplish that goal of getting people to really pay attention. That shouldn't be an easy goal for the artist or the audience.[69]

Wall cites Huebler's *Duration Piece #7, Rome, March 1973* to make his case. This particular piece involves photographs of the famed Trevi Fountain taken at thirty-second intervals, which, according to the accompanying statement, are intended "to document specific changes in the relationship between two aspects of the water falling from the rocks in one area of the Fountain of Trevi." Wall willfully ignores the actual content of the image, claiming only that it is "emptied of what could normatively be considered to be compelling social subject matter."[70] A critical counter-reading would ponder Huebler's statement for the piece, noting its facetiousness (at least in part), especially bearing in mind that these photographs depict groups of tourists posing for souvenir photos in capricious and often-exaggerated positions, and with varying degrees of comportment ranging from seriousness to comedic parodies in front of Nicola Salvi's baroque masterpiece. Despite the fact that Huebler's statement calls attention to the water, how can one ignore these figures and their theater so easily? Especially since some of them appear to be vying intently for the camera's, and by extension the viewer's, attention. Their expressions solicit "Look at me!" while their behavior declares "I was here." Their inclusion in the piece, though seemingly haphazard, should not be overlooked. Their act of photographing within Huebler's photographs serves as yet another meta-commentary on the multivalence of photography, particularly as it functions in the "second-degree." In this regard,

Sontag's remarks from the 1970s seem apt: "The camera makes everyone a tourist in other people's reality, and eventually in one's own."[71] As emblems of tourism and tourist photography, Huebler's piece engages questions about yet another economy of the photograph and "social subject matter" while exposing an alternative version of photography's promise and failure to capture and contain the world outside the parameters of fine art.[72]

The magnetic and symbolic pull of the Trevi Fountain bears noting, as the site reappears in duplicate in Huebler's *Duration Piece #25, Rome, 1973* (1973), a work that compares a photograph by Huebler to an appropriated postcard, again raising questions involving the reproducibility and mass circulation of both images and people. Notably, as a tourist destination, the Trevi Fountain soared to iconic status after it was glamorously featured as the enchanting set of one of Federico Fellini's most unforgettable cinematic scenes, when Anita Ekberg and Marcello Mastroianni wade in the fountain in the 1960 comic-drama *La Dolce Vita*. The protagonist Marcello follows the impulsive Sylvia into the water and declares softly, "We're all making a mistake." His character's dilemma throughout the film, as a writer grappling with the existential crisis of choosing between journalism and literature, or we might say, popular culture versus fine art, sheds additional light on Huebler's evocation of the Trevi Fountain as backdrop. It seems appropriate to consider the implied tensions between illusionism versus realism here, and elite versus commonplace (or avant-garde versus kitsch), that course through both Huebler's and Fellini's narratives.

In contrast to the modernism Wall desires to align Huebler with, Huebler's photographs affably test the certainty of the modernist program and the modernist grid to the point where its infinite ungroundedness, and in Huebler's words, his "infinite extension,"[73] become apparent. We saw similar engagement with concepts of expansion and ungroundedness in Bochner's use of photography. In a related vein, through photography, Huebler unveils the contingency of the system itself as well as the instability of subjectivity and perception. Noting how Huebler is "methodical rather than formulaic,"[74] the painter, art critic, and theorist Jeremy Gilbert-Rolfe claimed emphatically that "Huebler's work is about the 'deconstruction' of the familiar."[75] This observation allows for a comparison with other readings of abstract art that segues back to Huebler's possible connection to Mondrian, with a difference.

Krauss perceptively noted the "curious paradoxes by which the use of the grid is marked at every turn,"[76] including its ability to be read in opposing and even contradictory ways. Not surprisingly, Mondrian is also the artist evoked by Krauss to illustrate this point, demonstrating that the grid can function in both "centrifugal" and "centripetal" ways. In the centrifugal reading, the grid presents the given work of art "as a mere fragment, a tiny piece arbitrarily cropped from an infinitely larger fabric . . . operat[ing] from the work of art outward, compelling our acknowledgement of a world beyond the frame."[77] The centripetal reading works oppositely, moving inward from the frame, declaratively separating the work of art from the world.[78] Wall sees only the centripetal reading, and for him, this is the connection between Huebler's art and Mondrian's. This is only one possible approach, however.

Arguably the art of both Huebler and Mondrian can be read quite convincingly as simultaneously centripetal and centrifugal, a tension that suspends their work from any essential understanding. Krauss mentions Mondrian's *Composition IA* (1930), an example that functions similarly to *Composition in White and Black (Painting I)* (1926), the work with which Meyer Schapiro famously buttressed his claims in "Mondrian: Order and Randomness in Abstract Painting" (1978), published in *Mondrian: On the Humanity of Abstract Painting* (1995). This correlation is useful because it is precisely "humanity" and its fallibility that Wall dismisses. Instead, in using Mondrian as an example of an inflexible commitment to art for art's sake, Wall neglects the works by Mondrian that conversely propose questions about the contingency of life within and without the frame of art.

Mondrian wrote that his goal was to achieve an art of "pure relations"; however, many of his works suggest that there is no knowable absolute or comprehensive purity in art. The works cited by Krauss and Schapiro, for example, seem "at first glance [as] a square set within a diamond square," yet they become "to the probing eye a complex design with a subtly balanced asymmetry of unequal lines."[79] A caesura in understanding occurs, in which the whole is recognized "as a cropped representation. . . . The missing parts are cut off from view at the limits of the diamond field,"[80] and the illusion of autonomy is shattered. One is confronted with the incompleteness of the forms, as well as with how the forms exceed the limits of the frame, causing what seemed at first legible and clear to become discontinuous and problematic.

A similar dynamic occurs in Huebler's projects, and his dubious documents ask viewers to question their own preconceptions about the boundaries between art and life. The photograph in particular implies a contained space because of its geometric and modular form; however, as the comparison with Mondrian reveals, counter to Wall's reading, the pronounced asymmetries and the continuation of the work into an unknown space beyond the frame can never entirely be repressed. This is especially true when presented with human faces as subject matter.

Consider the doubt this casts on the concept of objectivity. It becomes apparent why the grid was attractive to conceptual artists as a way to address accumulation while defying categories. Measured and deliberately banal, as seen in the logic of the Bechers' archival project, the use of the grid as an organizing principle appealed to conceptualists, who saw it as a format with which to challenge the so-called objectivity of institutional rhetoric by turning it against itself.

To extend this genealogical lineage even further, clearly both the Bechers and Huebler were influenced by the early twentieth-century portrait photographer August Sander and his famous attempt to record a pictorial sociology of faces of the German people compiled under the title *Face of Our Time* (1929). Starting from the premise that "we know that people are formed by the light and air, by their inherited traits, and their actions. We can tell from appearance the work someone does or does not do; we can read in his face whether he is happy or troubled," Sander photographed subjects from all walks of life and created a typological catalog of more than six hundred photographs of the German people.[81] Sander's nearly mystical allusion to "light and air" may also be taken as an equivocal reflection on the abstract genesis of people and of photography.

The Nazis banned Sander's portraits in the 1930s because the subjects did not adhere to the ideal Aryan ideology, somewhat ironically condemning the project as "anti-social."[82] To put it another way, these photographs admitted their inability to either contain or maintain an objective type or face, or a readable map of the nation. Sander nevertheless continued his photographic archive until his death. Though the project was intended to be a comprehensive picture of the German people, it resulted in revealing the poignant incompleteness theorem of the photograph and the archive. *Face of Our Time* displayed the differences that could not be assimilated, and this categorical refusal earned Sander the distaste of the Third Reich. Sander's archive of portraits, like Huebler's *Variable Piece #70,* was never finished, and remained a work in progress as long as he lived.[83] The impracticality and obsessive seriality of such projects were one of the main fascinations for conceptualists, many of whom, like Huebler, were devoted to dissembling and disassembling conventional organizational, linguistic, and visual systems of representation.

Methods of collection and uniformity were a way to challenge dominant understandings of typologies as well as the construct of history. In fact, the notion of history as rational, causative, and accumulative provides a rich counterpoint to Huebler's aspirations for democratic representation enacted via photography's phenomenological and epistemological questioning. With his distinct disavowal of "purity" and of the "art" of photography, Huebler's snapshots consistently connect life beyond the frame with life within the frame. As Huebler explained, "I have never been as 'correct' or pure, as my friends Barry, Weiner, and Kosuth. I have always been interested in social/political content within the subject matter of the work. The 'everyone alive' format has provided me with a strategy whereby I can make a bridge between 'art' and ongoing social reality."[84] In contrast to the other artists who exhibited under the leadership of the gallerist Seth Siegelaub between 1968 and 1970, Huebler was not known for either a committed rejection of visuality or a strict emphasis on dematerialization in favor of language. Instead, Huebler explored the boundaries of language, visuality, and representation in relation to experience in the social world. The egalitarian potential of photography provided the ideal means for this investigation, with the emphasis placed on the "potential" without illusions of actually achieving the professed goal.

In addition to complicating the legibility of photographic representation, these photographs act as documents of their time by evoking Fredric Jameson's discerning description of the fate of the referent under pressure from the structural concept of the sign. According to Jameson, representation was pushed "to the point of imagining a map so rigorous and referential that it becomes coterminous with its object";[85] in other words, it collapses upon itself. Much like this excessive mapping, Huebler's radical and obsessive practice interrogates the equation between how "ways of knowing and ways of representing merge and inform one another."[86] As evidenced by previously discussed examples, the photograph, like the map, does indeed put one "into a certain relation with the world that feels like knowledge—and, therefore, like power."[87] Huebler himself noted the fallibility of this correlation. Discussing such conceits of mastery, the artist explained:

> Of course, by making a dot on a map, you are really covering perhaps twenty or forty square feet, or circular feet. And there's no proof that when you get there you're pointing your camera, or putting your marker on the exact spot, which of course is the point too. It doesn't matter, you see. It could have been three or four feet over, or you could have miscalculated just because your pencil was too thick . . . any number of things. So what it finally comes back to is the idea of these locations, the idea of the system.[88]

The map, like the photograph, is unable to truly cohere with real lived experience. This analogy is explored further in my discussion of Baldessari's *California Map Project / Part 1: California* (1969) in the following chapter. In both the photograph and the map it may seem that one can hold the world in one's hands, but this is illusory. It is not by chance that mapping as a methodological approach reappears repeatedly throughout Huebler's work, primarily as a duplicitous way to deny, rather than grant, access to the real, highlighting instead the discrepancies between perceived reality, objectivity, and lived experience. Through this lens, the nonidentical status between any two corresponding images is precisely what becomes most obvious in the cases of Huebler, the Bechers, and Sander.

Counterfigurations

In an era characterized by an unprecedented casualness toward picture making and circulation, public and private images have become increasingly elided, and Warhol's prophecy that everyone will be famous for fifteen minutes has become all the more prescient. The imagined uniqueness of fame is continually countered by the ubiquity of the photograph, even as the photograph is often the very means by which that fame is generated. How can we understand this desire for the photograph and the strange relations it provokes?

In his 1958 essay "The Ontology of the Photographic Image," André Bazin traced what he called the "mummy complex" of the plastic arts—namely, that drive to preserve life by a representation of life or, in other words, a view of the development of artistic methods over time as the advancement of progressive insurance policies against death.[89] One of the underlying questions is how much life can, in any case, be preserved. In a footnote, Bazin briefly mentions the contest between photographic reporting and the use of drawings in illustrative magazines during the early twentieth century, saying that the latter fulfilled a "baroque need for the dramatic." By contrast, he explains that photographs functioned as documents of objective information, irrevocably tied to the plainness of reality through their automatic genesis, rather than having the ability to evoke as persuasively as drawing or painting the suggestive nuances of either comedy or tragedy in life. Bazin states explicitly that "a feeling for the photographic document developed only gradually."[90]

This curious statement further incites my inquiry into photographic portraiture under the aegis of conceptual art in the late 1960s, especially into Huebler's multifaceted projects. The question of photography's theatrical power and affective wiles remained relevant, for even in 1970 it seemed that this "feeling for the photographic document" that Bazin noted was still nascent. To "feel photography" in opposition to, or at least in conjunction with, thinking photography, the medium needed to have the boundaries of its "resemblance complex" investigated,[91] and to be considered akin to language, as messages of relative affect—having meaning only in relation to others. Each photograph possesses a singularity yet is also intimately and ontologically connected to all other photographs, and thus needs to be read among others if any convincing legibility is to be gained. This realization acquires even more resonance when considering portraits. Moreover, any inquiry into the affective logic of photography needs to consider how the complex relationship between objectivity and subjectivity functions within this peculiar medium.

Affect in photography generally cleaves to subject matter as a way to understand the subject. Be it the pained or elated look of a face, or the pleasure or poignancy in a gesture, these are the signs and symptoms that one looks for to read the image. This cleaving between the affect and the subject plays provocatively on the polysemic significance of "to cleave": meaning at once brought together, tied as one, as well as separated and wrought apart. The instability of this verb itself makes it the perfect fit for describing Huebler's paradoxical photographs and his portraits' affective logic. What we might believe we understand in one moment is contradicted in the next, playing on assumptions, playing on the deceptive nature of reality and the ontology of the photograph. By analyzing photographic representations that claim technologically to "capture" emotion, we see how Huebler's practice works against the commodification of feeling presented by popular advertising. Moreover, it suggests a counterdiscourse to the narrative of rationalized dematerialization that is often attributed to conceptual art.

A direct example of the influential connection between Huebler and the Bechers that goes beyond the formal logic I have already discussed, and that gives insight into the counterdiscourse offered by Huebler, is *Variable Piece #101, West Germany, March 1973* (Figure 3.13). For this piece, Huebler took photographs of Bernd Becher, whom he asked to act out stereotypes of various roles, including a priest, a criminal, a spy, a philosopher, a nice guy, a policeman, and a lover. In a clever and nearly anachronistic reversal of roles, the question becomes: who is under the influence? It has been suggested that this piece be read as two friends getting drunk together.[92] And yes, images and concepts are indeed as contorted as Bernd's face. Becher, as an icon of deadpan seriousness and the advent of early photoconceptualism, here becomes the embodiment of serial typologies. Read as an inebriated friend, these images playfully challenge the sobriety of Sander and Neue Sachlichkeit (New Objectivity), here exposing objectivity in photographic terms as always compro-

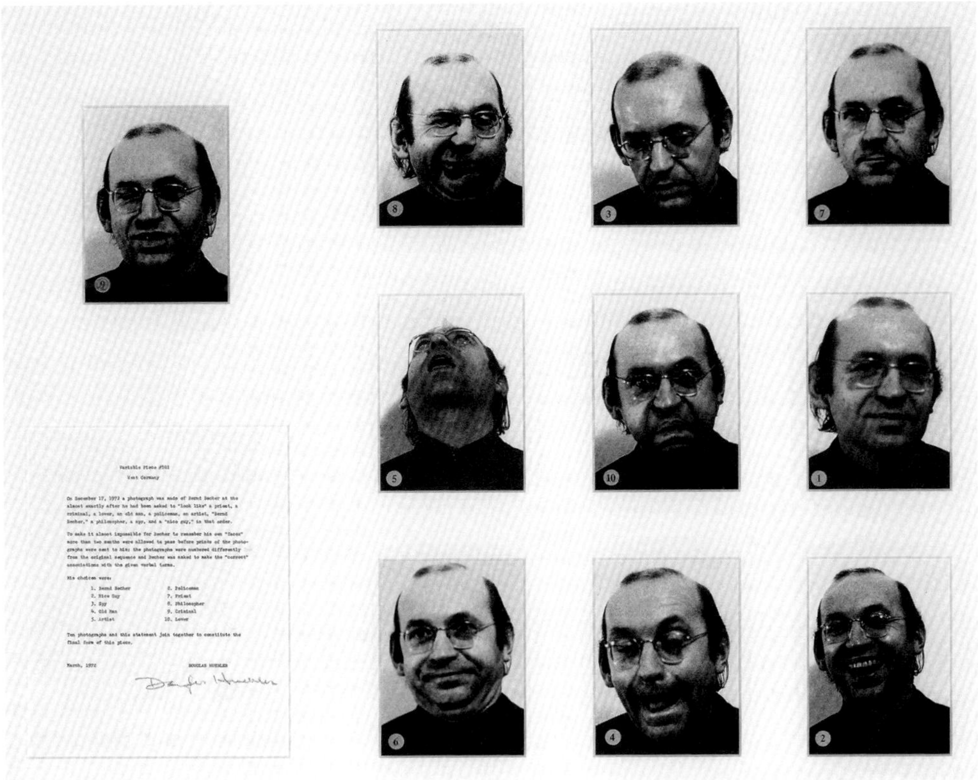

Figure 3.13. Douglas Huebler, *Variable Piece #101, West Germany, March 1973,* 1973. Copyright 2019 Estate of Douglas Huebler / Artists Rights Society (ARS), New York. Courtesy of Darcy Huebler / Artist Rights Society (ARS), New York and Paula Cooper Gallery, New York.

mised, and with one's perceptual subjectivity continuously questioned and contingent. As demonstrated in Hughes's astute analysis, it becomes impossible to trace the stereotypes to their corresponding representations.[93] The portraits are shot in a straight-on manner similar to the assiduousness of the Bechers' photographs, yet they do so in order to challenge the Bechers and other photographers who claimed that they do "not hide or exaggerate or depict anything in an untrue fashion."[94] Huebler's counterfigurations point instead to an overriding inability to map any singular identity with or within any particular system. Whereas Sander's documentation of faces was systematized with the goal of being comprehensive, here these grimaces present themselves as fragments of a greater whole and mimic the very idea of a system by pushing the limits of a singular subject's multiplicity of identities. In performing this system, they reveal the absurdity of the system itself.

These portraits, together with a written statement, constitute the final form of the piece. Two months after the shoot, Huebler mailed the photographs to Bernd, asking him to order them in relation to the list of verbal terms he had been asked to portray. His acting out for the camera and the word-to-image correlation are never clearly retraced, however. Humorously, they seem to become increasingly mixed up, as they play provocatively on the viewer's desire to believe the associations based on our own conventions of these terms. This game of mismatched identities lacks coherence. The chronology of the system is disturbed by chance, interrupted by time, and it is hard to sort through which images might be more convincingly natural (e.g., "artist" or "Bernd Becher") and which are more staged (e.g., "spy" or "criminal"). Twice removed and once doubled, Becher's attempts to decipher which photographs of himself are which further relay the question of "who's who?" Beyond ridiculing the exaggerated animation of subjects photographed by the fast and loose style of New York School photographers such as Garry Winogrand or Richard Avedon, these images also demystify the restraint of Becher's signature systems-based categorical photography.[95] The grimaces captured by the photograph remain fugitive. They collapse "the structure of the system into an undifferentiated system of indifference";[96] despite the orderly grid and the conventional frame, the subject remains untethered.

Instead of allowing the photographic subject the sense of being a unified whole, Huebler's images resonate with both Walter Benjamin's and Siegfried Kracauer's observations that the increasing technological sophistication of photography divests both the object and the subject of uniqueness. Further to the camera's claims to scientific objectivity, it is important to note how the link between photography and physiognomy, particularly in Germany, is being marked and mocked in *Variable Piece #101.* Physiognomy, the discredited pseudo-science of reading difference between faces across images, implicates photography in a slippery history of surveillance culture and categorization. As a mode of resistance, Huebler consistently destabilizes the photograph's documentary status by pointing to the kinds of information it cannot convey.[97] In refusing to take themselves too seriously, these photographs deliberately provide comic relief from modernism's solipsistic position; they are denial of any concept of "true" knowledge grounded in the self.

Huebler's *Variable Piece #28, Truro, Massachusetts* (1970) may be seen as a foil to the work with Becher as pliable subject (Figure 3.14). Here, Huebler's daughter posed for a series of close-up portraits, being instructed to keep a "straight face" while her siblings, outside the frame of the image, tried to make her laugh. The touching failure of this piece, resulting in this case in the recording of the laughing child, is again the source of the work's conceptual and humorous success. As in his other works, in performing the system and testing the premise, the photographs reveal the absurdity of the system itself. Presenting the photographs in the form of documentation alongside the text does not allow one to map out certainty.[98] The format might suggest that rationalism underpins this information, yet the text and the images tell us otherwise. Instead, each of Huebler's pieces is open-ended, revealing a profound suspicion of dogmatism and unfastening the very idea that meaning can be decisive.

Huebler's desire to frustrate legibility, to simultaneously challenge and contradict affective logic manifests itself (as I am describing) through numerous strategies. One of the most dominant ways, as seen in the Becher piece, is the seemingly arbitrary

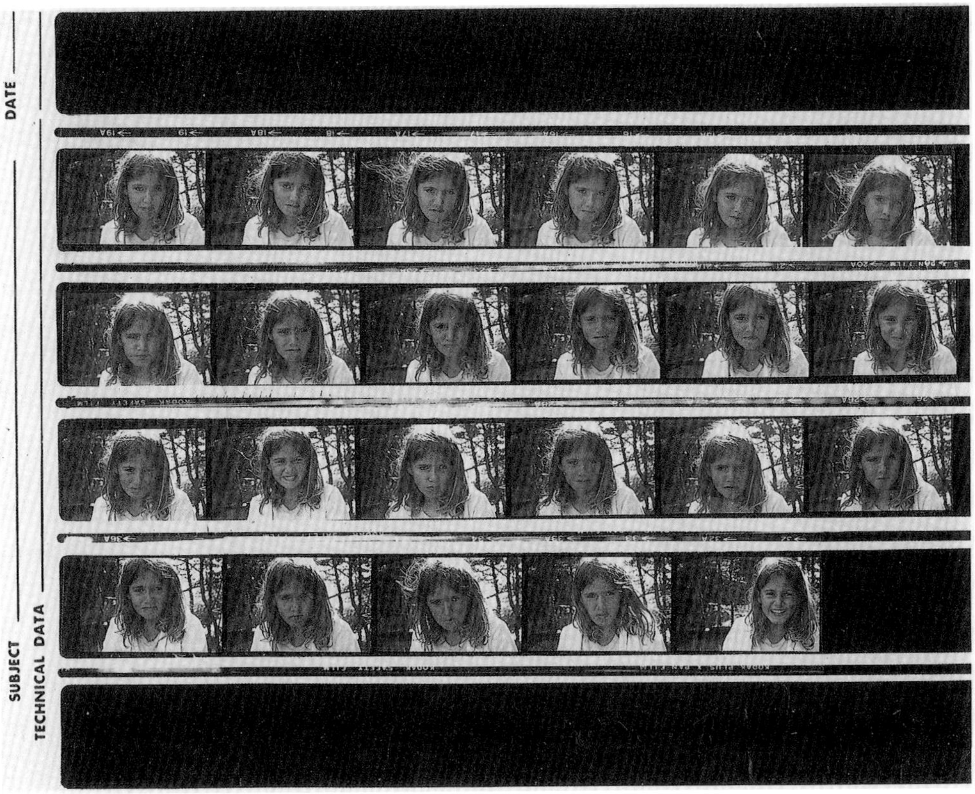

Figure 3.14. *Variable Piece #28, Truro, Massachusetts, 1970,* 1970. Copyright 2019 Estate of Douglas Huebler / Artists Rights Society (ARS), New York. Courtesy of Darcy Huebler / Artist Rights Society (ARS), New York and Paula Cooper Gallery, New York.

shuffling of photographs out of sequence so that their meanings can never be entirely resolved. Huebler deliberately confuses the "one thing after another" sequential logic of serial and systems-based art coming out of minimalism and highlights the succession of temporal disjunctures that inhabit all photographs. As Huebler wrote in a catalog statement for his exhibition at the Palais des Beaux-Arts in Brussels in 1997: "The photographs which have been made in sequence are presented in a scrambled order," thereby challenging the structure of the system with the irrepressibility of difference.[99] This rupture in Huebler's work, in contrast to the interpretations of many writers on the subject, is about more than exposing the enclosed logic of the system. After 1970 Huebler works almost exclusively with photographic portraiture, thereby questioning the very human affects of systems. Using faces instead of impersonal structures such as blocks or numbers is not haphazard, even if the order of the work overall is given up to chance.

Conceptual artists like Huebler used the camera's instantaneity to their advantage; it was employed as a seemingly innocent form of documentation. Without artistic considerations of form and composition, lighting and lenses, *Variable Piece #34,*

Bradford, Massachusetts, December 1970 resembles a sociological survey, but very different from Sander's (Figure 3.15). Less overt than Becher's theater for Huebler's camera, but nevertheless performative and random, Huebler photographed anonymous people on the street at the exact instant after each had been told "You have a beautiful face." Bringing to mind Barthes's comments on the self-conscious feeling of being photographed and becoming other in that instant, *Variable Piece #34* documents the interaction of the self with the other, and the self-as-other, in social space. Barthes also marked what he called "a cunning dissociation of consciousness from identity,"[100] that was chiefly enacted not within a singular photograph but as a result of any photograph. This complication suggests that while photography might be inherently an index of the real, it does not preclude the difficulty of putting one's finger on that "real." In a 1977 interview with the curator Michael Auping, Huebler shared this sentiment about his designation of beautiful faces:

> I can say that about any face because every face is. That has to do with my interest in appearance and suspending these kinds of value judgements about appearance. It also developed out of me being in the streets, using the camera and finding out the power the camera has and the social reactions that people have to it, how they duck, how they cringe and so forth. To pose for your photograph or in front of a television camera is to be the most self-conscious that you can be, and it's a self-conscious without a reflection. . . . there's no reflective feedback. It's a risk.[101]

The arbitrary selection of subjects, because of the a priori decision that every face is beautiful simply because it is a human face, exemplifies the tension between individuality and universality. This affirmative rhetorical intervention also works against the reigning social principles of advertising, which incessantly remind us of what we lack as opposed to reassuring our individual wholeness. Here, all typologies are obfuscated even as the presentation of these portraits is systematized, allowing for a situation in which all individuals may be regarded as equally beautiful rather than erratically lacking. Their seriality as photographs works to show how meaning is constructed across signifieds while further critiquing the modernist values of purity, autonomy, and beauty.

An essential property of this project for Huebler was recording the reactive positioning of those confronted with his camera and his flattery, or in other words, how they composed themselves in the moment of exposure.

> To turn [the] situation inside out I designed a project which I thought would relieve the subject of the classic anxiety associated with posing for the camera: I asked passersby on public streets if I could photograph them for a study that I was making of faces (I never mention "art" when doing such projects), and to those willing to pose I would say at just the instant before clicking the shutter, "you have a beautiful face . . ." or, "an interesting face . . . ," or whatever seemed appropriate

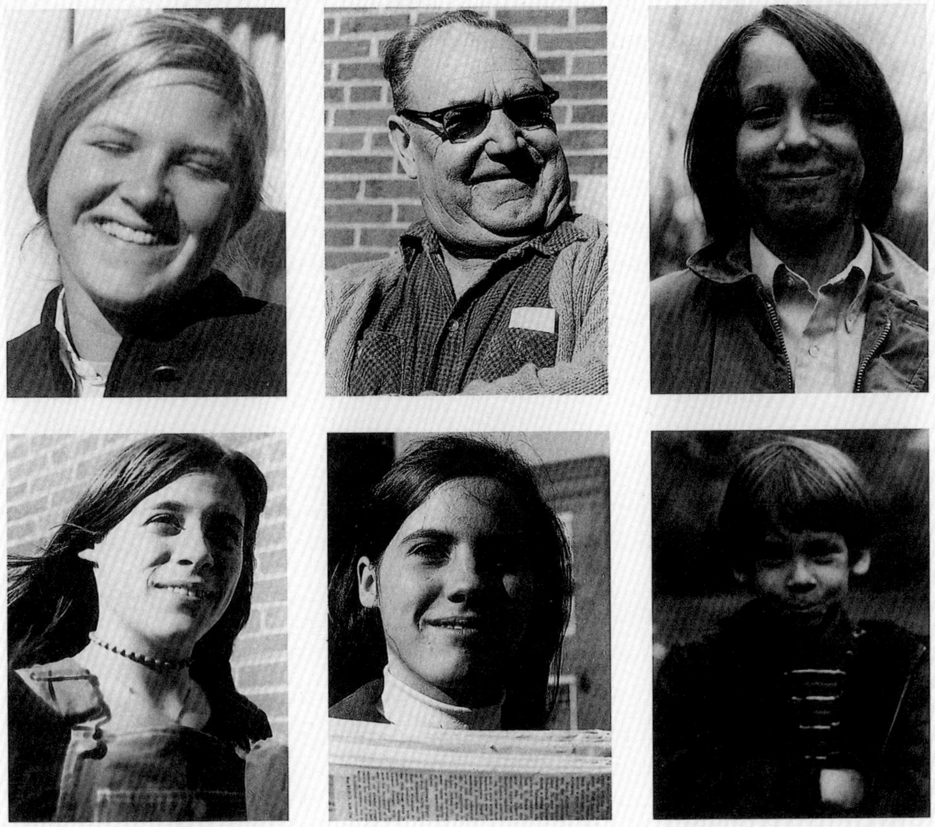

Figure 3.15. Douglas Huebler, *Variable Piece #34, Bradford, Massachusetts, December 1970,* 1970. Copyright 2019 Estate of Douglas Huebler / Artists Rights Society (ARS), New York. Courtesy of Darcy Huebler / Artist Rights Society (ARS), New York and Paula Cooper Gallery, New York.

> to say in each case. My objective was to record the look on the face of the subject when his or her normal anxiety was alleviated by highly supportive comments which filled in for the missing "mirror." Furthermore, I felt that the camera had been transformed from an instrument of intimidation into a means of mediating the usual social distance that exists between strangers.[102]

The category of beauty is brought to the fore, as an aesthetic equivalent that is here challenged by random selection. The photographic archive of beauty harks back to yet another project emerging from Weimar's Neue Sachlichkeit photography: that of Albert Renger-Patzsch's book *The World Is Beautiful (Die Welt ist schön)* (1928) in which he systematically monumentalized a broad range of subjects via attentive close-ups, among them flora, fauna, and the factory. Whereas Bertolt Brecht criticized the image of the factory for telling us next to nothing about the conditions of production, Huebler's documentation that "the world is beautiful" as constituted by humans as opposed to machines tells us important things about social relations well beyond those of production.

Familiar Resemblances and Irreconcilable Differences

Location Piece #17, Turin, Italy, 1973 continues Huebler's mobilization of the tension between equivalence and difference by demonstrating how the devices of resemblance and make-believe constitute the ontology of the photograph (Figure 3.16).

> Location Piece #17
> Turin, Italy
>
> After photographing an arbitrarily chosen location lying just beyond the limits of ordinary perception, the artist walked directly to the site (the corner of Via Cosmo and Via Villa d. Regina) to learn what might actually be seen there. After taking one photograph he left, with no expectation of ever visiting that location again.
>
> When, at a much later time, the film was processed it revealed the fact that at the instant when the second photograph was taken a man was looking directly at the artist, a man bearing a strong resemblance to the artist—at least more so than almost everyone else in the world.
>
> March/December, 1973

Here Huebler dramatizes the uncanny notion of resemblance, and with that the somewhat absurd yet implicit desire for recognition based on shared appearance. Seeing himself in a stranger seems to at once challenge and confirm his sense of self. As a meta-reflection on the ways photographic representation is often premised on resemblance or verisimilitude, Huebler points to photography's stealthy, almost mask-like ability to distract awareness from its distortions and abstractions. Instead, the photograph insists on the reality of its appearance. In the instance of Huebler's Italian look-alike, the viewer's task is to connect the narrative dots, despite the confessed randomness of the overall project. Again, an allusion to the traditions of street photography comes into play, as a subtext of Huebler's scheme—but it is significant that the fleeting quality of the "decisive moment" remains unremarked until after the development process as opposed to before the clicking of the camera's shutter. Indeed, a lack of precision and decision seems heightened here.

With the inclusion of a small map, as in many other pieces, the unreliability of mapping positions is again exposed. Once more, the map is like the photograph in two seemingly contradicting ways: it can act as an instrument of analysis and pinpoint exactitudes and locations, and it is inescapably linked to a kind of self-deception necessary for its believability. In a 1969 interview, Huebler observed that the map is "never really a real thing, and yet we begin to assume it is a real thing. Most people experience maps or clocks or charts and so forth as very real

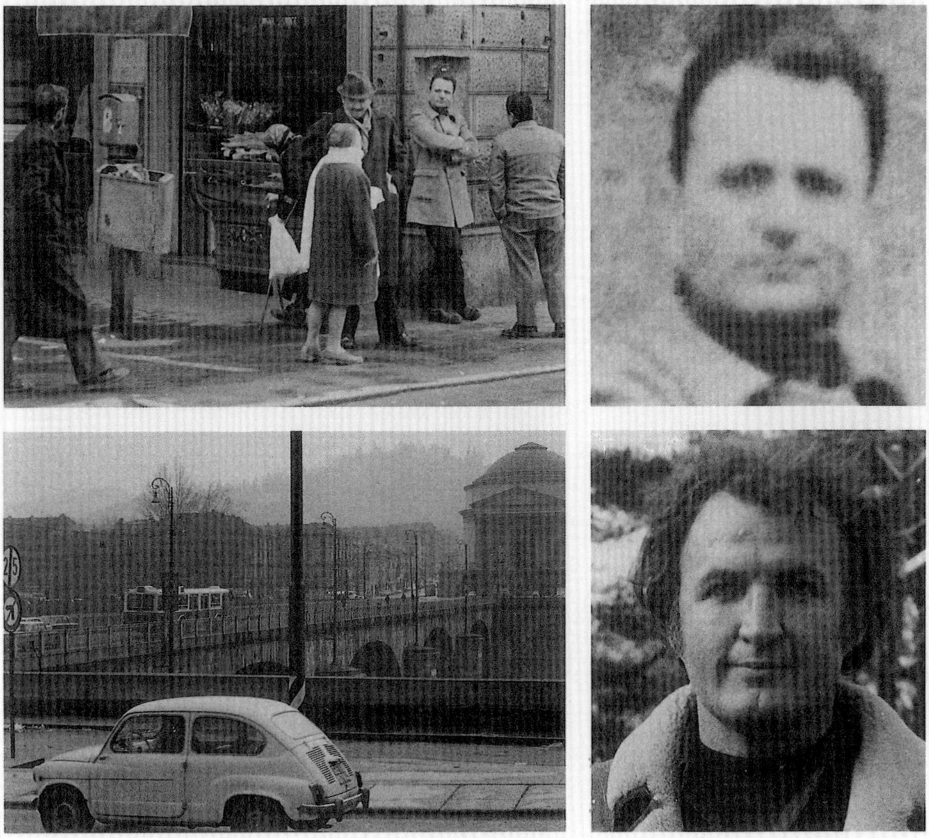

Figure 3.16. Douglas Huebler, *Location Piece #17, Turin, Italy, 1973,* 1973. Copyright 2019 Estate of Douglas Huebler / Artists Rights Society (ARS), New York. Courtesy of Darcy Huebler / Artist Rights Society (ARS), New York and Paula Cooper Gallery, New York.

life-defining phenomena, or whatever."[103] The viewer is made aware of the fact that pointing to something on a map or a photograph makes that point as abstract as it does concrete. All the empirical investments of such media show themselves to be pseudo-scientific and disorienting in the end, exponentially setting into motion a series of doubts alongside a series of proposed certainties.

The basic doubling effect of photography is further philosophically nuanced by *Location Piece #17.* According to John Berger's germinal estimation of 1972, "Understanding a Photograph": "The very principle of photography is that the resulting image is not unique, but on the contrary infinitely reproducible."[104] In this case, while "doubling" is underscored as the common denominator of all photographic devices, here the specific doubling of the "artist" further complicates the easy absorption of the subject. The frisson of the uncanny created by the doppelgänger effects the nomination of the artist, as his identity becomes effectively dispersed, his intention renounced. He could be someone else. He could be a stranger.

He could be the subject. In a reversal of fortunes, he could be almost everyone else in the world, and thus anyone else could be the artist. The position of the perceiving subject asked to evaluate these claims and make judgments about the narrator's reliability not only decenters authorship in this piece but sets in orbit various chances, operations, and possible resemblances. This piece, like Huebler's other definitively dubious documents, does not simply represent social reality; rather, it is part of social reality.

Huebler's practice embodies a broad critique of categorical photography, using photography and especially the portrait genre to constitute a radical destabilization of the Cartesian subject.[105] Asking the viewer to question subjective and objective identities occurs repeatedly in Huebler's photographs, and in every instance the uncanny seems to remain at large. Take, for example, *Duration Piece #15, Global, September 1969,* in which Huebler reproduced an FBI "Wanted" poster as a readymade, joined with a text in which Huebler personally offers to pay a $1,100 reward to anyone who apprehends the depicted criminal (Figure 3.17). The piece is for sale for $1,000, and the reward shrinks by $100 a month from the starting date of January 1, 1970; thus the artist risks losing money if the criminal is apprehended in the first three months. It is a game of risk and a jest/gesture to the burgeoning art market. The man arrested by the photograph remains a fugitive, captured by the camera yet on the loose. And, like all photographic referents, he deviates from expected norms and conventions.[106] His crime is as a suspected bank robber, but we are also told that he works as a commercial artist and as a silk screen worker, details that sound stranger than fiction but may very well be fact.[107]

Using this readymade from the official authorities draws attention again to the prevalent understanding of the term *information* at this juncture, especially *official information,* as endowed with directness, objectivity, and transparence—indelibly linked to the photograph itself. On the contrary, this piece solicits the viewer's participation to test the believability of the wanted poster and by extension the photograph. Notice, for example, the discrepancies between the two frontal portraits bookending the profile shot. The caption claims that one was taken in 1966 and the other in 1968. The photographs appear to be the same person, but only in the most superficial way. After looking at them for a few moments, irreconcilable differences begin to emerge, forcing one to question one's own perception and judgment. Calling attention to the ubiquity of law enforcement, surveillance culture, and the ways in which photography assists these judicial systems in public space, it refamiliarizes the viewer with what is perhaps most familiar and thus most readily invisible: the everyday and its intricate and underlying social relations. Connoting associations to Warhol's infamous silk screen *Thirteen Most Wanted Men* at the 1964 New York World's Fair, pointing accusations at these neutrally gridded images shows the system itself to be far from innocent.

These incriminating photographs belong to the arsenal of categorical photography and judicial regimes, as a way to expose not only incongruous characteristics

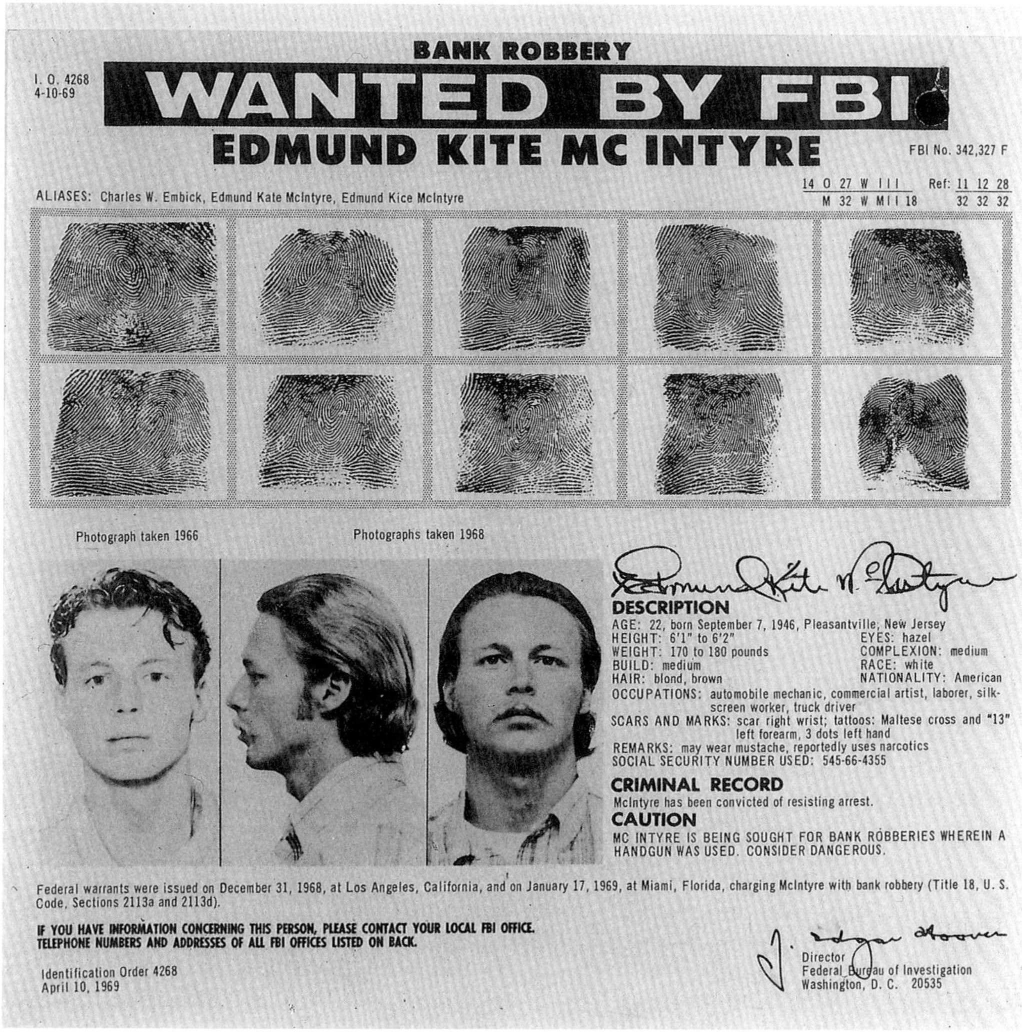

I. O. 4268
4-10-69

BANK ROBBERY

WANTED BY FBI

EDMUND KITE MC INTYRE

FBI No. 342,327 F

ALIASES: Charles W. Embick, Edmund Kate McIntyre, Edmund Kice McIntyre

14 O 27 W III Ref: 11 12 28
M 32 W MII 18 32 32 32

Photograph taken 1966

Photographs taken 1968

DESCRIPTION

AGE: 22, born September 7, 1946, Pleasantville, New Jersey
HEIGHT: 6'1" to 6'2" EYES: hazel
WEIGHT: 170 to 180 pounds COMPLEXION: medium
BUILD: medium RACE: white
HAIR: blond, brown NATIONALITY: American
OCCUPATIONS: automobile mechanic, commercial artist, laborer, silk-screen worker, truck driver
SCARS AND MARKS: scar right wrist; tattoos: Maltese cross and "13" left forearm, 3 dots left hand
REMARKS: may wear mustache, reportedly uses narcotics
SOCIAL SECURITY NUMBER USED: 545-66-4355

CRIMINAL RECORD

McIntyre has been convicted of resisting arrest.

CAUTION

MC INTYRE IS BEING SOUGHT FOR BANK ROBBERIES WHEREIN A HANDGUN WAS USED. CONSIDER DANGEROUS.

Federal warrants were issued on December 31, 1968, at Los Angeles, California, and on January 17, 1969, at Miami, Florida, charging McIntyre with bank robbery (Title 18, U. S. Code, Sections 2113a and 2113d).

IF YOU HAVE INFORMATION CONCERNING THIS PERSON, PLEASE CONTACT YOUR LOCAL FBI OFFICE.
TELEPHONE NUMBERS AND ADDRESSES OF ALL FBI OFFICES LISTED ON BACK.

Identification Order 4268
April 10, 1969

Director
Federal Bureau of Investigation
Washington, D. C. 20535

Figure 3.17. Douglas Huebler, *Duration Piece #15, Global, September 1969,* 1969. Copyright 2019 Estate of Douglas Huebler / Artists Rights Society (ARS), New York. Courtesy of Darcy Huebler / Artist Rights Society (ARS), New York and Paula Cooper Gallery, New York.

but also inassimilable characters in the greater social system, for example, those who break laws. This unknown and anonymous man may be caught by the frame of the photograph and suggestively "framed," but remains at large.[108] Tapping into photography's long history of criminalizing particular identities on the basis of "appearance," Huebler acknowledged his understanding of the aggressive and disciplinary dangers of photography:

> Indeed, I began to understand that for most people the camera represents a "threat" of a certain kind, with which I could identify, that being a profound feeling of vulnerability in front of the camera because it symbolizes a one-way mirror, an eye that sees its subject in an unconditional manner while denying him or her any possibility of seeing his or her "reflection": in front of an everyday mirror one can pose until his or her "best face" is reflected, but too often the camera kidnaps one's worst face.[109]

Like other floating signifiers, and as a kind of meta-commentary on photography itself, the subject "captured" by *Duration Piece #15* exemplifies how all photographs evidence a presence only as a trace while actually marking the absence of any concrete entity. To appropriate Bazin's analysis of the ontology of the photographic image once more: "The photograph as such and the subject in itself share a common being, after the fashion of a fingerprint."[110] The displayed series of ten blurry fingerprints included with the final piece are presented as concrete evidence, yet alongside the photograph, they begin to appear increasingly abstract. They, like the rebel index of the photographic image, ironically evade capture.

Viewed in this light, works such as *Location Piece #17, Turin, Italy,* in which the artist believes he has inadvertently discovered his doppelgänger, or *Duration Piece #15,* in which the artist reproduces an FBI poster, offering a reward for the "capture" of an imaged fugitive (who notably has a record of "resisting arrest"), constitute a radical destabilization. The decisive moment escapes, and photographic doubling complicates the easy absorption of the subject. The blurry index of the convict's fingerprints is paralleled by the equally blurry index of the artist's Italian look-alike. Such photographs refer to the arsenal of categorical photography and judicial regimes dating back to the nineteenth century, yet they function here to expose not only inassimilable or even unlawful characteristics but also the renegade potential of photography in the greater social system.[111]

A tattered front page from the Thursday, November 7, 1968, edition of the *Boston Globe* is foregrounded in *330/Variable Piece #70: 1971* (1974) (Plate 19). The headline tells us of President Richard Nixon's uproarious election to office two days earlier. From the vantage of the present, let alone 1974, it is not Nixon's electoral success that first comes to mind but rather the five thin words he uttered publicly in defense of his involvement with the Watergate scandal: "I am not a crook." Less than a year later, speaking from the Oval Office on August 8, 1974, Nixon announced his resignation. Moments before doing so, somewhat ironically, he professed, "I have never been a quitter." Lacking a single cohesive through-line, Huebler's collection of ephemera in *Number 330* functions in incredibly multivalent ways, redoubling Nixon's duplicity. A selection of Becher portraits appropriated from the earlier *Variable Piece #101* appears to the left of the newspaper print, two of them exact duplicates. Bernd's own described "failure" to "match a single 'face'" echoes Tricky Dick's charade. The more one looks at the photographs of Becher and Nixon in tandem, the more their associations arise: even their noses begin to resemble one another. Beneath Becher, we find another appropriated FBI Wanted poster, again random and incriminating. And then there is Huebler's attendant distinctive statement: AT LEAST ONE PERSON WHO WOULD CUT OFF HIS NOSE TO SPITE HIS FACE. Functioning on multiple levels, the aphorism insinuates references to Nixon's infamous negotiating strategies and needlessly self-destructive spite, a caricature reference to Nixon's notorious nose and, by way of extended metaphors reaching back to Pinocchio, the connotation of the long-nosed liar. Distrust, and by extension contingency, undercut the entirety of *Variable Piece #70*.

Huebler insisted: "I don't want to celebrate absurdity, but I do mean to challenge a lot of premises."[112] By extension, Huebler's projects are reinforced by both ambiguous and poignant logics, and a doubt-producing rationale that keeps the viewer guessing. They demonstrate how, with the collaboration of photography and conceptualism, nowhere in the dispersed and expanded field of so-called post-object art was the potentiality of either object or image finally outlawed. Indeed, together, photography and conceptual art transformed the very idea of the document into a contest of meaning, obliging current acts of writing and thinking through the history of conceptual art, especially its relationship to photography, to grapple with the pressures this places on the methodologies of art history within this suspended, and often equivocal, yet intensely productive state of openness.[113] A closer consideration of Douglas Huebler's art at this juncture advances one foray into this highly contingent matrix. Visuality in the late 1960s persisted as a disputed site, in which established dictums of sight and photographic impetus converged and ultimately shaped the practice, meaning, and historicization of conceptual art.

Four
This Is Not to Be Looked At
John Baldessari and Photography's Insistent Visuality

A hazy, pixelated black-and-white photograph shows spindly palm fronds, pavement, and rows of parked cars (Figure 4.1). A generic Southern California setting, bereft of particular intrigue. Bisected by what appears to be a tree trunk (though it could just as easily be a telephone pole or a lamp post), we have either a precise diptych or an awkward composition (depending on how one reads it). The image appears arbitrary yet highly measured. There is a sense of stark, midday sunlight, marked by the near absence of shadow. It is a calm picture of order, where plants and shrubbery seem as planned and organized as the immobile vehicles in the background. One searches the picture, and significance is difficult to detect: a low-resolution image, both visually and conceptually. Beneath the photograph's frame, against a blank background, hand-painted black capital letters spell out the following: AN ARTIST IS NOT MERELY THE SLAVISH ANNOUNCER OF A SERIES OF FACTS, WHICH IN THIS CASE THE CAMERA HAS HAD TO ACCEPT AND MECHANICALLY RECORD.

An Artist Is Not Merely the Slavish Announcer of a Series of Facts, Which in This Case the Camera Has Had to Accept and Mechanically Record (1966–68) counts among John Baldessari's early works, from a series Peter Schjeldahl referred to plainly in

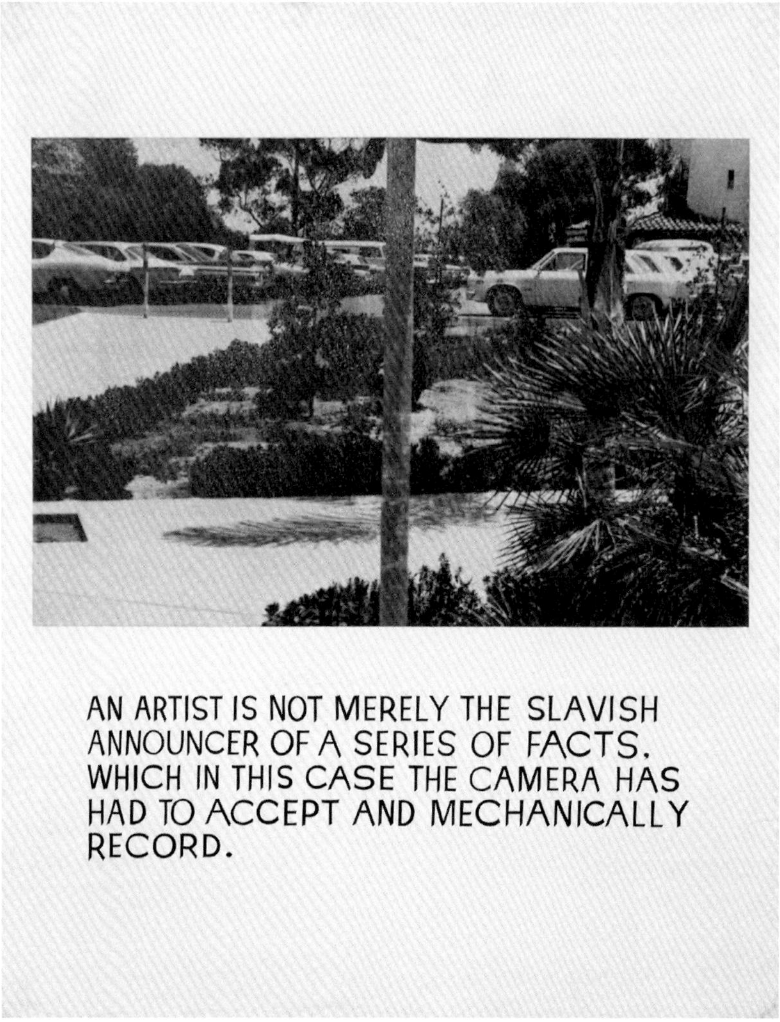

Figure 4.1. John Baldessari, *An Artist Is Not Merely the Slavish Announcer . . .*, 1966–68. Photographic emulsion and acrylic on canvas, 59⅛ × 45⅛ inches (150.2 × 114.6 cm). Courtesy of the Estate of John Baldessari and Marian Goodman Gallery.

the late 1990s as "banal photographs blown up on canvas with gnomic captions lettered by a professional sign painter."[1] Baldessari's text here is appropriated from an art book asserting the superiority of painting over and above photography. Spurred to spite this judgment, Baldessari decided to put photography into direct tension with painting. Canvas coated in emulsion, Baldessari's painting is "developed" literally and sardonically via a photographic process, thereby complicating the decisiveness of either painting or photography. The choice of canvas here is significant, since Baldessari maintains (somewhat sarcastically) that he wanted to keep the "sign" of art.[2] The use of a "professional" sign painter for the text ironizes the missing hand of the artist and, despite the seemingly perfunctory regularity of the sans serif text, suggests the paradoxical and inescapable aesthetic dimension of language itself.[3] In fact, the authority of the reproduced text is undermined by the very work of art on which it is magnified, positing at once the artful possibilities of photography while insinuating the mechanical aspects of painting. The choice of this particular image, of the desolate, anonymous, and ordinary parking lot with plants, has been regarded partly as a "non-choice," according to the discernment of the Whitney Museum of American Art's online collection guide, among others.[4] Yet Baldessari himself states explicitly on the same museum's website that he was consciously trying to "violate the rules of photography."[5] In this way, the artist *decides* to make a nonchoice, foregrounding the entanglement of indecision and deliberation at the outset as both subject and method in his conceptual use of photography.

More than a one-liner, the selection of accompanying text deserves renewed attention, particularly since a surprising degree of ambivalence is buried in this seemingly self-assured proclamation, "An artist is not merely . . .": an artist might be something else in addition to, and therefore possibly also, a "slavish announcer"? And what about the status of the camera in this equation—there seems to be a presumption that the monolithic camera is inevitably "slavish" and functions without agency, since the "camera *has to*." Yet this same logic also paradoxically characterizes the camera as having ultimate control and urgency, thanks to its nearly voracious compulsion. For, after all, there is no mention of a human operator. Furthermore, the notion of "facts" as the alleged territory of the camera is curious, as though implying that the camera's presumed lack of subjectivity results necessarily in truth by mechanical means. This apparently neutral work of art provokes many questions in terms of form, content, and ultimate meaning in ways that reexamine many of the foundational presumptions surrounding the contradictory nexus of photography and conceptual art.

How are we to distinguish the artist from the camera, especially if that artist "uses" photography? More broadly, if the artist "in this case" is aligned with a photographic point of view, what are the stakes of being "slavish"? And what of the position of the viewer? Does "in this case" suggest that there could be exceptions to the rule? The text passage implies an alignment, or misalignment, of positions, oscillating between the artist and the camera and the world that surrounds and regards them. In this way, by subtle and easily overlooked means, Baldessari inserts photography as a medium and as a way of seeing, thereby suggesting dilemmas of photographic visuality that can be understood in relation to, and as analogies for, larger social and political anxieties of the time. Deciphering and distilling these unwieldy and systemic conditions of photographic visuality are precisely the subject of this chapter.

What does it mean to be a "slavish announcer"? The adjective *slavish* rings with obsolescence, yet this barbed word takes on expanded associations in this context. Derived from the word *slave*, it denotes not simply being servile and submissive but also uninventive, with a distinct lack of originality. These are heavy accusations, especially if they indict not only the camera (as a stand-in for photography) but also the artists who use photography (as a stand-in for themselves), who, with the click of their impersonal shutter, invariably relinquish creative control. Of course, this is a false dichotomy. As discussed in the preceding chapters, this kind of simplification seems well in line with polarized arguments over the artistry (or lack therefore) of photography in the United States in the late 1960s. Baldessari admits that this was one of the absurd tenets that he took aim at, explicitly wanting to violate the rules. But again, with reference to the image itself, how seriously can one take this supposed violation of rules? How daring a "violation" is the inclusion of the tree in the center of a photograph, or the banal nonchoice of the overall picture? Decades later, Baldessari confessed how "after a while you learn all the tricks of how to make things beautiful and you get really suspicious."[6] His rebellion was thus to sabotage and satirize the quest for "beautiful" pictures, or photographs that conform to the established ideals of art. Is it possible that something deeper is at play here—something more incisive and revealing about the context in which Baldessari devised these maneuvers? Perhaps loaded language such as *slavish* and *violation* can provide some direction.

Understanding Baldessari's artwork as an address to the conditions of photographic visuality that characterized the late 1960s well beyond the scope of the art world indeed reveals a more radical intervention. By *visuality* I am referring to the definition outlined by the visual culture theorist Nicholas Mirzoeff, in which *visuality* is "not a trendy theory-word meaning the totality of all visual images and devices, but it is in fact an early nineteenth-century term, meaning the visualization of history."[7] In his analysis of Thomas Carlyle's writings from 1837 to 1841, around the time of photography's official invention, Mirzoeff explains the ways Carlyle, who coined the term *visuality,* opposed a physiology of vision in which seeing and understanding were the same process. Mirzoeff writes, "Visuality is very much to do with picturing and nothing to do with vision, if by vision we understand how an individual person registers visual sensory impressions."[8] This notion of picturing and the ability to "visualize," moreover, is described as the domain of power and authority, manifesting "visuality" as a way to order and narrate the chaotic events of modern life.[9] Arguably, Baldessari too was invested in thinking through the very notion of picturing and, by extension, the authorial structures and strictures of visuality. From this angle, Baldessari's nonchalant "violations" of the "rules" of photography and art become an address to power that, in addition to challenging the slavish status of photography within the established schema of art, demystify constructed ways of seeing the world, thereby challenging the will to power and the potentially "slavish" position of the viewer. For in defying the expectation of resolution (both pictorial and conceptual), Baldessari raises the specter of visuality, showing its contradictions to the attentive viewer, and slyly proposes a way to resist unequal and exploitative power dynamics, claiming subjectivity, and overhauling the inevitability of the "slavish" announcer. Particularly within the framework of the circulation of images during the Vietnam War era, this understanding of visuality as both what is seen and what remains occluded has poignant implications. Moving through select examples of how Baldessari mobilized photographic conditions for conceptual ends, this chapter reassesses Baldessari's practice through the critical lens of visuality and suggests ways that the status quo of looking, being seen, and picturing history was under dispute in the late 1960s.

Mobility of Meaning

As early as 1963, Baldessari was producing photographic works that emphasized process, de-emphasized the end product, and decentralized the role of the artist.[10] Beginning with a preconceived proposition, like much conceptual art of the time, his work remained open to the effects of chance, to the elements of life that the artist cannot control. *The Backs of All the Trucks Passed While Driving from Los Angeles to Santa Barbara, Calif., Sunday 20 January 1963* (1963), for example, introduces itself with a title that sounds like a straightforward statement of the facts (Plate 20). Thirty-two images shot over the dashboard of Baldessari's car are arranged in a suspiciously perfect grid. Yet despite the cohesiveness implied by their categorical seriality, the photographs that compose the piece seem unresolved, uncanny, and inconclusive. His photographic approach anticipates the facility and excess of mobile phone photography, in which ordinary and often nondescript archives are amassed easily, on the move. Reminiscent of Edward Ruscha's programmatic, banal, yet absurdly unexpected photographic books, such as *Twentysix Gasoline Stations* (1963), *Various Small Fires and Milk* (1964), and later *Every Building on Sunset Strip* (1966), Baldessari's work shows itself as inextricably linked to the contexts of California conceptualism from the outset, including the subversive attempt to contest the popular perception of the experience of reality as being governed by pictures and promulgated by the movie industry. Embracing the contingency of partial knowledge rather than the drive for complete mastery, Baldessari's practice lends itself to unexpected associations and inferences. Generations later, Baldessari's mode of approach still evidences viable traction and influence. Works such as Armando Andrade Tudela's *Camion* (2003), for example, a series in which seemingly haphazard photographs document freight lorries on Peruvian motorways, and which recalls Baldessari's precedent both in its amateurish photographic style and in moving vehicle subject matter, spark new assessments of Baldessari's work. Prompting questions of how mobility, geography, and economic circulation were already at stake in this earlier moment of postwar globalization, one wonders how the conceptual use of photographic deskilling and the process of quick camera clicks may have served as an analogy with larger sociopolitical implications. "Everybody knows a different world, and only part of it," Baldessari has elaborated. "We communicate only by chance, as nobody knows the whole, only where overlapping takes place."[11] The fugitive overlaps and disjunctures of everyday life were central preoccupations in Baldessari's early use of photography. And it is photography's potential to expose sameness and difference, coherence and simultaneous confusion, that mobilized his propositions into play. Somewhat ironically, however, the opacity of "overlaps" can be both productive and elusive, as I demonstrate in this chapter.

Originally a painter, throughout the 1960s Baldessari challenged questions about how the discourse that surrounds art (as concerns the circuitry of practice, exhibition, and dissemination) influences the way one is able to conceive or "know" what art in fact is or, perhaps more aptly, *might* be. An overwhelming inability to adhere to any single definition became Baldessari's signature, as he somewhat paradoxically used his pedagogical position as an art teacher to interrogate whether "art" was something a person could ever know, let alone learn or teach. Uncertainty characterizes Baldessari's heuristic practice, sometimes in the form of irony, other times as satirical literalness. Like the familiar paradox attributed to the Greek philosopher Socrates, *scio me nihil scire,* which translates imprecisely to "I know that I know nothing," Baldessari similarly ponders the formative role of questioning in the pursuit of knowledge and, in his case, through art. Socrates's statement is, of course, not about the impossibility of knowing anything. Rather, it is the assertion of complexly knowing through the process of unknowing that nothing can be known with absolute certainty. Arguably, Socrates's statement sets Western philosophy in motion. Baldessari uses this somewhat vexing approach to offer a contemporary engagement with the question of questions in art, which returns art to its philosophical beginnings. Socrates's formulation that all wisdom begins with wondering accepts the fact that all knowing must begin with admitting one's own essential ignorance. Baldessari takes up the relevance of immanent ignorance in the late twentieth century by considering the tensions and contingencies between art and any concept of understanding, as a way to redress the foundations of Western aesthetics and prod the limits of art's social relevance. As opposed to being slavish, Baldessari's conceptual photographic work interrogates visuality itself.

A 1966 photograph of Baldessari opens Max Kozloff's 1975 *Artforum* article "Pygmalion Reversed" (Figure 4.2).[12] This image of Baldessari, *Artist as Renaissance Man,* is the first thing that strikes viewers before they read Kozloff's account of body art and performance. A picture of the artist, looming large at the unusually tall height of six foot seven in a pose reminiscent of Leonardo da Vinci's *Vitruvian Man* (circa 1487), his body doubled, one posture overlaid on another, is captured in a single frame. Kozloff opens with a query: "Question: can a work of art ever be in pain? Answer: yes, if it is *incarnated* in a body; if, somehow, the body acts as the ground upon which an art meaning may be inscribed."[13] Though it is never entirely clear what Kozloff means by "art meaning," he does acknowledge that in body art, the "hidden instrumentality of the work becomes, not so much its visible motif, but the receptacle of the art action, the corporeal base that has been acted upon by the artists' process."[14] Nevertheless, the radical potential of body artists to reveal the "hidden instrumentality" of the modernist artistic subject is abandoned by Kozloff in his next breath, when he concludes that the body is a "corporeal base" that is "acted upon," rather than a critical agent in its own right.[15] The article continues by discussing performances by Vito Acconci, Chris Burden, Hermann Nitsch, and others, in detail: all artists who famously combined violence and the body to test the limits of "art meaning" located in the body. In this respect, the inclu-

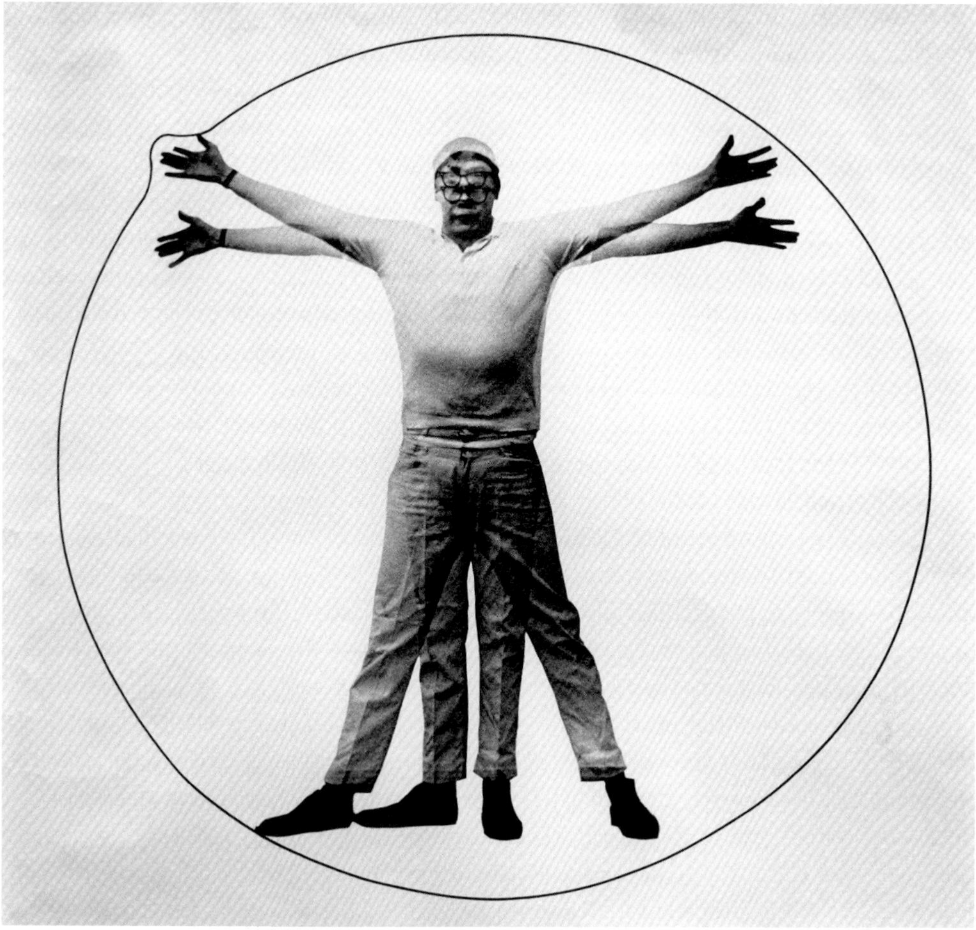

Figure 4.2. John Baldessari, *Artist as Renaissance Man,* 1966. Black and white photograph, 8 × 8 inches (20.3 × 20.3 cm). Courtesy of the Estate of John Baldessari and Marian Goodman Gallery.

sion of Baldessari's photograph seems to be a stark anomaly. How does Baldessari's emblematic photograph re-present a "corporeal base" to be "acted upon"? And how is it that he enters into a discussion of body art when neither he nor his critical reception at large regards him in connection to the discourses of body art more broadly?

Kozloff at no point engages the image or relates Baldessari's practice to the other "corporeal" works he addresses, instances where he claims that "the animate body . . . doubles back into inanimate art."[16] The action of doubling back is indeed imaged via superimposition in this photograph yet not addressed as an action that either explicitly relates to or evidences Kozloff's claims. The inclusion, though baffling in terms of Kozloff's thesis, presents an important clue to understanding Baldessari's artwork. He is not an artist commonly associated with performance, yet here he is; he is not an artist typically named in association with body art: in fact, he is more often discussed in terms of conceptual art as disembodied and as a challenge to materiality.

Obviously something in this formulation is missing. How do materiality and the body figure in Baldessari's so-called dematerialized art?

At first glance it may seem that Baldessari's imitation of the Vitruvian Man is flawed, the subject/artist's feet slightly akimbo, one foot turned out and the other facing forward. However, by comparing this image to Leonardo's original, it becomes clear that Baldessari's imitation is indeed a studied replica. The original Vitruvian Man comports the same slightly askew stance. Leonardo's Canon of Proportions, which includes a drawing in pen and ink on paper, and his notes on the architect Vitruvius, depicts a male figure in two superimposed positions with his arms and his legs apart, inscribed within an overlapping circle and square.

The drawing is based on the correlations of ideal human proportions with geometric measurements described by the ancient Roman architect Marcus Vitruvius in book 3 of his treatise *De Architectura* (circa 30–15 BC). Baldessari's image includes the square, while the circle is not present at all. The square, in fact, is only present through the stand-in of the generic square frame of the photograph. Perhaps it was not considered necessary, for the reference is clear enough, and added prompts might be forcing the issue. But ultimately, what is at issue? The image as a representation of the blend of art and science that characterized the Renaissance worldview is plain, and brought into the twentieth century, with its weighty symbolic signification and implication that man remains the measure of all things. This iconic image affirms the belief that the workings of the human body can be an analogy for the workings of the universe, that investigations into the material form of the body can be a way to understand the world. As historians have noted, this study of proportion proposes to fuse artistic and scientific objectives, as Leonardo, not Vitruvius, provides one of his simplest illustrations of a shifting "centre of magnitude" without a corresponding change to the "centre of normal gravity."[17] Baldessari similarly investigates the limits of the body and materiality as linked to visuality and perception through photography, yet with distinct reasons for doing so. For Baldessari, photography provides a way to confront traditional divisions between art as form and art as idea with a profound sense of doubt, moving from a consideration of objects toward a performance of effects.

As the formalists had rejected conceptual elements from their work, the conceptualists, wanting to emphasize their break from the traditional practices of painting and sculpture, began to reject physical elements in favor of conceptual ones. This in turn created a solipsistic and seemingly impassable situation, and by 1974 conceptual art appeared dominated by linguistic form. Thomas McEvilley noted this shift, explaining how artists such as Terry Atkinson, Michael Baldwin, and others offered theoretical essays on art as works of conceptual art: "In moving to reclaim the intellect, artists seemed to have incorporated the role of the critic."[18] Baldessari, however, never fully accepted the separation of concept from form or mind from body. It was never about an intellectual overhaul above all—indeed, if anything, his was much more of a preoccupation with preceptual conundrums. As illustrated by the portrait *Artist as Renaissance Man,* Baldessari's interest lay in the overlap between categories—both imagined and imaged. Like the *Renaissance Man,* he highlights the possibility to move through and across disciplinary borders. In this way, this gesture employs the form of the artist's own body as an ironic antiformalist refutation of Clement Greenberg's doctrine of medium specificity.

Moreover, Baldessari wanted to exceed iterable categories, thereby challenging the stability of the "order of things," particularly in the instance that man is posed as the measure. Another version of Baldessari's *Renaissance Man* appeared on the poster announcing his 1966 exhibition *Fragments* at the La Jolla Museum of Art. The show centered on the question "When is a part a whole, and when is a whole a part?"[19] Tellingly, this conundrum is one that has concerned thinking on photography nearly since its inception. It focuses on the illusion that individual photographs contain whole worlds yet are actually only fragments that deny any view of the whole. In other words, photographs exist as what Jacques Derrida termed "abyssal synecdoches."[20]

Baldessari felt that the double-exposed photograph of himself inside a drawn circle, outstretched as the axis, was representative of this theme. In Baldessari's image Vitruvius's code of ideal proportions is mocked by the uncontainable body of the artist; he is pictured as the veritable embodiment of the rule breaker. With one arm longer than the other, his body refuses to fit into a calculated geometric form. Instead, to accentuate this "flaw" further, Baldessari humorously corrects Leonardo's circle by distorting its line to accommodate his body.

In opposition to the Cartesian worldview, derived from Plato's mind–body dualism, Baldessari redresses the flaw McEvilley sees in the division between the material body and the supposedly immaterial mind. In so doing, Baldessari also challenged Kozloff's thorny complaint from 1973, that "conceptual art's questioning has no form."[21] Baldessari's artwork refuses this material/immaterial dualism and gives form to thought and thought to form. Perhaps his most powerful way of doing so is by evoking overlapping meanings and categories, which is again, by extension, the provocation of the Renaissance Man.

Death-Defying

Several early works by Baldessari address the body of the artist, though not as a presence. Rather, they reveal the artist's body as an absence in tension with an assumed presence. Tellingly, the main vehicle for these works is the photograph. One of the first pieces that can be associated explicitly with the conundrum of the *missing* body of the artist is *Evidence (Bowl Handed to Helene Winer, Dec. 1, 1970)* (1971), which the film theorist Peter Wollen argued engages the forensic gaze,[22] a motif prevalent in contemporary art practice (Figure 4.3). Staging the piece as a scene of a crime, however equivocal the so-called crime, reflects a brand of Hollywood melodrama and film noir aesthetic of recurrent interest to Baldessari. In turning these tropes to the context of art, Baldessari accentuates "an art of enigmatic traces, reduplicating the already enigmatic traces of the real life crime scene."[23] This play on the aestheticization of the neutral and purportedly evidentiary document is not haphazard. Rooted

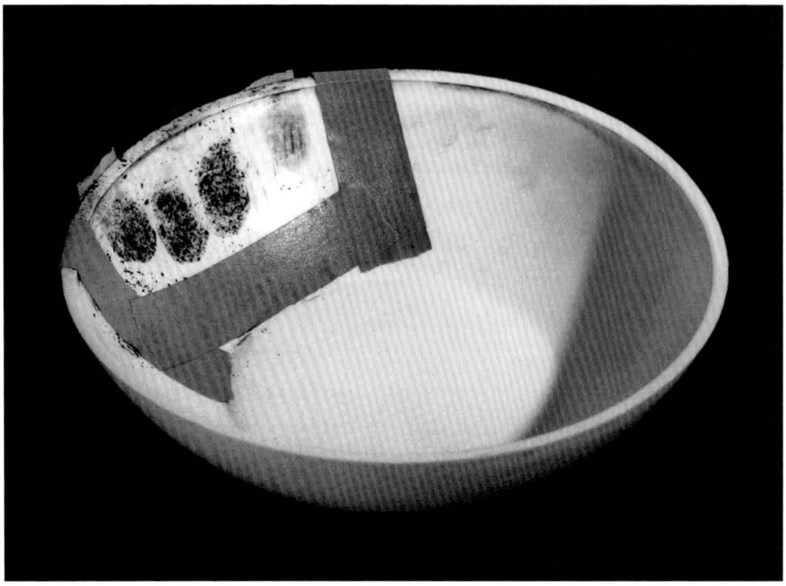

Figure 4.3. John Baldessari, *Evidence (Bowl Handed to Helene Winer, Dec. 1, 1970)*, 1971. Black and white photograph. Courtesy of the Estate of John Baldessari and Marian Goodman Gallery.

in conceptual art, the tactic builds off minimalism's investigations into objectivity and deliberately calls into question anything that claims to be unmediated.

Evidence consists of a photograph of a broken bowl dusted with lampblack powder, showing four of Baldessari's fingerprints. The image immediately evokes the discourse of traditional art predicated on the hand of the artist as a trace of authenticity, originality, and authorship. Now considered the stuff of myth, the artist's touch has been said to connote the individual artist's brushstrokes as the mark of true artfulness. Rather than simply assert the artist's presence, however, *Evidence* emphasizes the fact that the artist has fled the scene. The absence evoked by the piece indicates that, by contrast, "evidence [is] needed to confirm the artist's physical existence and, in a last-gasp effort, assert his unique identity."[24] Thus enters, stage left, the trace as photography's figure of itself.

A common trope in late-sixties art was works that announced the artist's absence, including the artist's increasingly nomadic character, while offering reassurance of the artist's existence and presence via traces (often photographic) and statements. On Kawara's *I GOT UP* postcard project begun in 1968 is exemplary in this respect.[25] Each postcard featured the precise time (e.g., 7:48 a.m.) the artist woke up each day, functioning as "a kind of self-reassurance that the artist does in fact exist."[26] The fact that Kawara's postcards were then mailed to his friends indicates that this reassurance was not entirely for the benefit of the artist, or at the very least that his existence was not entirely affirmed unless its fact was shared with others. Baldessari's piece also displays this need for public affirmation beyond private assertions, yet here it is even less stable. Though Kawara's postcard inscriptions are rubber-stamped, not allowing the hand of the artist to be directly traced, Baldessari's use of his actual fingerprints, despite the implication of the "hand of the artist," nevertheless remains no more expressive, locatable, or certain. His evidence of the self is deliberately cast in doubt and made contingent. The title and the material of the work suggest that we as viewers are witnesses to the remaining evidence of an "art disaster"—yet what is the disaster? The circumstance is never clear and, in this case, neither is the context. Perhaps that is the point. After all, how can we even be certain that these are actually Baldessari's prints? Baldessari subtly suggests the presumptions that inevitably enter the act of looking at art and making art. His installation "cannily conflates a means of criminal identification with an ironic commentary on the artist's signature 'touch,'"[27] challenging the myth of the singular artist with suggestive, albeit inconclusive, nuances.

As a photograph, it highlights further the question of photographic indexicality, which is both physical and metaphysical, or as Rosalind Krauss described, "By index I mean that type of sign which arises as the physical manifestation of a cause, of which traces, imprints, and clues are examples."[28] The photograph is moved from a discourse of truth telling to one of having the potential for lying, so that photography is inevitably staged, recalling Walter Benjamin's observations, as the scene of the crime.[29] Similarly, Baldessari calls documents into question and, in so doing, undermines the possibility of viewing photography under the aegis of conceptual art as neutral, or in any context, for that matter. Instead, Baldessari shows that the camera, the photograph, and traces in general (from which photography is inseparable) are not simply suspect but run the risk of incrimination.

The plural practices of conceptual art and the notion of the document at the center of contemporary art destabilized and disavowed the privileged position of painting. Often this move was a performative one, and a deliberate affront to any modernist desire for certainty. It is not mere chance that Jackson Pollock reappears in art after 1960 as the artist to contend with—or at least to ironize. As elaborated in the previous chapter's discussion of Bruce Nauman's practice, the exposure of Pollock's agency and artwork as a gateway to radical performance as noted by Harold Rosenberg and Allan Kaprow marked not only a gesture toward performance but also a revealing glimpse of the performance and theatricality that underscore all art.

In his later work *White Shape* (1984) Baldessari appropriated a famous Rudy Burckhardt documentary photograph of Pollock "performing" for the camera. It is difficult not to read this piece as Baldessari exposing the larger implications of Pollock's work, as well as the contentious significance of Pollock as an artistic figure for conceptual art. In this refashioned photograph by Baldessari, the artist is literally and figuratively missing in action. Where Pollock's figure had been, there is now only white vinyl paint, an outline of the "heroic" artist at work or, as Pollock might have formulated it, *in* his work. Because this photograph pictures Pollock posing in his studio between a "drip" painting on the floor and one on the wall behind him, it is nearly impossible not to read the man and the art in tandem, as part and parcel. Akin to the chalk outline of a victim's body at a crime scene, Pollock's figure remains only as an absence. Furthermore, this blanking out of the artist/protagonist opens a space in which to consider the enframing capacity, rather than the artist, as central. The parergonality of both Baldessari's piece and Pollock's is brought into focus for questioning.

Considering the fact that Pollock's art emphasized its function as the trace of a physical action further connects the body of the artist to the work of art. However, there remains a way to read this connection as actually disaffirming the artist's control and mastery. Linking the artist's living existence to the art object means allowing human fallibility and mortality to enter the equation. No one lives forever. This unavoidable human vulnerability by extension challenges the idea of timeless and immortal art, and calls into question the ways that conventions of traditional art depend on deliberate misrecognitions to be believable, to avoid acknowledging the ominous limits of art.

Baldessari's *White Shape* further alludes to this problematic paradox. More than literalizing the abstraction of the figure heralded by abstract expressionism, the body of the artist is obliterated, rubbed out, so to speak. Picturing Pollock's body blotted out in white contradicts Pollock's own denial of accident by picturing his aesthetic arena as though it were an accident. Moreover, given the formal affinity of the paintings with blood-spattered floors and walls, particularly as arranged in this black-and-white photograph, as Ralph Rugoff notes, "the altered photograph hints that the linking of art and action subtly transforms the studio into a forensic site."[30] The idea of the chalk outline also implies the double-bind of the photograph as evidence: it is always a ghostly presence combined with a concealed absence. The visual allusion of Pollock's white form to the cliché image of a ghost is compelling in this regard as well. Notably, suspicious and suspiciously blanked-out figures recur throughout Baldessari's oeuvre. Though not always whited out, more frequently colored in vibrant hues, Baldessari repeatedly plays with the suggestive qualities of this strategy, sometimes applying it only to faces rather than full bodies.[31] In either case, the omissions suggest a strategic "cover-up" and contingent narratives. Fittingly, these photographs offer only partial and limited truths.

To highlight the contingency of perception and its basis in experience, Baldessari has frequently created pieces that revolve around different versions of stories. His photographic images often contain inconsistencies meant to push viewers into a place where it becomes difficult to keep their story straight as they recount what they were, or are, witnesses to. This inability to pin down a singular truth forms the groundwork of pieces such as *Story with 24 Versions* (1974), the artist's book *Brutus Killed Caesar* (1976), *A Sentence of Thirteen Parts (with Twelve Alternate Verbs) Ending in FABLE* (1977), and countless other works that evoke the concept of "versions" in the title, or "tales" (e.g., *Close-Cropped Tales,* artist book [1981]), which test the reliability of, and correlation between, experience and documentation. This emphasis on investigation as a mode of viewing, counter to passive looking, further challenges the modernist paradigm of viewership. Often these works by Baldessari are sardonic in tone. Even when the titles seem to be forthright in declaring the puzzle they pose or the duplicity they contain (e.g., *A Sentence with Hidden Meaning* in *The Way We Do Art Now and Other Sacred Tales* [1973] or *Binary Code Series: Lily (Yes/No)* [1974]), these series nevertheless provoke our instincts to try to assemble the pieces, divine coherence, and make sense of our experiences by matching them with the images presented.

In *Police Drawing* (1970) the body of the artist is once again at stake, at least insofar as our ability to affirm and locate it is concerned, and the perception of viewers is again put to the test. Like Baldessari's other projects based in photography, there is a sense of indeterminacy around the framing of the work, and certainly of the subject. The viewers in this instance assist in the creation of the work both during and after its execution. In a game of perception and memory, once more staged as a kind of ambiguous art crime, Baldessari made an unannounced visit to an instructor friend's art class in San Diego for fifteen minutes. After his departure, a police artist was called in, and the students were asked to describe him as they would a suspect or perpetrator, so that a "wanted" sketch could be drawn. A full-length photograph of Baldessari, a photograph of the police artist talking to the students, a photograph of the police artist drawing, the resultant conté drawing, as well as a thirty-minute videotape of the exercise, combine to form the final piece. Like the role of the trace in *Evidence,* the other forms of documentation of the artist's existence corroborate the photograph at the same time that mediums are put in tension with one another vying for the role of proof. We are shown how photography always contains a trace of the thing that was once there;[32] as a result, "it's all about the return of the departed. . . . The spectral is the essence of photography."[33] This observation clearly resonates with *White Shape.* As is frequently the case in conceptual photography, it is not a remarkable aesthetic that preoccupies the viewer but, rather, a typically unremarkable one, which encourages the frustrating sense that something is missing.

Following in the footsteps of Duchamp, these works are more cerebral than retinal, with the focus remaining always on the issue of information through documentation and the process of understanding how this information does or does not engage in relation to one's experiences. Aesthetics are not a priority. Describing these works from the 1970s, Coosje van Bruggen has referred to Baldessari's work as "mind games," in which the artist leaves clues for the spectators "to decipher the crime, or the art."[34] This so-called crime, or the idea of the art as crime, is of course speculative. Baldessari recounts how he was motivated by the story of a friend of his, who had worked in the photography archive of the San Diego Police Department, eventually quitting because he found the constant inspection of pictures of traffic accidents, murder cases, and so on "too eerie": "I think that story got me interested in photographs that weren't done to be beautiful, and the whole idea of photographs as document rather than as art began to emerge."[35] The coy ordinariness of the photograph as an object takes on disconcerting meanings, sometimes as a result of what is missing rather than what is present. The photograph exists at once as evidence to assure us of the artist's existence, as a sign of life, as well as evidence that suggests what or who has vanished, echoing Benjamin's axiom: "To live means to leave traces."[36] This photographic observation stages a crucial aporia. Without traces, our lives are thrown into doubt (insofar as photographic documentation establishes a sense of self and of one's history); yet, paradoxically, traces also become source material for the existential doubt that demands interpretation and that always contains missing pieces.

Baldessari's *Rolling: Tire* (1972) pushes the concept of the photograph as evidence to the next violent and threatening level, and again insinuates the artist in the role of culpable escape artist, with life hanging in the balance (Figure 4.4). This conceptual performance piece and its attendant documentation call Ruscha to mind again, namely, connecting to his free-flying typewriter and looming shadows in the documentation of *Royal Road Test* (1967). In *Rolling: Tire,* which indeed has an experimental and experiential dimension akin to *Police Drawing,* it is once more ambiguous about whether the body of the artist is in danger, as it would most likely be in Burden and Acconci as discussed by Max Kozloff. Instead, the threat and target seem untethered, and pointed outward. Building on the surrealist tradition of objects that gather meanings that seem to have little to do with their everyday use, Baldessari's meanings seem even more excessively random. *Rolling: Tire* was among the artist's first works to use hidden hostility as a motif and is suggestive once more of the fine line between an accident and a crime, or chance and premeditated action. Consisting of five juxtaposed snapshots of a rolling tire with a newspaper clipping about a fatal collision between a perilous tire truck and a pedestrian,[37] "we are left to ponder whether the tire in the snapshots is a potential agent of death or a harmless object; its definition, as Baldessari wryly implies, cannot be based on 'inherent' characteristics, but instead is contingent on how it 'behaves.'"[38] Like the photograph, function and context inform meaning at least as much as material or content. Interested in the open "character" of objects, Baldessari has commented: "We tend to live too much with our heads. A thing, for instance a garbage can, has no life. I know that it is only a receptacle, but I also think of a garbage can as having a life. Anything around me can be invested with lifelike qualities."[39] This unpredictable quality of living experience confounds rational expectations and resonates with the uncanny expectations projected onto photographs.

A connection between *Rolling: Tire* and Andy Warhol's deadpan delivery of fatalistic information in his *Death and Disaster Series* of the early sixties is obvious. Warhol's series included an array of seemingly despondent subjects such as race riots, car crashes, and nuclear explosions. All were cropped, removed from their journalistic framework, and silk-screened into the context of art. Using monochrome colors and repetitive patterns, Warhol made these tragedies appear as mundane as wallpaper. Certain images in the series connect more blatantly to Baldessari than others, namely, those images that picture the dark side of ordinary life and point to the nearly absurd terrors lurking in ordinary objects. An analogy to the prints for

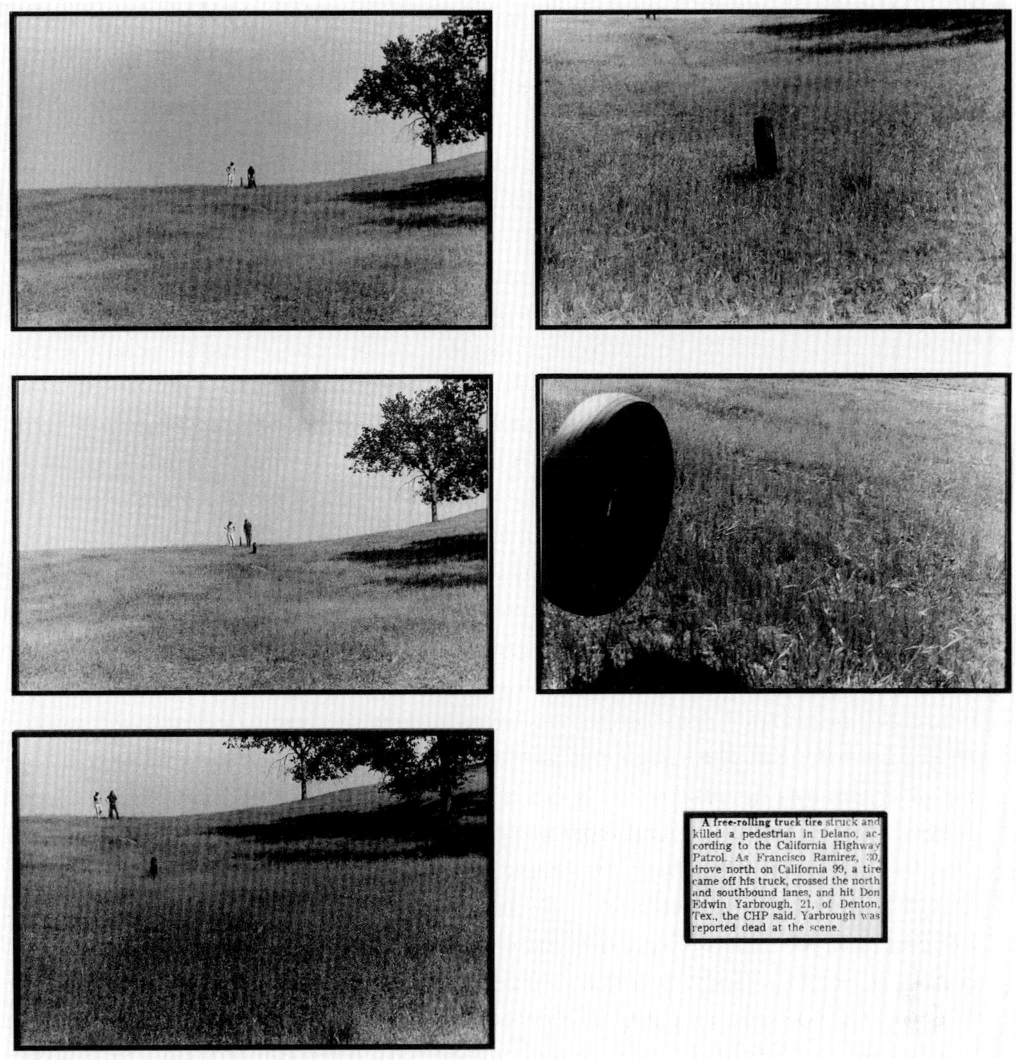

Figure 4.4. John Baldessari, *Rolling: Tire,* 1972. Five black and white photographs and photocopy. Photographs 16 × 24 inches (40.6 × 61 cm); photocopy 6¼ × 10 inches (15.9 × 25.4 cm). Courtesy of the Estate of John Baldessari and Marian Goodman Gallery.

Warhol's *Tuna Fish Disaster* (1963) is a touchstone in this regard. Warhol's piece, like *Rolling: Tire,* demonstrates the vital joints between life-threatening danger and absurdity. Warhol's smiling portraits of Mrs. McCarthy and Mrs. Brown overlaid with images of toxic tuna and text that reads "Seized shipment: Did a leak kill . . ." expose the anxiety of ordinary objects. Delivered in a seemingly affectless tone, they exemplify the irony of Warhol's reticence to explain his work, saying duplicitously that all anyone needed to know about Warhol or his artworks was already there, "on the surface." Like the cans of tuna fish imaged, the surface is never really a sufficient source of information. The incredibility of photographs is ironically alluded to in Warhol's rumination on the subject of death; "I don't believe in it because you're not around to know that it's happened."[40] Despite the photograph's claim to truth and reportage, it is always removed from the moment before and after, like death. We may desire the photograph to bear witness, but there is always a delay, and what inevitably takes place after that singular instant throws the picture itself into uncertainty. How can one believe in the photograph, when the photograph alone never provides the conclusive presence to know what happened? In the case of both death and the photograph, direct experience is not possible.

Writing one year before Warhol's death in 1987, Kay Larson observed how little critical attention the gruesomeness of Warhol's images had garnered: "What nobody talked about was the horror of the message—perhaps because nobody could see it."[41] As though hiding in plain sight, the silk screens of death and pain were largely celebrated as though decorative, or pleasant to look at. *Foot and Tire* (1963–64), also from the *Death and Disaster Series,* imprints once more Warhol's fascination with fleshing out fatality (Figure 4.5). The work, particularly with its vicious tire, further suggests a conceptual continuum treading from his practice to Baldessari's. The laconic, straightforward title belies the brutality of what can be seen in the image. A photograph of a traffic accident is repeated four times against a disarming silver background. Not clearly a foot per se, but certainly the sole of a shoe emerges from underneath the crushing double wheel of a massive tractor-trailer rig. Upon closer inspection the embodied dimensions of the shoe become apparent, triggering an abject gut-reaction. Indeed, the violence of these images reveals a crucial aspect of photographic ontology: the ways violation is always built into the photographic reproduction of appearances. In *Photography and Its Violations* (2014), John Roberts offers a compelling argument that photographs should be understood by their conceptual underpinnings, as opposed to the visually apparent subject matter. Roberts describes photography's particularly "unstable and destabilizing character" and the ways it is "entangled with what is unconscious, half-hidden, implicit."[42] This mode of reorienting attention and questioning the candor of photography offers a productive and political reimagining of photography's social capacity, and a way to tease out tendentious layers of nuance in the artwork of Warhol, Baldessari, and others.

Complicated by the unstable character of the photograph, the most mundane objects and details show themselves to be filled with excessive and uncontainable meanings and possibilities—ones that implicate life and death stakes. In this way,

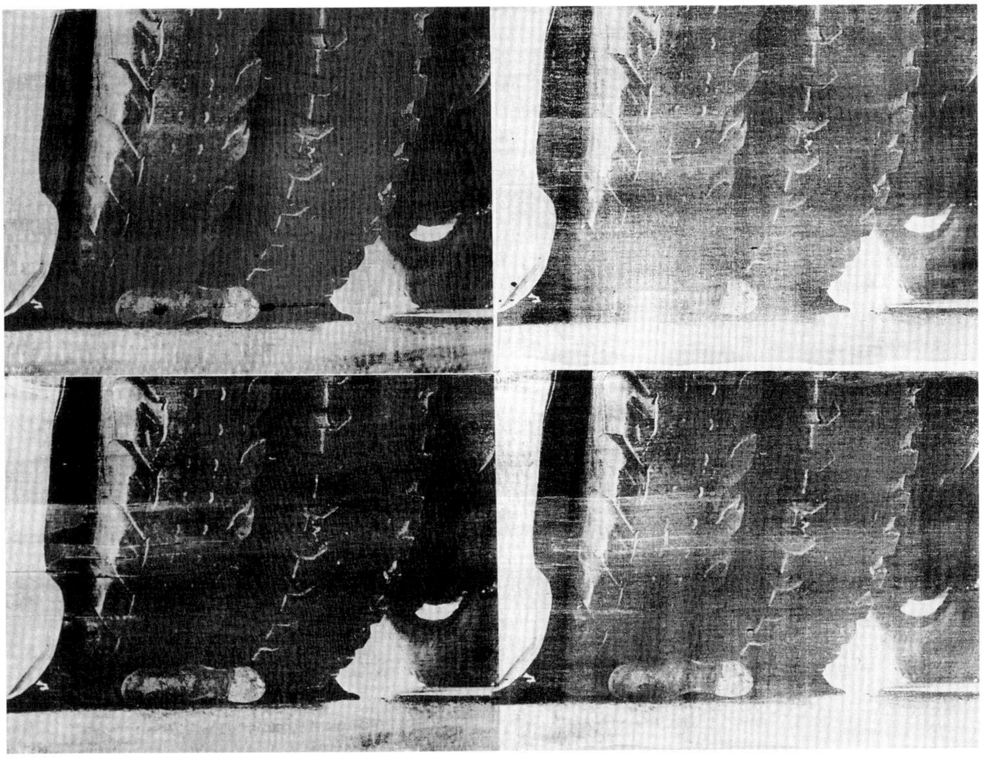

Figure 4.5. Andy Warhol, *Foot and Tire,* 1963–64. Copyright 2019 The Andy Warhol Foundation for the Visual Arts, Inc. Licensed by Artists Rights Society (ARS), New York.

the postmodern sensibilities of objects in the world—and specifically objects in Baldessari's art practice—are exposed, demonstrating their uncanny ability to shift between opposing and contradictory categories. As the hard-boiled detective novelist Philip Kerr observed, detectives have always been postmodern investigators (a role Baldessari often assigns his viewers), since to the detective "a cigarette end was never just a cigarette end: it was also sometimes a sign, a clue, a piece in a puzzle awaiting connection with something else."[43] Baldessari creates a Hitchcock-like ambiance, insinuating that something dangerous is always around the corner, something is always about to happen, everything is under suspicion, and therefore the viewer, like the detective, must pay attention to the signs. Film-noir and pulp-fiction sleuth allusions reappear throughout Baldessari's career, nearly exclusively in photographic form: for example, his serial *Six Gags (Male)* (1991), *Violent Space Series: Six Vignette Portraits of Guns Aligned and Equipoised (Violet)* (1976), *Violent Space Series: Six Situations with Guns Aligned (Guns Sequenced Small to Large)* (1976), *Violent Space Series: Two Stares Making a Point but Blocked by a Plane (for Malevich)* (1976). The list goes on. Each of these is playful yet cynical and foreboding. With scenes staged expressly for investigative purposes, sites of interrogation abound, for example, in multiple iterations of *Two Crowds (With Shape of Reason Missing)* (1984).[44] Baldessari's attraction to what is missing is repeatedly put in tension with the viewer's desire and inclination to fill in the blanks while intimating close connections between notions of "pointing" and being "loaded" in terms of social violence and photography.[45] In outlining what he dubs Baldessari's "conceptual comedy," John Welchman insists foremost on the strategy of deadpan, which he identifies as "distinctively American." In a description that sounds uncannily, uncomfortably similar to popular modes of documentary photography, Welchman defines deadpan's attributes as "eschew[ing] expression, emotion, or motile physicality," using "physiognomic reduction and impassive restraint."[46] Akin to the deadpan discussed earlier in the work of Douglas Huebler, deadpan here revives its etymological origins going back to the nineteenth century, literally signifying "deadface." Such a somber reading is particularly apt in reference to Baldessari's art, a practice persistently syncopated with morbidity and violence veiled in humor.

The Execution Is a Perfunctory Affair

In what is now a well-rehearsed historical narrative, painting was at its apotheosis by the 1960s, so much so that the authority of abstract expressionism had become nearly cliché. Photography of this time therefore often acted as painting's character foil. Baldessari, trained as a painter, nevertheless sought to push the boundaries of painting and high modernist criticism's hold on the art world through photographic thinking. A photograph such as John Baldessari wearing a Born to Paint jacket, (1968), a portrait of the artist from behind dressed in a black leather motorcycle jacket decaled with a skull and flames and the tagline "Born to Paint," can be seen as parodying this rebellion and the stakes of waging this aesthetic war (Figure 4.6). Similarly, his 1970 decision to formally cremate all his unsold extant paintings in a performative act, resulting in both an official newspaper obituary and cookies baked from the ashes, pokes fun at the anxieties around the purported death of painting.

Couched in humor and ironic reticence, Baldessari's practice offers a complex case. Despite his reservations about painting, Baldessari never entirely let go of the medium or its influence. Instead, he manipulated the conventions that equated painting to Art—as if the bond were formed in nature—to question the culturally constructed status of the art object more broadly. This is significant, because even though Baldessari moves away from painting in the early 1960s and toward mechanical reproduction and photographic investigation in the late 1960s, he retains an interest in the conceptual dialectic between these two media, refuting the discourse of medium specificity.

From another perspective, these shifts can also be seen as Baldessari's development of his own version of Sol LeWitt's injunction of June 1967, in his now-famed "Paragraphs on Conceptual Art": "When an artist uses a conceptual form of art, it means that all of the planning and decisions are made beforehand and the execution is a perfunctory affair. The idea becomes the machine that makes the art."[47] LeWitt's ideas were formative for conceptual art and also for Baldessari, who was in close conversation with LeWitt throughout the late 1960s. Baldessari's interest in ideation

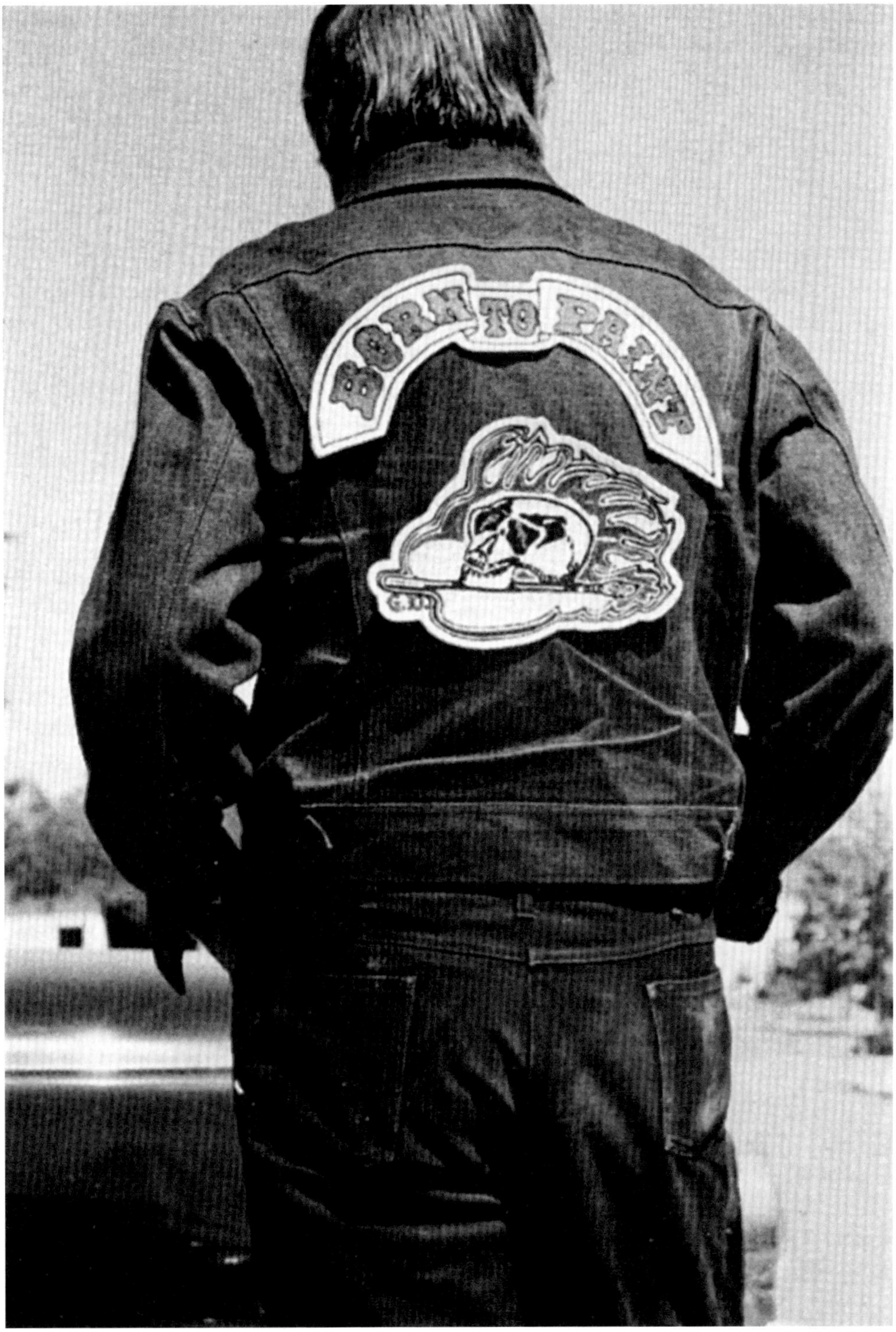

Figure 4.6. John Baldessari wearing a Born to Paint jacket, 1968. Courtesy of the Estate of John Baldessari and Marian Goodman Gallery.

as "machine" is manifest across his practice. But so too is his desire to punningly push against prescribed tenets. What can be made of the archaic tone or the severity of LeWitt's dictum? What of its implied callousness? While Baldessari took LeWitt to task with his own refrains, including a mock version of LeWitt's "Sentences on Conceptual Art" titled *John Baldessari Sings Sol LeWitt* (1972), in which each of the thirty-five statements was sung to the tune of popular songs, including *The Star Spangled Banner* and *Tea for Two,* he also attenuated the concept of art's "execution" as a site of investigation.

Like Jasper Johns—who used commonplace objects as his subject, blurring the categories of both the index and the icon while criticizing the completeness of any singular system—Baldessari's art was also less matter-of-fact than it appeared at first glance. Both Johns and Baldessari invested in a reorientation of the picture-as-art. As Johns himself perceptively declared, "Nothing in art is so true that its opposite cannot be made truer."[48] Truth is posited as relative and potentially reversible, thereby offering a mutable alternative to Greenberg's formalist criticism and to high modernism more generally.

Frank Stella, in contrast to Johns or Baldessari, was reportedly not amused by ambiguities; instead, he saw them as "dilemmas to resolve rather than paradoxes to indulge."[49] Wanting completely to expunge the figure-ground relation, he famously stated in 1964 that "what you see is what you see." But of course seeing Stella's work as the eradication of the figure-ground relation is only one point of view, namely, the one advocated by Greenberg's disciple, Michael Fried.[50] A counterpoint to Fried's orthodoxy and his call for autonomy is made manifest by Carl Andre's writings in the sixties, which characterized Stella as the move to minimalism, an argument that would become increasingly convincing when Stella began to shape his canvases.[51] In either case, Stella's terse delivery that "what you see is what you see" suggests a kind of closed-circuit relay between the viewer and the work of art, and moreover, such a stance lacks the unpredictability of Baldessari's witty aphorisms.

Baldessari's *This Is Not to Be Looked At* (1966–68) presents an appropriated image of an *Artforum* cover from 1966–67 showcasing Stella's painting *Union III* (1966) and is an ironic example of Baldessari's challenge to both didacticism and hermetic readings of art, covertly suggesting that what you do not see, what lies beyond the frame, matters as well (Figure 4.7).[52] Baldessari undercuts the overwhelming scale of Stella's original (measuring over eight feet by fourteen feet) by reducing it in size and rendering it in pixelated black and white, while draining the intensity of its color. Gone is the vibrant clash of Stella's neon orange, powder blue, and pallid yellow. Instead we are met with the humble and the unspectacular. *Union III*'s rigid geometry against an unplaceable mottled surface in this reproduction recalls my earlier discussion of Bochner's photographic experiments from the same era. Moreover, particularly in this case, Baldessari's photographic appropriation of Stella's painting challenges presence and painting, and the presence of painting, as the be-all and end-all in art. This piece contains numerous "signs" of painting—foremost being the canvas and the reproduction of Stella's painting printed on it. The fact that part

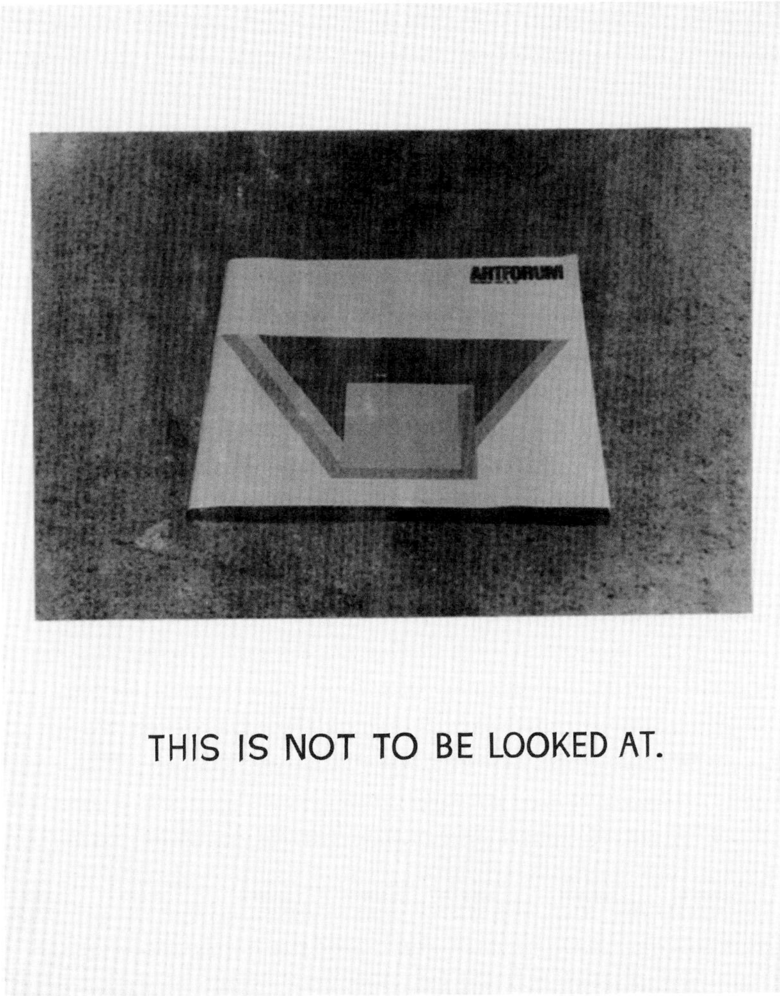

Figure 4.7. John Baldessari, *This Is Not to Be Looked At,* 1966–68. Photographic emulsion and acrylic on canvas, 59 × 45 inches (149.9 × 114.3 cm). Courtesy of the Estate of John Baldessari and Marian Goodman Gallery.

of Baldessari's canvas is left bare and the rendering of Stella's reproduced reproduction (the photographic image of Stella's work on the cover of *Artforum*) is shoddy, due to the photo emulsion with which it has been placed on the canvas, multiplies exponentially the ways of understanding what we are looking at. This observation is the tip of the semiotic iceberg, especially considering the ban on looking that the iconoclastic caption demands. This may be interpreted in deconstructionist terms, as a call not to look but to *read*. Deconstruction beneficially exposes the impossibility of self-sufficiency and self-evidence—the work cannot stand alone. By contrast, delving into the overlooked aspects of image and text and image *as* text, we are encouraged to recognize that "photo*graphy*" should be understood as writing, which has to be read as well as viewed.[53]

According to Derrida, photography's referential function is precisely why it necessitates distancing more than any other medium. Importantly, acknowledging the gap between one's self and the image allows the work to be read within and without the frame, rather than accepting that "what you see is what you see." Here Baldessari exploits not only photography's need for distance but also its potential creation of distance. By reproducing a photograph of a Stella painting, Baldessari denigrates vision as the epitome of access to art. At the same time, he creates the necessary distance for the viewer to *think* about the system he is presenting to them, including the nexus of entanglements between Stella, modernist painting, modernist criticism, *Artforum*, painting more broadly, mechanical reproduction, and surface. Somewhat paradoxically, by interrogating the salience of the reproduced image, this approach also questions the growing trend in 1960s art magazines that were increasingly "designed to be 'seen' rather than 'read.'"[54] In a related way, *This Is Not to Be Looked At* also humorously addresses one of the central aporias of conceptual art—namely, the tension between ideation and the visual form. Baldessari's stated prohibition on looking ironizes conceptual art as an alternative to the opticality of post-painterly abstraction, the physical presence of minimalist sculpture, and the mass media saturation of pop art.[55] It is also suggestive of the backlash against *Artforum*'s move from California to New York in the summer of 1967.[56] The list of possible considerations and inflections grows exponentially as one steps back to contemplate the text. As Derrida explained in *The Deaths of Roland Barthes* (1988), "Where the referent is itself framed within the photographic frames, the index of the completely other, however marked it may be, nonetheless makes reference endlessly refer. The notion of the chimera is then admissible. If there is an art in photography . . . it is here. Not that it suspends reference, but that it indefinitely defers a certain type of reality, that of the perceptible *referent*."[57] Much like the conspicuous instability of the body as subject and the frame as context in *White Shape* or *Rolling: Tire*, this indefinite deferral again marks the inability to secure or fix meaning as well as the dubious character of perception. Or, as John Tagg has eloquently described the unwieldy capacities of the frame and the mutual suspicion it adds to photographic ontology, "the frame is seen and not seen, disavowed, already at work in fixing the look and the givenness of difference, yet always denied or multiplied to infinity."[58]

This Is Not to Be Looked At acknowledges the ways that linguistic text, especially in the form of titles and captions (here they are colluded), mediates our understanding of images. Our look is filtered through the caption, which, in its forbiddance of our looking may in fact provoke our desire to look all the more. Combined, the caption/title and the image exemplify the inadequacy of language and images to ground one's understanding of the world. Though pithy text in Baldessari presents itself as self-evident, the words, like the images, are more frequently the signs of illiteracy, or certainly the limits of literacy. This accounts for their gnomic status; they are perplexingly straight and seemingly transparent at the same time that they are overwhelmingly opaque. Though these texts trade in appropriations from popular culture and the history of art, from Hollywood film stills to Jean-Auguste-

Dominique Ingres, they do so to undermine the myths that circulate around and within these images/texts when taken as a given. By exposing the very layered construction of meanings therein, they demonstrate how vision is always lodged within larger epistemological issues. Benjamin was the first to mark the risk of this precarious ignorance, particularly in relation to photography, writing in "A Short History of Photography" (1931): "'The illiterate of the future' it has been said, 'will not be the man who cannot read the alphabet, but the one who cannot take a photograph.' But must we not also count as illiterate the photographer who cannot read his own pictures? Will not the caption become the most important component of the shot?"[59] Building on Benjamin's invocation of the crucial role of the caption to ground the image, for both the photographer and the viewer, Baldessari exposes how naively trusting we have become in relation to directives on looking and, by extension, grasping the image (let alone the world) at hand.[60]

The lack of quality in this "poor" printed image returns one's thoughts to Hito Steyerl's theorization of displaced, low-resolution images, discussed earlier in the context of Huebler. More than pointing to the compromised position of modernist "opticality," re-presenting *Artforum* re-presenting Stella, who represents the then-dominant paradigm of modernist painting, further complicates legibility in Baldessari's work. On the one hand, its mechanically reproduced image could be a wink at photography imitating painting in order to attain the status of art by appearing more "painterly." On the other hand, it could be the exposure of a mechanical impulse behind Stella's own production. After all, this is not the only instance in which Baldessari has appropriated Stella's work. Yet another ironic reproduction of a signature Stella is the focus of Baldessari's *A 1968 Painting* (1968). Perhaps the repeated use of Stella is precisely due to its recognizable standing (and commodity status) as art at the time,[61] useful in that it also functions as a way to engage a counter-discourse to the "presentness" that Fried insisted on as grace.[62]

Against the "perpetual present" trumpeted by Fried, Baldessari recognizes duration as valuable in art, believing that all art exists in temporal space and is thus subject to changing perceptions; the present itself is always in the midst of change. Friedrich Nietzsche wrote that "our eye finds it more comfortable to respond to a given stimulus by reproducing once more an image that it has produced many times before, instead of registering what is different and new in an impression."[63] This sentiment accords well with the internal logic of Baldessari's work. Seeing differently requires going beyond one's comfort zone. Thus, in Baldessari's art practice, medium and subject matter frequently put the viewer in the confounding place of discomfort rather than complacency. They interrogate the status of subjectivity.

As the piece *The Spectator Is Compelled to Look Directly Down the Road and into the Middle of the Picture* (1967–68) expresses, viewers are not merely guided but even more forcefully dictated by culturally constructed perspective and habit to look at art in a particular way (Figure 4.8). Incongruously, in the aforementioned work a figure (the artist's body) is literally placed in the middle of the road with his back to the viewer, blocking our vision despite the picture's rigorous Cartesian perspective.

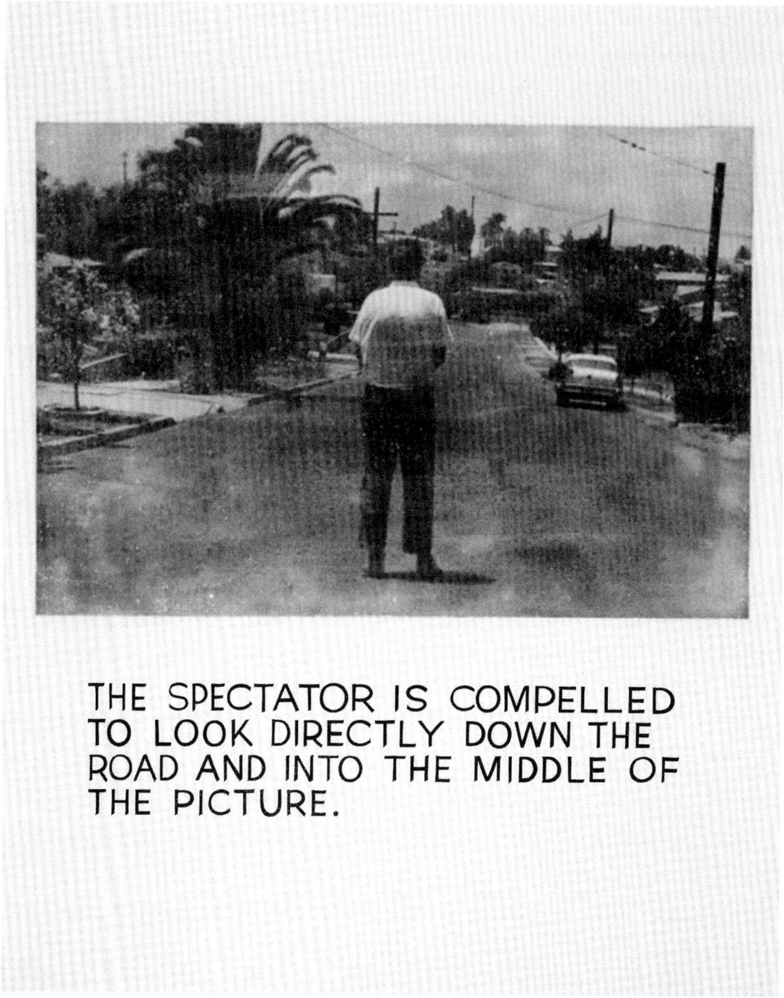

Figure 4.8. John Baldessari, *The Spectator Is Compelled . . .*, 1967–68. Photographic emulsion and acrylic on canvas, 59 × 45 inches (149.9 × 114.3 cm). Courtesy of the Estate of John Baldessari and Marian Goodman Gallery.

Even when it is "right," it is wrong. Another way to interpret this verso of a figure in the middle of the suburban landscape is as an ironic reference back to the traditions of German Romantic landscape painting, such as the painting of Caspar David Friedrich, in which the figures turn their backs on the reality of the viewer and turn instead to face the infinity of the landscape in front of them.[64] The infinite implications of the vanishing point in Baldessari's image thus become more of a deadpan dead-end for the viewer's perception than an experience of the immersive sublime. Commenting on his deliberate resistance to Romantic ideals, Baldessari explained, "I didn't want to have a hazy, romantic view about things and take out telephone lines and poles just because I didn't want them there, which is what a painter, of course, can do."[65] Deadpan plays out in yet another, not so romantic, sense, as well.

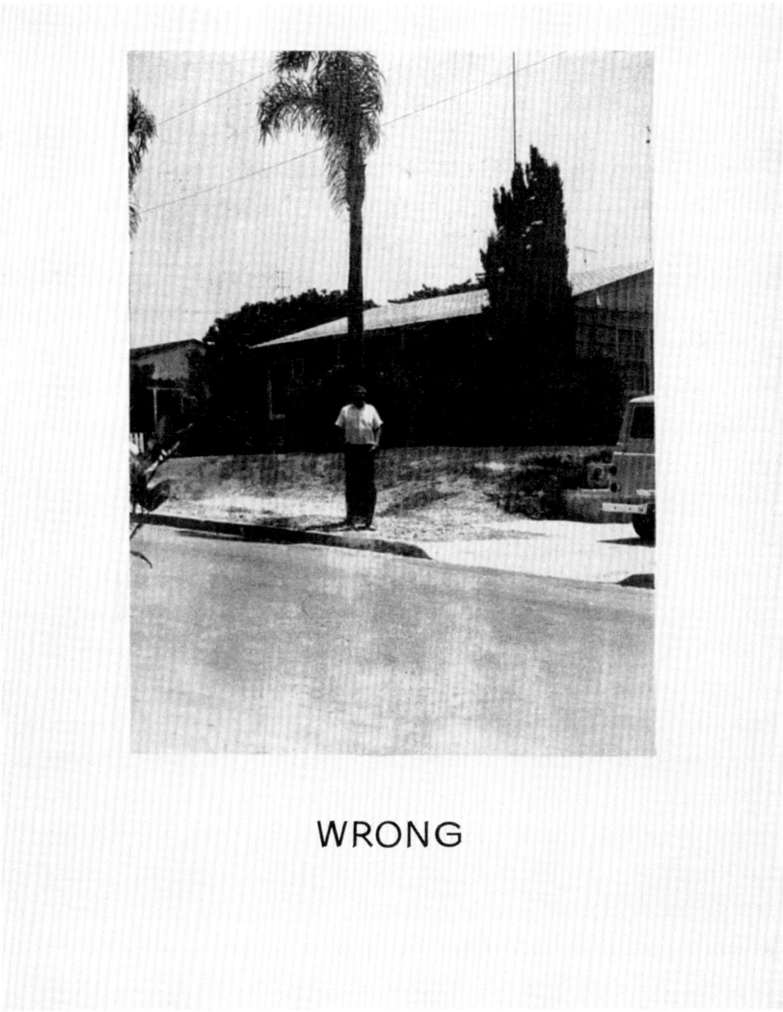

Figure 4.9. John Baldessari, *Wrong*, 1966–68. Photographic emulsion and acrylic on canvas, 59 × 45 inches (149.9 × 114.3 cm). Courtesy of the Estate of John Baldessari and Marian Goodman Gallery.

Seemingly unaware, standing in the middle of the street, the artist hazards the violent possibility of being struck by a car. Less an accident involving a random free-rolling tire than the carelessness of the protagonist, despite the pedestrian presentation, this scene is not in fact pedestrian-friendly. In this way, the privileged position implied by the artist's central vantage point within this perspectival scheme faces possible threats from beyond the frame of this pictured instant.

Similarly in *Wrong* (1966–68), another photo-text canvas, with the same standard fifty-nine by forty-five inches measurement (the dimensions determined by the size of the door of the artist's Volkswagen bus),[66] Baldessari again plays with the conventions of so-called correct composition (Figure 4.9). Here the artist is pictured standing in front of a palm tree, which through an illusion of cognition and seeming accident appears to be growing out of his head. It is a blatant violation of the basic rules that even an amateur photographer obeys, recalling the ploy of the contemporaneous piece *An Artist Is Not Merely . . . Wrong* seems to say that this is neither good nor correct photography, let alone art. The caption is bold and disciplinary, but nevertheless confusing. These images render visual pleasure absurd at the same time that the image is elevated to the status of high art via the canvas. By such turns, Baldessari's work is not "anti-art," as it has popularly been dubbed, but the sign of a postwar cultural shift in the redefinition of art. For if *Wrong* continues to have its humorous effect upon each viewing, we might best understand it in the terms laid out by Abigail Solomon-Godeau, in that "Baldessari's deadpan if deceptively casual expulsion of centuries of aesthetic precepts still carries its punch, because aestheticism, notwithstanding its aggregate onslaughts from Dada through various postmodernisms, is still alive and kicking."[67] The persistence of these problematics despite everything we "know" returns with a surprising, albeit familiar, thud.

Thirty years later, Baldessari would revisit the old tree-through-the-head trick, with an updated version of *Wrong (Version #2)* (1996) (Figure 4.10). And though the artist has visibly aged, bearded face and partly balding brow, the hedges around the home in the background are less full and his hands remain idly tucked away in his pockets, the punch line this time around seems to cue the disheartening platitude that the more things change, the more they stay the same. Perhaps it is no coincidence that a year earlier, in May 1995, a public debate on the subject of journalistic integrity and photographic manipulation centered on the misleading removal of a post from a head. John Filo's iconic 1970 Kent State shooting photograph, of Mary Ann Vecchio kneeling over the body of Jeffrey Miller, had been published innumerable times over the years, until someone had at last noticed, that somewhere along the way, the fence post that had originally appeared behind Vecchio's head had vanished (Figure 4.11). David Friend, *Life* magazine's director of photography, issued a public statement, denying any intent: "Amazingly, the fence post had been airbrushed out by someone, now anonymous, in a darkroom sometime in the early 1970s. The picture had run numerous times, without the fencepost, and without anyone taking notice: in TIME (Nov. 6, 1972, p. 23) PEOPLE (May 2, 1977, p. 37), TIME (Jan. 7, 1980, p. 45), PEOPLE (April 30, 1990, p. 117), to name just a few publications." This is but one example in a long-standing history of photographs not quite looking "right," which nevertheless shape collective and historical memory. Whether Baldessari was thinking of this controversy when he decided to update *Wrong* is unclear. However, in any case, Baldessari's sustained critique of the constructedness and the limitations of visual rules resonates. The artist's preoccupation with contrived aesthetic "correctness" was further evidenced when Baldessari's titular *Wrong* was editioned by the Los Angeles County Museum of Art, as an eraser in 2010 (Figure 4.12). Priced modestly at $6.95 and wrapped in cellophane, this slight commercial object makes light of the loaded erasure Baldessari's work evokes. Though playful and punning, the WRONG eraser subtly summons a needed reassessment of what has been occluded both by Baldessari and by the historical

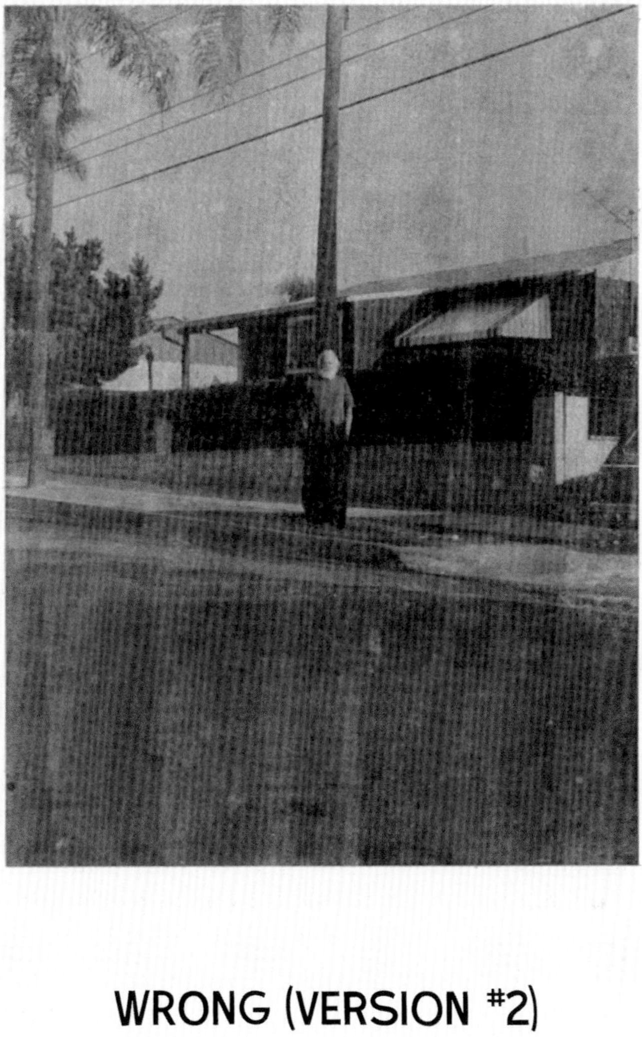

Figure 4.10. John Baldessari, *Wrong (Version #2)*, 1996. Photographic emulsion and enamel paint on canvas, 59 × 45 inches (149.9 × 114.3 cm). Courtesy of the Estate of John Baldessari and Marian Goodman Gallery.

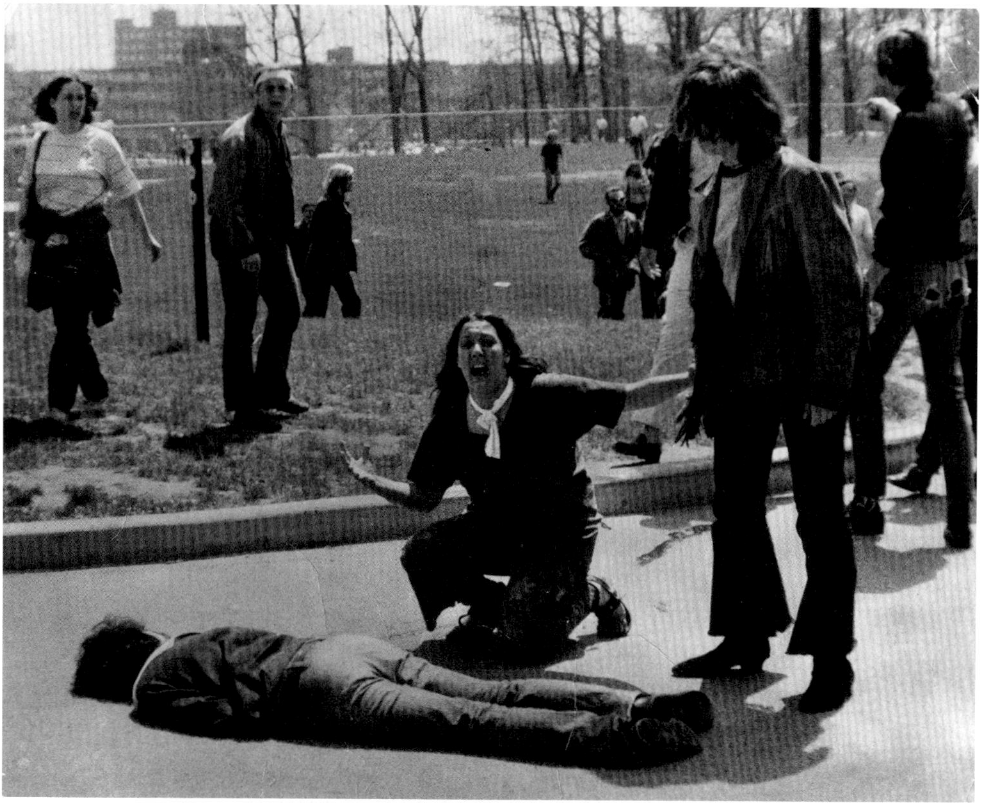

Figure 4.11. John Paul Filo, [Mary Ann Vecchio grieving over body of college student Jeffrey Glenn Miller shot by National Guardsmen during an antiwar demonstration, Kent State University, Ohio], May 4, 1970. International Center of Photography, The *Life* Magazine Collection, 2005 (1919.2005).

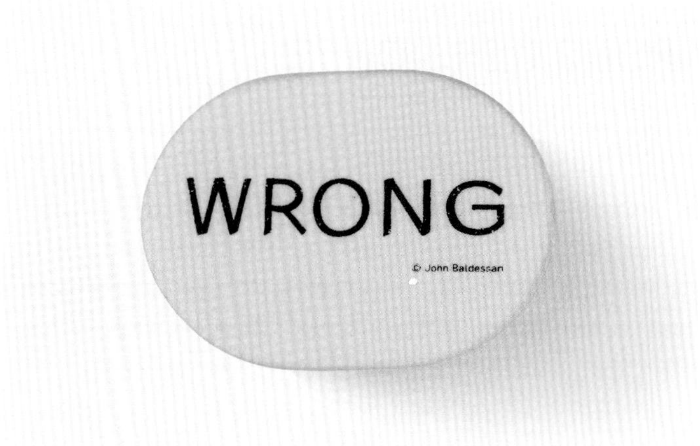

Figure 4.12. John Baldessari, *Wrong eraser,* 2010. Produced by Los Angeles County Museum of Art, 2½ × 2 × ⅝ inches (6.4 × 5 × 1.6 cm), latex free, nontoxic, and non-PVC. Courtesy LACMA, copyright Museum Associates.

accounts of his practice. Notably, in this case, though the allusion remains, the photographic image has been removed altogether.

Uncomfortable and obscured vision marks *This Is Not to Be Looked At*. Baldessari fashions disconcerting anxiety by taking the photograph from one source and the text from another, thereby creating compounded signification. While the Stella-clad *Artforum* may appear apolitical, the title *This Is Not To Be Looked At* is in fact appropriated from an etching in Francisco Goya's affecting *Disasters of War* series, produced during the Napoleonic invasion of Spain and the Peninsular War of 1808–14. Comprising eighty-five images of graphic exploitation, merging sadism with empathy, *Disasters of War* provides a touchstone in Western art history, which poignantly complicates the visuality of violence and the stakes of representing vulnerable bodies.[68] Goya's series viscerally questions the viewer's engagement with such images when, as Sontag memorably phrased it, "regarding the pain of others." It is of course no coincidence that the first edition of Sontag's poignant book features a Goya etching from this series on its cover, Plate 36. Sontag does not reproduce the attendant caption, which translates to "Not [in this case] either," which sounds obfuscatingly close to Baldessari's language. As Lela Graybill has eloquently argued, Goya's images trace the shift in cultural attitudes of his time toward the body, namely, "the rejection of an epistemology of pain wherein truth was seen to be lodged in the physical body, where meaning was thought to be discoverable by a mastering gaze attuned to reading the language of the suffering body."[69] Both Goya's series and Baldessari's early work mark changes in their particular cultural and political contexts, which affect the body as well as the mind. A closer consideration of Baldessari's artwork through the lens of Goya's series reveals compelling connections and uneasy political resonances.

Plate 26 of Goya's series describes a cruel execution scene by picturing the moment before (Figure 4.13). Its dramatic frieze and the emotional reactions of the victims pictured anticipate the moment of execution, and the captioned title beneath reads: "No se puede mirar," or "This is not to be looked at," which has also been translated as "One cannot look."[70] The act of looking itself links power to violence, and as this slippage in translation points out, one's subjective choice as a viewer is called into question. We do not see the executioners. Nevertheless, their bayonets enter the frame from the right, marking what Graybill identifies as their presence and our own "contingent field of vision," thereby problematizing the very act of looking.[71] As a precursor to the war photography of figures such as Robert Capa and Nick Ut, Goya exemplifies the painful limits of representation, particularly when looking at atrocities. Though etchings rather than photographs, Goya's images connect directly to histories of the photographic embodiment of atrocity. In many ways, Goya's series anticipates the horror of not only mechanized warfare but also the mechanized viewing of war. The viewer is always at a distance. This distance is enforced by the representation itself as well as imposed by the viewer's own defenses, which, in turn, are both invited and vaunted by the image, haunted by the inability to ever fully assimilate the information seen as an image before us. Seeing violence

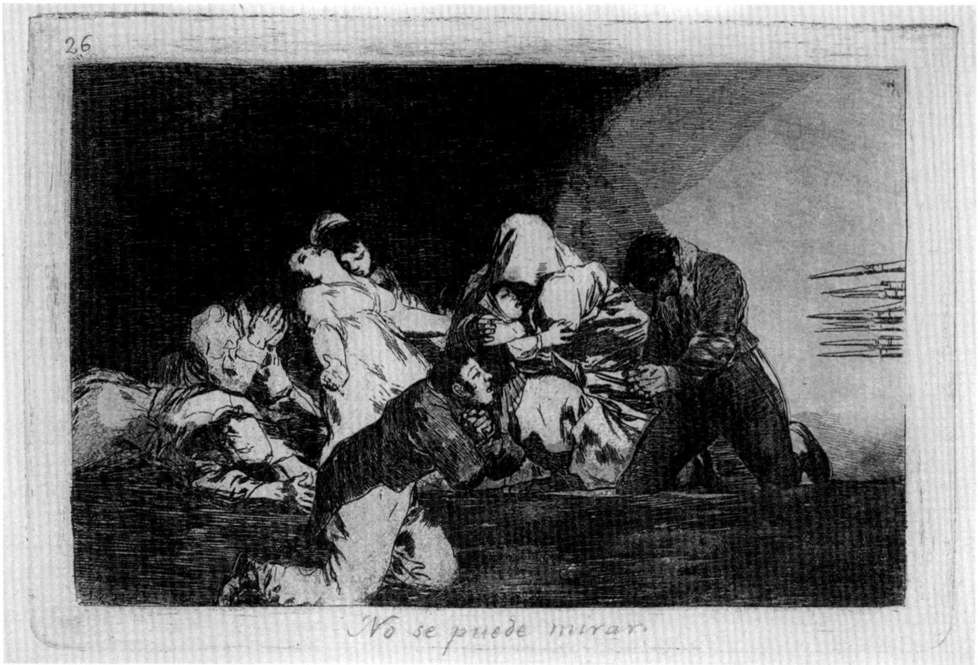

Figure 4.13. Goya (Francisco de Goya y Lucientes), Plate 26 from *The Disasters of War (Los Desastres de la Guerra): "One can't look." (No se puede mirar.),* 1810–20, published 1863. Etching, burnished lavis, drypoint, and burin. Plate 5¹¹⁄₁₆ × 8¼ inches (14.5 × 21 cm); sheet 9¹⁵⁄₁₆ × 13½ inches (25.2 × 34.3 cm). Inv. PD 1975, 1025.421.28. Copyright The Trustees of the British Museum / Art Resource, NY.

in images of war, it seems, suspends the ability to ever fully understand such an event, because the horror suppresses the social and historical context and meanings as well as the realities of brutality on the body. This repression shares an affinity with modern art's reluctance to acknowledge that all cultural practices, objects, and subjects are embedded in the social. Such an observation is made all the more poignant, since, as Amelia Jones has argued, "it is the body that inexorably links the subject to his or her social environment."[72]

Michel Foucault's interrogation of the empire of the gaze in his discussion of surveillance in *Discipline and Punish: The Birth of the Prison* (1979) demonstrates how power in the nineteenth century was intertwined and veritably equated with the concepts of seeing and knowing (e.g., *voir, savoir, pouvoir*). Goya's etchings similarly put these stakes on the line, but they do so in a way that problematizes their evidential function. Foucault wrote ironically of "self-evidence" to emphasize the artifice of visual experience, stating that "what was self-evident, taken for granted as natural, was precisely what had to be called into question."[73] The composition of Goya's etching, and by extension Baldessari's artwork, points outside the frame literally and figuratively to what one cannot see. Combined with the injunction against looking, Derrida's writing on the internal contradictions of framing applies here: "The frame makes a work of supplementary *désoeuvrement*. It cuts out but also sews back together."[74] A remarkable and unresolvable tension is created between the bayonets pointing our gaze inward and the strained visages of the victims facing outward, directing our gaze to the menace beyond the frame. Stella's famed reliance on the frame to organize his compositions is parodied as a way to expose the exclusions. Via photography, Baldessari literalizes this reliance and makes the viewer think about what supports prop up not simply the internal structure of Stella's work but also, and more pointedly, its external currency within culture and its occlusive function. In other words, what might a focus on art prevent us from recognizing?

On this point, it makes sense to insist that the war raging in Vietnam between 1959 and 1973 inevitably bled into the larger culture of representation in the United States. Without question, Baldessari, who was always mass media savvy, would have seen horrific photographs depicting the violence, including that which was perpetrated by the U.S. military against the North Vietnamese. In substituting Goya's image with Stella's painting in photographic form on canvas, Baldessari challenges the link between disinterest and the disembodied subject while raising the specter of a political unconscious. By interpreting *This Is Not to Be Looked At* in connection to Baldessari's lived experience within U.S. culture of the time, the substitution becomes an oblique critique of an insular and ineffective art world. His highlighting of Stella's iconic emphasis on the frame becomes an ironic analogy to the U.S. political policy of containment, so that in place of seeing Stella, we might instead see an image covering over the *Disasters of War,* which in Baldessari's context would be the Vietnam War.

The captions in Goya's series, and their specific invocation through Baldessari, tell us not what the images are of but how they are to be seen. This situation is complicated by the paradox of being repeatedly "reminded that the scene is always subject to a multiplicity of looks and is thus never wholly visible to our own contingent sight."[75] And moreover, deciphering events becomes even more intricate when an injunction against looking formulates the very directive of viewing. As viewers, we are conscripted as witnesses, integral to confirming the scene; however, we are never master of it as "wholly present" or ever completely in control of its meaning. Like the deferring function of the referent in photography, the violence is ultimately unlocatable. In fact, it appears that what we do not see controls the image. This unseen threat can also be connected, as mentioned, to the intensive circulation of photographs reporting on gruesome violence in Vietnam at this time and the absence of its literal presence in modernist art. The restriction against imagery, let alone suffering, in modernist art would eventually be paralleled by the government censorship of war photography. Baldessari's appropriation of these meanings suggests the confusing seriality of the violence of looking itself. Counter to the modernist proscription, both Goya's and Baldessari's complex images and their relation to text disrupt us from our absorption. As a work of conceptual art, Baldessari's *This Is Not to Be Looked At* subtly uses dark humor to question whether the "execution," to borrow LeWitt's language, is indeed "a perfunctory affair."

Eddie Adams's notorious February 1968 photograph of Brigadier General Nguyen

Ngoc Loan executing the Vietcong suspect Bay Lop at point-blank range in Saigon coincides with Baldessari's allusions to executions. Said to be stunning for its casualness as well as its severity, the photograph was first published in the *New York Times* that same year. In this image, the decisiveness of the shooter's resolve is palpable: it is as if the piercing sound of the shot were audible through the still. Deafening, too, is the unsettling expression of the flinching victim, which has been morbidly likened by the communications scholars Robert Hariman and John Louis Lucaites to one that might be seen at the dentist's office.[76] A third man, a witness within the frame, is seen recoiling in tandem, in the upper left-hand corner. Adams's photograph and other wretched moments from the conflict in Vietnam brought attention to the war and, at least in popular memory, are said to have galvanized the American public's resistance to it. Though there is little evidence to substantiate this belief, it is true that a handful of powerful and complex photographs remain cultural icons of the time, shaping the memory of war retrospectively.

Among the shocking images of the war in Vietnam, one particularly searing series stands out: namely, army photographer Ron Haeberle's documentation of the My Lai massacre on March 16, 1968. Published nearly a year after the fact, in late November 1969 in the *Cleveland Plain Dealer* and *Time* magazine, and in early December 1969 in *Life* magazine, these grisly photographs are notorious and traumatic.[77] The most extreme, showing mutilated bodies, split skulls, and spilled intestines, were not shared publicly. Shot in color, the intense realism of the images suffocates the viewer, exacerbated further by their close-up view and tight cropping. These photographs document the murder of more than five hundred unarmed civilian women, children, and old men by U.S. soldiers serving in a unit known as Charlie Company. Despite their evidential status, the photographs were nevertheless met with incredulity by some factions in the United States. Rep. Mendel Rivers, chair of the House Armed Services Committee, voiced a popular sentiment, "You know our boys would never do anything like that." Still others believed the photographs were planted by antiwar sympathizers.[78] With the exception of the fact that they are in color, these intimate images share much in common with Goya's *Disasters of War*, in their graphic depiction of inhumanity and the fragility of humanity, in their close-up range, and in their complex matrix of looks. One unforgettable photograph frames dozens of dead bodies, women and children, sprawled along a desolate blood-soaked dirt path. Appropriated in poster form, this horrific image was mobilized in antiwar protests by the Art Workers Coalition.[79]

Though not circulated publicly until the following year, Haeberle's visceral photographs of the My Lai massacre count among the most excruciating photographs of atrocity perpetrated in Vietnam and also resonate with Baldessari's *This Is Not to Be Looked At*. Possibly the most thoroughly documented action in the Vietnam War, complete with army investigations, congressional hearings, court-martial transcripts, articles, books, and documentaries, this "American Atrocity," to use the historian Claude Cookman's terms, might never have received any attention if Haeberle had followed the rules.[80] Dubbing them retrospectively "the Abu Ghraib pictures of the Vietnam era," Andy Grundberg explains: "If he had followed the rules, his pictures might never have been seen: he handed in his black-and-white shots to his superiors but kept for himself those shot in color with a second camera. This subterfuge allowed news of the My Lai killings to escape government control. It was only after Haeberle returned to the United States months later, however, that the pictures came to be published."[81] The officers of Charlie Company and their superiors covered up the massacre. In fact, it was only after U.S. Army Specialist Ron Ridenhour, who heard about the events from friends who had participated in the massacre, wrote a letter to President Richard Nixon, as well as several senators and Pentagon officials in March 1969, reporting the inhumane slaughter. Even with the photographs, the complex reality of this atrocity remains difficult to comprehend.

One particular photograph seems to concretize the massacre more than others. Seven terrorized villagers are huddled together, bracing themselves seconds before being executed (Plate 21). A small girl tries to hide behind a woman who, seen only in a blur, lifts her arm as a shield. With the knowledge of what comes next, the photograph is unbearable. Notably, none of Haeberle's published photographs put U.S. soldiers in the same frame with the villagers. Instead we have only the victims, and with that, the viewer seems aligned with the invisible assailants. Among the painful details, one is hidden in plain sight: a young woman wearing a black shirt fiddles to fasten her buttons. Why the preoccupation with buttons in such a crisis situation? Fifty years later this fragment has at last been widely acknowledged as indicating that this is a scene between the moments of sexual assault and mass murder. The court-martial excerpts attest to the brutal rape of numerous women and children. The melee of ethics, emotions, and violations in this photograph is impossible to untangle. Add to this the account of the photographer himself. "I yelled, 'Hold it,'" Haeberle recalled, "and shot my picture. As I walked away, I heard M16s open up. From the corner of my eye, I saw bodies falling, but I didn't turn to look."[82] Though at first the connection might seem to come out of left field, Haeberle's tone as he describes the moment before he turned his back is not so distanced from Baldessari's. More surprising is the fact that even in the capacity of a combat photographer, beyond the question of morality and mortality, Haeberle's photographic composition has been questioned. Criticized by some for not stopping the killing, he was also critiqued for visually cutting off the feet of the woman in the foreground and the body of the boy on the right-hand side. Comments such as "Haeberle, who probably felt rushed, failed to observe a rule taught in beginning photography classes—'Watch your edges!'" disconcertingly underscore how aesthetic rules rear their compassionless heads even in the most unseemly of places.[83] Following the rules, whether given in the form of a photography manual or a military order, embeds larger questions connected to individual agency and the role of indifference.

Three decades later, Baldessari returned to Goya, this time as an explicit reference point in the creation of his *Goya Series* (1997) for presentation at the Venice Biennale:

"I've always been a fan of Goya, and in this series I took off from his titles, which are so ambiguous that I realized you could move them to another subject and wouldn't know it. If someone's body is being mutilated and you're saying that this is bad, what's bad? If you take the subject matter away, you can apply the title to another subject. I like that kind of mobility of meaning."[84]

With a remarkable degree of callousness, Baldessari defers the violence and viscerality with which he knowingly, if cursorily, engages. Truly seeming "perfunctory," this later series reinforces the taciturn thread that was implicit in Baldessari's earlier work with photography. A plain, overturned white coffee mug is accompanied by text that reads "Wrong": a pun on the mug-shot genre perhaps? An empty bowl, right side up, captioned "This is Bad," possesses the vacancy of a generic stock photograph. Accusations of banality, laconicity, cynicism, and opacity seem fitting for this popular series. *No One Knows Why* pictures a mangled pair of glasses, warped frames without lenses, an image that lends itself to thinking about how vision and visuality are shaped by the specificity of those fragile parts. The caption throws up its hands, existentially shrugs off the ability to make coherent sense, yet, by way of a return to Goya and the *Disasters of War,* this aspect of unknowability becomes much more than stated indifference. *And* shows a basic paper clip, evoking ideas of linkage, but again, in the absence of specifics, connections are obscure if only inferred, more slippages than fixtures.

There is reason to be suspicious of the frequently naive appearance of Baldessari's work. His series of *Commissioned Paintings* (1969) are a case in point and pivot on their apparent banality and embedded polemical motivation (Figure 4.14). The canvasses are deceptively ordinary, featuring fourteen paintings in which a different object is shown in conjunction with a pointing finger. Or, more precisely, a hand gesture mimicking a gun, with the index finger standing in for the barrel. Uniform in size and principle, a caption beneath each painting reads "A Painting by [the person's name]," in the lower frame of the canvas. For example, *A Painting by Helene Morris* shows an index finger pointing at tangled cord and wires in an ordinary-looking cardboard box; *A Painting by Dante Guido* shows an index finger pointing at two commonplace lightbulbs in a recessed hole in a wall (one on and one off); *A Painting by Jane Moore* shows an index finger pointing at two conventional deep-set stovetop elements. This series developed out of what Baldessari refers to as his fascination with Sunday painters, and the thematized domesticity of each scene, characterized by ramshackle storage and banal details around the house, seems to indicate as much.[85]

The process of creating *Commissioned Paintings* began with Baldessari asking his friend George Nicolaidis to randomly point out things that interested him, and then Baldessari would photograph Nicolaidis in the act of pointing (Plates 24 and 25). Like the process of the readymade, the documentary slides of these excursions were concerned with selection rather than beauty. Baldessari then commissioned four-

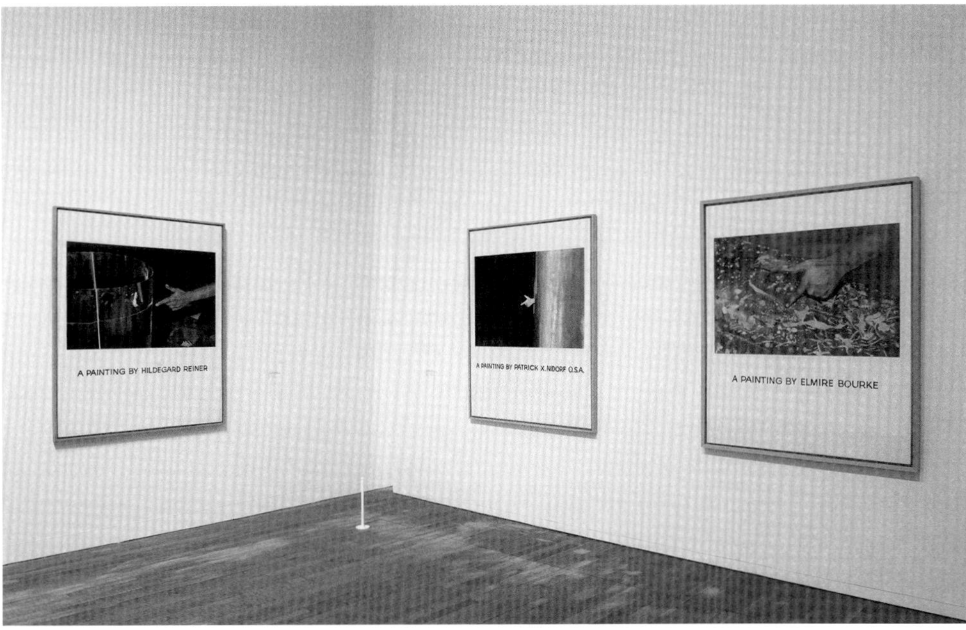

Figure 4.14. Left: John Baldessari, *Commissioned Painting: A Painting by Hildegard Reiner,* 1969. Oil and acrylic on canvas, 59¼ × 45½ inches (150.5 × 115.6 cm). Center: John Baldessari, *Commissioned Painting: A Painting by Patrick X. Nidorf O.S.A.* Oil and acrylic on canvas, 59¼ × 45½ inches (150.5 × 115.6 cm). Right: John Baldessari, *Commissioned Painting: A Painting by Elmire Bourke,* 1969. Oil and acrylic on canvas, 59¼ × 45½ inches (150.5 × 115.6 cm). Installation view of *John Baldessari, Pure Beauty* at the Tate Modern, London, 2010. Courtesy of the Estate of John Baldessari and Marian Goodman Gallery.

teen "Sunday painters" he had met while visiting art fairs in Southern California to copy a slide from the series. Each painter had the choice of a handful of slides. Duplicated as precisely as possible, in a kitschy photo-realist style, the works in the *Commissioned Paintings* function more akin to photographs than paintings.[86] In this respect they further expose the latent photographic impulses of representational painting. They also expose the framing conventions of photography as inherited from the history of painting. In Baldessari's involvement as documentary photographer, while exempting himself from the selection as well as from the final execution of the piece (including the painting, done by a "Sunday painter," and the text, done by a professional sign painter), the artist stages issues regarding the implied and complicated contingency between decision-making and artistry, democracy and order, lest we forget that the initial parameters of this pseudo-performance piece are outlined by Baldessari himself.

The choices of supposedly interesting objects in these images seem to be haphazard. However, the longer one contemplates them, the more commonalities and differences start to emerge. Two dominant aspects recur in each of these photo-based paintings: the frame and the index. Both are present yet under varying guises.

As Dave Hickey has argued, in contemplating whether Baldessari is indeed a "conceptual" artist at all: "Simply stated, the 'conceptual' aspect of Baldessari's work resides in its treatment of all media as nested extensions of the body's demonstrative gesture—Baldessari's trademark pointing finger."[87] Hickey explicitly identifies the index (literally and figuratively) in Baldessari and implicitly identifies the frame by evoking the term *nested*. Each composition in *Commissioned Paintings* has a multiplicity of frames within frames. Echoing the bayonets in Goya or the centerpiece on the cover of *Artforum*, the gesture of pointing opposes the dictum "This is not to be looked at." Emphatically, demonstratively, it says instead, "Look at this!" But look at what? The pictures contain only humdrum objects of everyday life. As such, they become meta-commentaries on the most basic principle of the photographic index. As Charles Peirce related, "The index asserts nothing: it only says 'There!'"[88]

An ensconced sequence of visual arrows and targets combines in Baldessari to at once orient and disorient the viewer. This index, which directs looking, underpins Baldessari's diverse body of work, so that, for example, the thirty-three photographs that compose *Lines of Force (Photos in Line)* (1972–73) and the twenty-eight photos in *A Movie: Directional Piece (Where People Are Looking)* (1972–73) are linked by a sequential reliance on pointing and looking. The two acts are nearly inseparable. Gesture and vision are connected, as are the act and the idea, always suspended within the question of the frame of reference. The index finger, that mnemonic reference to the photographic index, underscores all these pieces, just as the frame, the mnemonic reference to the quintessential properties of art, is always present. The oblique critiquing of the frame and the instability of the index connect directly and point a posteriori to his later series *Choosing* (1971).

During the 1970s, Baldessari asked himself, "why photographers do one thing and painters another." He stated: "The real reason I got deeply interested in photography was a sense of dissatisfaction with what I was seeing. I wanted to break down the rules of photography—the conventions. I began to say photographs are simply nothing but silver deposit on paper and paintings are nothing more than paint deposited on canvas, so what's the big deal? Why should there be a separate kind of imagery for each?"[89] With this connection in mind, Baldessari returns repeatedly to an investigation of the dialectic between painting and photography as an intermedia gesture.

"Painterliness" continually seeps into Baldessari's art, particularly through his use of color. Though most of his photographs are black-and-white (as was the case with most early conceptual photography), they are typically put in conversation with color fields. Solid colored shapes evoke the monochrome even as Baldessari criticizes the disappearance of the figure in modern art. Two works from the *Pathetic Fallacy Series, Injured Yellow* and *Stoic Peach* (both 1975), present only the most minimal photographic information. Their washed-out colors connote overexposed and sun-drenched film. The titles anchor their meanings in one sense, playing on the associative relation between colors and states of mind. But how fastened are they as evidence of anything? Removed from the facts, these documents serve as floating signifiers, linked to emotion-charged titles. In other words, their meaning is colored or shaded, suggesting that they are in fact misleading information at best.

Baldessari's works of the late sixties—especially those that included enlarged photographs of nondescript street corners of National City, drive-by snapshots of his hometown in California—have frequently been associated with the look and the poker-faced attitude of Ruscha's photographic works.[90] Claiming the use of the camera as "a sort of note-taking rather than carrying around a notebook," Baldessari's professed haphazard attitude about image making and picture taking seems to be a similarly expressionless enumerations of "facts."[91] Akin to what Ruscha dubbed "capers," Baldessari's self-consciously narrative visual jokes use a laconic presentation to problematize visuality.[92] In contrast with the democratic gesture of Ruscha's artist books, however, Baldessari's decision to print on canvas adds an extra dimension of irony and, by extension, questions the photograph as art and as a cultural sign.[93] Notably, the assumed speed of photographic capture and transmission contributed to Baldessari's shift to photography. As he described retrospectively in 1980, "I discovered I was more of a 'thinking' person than a 'working' person. Photography allowed me to register my ideas more rapidly than painting them. They grew out of a sense of urgency. If you're stranded on a desert island and a plane flew over, you wouldn't write 'HELP' in Old English script."[94] The analogy to desert island–level desperation is at once humorous, revealing, and misleading. Moreover, it is out of sync with the apparent content of most of Baldessari's images and his inclusion of the apparatus of painting. After all, what is so pressing about a blurry picture of an Oldsmobile? What or where is the exigency? The attendant script that Baldessari included on his text canvas works in 1967–68 might as well have been written in Old English for all the clarity they provide. Moving from captions that were plain statements of content, Baldessari began to include increasingly sophisticated quotes, appropriated from increasingly obscure sources, only to become popularly identified in the art press as "American art's most prolific commentator on photography's social workings."[95] Returning to *An Artist Is Not Merely the Slavish Announcer of Facts, Which in This Case the Camera Has Had to Accept and Mechanically Record* suggests at least part of the artist's magnetism. Using an uncanny mix of blatant banality and covert criticism, Baldessari turns a simultaneously dismissive and attentive eye on our assumptions about art, photography, and visuality. The art does not reside in the undistinguished black-and-white photograph of a California parking lot, greenery, with a tree in the center of the picture; nor is it in the text—copied by a professional sign painter from a book. Nor is it in the "artistic" material of stretched canvas or an "artistic" arrangement of pictorial ingredients. It is in the artist's sardonic combination of these elements and his choice of an elusively straight image that breaks the most rudimentary, photo-manual rules of composition, thereby questioning the conditions of visuality at the outset. In other words, Baldessari points to the inevitable interventionist artistry of the camera, magnifying the medium's mechanical conditions only to make clear our inability to grasp its ever-morphing complexity.

C-A-L-I-F-O-R-N-I-A

California Map Project / Part 1: California (1969) was the first time Baldessari employed photographs independently from canvas (Plate 22).[96] Ten color photographs, a photograph of a map of California, and an explanatory text constitute the work. Structured around the word *California,* which is printed across the geography of the state on a found map, Baldessari undoes the logic of the map and the photograph in tandem. Traveling the length of the state to the geographic coordinates marked by each letter, Baldessari created, or "found," each letter's shape in the land itself at the sites where the individual letters happened to *land.* The project contributes to Baldessari's investigations into randomness and objectivity, and moreover, the ways in which these categories collapse under their own weight. The *C* is made of logs on a beach; *L* is created by a telephone pole and the adjacent shadow it casts along the side of the road; *R* is formed out of rocks in a stream. Uncertainty marks each one, with some more gag-like than others. As Larisa Dryansky has pointed out, the unpredictable shadow of the *L* would only read as such at a particular time of day, from a specific angle.[97] Grouped together, the eleven photographed sites parodically spell out "California." The photographs are linguistically keyed to the found letters of the location, thereby serving, in the curator Anne Rorimer's estimation, "to bring geographically disparate segments of observed reality together in one place"[98] while calling into question the absurd quality of maps, in opposition to their professed ability to act as objective representations. A similar investigation into the instability of maps occurs in Huebler's work. Maps, like photographs, are real only insofar as the meaning one attributes to them or the confidence one invests in them to provide directions. They defy the ideal of the perfect analog. More than a game about the arbitrary "nature" of language (though the letters do seem camouflaged in their habitat), this piece is also striking as a demarcation of the territory in which Baldessari's art practice has itself come to be representative, namely, as a pioneer of photographic experimentation in California. Additionally, from the vantage of the present, *California Map Project* takes on amplified resonance, with the recognition that though maps and borders might be arbitrary, the effects they exert on real lived experience can indeed be treacherous and in some cases deadly.

An exhibition curated by Charles Desmarais in 1992 at the Laguna Art Museum, titled *Proof: Los Angeles Art and the Photograph, 1960–1980,*[99] set the task of explaining the commonalities in Los Angeles art of this period by referring to the work of some forty-five artists experimenting with photography. Among the central questions underpinning the show were why so many artists were using photography the way they were, and how these practices were distinct to a West Coast sensibility. Among the conclusions Desmarais draws is the "realization that this art, ultimately, is the expression of profound doubt" as a result of the overall "unreliability of modern social and political structures, anchored in the liberating revelation that there is no such thing as proof—that we can communicate nothing but interpretation."[100] Echoing Nietzsche's late nineteenth-century adage that "there are no facts, only interpretation," this use of photography in the sixties visibly anticipated current concerns in contemporary art.

Like much of today's media-savvy work, these conceptual photographic practices owe a heavy debt to the pop art of the early 1960s as well as to earlier reflections on the medium in relation to cultural phenomena, namely, Benjamin's writings from the 1930s.[101] While Douglas Crimp's writings on pictures and the Pictures Generation might lead one to believe that the brand of photoconceptualism based in media appropriation has its genesis in New York, Desmarais argues quite convincingly for a reconsideration of the origins of postmodernism in earlier Los Angeles art when, by some seemingly strange coincidence of geography, these photographers took up the photograph's essence as a subject of investigation: "Searching for the answer to what the photograph *is,* they often tested assumptions about what it *is not.* Challenging its authority as repository of fact, they used it to lie, or to detect lies, or to rethink the conventional distinction between lie and truth."[102] Beginning with works such as Ruscha's *Twentysix Gasoline Stations* portfolio of 1962, the use of photography in art on the West Coast has been dominated by the experience of reality governed by pictures, or to use Crimp's observation about the role of pictures more broadly: "While it once seemed that pictures had the function of interpreting reality, now it seems that they have usurped it."[103] Countering the idea that art is synonymous with either stable truth or entrenched power, California artists in the late sixties turned to photography as a way to encourage doubt and contradiction under the guise of the blasé delivery of information, working against the double sense of Nietzschean mastery. According to the German philosopher, "Our so-called will to truth is the will to power because the so-called drive for knowledge can be traced back to a drive to appropriate and conquer."[104] The paradox of being unable to distinguish between reality and representation is a truism of Californian reality. This is particularly the case in Los Angeles, where the visual arts are often enmeshed with the tradition of movies and television, of billboards and advertising, of the Hollywood dream-machine and Disney.

Art in California has always been deeply connected to the film industry. Walt Disney employed painters as animators during the Great Depression; today, Disney funding continues to be one of the most important lifelines of the top regional art school, the California Institute of the Arts. In addition, actors and directors, and other film workers, have been among the wealthiest and most vigilant art collectors, from Cary Grant to Dennis Hopper to Steve Martin.[105] As Ruscha described his attraction to Southern California, "LA possessed vulgar magic with no history except that of the movie industry."[106] This is the California zeitgeist of which Baldessari was part and parcel, constantly oscillating between concepts of what is "real" versus "illusion." Hollywood's influence was nearly omnipresent, including what the artist Suda House has described as "the set-building—constructed for the camera—sensibility."[107]

Significantly, the fact that Southern California as a whole lacked serious exhibition spaces and critics, especially by contrast with New York's preeminence, created a sense of freedom and experimentation.[108] Until 1965, when a new Los Angeles County Art Museum was built, there was no independent art museum in the entire city of two and a half million people.[109] And though *Artforum* magazine was founded on the West Coast in San Francisco in 1962, and moved to LA in 1965, it had relocated to New York by 1967. There was momentarily a glimmer of hope made possible by the sophisticated programming of both the Pasadena Art Museum and the Ferus Gallery; however, Ferus closed in 1966, and the Pasadena Art Museum followed suit in 1974.

Perhaps partly because of the lack of dominant institutions, the few major exhibitions that took place were extremely influential. The most significant exhibitions of this era were also ones that "encouraged experimental attitudes towards photography,"[110] namely, *The New Painting of the Common Object* (1962) and *By or of Marcel Duchamp or Rrose Sélavy* (1963). Both shows were held at the Pasadena Art Museum and organized by Walter Hopps. *New Painting* was the first museum exhibition of pop art in the United States, and the Duchamp exhibition was the artist's first retrospective. Each was influential in further developing the freewheeling Southern California outlook. Both exhibitions were also crucial to the specific interests of emerging artists working with photography: "the first validated the Image in an Abstract Expressionist's world, pointing an ironic and self-referential way for artists more or less stuck with Image as a given; the second discredited the merely 'retinal.'"[111] Hopps's curatorial efforts opened up entirely new possibilities for the very conception of art. The Pasadena Art Museum was also the site of Warhol's first museum exhibition in 1970. The Ferus Gallery hosted Warhol's first one-man show, a deadpan presentation of thirty-two paintings of *Campbell's Soup Cans* held in 1962 (the same year as Ruscha's debut exhibition in the same space).

Among the advantages of this lack of prominent institutional structures for artists was an abiding "sense of freedom from artistic rules and institutional strictures,"[112] the very things Baldessari was interested in putting on trial. As Eleanor Antin expressed it, "New York was always formulating the correct ways to work and think while back here we were always eager to be surprised and engaged in new ways."[113] In addition to the Ferus Gallery and the Pasadena Art Museum, the Chouinard Art Institute (which later became known as the California Institute of the Arts) and the University of California, Los Angeles were the centers of gravity for nearly everyone involved in progressive art. Significantly, in 1970 (the same year he burned his paintings), Baldessari moved from San Diego to join the faculty at California Institute of the Arts (CalArts), where he began to work "almost exclusively in photography and related media, unleashing a frenzy of production that has gone unabated since."[114]

In the art school context, teachers and students alike were beginning to think of the photograph as an art *object,* rather than simply a medium. Seeing photography not as the transparent transmission of information or as pure information itself but as a material entity with its own formal properties ran completely opposite to conservative and modernist-informed artistic ideologies about the limits of medium-specificity. The formal surface of the photograph—completely out of keeping with traditional sculptural materials—introduces a pictorial space as a counterpoint to, and extension of, sculptural space, positing a powerful break from the illusory concept of photography as a window on an infinitely receding world,[115] deliberately against modernism's "truth to materials" and the belief in truth as a stable category more broadly. By contrast, critics like Hilton Kramer could not conceive of the possibility of a photograph being understood as an object beyond any object that it might name as an image.[116]

The very notion that photography was in some ways suspect to the art world overall as an aesthetic medium, let alone an aesthetic object, was precisely the attraction for artists such as Ruscha, Wallace Berman, Allen Ruppersberg, and of course Baldessari. According to Desmarais, Baldessari is one of the most prevalent figures to emerge at this time as especially powerful from this nexus of Los Angeles photography.[117] Having been hired at the inception of CalArts, Baldessari had a major impact on the school and, thus, on contemporary art in Los Angeles and the ways in which it was perceived nationally. Dubbing the school a "coolbed" of conceptual art, Baldessari was instrumental in bringing Douglas Huebler to CalArts, who had close affinities with the Los Angeles conceptual scene, as dean in 1976. Others who came to teach at Baldessari's invitation included Acconci, Laurie Anderson, Robert Barry, Daniel Buren, Dan Graham, Hans Haacke, LeWitt, Robert Smithson, and Lawrence Weiner. Among his students Baldessari can count some of the most visible contemporary artists, many of whom, even among the painters, demonstrate an awareness of the power contemporary culture grants the photograph, including Barbara Bloom, James Casebere, Meg Cranston, Eric Fischl, Mike Kelley, Matt Mullican, David Salle, and James Welling.[118]

Noting that other artists, such as Acconci, Joseph Kosuth, and Richard Long, had made far-reaching use of photographs in complex ways that went beyond mere documentation, Desmarais nevertheless distinguishes between West Coast and East Coast sensibilities: "In Los Angeles, however, we can discern a particularly tenacious strain of works primarily dedicated to unmasking the photographic lie."[119] Additionally, a "goofy humor and self-deprecating humility are marks of this work of the early seventies"—characteristics Baldessari's work shared with other artists in his milieu, namely, Ruppersberg, Antin (who knew Baldessari from San Diego), and William Wegman (who shared a studio with him in 1973).[120]

Peter Plagens and others have continued to develop narratives around the idea of scholastic conceptual art in New York versus a prankster, laissez-faire-style conceptual art on the West Coast.[121] Considering Baldessari's pedagogic legacy, this mythology makes for an oversimplification of the facts. The complex and often contradictory realities of California life, and its relation to art, have been explored with renewed interest in projects such as the Getty Foundation's *Pacific Standard Time*. Such efforts call out the fact that, as noted by the political activist and academic Angela Davis, "Although the history of this state is often told as a story of renewal, hope, and utopian possibility, a parallel story of disaster and catastrophe—of a dystopia shaped by fires, earthquakes, war and prisons—also informs California imagery."[122] This sentiment echoes in the words of the artist and photo-theorist Allan Sekula, when he wrote, "Los Angeles is perpetually in the grip of a generalized, often hallucinatory idealism. The art world perpetuates this in various ways. It's logical that Los Angeles should be the site of the counter-myth that photographs 'don't tell the truth.'"[123]

Sekula's extremely influential essay of 1975 provided a more dialectical approach to these two positions. "On the Invention of Photographic Meaning," originally published in *Artforum,* was among the first widely read political critiques of the medium of photography. His statement that "the meaning of a photograph, like that of any other entity, is inevitably subject to cultural definition" seemed obvious but was nevertheless radical based on the obedient ways in which photographs were being used and circulated at face value. Sekula made explicit the ways that photographs are loaded signifiers replete with interpretation: "Photographs are used to sell cars, commemorate family outings, to impress images of dangerous faces on the memories of post-office patrons, to convince citizens that their taxes did in fact collide gloriously with the moon, to remind us of what we used to look like, to move our passions, to investigate a countryside for traces of an enemy, to advance the careers of photographers, etc. Every photographic image is a sign, above all, of someone's investment in the sending of a message."[124] Baldessari, like Sekula, was an exception to the rules of so-called California anti-intellectualism. Each was engaged with issues of critique from the outset—demonstrating a West Coast subversion of the standards of East Coast "legibility." Baldessari's photographs provide one of the many necessary countermyths advocated by Sekula as a way to call into doubt the photographic sign as well as the photographic message.

Choice, Chance, and Conscription

Many of Baldessari's students over the years have commented on the profound impact his approach to art and pedagogy had on them. In a 2004 interview, the artist Matt Mullican tried to convey the immense shift that had occurred in his own thinking due to Baldessari's teachings at CalArts during the 1970s. Mullican admits that he remains nearly dumbfounded as to how the simple act of "pointing" opened up a whole new way of seeing for him: "I still can't stop thinking about those works, the pointing issue. The fact that pointing is almost the first semantic act; it is the basic basic act."[125] In a near spoof of Michelangelo's *Creation of Adam* (1512), Baldessari connects creation, and by extension artistic creativity, back to the genesis of an effortless hand gesture. Certainly, Baldessari's series of photo-based projects from the early 1970s emphasized the importance of pointing to practice and, by extension, pointing as a practice. Moreover, by linking pointing explicitly to the act of choosing, through simple means Baldessari seemed to enact the credo of Duchamp, who famously stated: "To make art is to choose and always to choose."[126]

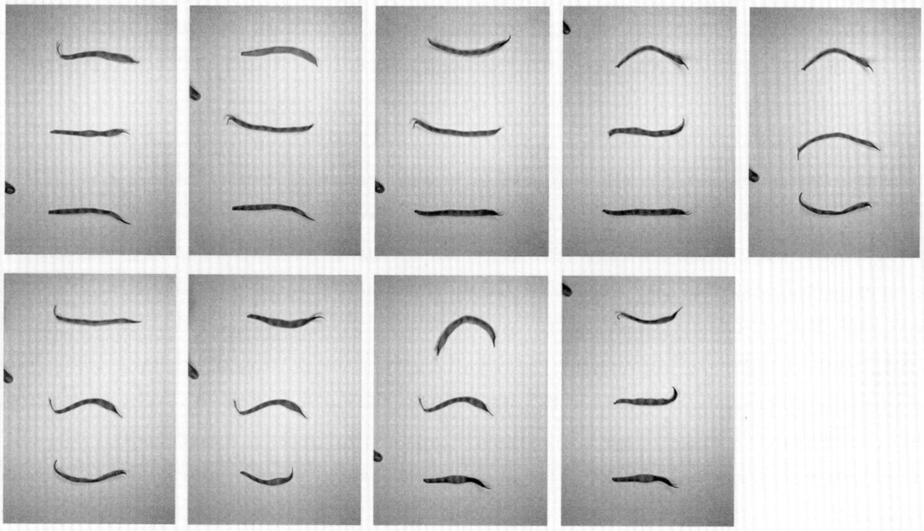

Figure 4.15. John Baldessari, *Choosing (A Game for Two Players): Green Beans,* 1971–72. Nine color photographs, 22 × 12¼ inches (55.9 × 31.1 cm). Courtesy of the Estate of John Baldessari and Marian Goodman Gallery.

Using nominalism as the name of the game (and the game of the name), *Choosing (A Game for Two Players)* (1971–72) poses a key case in "point." The series itself focused on the act of choosing and its connection to random impulse. For example, one version of *Choosing (A Game for Two Players): Green Beans* (1971–72) consists of nine color photographs arranged in three horizontal rows of three images (Figure 4.15).[127] As a rudimentary counterpoint to Edward Weston's esteemed beautiful photographs of individual vegetables, each blasé photograph by Baldessari documents three plain green beans. In Baldessari's own words, the instructions were as follows:

> A participant was asked to choose any three beans from the group for whatever reasons he/she might have at the moment. The three chosen beans were then placed upon a surface to be photographed. I chose one of the three beans for whatever reasons, I might have had at the moment. A photograph was taken of the selection process. The chosen bean was carried over; the two other beans not chosen were discarded; two new beans added. The next choice was made, and so on. Each of the participants develops strategies unknown to the other player as the selection process continued until all the beans are used.[128]

Each photograph of the set, though seemingly mundane, includes the omnipresent index finger pointing in the foreground, piercing the image frame. Played with not only green beans but also rhubarb and carrots, Baldessari's specific choices seem to suggest an overriding preference for vegetables that share a visual affinity with fingers.[129] This ostensibly self-contained and self-referential system seems more controlled than capricious, as if enacting some sort of assembly-line quality compliance. *Choosing,* like other works by Baldessari, performs the belief that rules (particularly as far as art is concerned) are a matter of perspective. But perhaps there is yet another way to regard the meta-commentary around pointing as intertwined with photography that Baldessari keeps pointing to.

Not surprisingly, *Aligning: Balls* (1972–73) also began with a set of instructions, directing a banal activity, with a set goal that seemed arbitrary if not completely useless (Plate 23). In *Aligning,* a red ball was thrown into the air and photographed in various scenes, on various streets, in front of various buildings or telephone poles, in front of the expanse of an anonymous expanse of the sky. In each snapshot the resolution of the image varies as does the location of the ball. Overall, the photographs appear excessively amateur and haphazard, one might even say meaningless. Always off center, the ball floats farther up or down the frame, more laterally or not. The completed project includes forty-one photographs arranged on the wall with an unorthodox installation logic. Rather than use the typical top or bottom edges of the photograph's frame to dictate the level at which they should be exhibited, the floating ball was used as a notational device. This built-in contingency became the somewhat absurd means of cohesively hanging the photographs. The random balls in each photograph are aligned across the installation to create an order all its own. "Art for John Baldessari has to do with . . . the establishment of certain qualitative levels of order while accepting the formation of other levels of disorder," one critic wrote in 1972, referring specifically to *Aligning: Balls* of that same year.[130] Exposing the capriciousness of rules, in this view, functions as a critique of modernist orthodoxy. As the viewer attempts to fill in the blanks, or in this case to connect the dots, one considers how the desire for narrative literacy often threatens to override reality.

Robin Kelsey's recent account of Baldessari's use of photography and chance cleverly analyzes the ways the artist satirized taste and skewered precepts surrounding photography's act of suspension. Focusing on Baldessari's *Throwing Three Balls in the Air to Get a Straight Line (Best of Thirty-Six Attempts)* (1973) (a series in the lineage of *Aligning: Balls*), Kelsey describes how this gesture at once mocks and asserts masculinist bravado (the artist throwing his "balls" in the air, the photographs taken by his uncredited wife), as well as suggesting "how much more meaningful than his simple 'straight line' rule our aesthetic demands on everyday photographs really are." By playing on the idea of playing it straight, in Kelsey's point of view, Baldessari calls attention to how the structures of snapshot photography have infiltrated quotidian ways of looking.[131]

Balls other than Baldessari's were contemporaneously up in the air, however. Though beyond the immediate reference points of art, the much feared and fateful balls of the U.S. draft were both random and potentially fatal. Whereas Kelsey argues foremost that "chance offers an opening from rule and routine but remains radically indifferent to anyone who enlists it," because photography is the vehicle by which chance is accessed, we must not lose sight of how seriously enforced rule and indifference characterized the push to actually "enlist" at this juncture. In other words, far beyond questions of aesthetic and artistic subjectivity, how was subjectivity at large contingent on and restrained within the culture of the Vietnam War era? Selection was indeed a fraught social concern. Kelsey rightly makes mention of the fact that the military-industrial complex instrumentalized chance during the early years of the Cold War, yet a significant, unacknowledged dimension remains.

On December 1, 1969, the United States conducted its first televised lottery, conscripting military service for the war in Vietnam. Public disapproval was growing while violence was escalating, and people gathered across the country to watch on television or listen on the radio to the outcomes of this macabre lottery. Colored balls with birthdates inscribed inside were drawn by hand from a Plexiglas container. The individual selection of balls determined the order of the call for induction for the 1970 calendar year, for all men ages eighteen to twenty-six as specified by the Selective Service law. Some twenty-eight million young men were at risk. A significant portion of the public believed that the professed randomness of the draft was in fact unfairly weighted to particular demographics. John Fogerty of Creedence Clearwater Revival remembers the moment in 1969 when he penned the song *Fortunate Son*: "Now I was drafted and they're making me fight, and no one has actually defined why. So this was all boiling inside of me and I sat down on the edge of my bed and out came "It ain't me, it ain't me, I ain't no senator's son!"[132] With this uneven sense of reality in mind, the stakes of photographic selection, pointing, and absurdity take on new resonance. Notably, the decisive act of using balls to efface identity recurs with renewed force throughout Baldessari's artwork in the 1980s, with adhesive color dots placed obstructively and enigmatically over faces, in a manner that suggests erasure and resistance to identification.

Admitting as much, Baldessari has perspicaciously explained, "For most of us photography stands for the truth. . . . It fascinates me how I can manipulate the truth so easily by the way I juxtapose opposites or crop the image or take it out of context."[133] Ultimately, Baldessari employs the photograph as a prosaic yet multidimensional material; it is at once his object and his subject. Indulging it its anonymity as well as its surfeit of detail, his interest in photography's simultaneous vulnerability and its insatiable truth claims is repeatedly manifest. Despite his use of the stuff of everyday life as both form and ideation, even Baldessari's plainest pictures show themselves to be filled with potential duplicity, distantiation, and contingency.

The indecisive quality of Baldessari's pictures can cut in the other direction as well, working against productive openness and materializing instead as impassive uncertainty. When asked to evaluate his photo-text canvases from the late 1960s, Baldessari remarked blandly with hindsight: "This is what it is. It's not great, it's not bad, it's just what it is, sort of ordinary, like Van Gogh painting a pair of old shoes."[134] Such a pointed lack of discernment might be understood as aligning happily with photography's own absence of judgment or its "slavish" self. As this chapter has demonstrated, however, we might do well to be suspicious of this kind of abdication from agency on the part of the artist and, by extension, the viewer. In the face of a complex and morphing contemporary image-driven world, Andy Grundberg's assessment seems apt: "merely declaring that we live in an image world does not make explicit the dire consequences of being unable to sort one image from another. Instead of offering us freedom, the uncontrolled flow of pictures distracts us from the task of determining for ourselves what might be real enough to really matter." After all, Grundberg explains, those in power benefit from this broader reluctance to choose, and with that "the liberty of an unchecked image environment may prove to be less a blessing than a subtle form of tyranny, and the democracy of the camera a perverse kind of fascism."[135] Whereas Baldessari's conceptual use of photography implies its unwieldy potential, it also points accusatorily to photography's public and social limits. One detects a tone of resignation in the artist's approach and his deliberate obfuscation. Yet there remains the possibility within this multivalent space of photographic contingency that viewers might nevertheless be spurred to decipher the stakes, the play of power and visuality, and to come to their own conclusions within and beyond the frame of the image.

Epilogue
Credibility Gap

The term *credibility gap* was widely used during the Vietnam War era to indicate a sense of pervasive skepticism in the United States. It alluded to the division between President Lyndon B. Johnson's administration's policies and statements about the war and the actual realities of that same war. Whereas the Johnson administration continued to paint an optimistic picture of the situation in Vietnam throughout 1967, the Tet Offensive in 1968 and the later leak of the Pentagon Papers in 1971 evidenced irrefutably that the government had knowingly lied to the public. The situation escalated even further after 1969, under President Richard Nixon, leading many to conclude that the credibility gap was irreparable. The prevalence of this crucial disconnect—between official information, pronouncements in the media, and actual occurrence—became increasingly normalized during the twentieth century. Photographic images were one of the key terrains on which these tensions were manifest. Conceptual artists gravitated toward the plainness claimed by photographs, their indelible surface appearance and their matter-of-fact positioning, partly to test this inevitable contingency and its irreconcilable surfeit of meaning.

The credibility gap was first evoked in connection with the conflict in Vietnam by David Wise in the *New York Herald Tribune* in March 1965. Wise noted the inconsistent rationales circulating to justify war, including the U.S. military intervention in the Dominican Republic the previous month.[1] Was it "to save lives," "to prevent a Communist takeover," or something else altogether? Reporting in the *Washington Post* on December 5, 1965, Murray Marder picked up the term to describe the "creeping signs of doubt and cynicism about Administration pronouncements, especially in its foreign policy. . . . It represents a perceptibly growing disquiet, misgiving, or skepticism about the candor or validity of official declarations." Johnson and his aides responded to such criticism by claiming the real problem was that their comments were too often taken out of context by what they deemed a hypercritical press corps. The 1960s notion of a credibility gap, and a growing chasm between public perception and knowledge, bears an unsettling similarity to our current political predicament. One echo of the credibility gap's contemporary relevance can be found in the *Oxford English Dictionary*'s 2016 announcement that *post-truth* was its international word of the year. On the heels of the Brexit referendum that summer and a fall that saw the most divisive and polarizing election in modern U.S. history, *post-truth* held tremendous traction. Defined by the *OED* as "relating to or denoting circumstances in which objective facts are less influential in shaping public opinion than appeals to emotion and personal belief," the cultural currency of this adjective seems to have only gained in momentum. One wonders how deep the divide runs and how a peculiar drive toward self-deception may haunt American culture more broadly. Recall that in the late nineteenth century, P. T. Barnum famously claimed, "American people love to be humbugged," spurring a preoccupation in the mass press to evaluate this national trait.[2] Through this lens, the distance between then and now becomes condensed. Looking back to the emergence of conceptual art practices in the United States in the late 1960s, particularly those using photography, sheds further light on the complicated nexus of credibility and visibility.

While teaching at the New School for Social Research in New York amid anti–Vietnam War protests, Hannah Arendt published a poignant collection of essays whose powerful preface seems to predict our post-truth moment. In *Men in Dark Times,* Arendt discussed how historical records and rational truths are subject to manipulation. As Lauren O'Neill-Butler explains, by acknowledging the proliferation of "official" government double-talk, Arendt points to "something subtler, harder to see, and foundationally carcinogenic: when lies overwhelm the truth."[3] In Arendt's own words, "there was nothing secret or mysterious" about this phenomenon, yet "it was by no means visible to all, nor was it at all easy to perceive it." Arendt refers to the importance of the public realm to shed light on what she calls the "space of appearances," before explaining that "darkness has come when this light is extinguished by 'credibility gaps' and 'invisible government,' by speech that does not disclose what is but sweeps it under the carpet, by exhortations, moral and otherwise, that, under the pretext of upholding old truths, degrade all truth to meaningless triviality."[4] Like the eerie indifference Arendt had observed in her earlier discussion of "the banality of evil," ordinary appearances can be misleading and, perhaps more terrifyingly, normalize endemic violence.[5] Distinguishing between the implicit violence of so-called alternate facts and actual lived realities requires a careful and vigilant level of critical discernment. The conceptual approach to the photographic embeds a call to individuals acting in the public realm to cultivate this mode of attention, to enact a cognitive justice that acknowledges complexity rather than reductive assumptions.[6] Too frequently dismissed for their apparent banality, such images nimbly ask the viewer to suspend easy conclusions and to engage thoughtfully.

Something akin to Walter Benjamin's notion of "that tiny spark of contingency" appears with increasing frequency when we look back on the uncertainties of the late 1960s and the conditions of photography in tandem. In his "Short History of Photography" (1931), Benjamin described how the "spark of contingency" that is ignited when looking back on particular photographs summons "the Here and Now, with which reality has so to speak seared the subject, to find the inconspicuous spot where in the immediacy of that long-forgotten moment the future subsists so eloquently that we, looking back, may rediscover it."[7] In ways disquieting, unnerving, and surprising, we find echoes of the seared subjects of conceptual art recurring throughout contemporary art practice.

Let me share a recent example. Writing shortly after hearing the results of the November 2016 presidential election in his recurring *New York Times Magazine* column, the photography critic Teju Cole described feeling blindsided: "I lay in my bed in grief and confusion. . . . I was derailed. All my work suddenly seemed pointless. . . . I lay in my bed aphasic and estranged from myself."[8] In a description sounding similar to Oppenheim's reading position on the beach, one pictures the author lying down, uncertain how to proceed. Yet, shortly thereafter, Cole reasserts the necessity of art and criticism, amid a world polarized like never before, a gaping hole where credibility once resided, with divisive and derisive hyperbole at the center. For Cole, art and its potential to "refocus attention on the workings of power" address how everything is charged with historical and political meaning, and nothing should be taken for granted or gauged by immediate appearances. Cole reminds us of the loaded significance of detail itself. In his view, attention to detail might provide a source of renewal and mobilization. Associating "the current predicament" with an overwhelming "erasure of historical nuance," Cole sees a series such as Taryn Simon's *Paperwork and the Will of Capital* (2015) as an ambidextrous antidote (Figure E.1).

Simon's series consists of thirty-six large-scale photographs of isolated flower arrangements in heavy mahogany wood frames, and twelve sculptures, each comprising two concrete columns supporting two identical concrete blocks, on which lie loose stacks of herbarium paper with pressed flowers sewn onto them. The format in which the pedestals pose as mantels for study harks back to Mel Bochner's *Working Drawings and Other Visible Things on Paper Not Necessarily Meant to Be Viewed as Art*. Akin to the notion of "working drawings," here we have a play on "paperwork,"

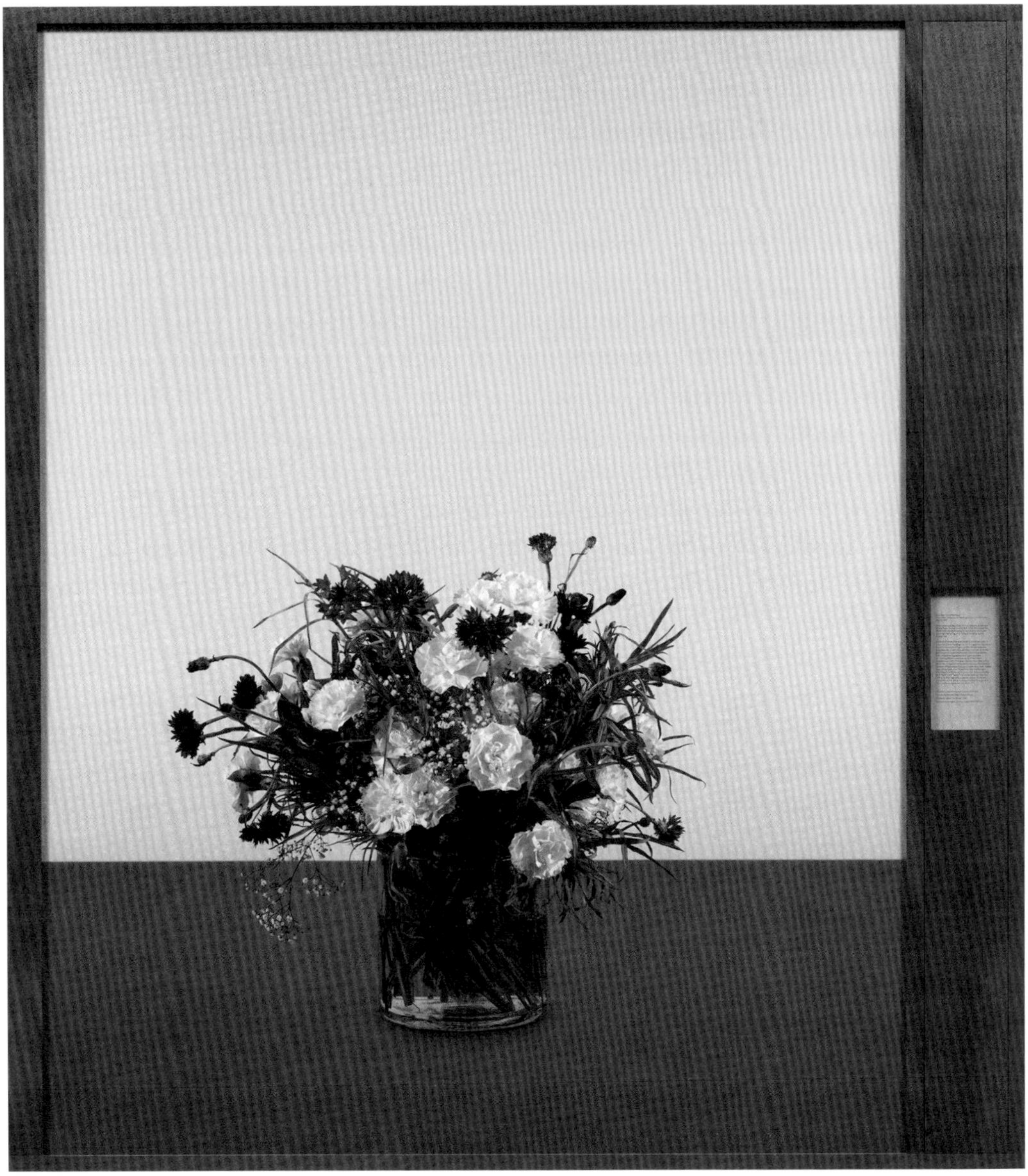

Figure E.1. Taryn Simon, *Classified "Spare Parts" Deal, Oval Office, White House, Washington, D.C., United States, May 16, 1975.* Part of the *Paperwork and the Will of Capital* series, 2015. Courtesy of the artist.

a conceptual motif implicating bureaucracy and the aesthetics of administration if there ever was one. And, like her early conceptual precursors, Simon's use of information is at once offered and obscured.

Some in color, some in black and white, each photograph presents a unique floral arrangement against a plain, unassuming backdrop. The bouquets suggest tropes of traditional art, still lifes to be contemplated on their own existential terms. And yet, despite this deceptively neutral appearance, closer examination reveals loaded significance. Simon noticed how incredibly staged photographs documenting the ratification of official treaties were and, oddly, how purposeful arrangements of cut flowers often adorned these scenes. Seeming to parallel the ceremonial arrangements and rearrangements of power marked by such occasions, Simon collected dozens of photographs from government signings dating from 1968 to 2014, including foreign and domestic affairs, dealings of trade and diplomacy, issues as vast as intellectual property, labor relations, nuclear armament, and land repatriation. To create *Paperwork and the Will of Capital,* Simon zoomed in on the flowers, in effect blowing up what had seemed only decorative and beside the point. Using these archival images as source material, Simon carefully and laboriously re-created these floral arrangements before shooting new photographs for exhibition. Giving pointed attention to such details opens additional layers of revelation, including the ways the fragility of form frequently parallels the tenuousness of geopolitical pacts.

Simon's *Classified "Spare Parts" Deal. Oval Office, White House, Washington, D.C., United States, May 16, 1975* (2015) features delicate spray carnation, baby's breath, cornflower, and oxeye daisy. The work evades easy legibility. An accompanying text describes the relevant treaty: "United States President Gerald R. Ford, United States Secretary of State Henry Kissinger and the Shah of Iran, Mohammed Reza Pahlavi, held a classified meeting in which they discussed a plan to provide material support to Turkey by funneling supplies through Iran." A longer paragraph explains how Ford and the Shah circumvented the arms embargo Congress imposed on Turkey for its invasion of Cyprus in 1974, clarifying further, how "In the 'Spare Parts' deal, the Pentagon overcharged Iran for the sale of arms so that Tehran could then send 'spares' on to Turkey. In a recorded meeting in the Oval Office, the Shah repeatedly expressed concern that his role in the deal could be leaked, insisting to Ford and Kissinger that 'your people must keep their mouths shut.'" An included appendix lists the scientific names of the flowers and discloses that the carnation originates from Colombia, the baby's breath from Kenya, and the cornflower from the United States. How to begin to make sense of this skirmish of information and signifiers? "It is in the deadpan meticulousness it embeds," argues Cole, "its unruffled testimony about the highways and byways of history." Looking back on the photographic traces of conceptual art, as *Documents of Doubt* has sought to do, we might both uncover and recover a shared impetus and a similarly double-edged charge.

An uncanny connection between Simon's project and an earlier work by Baldessari titled *Goya Series: There Isn't Time* (1997) brings this logic home (Figure E.2). Each depicts a black-and-white photograph of a seemingly ordinary vase of flowers,

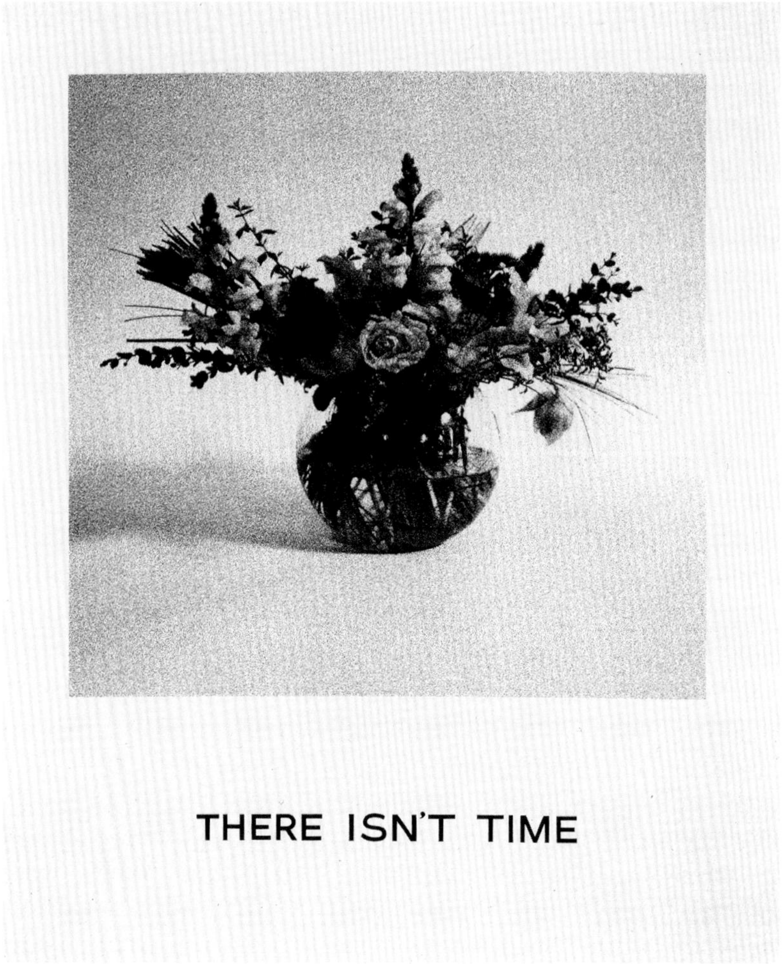

Figure E.2. John Baldessari, *Goya Series: There Isn't Time,* 1997. Ink-jet and enamel paint on canvas, 75 × 60 inches (190.5 × 152.4 cm). Courtesy of the Estate of John Baldessari and Marian Goodman Gallery.

against a blank background. Formally, they are nearly indistinguishable. Yet the operative possibilities of each lie in the details. They register the ambivalence of appearances that requires rethinking, the conceptual minutiae that buttress visuality, and the subtle yet profound power of photographic contingency. Baldessari's caption may be read as a sign of defeat; if there is no time, then why bother? Or, from another angle, it becomes a call to arms, immediate action. Despite the artful wink of the flowers, in both Baldessari and Simon, complicated questions emerge.

I have argued that, in relation to the work of some of the most paradigmatic conceptual artists, the photographic conditions of conceptual art disavowed and indeed dismembered art's autonomy. In place, they exposed inevitably contingent and ambiguous states and positions, pertaining not simply to the art world or art matters, but to lived experience more broadly. Particular case studies teased out early conceptual art's concern with depersonalized, a-subjective systems, quantification, and the "aesthetics of bureaucracy," calling for their reassessment in the light of current preoccupations with data collection and self-quantification, among other concerns. Despite knowing that what and how we see are shaped by culture and history, the complex negotiations of meaning instantiated by photography continue to disarm. The photograph's ubiquity and proposed self-evidence continue to necessitate careful and critical attention.

Just as the quest for a comprehensive picture of the world is bound to fail, so is the quest for essential photographic meaning. Photography is not and has never been an impartial recording device. Under the aegis of conceptual art, despite its often ordinary appearance, this reality was striking. The conceptual photography of Mel Bochner, Bruce Nauman, Douglas Huebler, John Baldessari, and others disavowed more than pure documentation and performed more than the role of coy amateur photography. In moving outside the boundaries of traditional aesthetics, these artists challenged the conventions of the aesthetic object. Moreover, as I have explored at length, each extended the problematics of Marcel Duchamp's readymade, repeatedly looking for the delays, seeking out the contingencies with broader social relevance.

All the artists studied here began with propositions that were at once logical and arbitrary. Each project's profound philosophical, artistic, and ethical questioning becomes all the more apparent as they are brought into dialogue with one another. Viewed together, Bochner's systematic undoing of measurements rejoins the apparent absurdity of Huebler's project to document the existence of everyone alive—both push beyond the limits of objective logic. Both depend on photography to do so, and in exchange, they reveal photography's unreliable yet persistent power to undermine systems. The distinctive banality of Nauman's photographs, from the artist's flour arrangements and attempts to drink coffee in his studio to his effort to levitate, speaks to the commonness and the implausibility of Baldessari's subjects, and questions what is art, as much as what is and is not to be looked at. The modernist logic of self-reference is displaced for a form of self-criticism that allows a space for deliberation, and often a space for humor. In the postmodernist sense, these works of conceptual art using photography make explicit the inevitability of mediation and the need for critique. The modernist claim to an original moment is exposed as a myth debunked by the possibility for proliferating infinite photographic copies.

I have deliberately avoided the nominalization *photoconceptualism* in regard to the artwork addressed in this book. On the one hand, this gesture recognizes the historic specificity of these works from the late 1960s and acknowledges the fact that it was not until the mid-1970s that a discussion of how these "conceptual" pieces relied on photography was available. Until that point, as I have described, critics, artists, and certainly art historians viewed photography as extraneous and incidental to the work rather than the mark of contingency on which the work pivoted. As Tony Godfrey noted, "Photography has had the widest possible effect on how photography is used in art, because it does not take the medium as a given, but as something whose mechanisms and use have to be analysed."[9] Beyond any one artist's position on or use of photography, it is doubtless that during the late 1960s and early 1970s conceptual artists participated in an important transformation of both art and the medium of photography in tandem. Photography's rise in prominence at this time was formative to the Pictures Generation artists of the late 1970s and early 1980s, and would continue to be relevant for every contemporary art movement that followed.

The need to question the rhetorical, ideological, and conceptual possibilities of the photograph remains prescient. Arthur Danto's summation of Ludwig Wittgenstein's emphatic doubt is relevant in this regard: "The things we 'accept' are what we are certain of only in the sense that we cannot imagine what life would be were they false, almost because they define the limits of imagination. Were we to attempt to set down these 'accepted' propositions, they would be simple, obvious, and useless. They would be all but uninformative."[10] Together, photography and conceptual art laid bare the unstable role of images in the late twentieth century, emphasizing the contingency and doubt that underscore any and every relationship between representation and the real.

Acknowledgments

In my early twenties, I worked as an archivist for the Press of the Nova Scotia College of Art and Design and became simultaneously perplexed and intrigued by conceptual art and its photographic forms. The work of the artists discussed across the pages of this book has influenced me in ways that I could never sufficiently put into words. My deep gratitude goes to the kindness and insights of Mel Bochner, Amy Plumb Oppenheim, Darcy Huebler, Paula Cooper Gallery, Baldessari Studio, Catherine Belloy at Marian Goodman Gallery, Eve Schillo at LACMA, Bruce Nauman Studio, Katherine Borkowski at Sperone Westwater, Jacqueline Simon at Artists Rights Society, and Robbi Siegel at Art Resource, NY, among numerous others. Sincere thank you to Amelia Rina for helping to clarify my thoughts and my voice, and to Kirstin Gotway's assistance navigating the labyrinth of image permissions.

I am grateful this book found a fitting home at the University of Minnesota Press under the wise guidance of Pieter Martin. Thanks to everyone at the Press who made this book a reality and shepherded the manuscript through the production process, including Anne Carter, Paula Dragosh, Rachel Moeller, and Laura Westlund. Sincere thanks go to Fred Kameny for his sharp-eyed and detailed work on the index. The perspicacity of anonymous readers enriched this text as well as its connective tissues. John Curley's attentive and thoughtful observations were incredibly productive, a testament to the most stellar ideals of the peer review process. I am grateful for the generous support of a Wyeth Foundation for American Art publication grant through the College Art Association.

Initial research for this project was supported by the Social Sciences and Research Council of Canada as part of doctoral work at the University of Toronto. I benefited from so many conversations over those years that cannot be recounted here, but the critique of and conversations with Elizabeth Legge, Mark Cheetham, and above all Louis Kaplan truly enabled this project to take root. Louis, as a mentor and a friend, has shaped my scholarship, and in turn my life, in innumerable meaningful ways. I also thank Amanda Boetzkes, Liz Kotz, Kaja Silverman, Alexander Streitberger, Blake Stimson, John Ricco, and Andres Zervigón for their discerning comments on early drafts of this material.

Seeing this project through over many years became possible as a result of the ongoing dialogue and motivation provided by numerous institutional and academic relationships. Foremost among these are the Whitney Independent Study Program, Whitney Museum of American Art, New York, especially Ron Clarke, Brendan Fernandes, and Marisa White Hartman; the Center for the Humanities at the University of Miami and the unparalleled collegiality of Erica Moiah James, Karen Mathews, Perri Lee Roberts, Tom Lopez, and especially Nathan Timpano; the Ryerson Image Center, Ryerson University, Toronto, in particular Thierry Gervais; and the Terra Foundation for American Art in conjunction with the John F. Kennedy Institute for North American Studies at the Freie Universität, Berlin, principally Frank Kelleher and Martin Lüthe.

So much family and so many friends have encouraged me along the winding road of this book, from ideation to publication, and all the contingencies in between. These include Jeff Thurlow and Cari Barrett, Carol and Jim Bradley-Williams, Jessica Thurlow and Todd Koffler. I am grateful to three unique sages, Angela MacDonald Vemic, Lisa DiQuinzio, and Farah Malik. The generosity and sheer tenacity of spirit of my parents, Bruce and Rachelle Diack, and my brother, Ian, have taught me to be endlessly curious yet steadfast, and open to embracing the unexpected. My greatest debt goes to my loving and brilliant husband, Erin Thurlow, and our sweet daughter, Eva, who have each stretched my heart and my mind in ways that have made, and continue to make, all the difference.

Notes

Introduction

1 Louis Kaplan, *Photography and Humour* (London: Reaktion Books, 2017), 171–72. See Kaplan for more on the humorous implications of Oppenheim's piece.

2 Douglas Crimp, "Pictures," *October* 8 (Spring 1979): 77.

3 Kynaston McShine, *Information,* exh. cat. (New York: Museum of Modern Art, 1970).

4 Alanna Heiss, "The Rightness of Wrongness: Modernism and Its Alter Ego in the Work of Dennis Oppenheim," in *Dennis Oppenheim: Selected Works, 1967–1990* (New York: P.S.1 Museum / Abrams, 1992), 27. Thomas McEvilley notes: "There is a humorous interplay between the ideas of leisure and sunbathing on the one hand, and self-endangerment on the other" (*Sculpture in an Age of Doubt* [New York: Allworth Press and School of Visual Arts, 1999], 95).

5 David Green, "From Presence to the Performative: Rethinking Photographic Indexicality," in *Where Is the Photograph?* (Maidstone, U.K.: Photoworks; Brighton, U.K.: Photoforum, 2003), 47–60. See Green and Joanna Lowry regarding the "event" of photography.

6 William Balck, *Tactics* (Fort Leavenworth, Kan.: U.S. Army Cavalry Association, 1915). This book has been identified by Robert Slifkin as the 1914 English translation of the second volume. See Slifkin, "Methodological Position for Second-Degree Art History," in *Photography and Doubt,* edited by Sabine T. Kreibel and Andrés Mario Zervigón (London: Routledge, 2016), 250.

7 Willoughby Sharp, "An Interview with Dennis Oppenheim," *Studio International* 182 (November 1971): 188. Also quoted in Slifkin, "Methodological Position," 239. Further, on page 250, Slifkin alludes to the additional connotations of the color red during this specific historical moment in terms of the spread of communism in East Asia.

8 Slifkin, "Methodological Position," 243.

9 Ibid., 245, 241.

10 "We can even become maniacs of the second degree: reject denotation, spontaneity, platitude, innocent repetition, tolerate only languages which testify, however frivolously, to a power of dislocation: parody, amphibology, surreptitious quotation" (*Roland Barthes on Roland Barthes* [New York: Farrar, Straus and Giroux, 1977], 66). See also Slifkin, "Methodological Position," 242.

11 Susan Sontag, "Shooting America," April 18, 1974, *New York Review of Books.*

12 James Meyer, "Second Degree: Working Drawings and Other Visible Things on Paper Not Necessarily Meant to Be Viewed as Art," in *Mel Bochner: Thought Made Visible, 1966–1973,* edited by Lesley K. Baier (New Haven, Conn.: Yale University Art Gallery, 1995), 96.

13 Taylor Walsh, "*Small Fires* Burning: Bruce Nauman and the Activation of Conceptual Art," *October,* no. 163 (Winter 2018): 33.

14 Between 1965 and 1973 the number of U.S. military casualties exceeded 58,000. Estimates of Vietnamese civilian deaths for the same period are 365,000. See Walter Russell Mead, *Special Providence: American Foreign Policy and How It Changed the World* (New York: Routledge, 2002), 219.

15 Dennis Oppenheim, quoted in Alison de Lima Greene, "Dennis Oppenheim: No Photography," *Spot* 12, no. 1 (1993): 5.

16 Henry Kissinger, *White House Years* (Boston: Little, Brown, 1979), 510. Kissinger added, "Emotion was not a policy." See also Robert Hariman, "Henry Kissinger: Realism's Rational Actor," in *Post-Realism: The Rhetorical Turn in International Relations,* edited by Francis A. Beer and Robert Hariman (East Lansing: Michigan State University Press, 1996), 35–53; and Hariman and John Lucaites, "Dissent and Emotional Management in a Liberal-Democratic Society: The Kent State Iconic Photograph," *Rhetoric Society Quarterly* 31, no. 3 (2001): 5–31.

17 Thomas McEvilley, *Sculpture in an Age of Doubt* (New York: Allworth Press and School of Visual Arts, 1999), 87.

18 For an in-depth discussion of the highly varied artistic practices that both directly and indirectly engaged with the contentious war in Vietnam, see Melissa Ho, "One Thing: Viet-Nam: American Art and the Vietnam War," in *Artists Respond: American Art and the Vietnam War, 1965–1975* (Princeton, N.J.: Princeton University Press and Smithsonian American Art Museum, 2019), 1–29.

19 Tony Godfrey, *Conceptual Art* (London: Phaidon, 1998), 15.

20 Anne Rorimer, "Photography: Restructuring the Pictorial," in *New Art in the 60s and 70s: Redefining Reality* (London: Thames & Hudson, 2001), 115.

21 Irene V. Small, "Believing in Art: The Votive Structures of Conceptual Art," *RES: Anthropology and Aesthetics* 55–56 (Spring–Fall 2009): 300.

22 Janet Kraynak, *Bruce Nauman Reiterated* (Minneapolis: University of Minnesota Press, 2014), 55.

23 For an insightful analysis of de Maria's relationship to photography and conceptual art, see Jane McFadden, "Earthquakes, Photoworks, and Oz: Walter de Maria's Conceptual Art," *Art Journal* 68, no. 3 (2009): 68–87.

24 Sianne Ngai, quoted in Adam Jasper, "Our Aesthetic Categories: An Interview with Sianne Ngai," *Cabinet* magazine, no. 43 (Fall 2011), http://www.cabinetmagazine.org/issues/43/jasper_ngai.php.

25 Susan Sontag, *On Photography* (New York: Farrar, Straus & Giroux, 1973), 86.

26 James Elkins, *What Photography Is* (New York: Routledge, 2011). Elkins argues that photography is also about meaninglessness.

27 Ngai, quoted in Jasper, "Our Aesthetic Categories," 45.

28 Jasper, "Our Aesthetic Categories," 50.

29 Michael S. Roth, "Photographic Ambivalence and Historical Consciousness," *History and Theory* 48, no. 4 (2009): 89. See Roth for an excellent discussion of the photograph's conflicted possibilities and the writings of Roland Barthes.

30 Matthew S. Witkovsky, *Light Years: Conceptual Art and the Photograph, 1964–1977* (Chicago: Art Institute of Chicago, 2011), 18.

31 Roland Barthes, *Camera Lucida,* translated by Richard Howard (New York: Hill and Wang, 1981), 3–4.

32 Ibid., 5.

33 See Alexander Alberro, *Conceptual Art and the Politics of Publicity* (Cambridge, Mass.: MIT Press, 2003).

34 Geoffrey Batchen, *Burning with Desire: The Conception of Photography* (Cambridge, Mass.: MIT Press, 1999). See Batchen on how the "invention" of photography was neither a singular nor a decisive historic moment but a combination of coincidences and social imperatives.

35 William Henry Fox Talbot, *The Pencil of Nature,* anniversary facsimile edition 1844–46 (New York: Larry J. Schaaf, 1989). See also Lars Kiel Bertelsen, "Reading Photographs Iconographically or Ichnographically," in *The Meaning of Photography,* edited by Robin Kelsey and Blake Stimson (Williamstown, Mass.: Sterling and Francine Clark Art Institute, 2008), 169–77. In his discussion of Talbot, Bertelsen surveys the multiple names Talbot indecisively suggested for photographs, including "specimens," "copies," "pictures," or "drawings."

36 Bertelsen, "Reading Photographs Iconographically or Ichnographically," 169.

37 Craig E. Adcock, *Marcel Duchamp's Notes from the Large Glass: An N-dimensional Analysis* (Ann Arbor, Mich.: UMI Research Press, 1983), 13.

38 Of course there are arguments against this understanding of Duchamp as well. See "Did Duchamp Deceive Us?," by Leslie Cambi, *ARTNews,* February 1999, 98–102. Rhonda Roland Shearer, a sculptor, contends that each readymade is a unique creation (98).

39 Susan Sontag, "In Plato's Cave," in *On Photography* (New York: Farrar, Straus and Giroux, 1977), 8.

40 See Marcel Duchamp and Richard L. Hamilton, *The Bride Stripped Bare by Her Bachelors, Even: A Typographic Version by Richard Hamilton of Marcel Duchamp's Green Box* (ca. 1934), translated by George Heard Hamilton (Stuttgart: Edition Hansjorg Meyer, 1976).

41 Sol LeWitt, "Paragraphs on Conceptual Art," *Artforum,* June 1967, 79–83.

42 Rosalind Krauss, "Notes on the Index: Seventies Art in America," *October* 3 (Spring 1977): 68–81.

43 Charles Baudelaire, "The Modern Public and Photography," in *Classic Essays on Photography,* edited by Alan Trachtenberg (New Haven, Conn.: Leete's Island Books, 1981), 86. "An avenging God has heard the prayers of this multitude, Daguerre was his messiah. And then they said to themselves: 'Since photography provides us with every desirable guarantee of exactitude' (they believe that, poor madmen!) 'art is photography.'"

44 Nancy Foote, "The Anti-Photographers," *Artforum* 15, no. 1 (1976): 46–54; my italics.

45 John Roberts, *The Impossible Document: Photography and Conceptual Art in Britain, 1966–1976* (London: Camerawork, 1997), 7.

46 For the most complete anthology to date of period debates and historiographical materials defining conceptual art, see Alexander Alberro and Blake Stimson, eds., *Conceptual Art: A Critical Anthology* (Cambridge, Mass.: MIT Press, 1999). For a concise synopsis of conceptual art, including an account of the development of the term, see Roberta Smith, "Conceptual Art," in *Concepts of Modern Art,* edited by Nikos Stangos (London: Thames and Hudson, 1989), 256–72.

47 The widespread interest in reevaluating conceptual art in the last three decades is evidenced by a handful of high-profile exhibitions, including *L'art conceptuel: Une perspective* (ARC, Paris, 1989); *Reconsidering The Object of Art: 1965–1975* (Museum of Contemporary

Art, Los Angeles, 1995); *Global Conceptualism: Points of Origin, 1950–1980s* (Queens Museum of Art, New York, 1999); and *Open Systems: Rethinking Art c. 1970* (Tate Modern, London, 2005).

Nonetheless, only three key exhibitions focus explicitly on photography and art during the juncture my book analyzes: Douglas Fogle's *The Last Picture Show: Artists Using Photography, 1960–1982* (Walker Art Center, Minneapolis, 2004), Matthew Witkovsky's *Light Years: Conceptual Art and the Photograph, 1964–1977* (Art Institute of Chicago, 2012), and Jill Dawsey's *The Uses of Photography: Art, Politics, and the Reinvention of a Medium* (Museum of Contemporary Art San Diego, 2016). Both Fogle and Witkovsky presented impressive surveys of the ways artists used photography as both medium and subject matter in this period, and their accompanying catalogs provide articulate overviews. Dawsey's exhibition catalog considers a network of artists who were active in San Diego in the late 1960s through to the 1980s, including figures such as John Baldessari, Allan Sekula, Martha Rosler, Fred Lonidier, and Carrie Mae Weems. This narrow focus provides fascinating insight into the work of a handful of Southern California artists. Two excellent edited volumes have assessed the impact of conceptual art on the work of contemporary artists using photography since the 1960s. I am referring to a special issue of the journal *Art History* (vol. 32, no. 5) in December 2009, "Photography after Conceptual Art," edited by Margaret Iversen and Diarmuid Costello, and a special issue of the journal *Critical Inquiry* (vol. 38, no. 4) in Summer 2012, "Agency and Automatism: Photography as Art since the Sixties," edited by Diarmuid Costello, Margaret Iversen, and Joel Snyder. These multiauthored journals develop various arguments about the impact of conceptualism on photographic practices, from a wide facet of angles including intentionality, control, chance, automatism, and labor. Again, though my study shares some terrain with these journals, my book offers a more sustained intervention into the late 1960s in the United States in particular.

48 Jeff Wall, "'Marks of Indifference': Aspects of Photography in, or as, Conceptual Art" (1995), in *Reconsidering the Object of Art: 1965–1975*, exh. cat. (Los Angeles: Museum of Contemporary Art, 1996), 253.

49 Ibid., 266.

50 Michael Fried, *Why Photography Matters as Art as Never Before* (New Haven, Conn.: Yale University Press, 2008).

51 Margaret Iversen and Diarmuid Costello, "Introduction: Photography after Conceptual Art," *Art History* 32, no. 5 (2009): 835.

52 Mary Ann Doane, "Indexicality and the Concept of Medium Specificity," in *The Meaning of Photography*, edited by Robin Kelsey and Blake Stimson (Williamstown, Mass.: Sterling and Francine Clark Art Institute, 2008).

53 John Roberts, "Photography, Iconophobia, and the Ruins of Conceptual Art," in *Impossible Document*, 9.

54 Donald Kuspit, "A Phenomenological Approach to Artistic Intention," in *The Critic Is Artist: The Intentionality of Art* (Ann Arbor: University of Michigan Press, 1984). See also Louis Kaplan, "Reframing the Self-Criticism: Clement Greenberg's 'Modernist Painting' in Light of Jewish Identity," in *Jewish Identity in Art History*, edited by Catherine M. Soussloff (Berkeley: University of California Press, 1999), 180–99.

55 Ihab Hassan, "Toward a Concept of Postmodernism," in *A Postmodern Reader*, edited by Joseph P. Natoli and Linda Hutcheon (Albany: State University of New York Press, 1993), 282.

56 Robert Smithson, *Recording Conceptual Art: Early Interviews with Barry, Huebler, Kaltenbach, LeWitt, Morris, Oppenheim, Siegelaub, Smithson, and Weiner*, edited by Alex Alberro and Patricia Norvell (Berkeley: University of California Press, 2001), 8.

57 Barthes, *Camera Lucida*, 85.

58 Ibid., 87.

59 Sigmund Freud, *Jokes and Their Relation to the Unconscious,* translated and edited by James Strachey (New York: W. W. Norton, 1960).

60 Arthur Rankin, "Tendentious Innocence: Chaplin's Use of Doubling in *City Lights* and *The Idle Class,*" http://archive.sensesofcinema.com/2007/feature-articles/charlie-chaplin-doubling.

61 Hal Foster, "The Passion of the Sign," in *The Return of the Real* (Cambridge, Mass.: MIT Press, 1996), 83.

62 Robert Smithson, "Cultural Confinement" (1972), in *Robert Smithson: The Collected Writings,* 2nd ed., edited by Jack Flam (Berkeley: University of California Press, 1996), 154; originally published in *The Writings of Robert Smithson,* edited by Nancy Holt (New York: New York University Press, 1979). Smithson wrote at length against the illusion that the art world or the gallery system was a neutral space, explaining, for example, that "cultural confinement takes place when a curator imposes his own limits on an art exhibition, rather than asking an artist to set his limits. Artists are expected to fit into fraudulent categories. Some artists imagine they've got a hold on this apparatus, which in fact has got a hold of them. As a result, they end up supporting a cultural prison that is out of their control." The remarkable lack of exhibition spaces for photography in the late 1960s is but one aspect of this system that conceptual artists using photography grappled with and, to a certain extent, inspired their commitment to using this particular medium.

63 Julia Bryan-Wilson, *Art Workers: Radical Practice in the Vietnam War Era* (Berkeley: University of California Press, 2009), 8.

64 Alexander Alberro, *Conceptual Art and the Politics of Publicity* (Cambridge, Mass.: MIT Press, 2003); Julia Bryan-Wilson, *Art Workers: Radical Practice in the Vietnam War Era* (Berkeley: University of California Press, 2009); Liz Kotz, *Words to Be Looked At: Language in 1960s Art* (Cambridge, Mass.: MIT Press, 2007); Frazer Ward, *No Innocent Bystanders: Performance Art and Audience* (Hanover, N.H.: Dartmouth College Press, 2012).

65 Joshua Shannon, *The Recording Machine: Art and Fact during the Cold War* (New Haven, Conn.: Yale University Press, 2017); Kate Palmer Albers, *Uncertain Histories: Accumulation, Inaccessibility, and Doubt in Contemporary Photography* (Berkeley: University of California Press, 2015).

66 Mel Bochner, "Seriality and Photography," in *Mel Bochner,* exh. cat. (Rio de Janeiro: Centro de Arte Helio Oiticica, 1999), 54.

67 In 1996 Lippard amended her original framing of conceptual art as dematerialization by including a new author's preface to *Six Years,* stating, "[Since] I first wrote on the subject in 1967, it has often been pointed out to me that dematerialization is an inaccurate term, that a piece of paper or a photograph is as much object, or as 'material,' as a ton of lead. Granted. But for lack of a better term I have continued to refer to a process of dematerialization, or a de-emphasis on material aspects (uniqueness, permanence, decorative attractiveness)" (preface to *Six Years: The Dematerialization of the Art Object from 1966 to 1972* [New York: Praeger, 1997], 5).

68 Siegfried Kracauer, "Photography (1927)," in *The Mass Ornament,* edited and translated by Thomas Y. Levin (Cambridge, Mass.: Harvard University Press, 1995), 259–64.

69 Ibid., 58.

70 See, e.g., McShine, *Information.*

1. Material Witness

1 "Hans Ulrich Obrist and Sandra Antelo-Suarez Interview Mel Bochner," projects.e-flux.com, accessed December 5, 2009, http://projects.e-flux.com/do_it/notes/interview/i003.html.

2 Scott Rothkopf, "'Photography Cannot Record Abstract Ideas' and Other Misunderstandings," in *Mel Bochner: Photographs, 1966–1969* (New Haven, Conn.: Yale University Press; Cambridge, Mass.: Harvard University Art Museums, 2002), 14.

3 Ibid. This process is clearly described in a study Bochner made for an artist's book, which he hoped would be editioned in 1969 by Marian Goodman's Multiples Gallery. The work was titled *Notes and Procedures: Photograph Series B / Part 2, 1966–1969,* and was never published by Goodman. It survives, however, in the form of a fourteen-page stapled booklet of ink drawings on graph paper.

4 Mel Bochner in conversation with Scott Rothkopf (1999), in Rothkopf, "'Photography Cannot Record Abstract Ideas' and Other Misunderstandings," 47n67.

5 Luis Camnitzer, *Conceptualism in Latin American Art: Didactics of Liberation* (Austin: University of Texas Press, 2007), 33.

6 James Meyer, "The Second Degree: *Working Drawings and Other Visible Things on Paper Not Necessarily Meant to Be Viewed as Art,*" in *Mel Bochner: Thought Made Visible, 1966–1973,* edited by Richard S. Field (New Haven, Conn.: Yale University Art Gallery, 1995), 96; Kynaston McShine, *Primary Structures: Younger American and British Sculptors* (New York: Jewish Museum, 1966).

7 Benjamin H. D. Buchloh, "Conceptual Art 1962–1969: From the Aesthetic of Administration to the Critique of Institutions," *October* 55 (Winter 1990): 109. Originally published in *L'art conceptuel: Une perspective* (Paris: Musée d'Art Moderne de la Ville de Paris, 1989).

8 Ibid.

9 Bochner was teaching at the School of the Visual Arts at the time and was asked to organize a "Christmas Show of drawings." See Meyer, "Second Degree," 95.

10 Ibid., 102.

11 Sol LeWitt, "Paragraphs on Conceptual Art," *Artforum* 5, no. 10 (1967): 80.

12 Ibid.

13 Mel Bochner, in conversation with the author, January 19, 2019.

14 Meyer, "Second Degree," 96.

15 Ibid.

16 John Brooks, "XEROX XEROX XEROX XEROX," *New Yorker,* April 1, 1967, quoted in Kate Eichhorn, "Copy Machines and Downtown Scenes: Deterritorializing Urban Culture in the Predigital Era," *Cultural Studies* 29, no. 3 (2015): 368.

17 Kate Eichhorn, *Adjusted Margin: Xerography, Art, and Activism in the Late Twentieth Century* (Cambridge, Mass.: MIT Press, 2016), 10.

18 Liz Kotz, *Words to Be Looked At: Language in 1960s Art* (Cambridge, Mass.: MIT Press, 2007), 104.

19 Meyer, "Second Degree," 96. Meyer quotes "infinite myopia" from Robert Smithson, "Interpolation of the Enantiomorphic Chambers," in *The Writings of Robert Smithson: Essays and Illustrations,* edited by Nancy Holt (New York: New York University Press, 1979), 39.

20 Craig Owens, "The Allegorical Impulse: Toward a Theory of Postmodernism, Part 2," *October* 13 (Summer 1980), reprinted in Owens, *Beyond Recognition: Representation, Power, and Culture* (Berkeley: University of California Press, 1992), 85.

21 David Joselit, "Conceptual Art 2.0," in *Contemporary Art: 1989 to the Present,* edited by Alexander Dumbadze and Suzanne Hudson (West Sussex, U.K.: Wiley-Blackwell), 159.

22 David Joselit, *After Art* (Princeton, N.J.: Princeton University Press, 2013), 94.

23 Rothkopf, "'Photography Cannot Record Abstract Ideas' and Other Misunderstandings," 6.

24 Greenberg wrote very little on photography, since he understood photography as helplessly bound to its inherent indexicality and thus without the capacity to be autonomous in the way that, for him, the best modernist painting was. He further likened any attempt at "ab-

stract photography" to an act of self-deception. See Greenberg, "Night Six," lecture delivered April 15, 1971, as part of the Bennington College Seminars; reprinted in Greenberg, *Homemade Esthetics* (New York: Oxford University Press, 1999), 155.

25 Donald Judd, "Specific Objects," *Arts Yearbook 8* (1951); reprinted in *Donald Judd Complete Writings: 1959–1975* (Halifax: Press of the Nova Scotia College of Art and Design; New York University Press, 1975), 184. Also quoted in Rothkopf, "'Photography Cannot Record Abstract Ideas' and Other Misunderstandings," 8.

26 Sasha M. Newman, "The Photo Pieces," in *Mel Bochner: Thought Made Visible,* 114.

27 John Coplans, "Concerning *Various Small Fires*: Edward Ruscha Discusses His Perplexing Publications," *Artforum* 3 (February 1965): 25. Also quoted in Rothkopf, "'Photography Cannot Record Abstract Ideas' and Other Misunderstandings," 9.

28 "By using the fabrication techniques of Minimalism, it gave me a certain objectivity" (Bochner in conversation with Rothkopf, in "'Photography Cannot Record Abstract Ideas' and Other Misunderstandings," 10).

29 Ibid., 11.

30 Ibid.

31 Rosalind Krauss noted a similar absurdity in Sol LeWitt's 1974 work *Variations of Incomplete Cubes.* See Krauss, "LeWitt in Progress," in *The Originality of the Avant-Garde and Other Modernist Myths* (Cambridge, Mass.: MIT Press, 1985), 245–58.

32 Rothkopf, "'Photography Cannot Record Abstract Ideas' and Other Misunderstandings," 12.

33 Notably, Bochner acquired a Muybridge in the sixties, featuring a bird in flight, head-on and in profile. In the essay "The Serial Attitude," Bochner describes Muybridge's work: "Muybridge simultaneously photographed the same activity from 180 degree, 90 degree, and 45 degree and printed the three sets of photographs parallel horizontally. By setting up alternative reading logics within a visually discontinuous sequence he completely fragmented perception into what Stockhausen called, in another context, a 'directionless time-field'" ("The Serial Attitude," *Artforum* 6 [December 1967]: 28–33); reprinted in Bochner, *Solar System and Rest Rooms: Writings and Interviews, 1965–2007* [Cambridge, Mass.: MIT Press, 2008], 42). Also quoted in Rothkopf, "'Photography Cannot Record Abstract Ideas' and Other Misunderstandings," 44. The concept of a "directionless timefield" reoccurs in numerous conceptual art projects using photography, including the work of Douglas Huebler, which is discussed in chapter 3. This phenomenon can be seen as yet another manifestation of doubting perception encouraged by the photograph as conceptual art.

34 Jeffrey Weiss, "Evidence of Sculpture," in *Photography and Sculpture: The Art Object in Reproduction,* edited by Sarah Hamill and Megan R. Luke (Los Angeles: Getty Publications, 2017), 247.

35 LeWitt, "Paragraphs on Conceptual Art," 80.

36 David Hopkins, "Modernism in Retreat: Minimalist Aesthetics and Beyond," in *After Modern Art, 1945–2000* (Oxford: Oxford University Press, 2000), 133.

37 Frances Colpitt, "The Shape of Painting in the 1960s," *Art Journal,* Spring 1991, 52. Judd asserted in 1965 that "several people are already stretching canvas into three-dimensional forms, and, while the possibilities are not used up, it is no longer very unusual to do so" (*Complete Writings, 1959–1975* [Halifax: The Press of the Nova Scotia College of Art and Design, 1975], 158). Colpitt notes that the list of artists making shaped paintings in the sixties should also include Robert Barry, Stephen Durkee, Michael Heizer, Peter Hutchinson, Patricia Johanson, Craig Kauffman, LeWitt, Clark Murray, Joe Overstreet, Edwin Ruda, Sylvia Stone, Peter Tangen, Richard Tuttle, and Lawrence Weiner (56).

38 *The Shaped Canvas* was curated by Lawrence Alloway at the Solomon R. Guggenheim Museum, New York, December 1964–January 1965, and included Richard Smith, Paul Feeley,

Sven Lukin, Neil Williams, and Stella. *Shape and Structure* was organized by Stella and Henry Geldzahler at the Tibor de Nagy Gallery, New York, in January 1965. Although Stella did not exhibit his own work in this show, his object-like canvases were important precedents for the other paintings presented.

39 Colpitt, "Shape of Painting," 52.

40 Michael Fried, *Three American Painters: Noland, Olitski, Stella,* exh. cat. (Cambridge, Mass.: Fogg Art Museum, 1965); reprinted in *Art and Objecthood* (Chicago: University of Chicago Press, 1998), 251. See also Fried, "Shape as Form: Frank Stella's New Paintings," *Artforum* 5 (November 1966): 18–23.

41 Hopkins, "Modernism in Retreat," 133.

42 Colpitt, "Shape of Painting," 55. See also William Rubin, *Frank Stella: 1970–1987* (New York: Museum of Modern Art, 1987), 15–20.

43 Rothkopf, "'Photography Cannot Record Abstract Ideas' and Other Misunderstandings," 20.

44 Ibid., 21.

45 Ibid., 22.

46 Carol Armstrong, "Mel Bochner: Photographs 1966–1969," *Artforum* 41, no. 1 (2002): 197.

47 Rothkopf, "'Photography Cannot Record Abstract Ideas' and Other Misunderstandings," 29. *Postminimalism* was a term coined by Robert Pincus-Witten in an article titled "Eva Hesse: Post-Minimalism into Sublime" in the November 1971 issue of *Artforum*. This broad term generally implies a reaction against the values of minimalism and has been used to embrace diverse phenomena such as conceptual art, land art, performance art, process art, and video art. See Robert Morris, "Anti-Form," *Artforum* 6 (April 1968): 33–35; and Morris, "Notes on Sculpture, Part 4: Beyond Objects," *Artforum* 7 (April 1969): 50–54.

48 See Larry Schaaf, *Out of the Shadows* (New Haven, Conn.: Yale University Press, 1992).

49 Talbot announced that he had discovered a method of overcoming the difficulties of temporality by "fixing the image." On January 25, 1839, Talbot wrote to John Herschel about "the possibility of fixing upon paper the image formed by a Camera Obscura, or rather, I should say, causing it to fix itself." On February 8, he wrote again, this time using the word more specifically and self-consciously ("my method of 'fixing'") to refer to the method whereby the induced image was to be made permanent. See Larry Schaaf, "Herschel, Talbot, and Photography: Spring 1831 and Spring 1839," *History of Photography* 4, no. 3 (1980): 185, 190.

50 Geoffrey Batchen, *Burning with Desire: The Conception of Photography* (Cambridge, Mass.: MIT Press, 1999), 241n148. "Never quite able to decide whether the origins of photography lay in nature or in culture (notice how his own photograms include both botanical specimens and samples of lace and handwriting), Talbot later conjured yet another descriptive phrase that contains elements of each: 'the art of fixing a shadow.'" Talbot elaborated: "The most transitory of things, a shadow, the proverbial emblem of all that is fleeting and momentary, may be fettered by the spells of our 'natural magic, and may be fixed for ever in the position which it seemed only destined for a single instant to occupy. . . . Such is the fact, that we may receive on paper the fleeting shadow, arrest it there and in the space of a single minute fix it there so firmly as to be no more capable of change" (William Fox Talbot, "Some Account of the Art of Photogenic Drawing" [1839], quoted in Beaumont Newhall, *Photography: Essays and Images* [New York: Museum of Modern Art, 1980], 25). Also quoted in Batchen, *Burning with Desire,* 91.

51 Rothkopf, "'Photography Cannot Record Abstract Ideas' and Other Misunderstandings," 29n70. For more on connection between Nauman and lunar photography, see Neal Benezra, Kathy Halbreich, and Paul Schimmel, *Bruce Nauman: Exhibition Catalogue and Cata-*

logue Raisonne, edited by Joan Simon (Minneapolis: Walker Art Center; New York: Distributed Art Publishers, 1994), 210.

52 Mel Bochner, in conversation with the author, January 18, 2019.

53 "One Step Photography," reprint by E. H. Land, 1949, Polaroid Corporation administrative records, circa 1930–2005, box I.48, folder 2, Baker Special Library Collections, Harvard Business School, Harvard University.

54 The organization E.A.T. was founded by Robert Rauschenberg and the physicist Billy Kluver in 1966, and was designed not only to make technology more financially accessible to artists but also to provide artists and engineers the possibility of collaborating.

55 See Christoph Grunenberg, ed., *Summer of Love: Art of the Psychedelic Era,* exh. cat. (London: Tate, 2005); and Paul Schimmel and Lisa Gabrielle Mark, eds., *Ecstasy: In and About Altered States,* exh. cat. (Cambridge, Mass.: MIT Press, 2005).

56 See Yve-Alain Bois and Rosalind Krauss, *Formless: A User's Guide* (New York: Zone Books, 1997).

57 Luke Skrebowski, "Productive Misunderstandings: Interpreting Mel Bochner's Theory of Photography," *Art History,* December 2009, 919.

58 My translation. "Un terme servant à déclasser, exigeant généralement que chaque chose ait sa forme. Ce qu'il désigne n'a ses droits dans aucun sens et se fait écraser partout comme une araignée ou un ver de terre. Il faudrait en effet, pour que les hommes académiques soient contents, que l'univers prenne forme. La philosophie entière n'a pas d'autre but: il s'agit de donner un redingote à ce qui est, une redingote mathématique. Par contre affirmer que l'univers ne ressemble à rien et n'est qu'informe revient à dire que l'univers est quelque chose comme une araignée ou un crachat" (Georges Bataille, "Informe," *Documents 7* [December 1929]: 382).

59 Yve-Alain Bois, quoted in "Down and Dirty: Lauren Sedofsky Talks with Rosalind Krauss and Yve-Alain Bois," *Artforum* 34, no. 10 (1996): 90.

60 Rothkopf also notes this comparison, citing Erwin Panofsky: "The surface is now no longer the wall or the panel bearing the forms of the individual things and figures, but rather is once again the transparent plane through which we are meant to believe that we are looking into a space, even if that space is still bounded on all sides" ("'Photography Cannot Record Abstract Ideas' and Other Misunderstandings," 33n8).

61 Ibid., 33.

62 Mel Bochner, "Primary Structures," *Arts Magazine* 40 (June 1966): 32–35.

63 Duchamp's first mention of the "infra-thin" was published in *View* magazine in 1945.

64 Dan Devening, *Infra-thin,* exh. cat. (College of DuPage, Ill.: Gahlberg Gallery, 2004).

65 Marcel Duchamp, *Notes,* arranged and translated by Paul Matisse (Boston: G. K. Hall, 1983).

66 Devening, *Infra-thin.*

67 Duchamp, *Notes,* 45.

68 Lucy Hunter, "The Untold History of Corporations Recruiting Artists to Inspire Their Employees," July 6, 2018, artsy.com.

69 Quoted in Rothkopf, "'Photography Cannot Record Abstract Ideas' and Other Misunderstandings," 36n84.

70 The full film was screened at the Clay Shaw trial in 1969. In 1975 the film was first shown on television by the assassination researcher Robert Groden and the television journalist Geraldo Rivera.

71 Marita Sturken, *Tangled Memories: The Vietnam War, the AIDS Epidemic, and the Politics of Remembering* (Berkeley: University of California Press, 1997), 26.

72 David Lubin, "Kennedy Assassination, Dallas, 1963," in *Getting the Picture: The Visual*

Culture of the News, edited by Jason E. Hill and Vanessa R. Schwartz (London: Bloomsbury, 2015), 85. 74.

73 "Death Found Him from This Window," *Life* magazine, November 29, 1963, 32H.

74 Mel Bochner, "Consumer Testing *The Warren Report*: Kennedy's Assassination as TV Serial," in Bochner, *Solar System and Rest Rooms,* 36.

75 Ibid., 35.

76 Ibid.

77 Ibid.

78 Anthony Quinn, "Freedom, Revolt, and Pubic Hair: Why Antonioni's Blow-Up Thrills Fifty Years On," *Guardian,* March 10, 2012.

79 For a fascinating discussion of the historically ambivalent role of photographic enlargements as both evidential indictments and evidential alibis, see Jordan Bear, "Blowing Up the World: On the Evidentiary Cultures of Enlargement, ca. 1893–1917," in *Photography and Doubt,* edited by Sabine T. Kriebel and Andres Zervigón (New York: Routledge, 2017), 44–58.

80 Rothkopf, "'Photography Cannot Record Abstract Ideas' and Other Misunderstandings," 39.

81 Ibid., 49n88. Yve-Alain Bois has also noted this connection: "The empty room had been transformed into an architect's blueprint" (Yve-Alain Bois, "The Measurement Pieces: from Index to Implex," in *Mel Bochner: Thought Made Visible, 1966–1973,* ed. Richard Field [New Haven, Conn.: Yale University Press, 1995], 167–88).

82 Douglas Crimp, *On the Museum's Ruins* (1980); reprinted (with photographs by Louise Lawler) (Cambridge, Mass.: MIT Press, 1993). See also Chrissie Iles and Russell Roberts, eds., *In Visible Light: Photography and Classification in Art, Science and The Everyday,* exh. cat. (Oxford: Museum of Modern Art, 1997).

83 Max Larkin, "A Conceptual Art Pioneer Who Doesn't Mince Words," *New York Times Style Magazine,* November 26, 2019.

84 Bochner, *Mel Bochner: Thought Made Visible,* 64.

85 Bois, "Measurement Pieces," 167.

86 Craig E. Adcock, *Marcel Duchamp's Notes from the Large Glass: An N-Dimensional Analysis* (Ann Arbor, Mich.: UMI Research Press, 1983), 7.

87 John Baldessari, *John Baldessari: A Different Kind of Order* (Cologne: Walther König, 2005), 275.

88 Transcript of Elayne Varian's interview with the artist (March 1969), in *Solar System and Rest Rooms: Writings and Interviews, 1965–2007* (Cambridge, Mass.: MIT Press, 2008), 57.

89 Rothkopf, "'Photography Cannot Record Abstract Ideas' and Other Misunderstandings," 37.

90 Bois, "Measurement Pieces," 168.

91 Transcript of Elayne Varian's interview with the artist, 58.

92 Robert Pincus-Witten, "Bochner at MOMA: *Three Ideas and Seven Procedures,*" *Artforum* 10 (December 1971): 233–35.

93 Mel Bochner, "How Can You Defend Making Paintings Now?" A Conversation with James Meyer," December 1993, in *As Painting: Division and Displacement,* exh. cat. (Columbus, Ohio: Wexner Center for the Arts, 2001); reprinted in Bochner, *Solar System and Rest Rooms,* 166.

94 See Daniel Soutif, "Pictures and an Exhibition—the Museum and the Photograph: Containers of Whatever," *Artforum* 29, no. 7 (1991): 83–89.

95 Luke Skrebowski, "All Systems Go! Recovering Jack Burnham's 'Systems Aesthetics,'" Tate Papers, accessed November 2, 2009, http://www.tate.org.uk/research/tateresearch/tatepapers/06spring/skrebowski.htm.

96 Bochner's tactic of taping up the room with vinyl has been appropriated by numerous contemporary artists as a mode of ideological and institutional critique. Carey Young's *Declared Void II* (2013), for example, questions the problematics of citizenship and free movement. Beside her outlined black box in the corner of the gallery, Young includes the following text: BY ENTERING THE ZONE CREATED BY THIS DRAWING, AND FOR THE PERIOD YOU REMAIN THERE, YOU DECLARE AND AGREE THAT YOU ARE A CITIZEN OF THE UNITED STATES OF AMERICA.

97 See James Putnam, "Framing the Frame," in *Art and Artifact: The Museum as Medium* (London: Thames & Hudson, 2001), 114–31.

98 Skrebowski, "All Systems Go!"

99 Walter Benjamin, section VI, "The Work of Art in the Age of Mechanical Reproduction," in *Illuminations,* translated by Harry Zohn (New York: Schocken, 1969).

100 Bois, "Measurement Pieces," 172.

101 Barbara Rose, *An Interview with Robert Rauschenberg* (New York: Vintage, 1987), 75.

102 Allan Sekula, "The Body in the Archive," *October* 39 (Winter 1986): 18. See also Josh Ellenbogen, *Reasoned and Unreasoned Images: The Photography of Bertillon, Galton, and Marey* (University Park: Pennsylvania State University Press, 2012).

103 "Hans Ulrich Obrist and Sandra Antelo-Suarez Interview with Mel Bochner."

104 Roland Barthes, *Camera Lucida* (New York: Hill & Wang, 1981), 3.

105 Ibid., 5.

106 See Bochner, "Thought Made Visible," in Field, *Mel Bochner,* 33. See also "Hans Ulrich Obrist and Sandra Antelo-Suarez Interview with Mel Bochner."

107 "The unbound envelope format was chosen to subvert any implication of a beginning, a middle, or an end (at least in that order)" (Bochner, *Solar System and Rest Rooms,* 180).

108 Skrebowski, "Productive Misunderstandings," 931n31.

109 Jonathan Benthell attempted to figure out which quotes are fakes and suggested the false "theories" are Mao, Proust, and Merleau-Ponty. See Benthell, "Bochner and Photography," *Studio International,* April 1971, 147–48.

110 Bochner, "Misunderstandings," *Solar System and Rest Rooms,* 180.

111 This is one quote whose source is indeed traceable. It is an abridged version of a well-known letter that Duchamp wrote to Alfred Stieglitz in 1922, criticizing Stieglitz's determination to have photography recognized as fine art. The full quotation reads: "You know exactly how I feel about photography. I would like to see it make people despise painting until something else will make photography unbearable" ("Letter to Stieglitz," in *Salt Seller: The Writings of Marcel Duchamp,* edited by Michel Sanouillet and Elmer Paterson [New York: Oxford University Press, 1973], 165).

112 As Walter Benjamin observed, "To ask for the 'authentic' print makes no sense" ("Work of Art," 224).

113 Lawrence Alloway, *Artists and Photographs* (New York: Multiples, 1970).

114 Mel Bochner, "*Misunderstandings (A Theory of Photography)* (1967–1970)," unpublished, printed in *Solar System and Rest Rooms,* 180.

115 Quoted in Godfrey, *Conceptual Art,* 301.

116 Quoted in "'How Can You Defend Making Paintings Now?': A Conversation with James Meyer," in *Solar System and Rest Rooms,* 159.

117 Allan Sekula, "On the Invention of Photographic Meaning," *Artforum* 13, no. 5 (1975): 36.

118 Ibid., 38.

119 Susan Sontag, "In Plato's Cave," in *On Photography* (New York: Farrar, Straus & Giroux, 1977), 24; first published in the *New York Review of Books* from 1973 to 1977.

120 Lucy Soutter, "The Photographic Idea: Reconsidering Conceptual Photography," *Afterimage* 26, no. 5 (1999).

2. Pressing the Point

1 Michael Fried, "Art and Objecthood," in *Art and Objecthood: Essays and Reviews* (Chicago: University of Chicago Press, 1998), 155; originally published in *Artforum* 10, no. 5 (1967): 12–23.

2 Clement Greenberg, "The Camera's Glass Eye: Review of and Exhibition of Edward Weston," in *The Collected Essays and Criticism,* edited by John O'Brian, vol. 4 (Chicago: University of Chicago Press, 1993), 60. Greenberg's position on photography was dismissive. His collected writings contain only two pieces on photography: "The Camera's Glass Eye: Review of an Exhibition of Edward Weston" and "Four Photographers: Review of *A Vision of Paris* by Eugène-Auguste Atget."

3 *The Photographer's Eye* included Walker Evans, Henri Cartier-Bresson, Edward Steichen, Paul Strand, Edward Weston, and others, alongside vernacular and snapshot photographs. *Towards a Social Landscape* included Bruce Davidson, Lee Friedlander, Garry Winogrand, Danny Lyon, and Duane Michals. Nathan Lyons invited Diane Arbus to participate, but she declined. The following year Arbus, Friedlander, and Winogrand would be included in Szarkowski's now-renowned exhibition *New Documents.*

4 Lucy Soutter, "The Visual Idea: Photography in Conceptual Art" (PhD diss., Yale University, 2001), 69.

5 See Anne Wilkes Tucker, "Lyons, Szarkowski, and the Perception of Photography," *American Art* 21, no. 3 (2007): 25–29.

6 Mark Pascale, "Studies for Holograms, 1970 by Bruce Nauman," *Art Institute of Chicago Museum Studies* 25, no. 1 (1999): 40.

7 Infrared photography records the image of an object by using film sensitive to invisible infrared radiation, or heat, instead of to ordinary light. Although it was probably used in this instance because Nauman was recording himself in low light, an analogy can be made between the heat of the body being captured on film and the artist's larger interest in the malleable human form; see Pascale, "Studies for Holograms."

8 Elizabeth Manchester, 2000, http://www.tate.org.uk/art/artworks/nauman-a-p77629.

9 Robert Slifkin, "Now Man's *Bound to Fail,* More," *October,* no. 135 (Winter 2011): 50.

10 Tony Godfrey, *Conceptual Art* (London: Phaidon, 1998), 188.

11 Eduardo Cadava, *Writing of Light: Theses on the Photography of History* (Princeton, N.J.: Princeton University Press, 1997), 135.

12 Despite the increased sales of televisions in the mid-1960s, television news did not surpass newspapers and picture magazines as a major source of information until the early 1970s; see Mary Warner Marien, *Photography: A Cultural History* (London: Laurence King, 2002), 364; quoted in Sabine T. Kriebel, "Theories of Photography: A Short History," in *Photography Theory,* edited by James Elkins (New York: Routledge, 2007), 44n34.

13 Peter Osborne, *Anywhere or Not At All: Philosophy of Contemporary Art* (New York: Verso, 2013).

14 Nauman, quoted in *Bruce Nauman: Work from 1965 to 1972,* edited by Jane Livingston and Marcia Tucker, exh. cat. (Los Angeles: Los Angeles County Museum of Art, 1972).

15 According to Catherine Morris, a curator at the Brooklyn Museum, Mendieta's art practice broadly concerns performance: "There's a way in which her work is about performance. It's about theater. It's about kind of capturing moments through various forms of documentation" (quoted in Monica Castillo, "Overlooked No More: Ana Mendieta, a Cuban Artist Who Pushed Boundaries," *New York Times,* September 9, 2018). See also Jane Blocker's discussion of Mendieta's artwork in relation to Judith Butler's notion of "performativity" in *Where Is Ana Mendieta? Identity, Performativity, and Exile* (Durham, N.C.: Duke University Press, 1999).

16 Kelley Baum, "Shapely Shapelessness," *Record of the Art Museum of Princeton University* 67 (2008): 81; see also notes 4 and 5 above.

17 Ibid., 82.

18 Though Mendieta did not explicitly self-identify as a woman of color, the elastic exaggeration of facial features in this series lends itself to being read nevertheless as a self-conscious evocation of racial stereotypes.

19 Eva Ehninger, "Bodies on Cool Surfaces," in *Bruce Nauman: A Contemporary* (Basel, Switzerland: Laurenz Foundation Schaulager, 2018), 123.

20 Roland Barthes, "The Rhetoric of the Image" (1963; English trans. 1977), in *Semiotics: An Introductory Anthology,* edited by Robert E. Innis (Bloomington: Indiana University Press, 1985).

21 October–December 1966 at LACMA, organized by Jules Langsner. Notably, the September 1996 issue of *Artforum* (vol. 5, no. 1) was a special issue dedicated to surrealism.

22 Laurence Sillars, "Bruce Nauman: Keeping Busy," in *Bruce Nauman: Make Me Think Me,* 10.

23 Ibid., 12.

24 Michal Raz-Russo, quoted in *Color Rush: American Color Photography from Stieglitz to Sherman,* edited by Katherine Bussard and Lisa Hostetler (New York: Aperture and Milwaukee Art Museum, 2013), 170.

25 See Janet Kraynak, ed., *Please Pay Attention Please: Bruce Nauman's Words: Writings and Interviews* (Cambridge, Mass.: MIT Press, 2002), 10.

26 See Thierry de Duve, *Pictorial Nominalism: On Marcel Duchamp's Passage from Painting to the Readymade* (Minneapolis: University of Minnesota Press, 1991). The performative aspect of the readymade is also the subject of debate between Rosalind Krauss, Yve-Alain Bois, Benjamin Buchloh, and Thierry de Duve in the roundtable discussion "Conceptual Art and the Reception of Duchamp," *October* 70 (Fall 1994); see especially pages 134–36.

27 Liz Kotz argues extensively for the important legacy of instructions in the work of John Cage in "Post-Cagean Aesthetics and the 'Event' Score," *October* 95 (Winter 2001): 55–90.

28 Roxana Marcoci, *The Original Copy: Photography of Sculpture, 1839 to Today* (New York: Museum of Modern Art, 2010), 219.

29 Sillars, "Bruce Nauman: Keeping Busy," 14.

30 For a more detailed discussion of *Coffee Spilled and Balloon Dog,* see Heather Diack, "Knot Again: Pratfall as Praxis in the Work of Bruce Nauman," in Ehninger, *Bruce Nauman: A Contemporary,* 27–51.

31 Willoughby Sharp, "Nauman Interview, 1970," in Kraynak, *Please Pay Attention Please,* 118.

32 Referring to his time in San Francisco, Nauman explained: "And a lot of things that I was doing in the studio didn't make sense so I quit doing them. That left me alone in the studio; this in turn left the fundamental question of what an artist does when left alone in the studio. My conclusion was that I was an artist and I was in the studio, then whatever I was doing in the studio must be art" (Ian Wallace and Russel Keziere, "Bruce Nauman Interviewed," *Vanguard* [Vancouver] 8, no. 1 [1979]: 18).

33 Bruce Nauman, interview with Michele De Angelus, May 27 and 30, 1980, 77, *California Oral History Project,* Archives of American Art, Smithsonian Institution.

34 Nauman, quoted in Coosje van Bruggen, *Bruce Nauman,* edited by Robert C. Morgan (Baltimore: Johns Hopkins University Press, 2002), 9.

35 "The place where it communicates best and most easily is also the place where language is the least interesting and emotionally involving—such as the functional way we understand the word 'sing' or the sentence 'Pick up the pencil'" (Christopher Cordes, "Talking with Bruce Nauman: An Interview by Christopher Cordes," in *Bruce Nauman: Prints, 1970–1989* [New York: Castelli Graphics, 1989], 25).

36 Constance M. Lewallen's account of Nauman's early works brought the allusion to Jelly

Roll Morton to my attention; see Lewallen, *A Rose Has No Teeth: Bruce Nauman in the 1960s* (Berkeley: University of California Press, 2007), 63.

37 The phrase is from the Bible (Daniel 2:31–40). This passage recounts the episode in which King Nebuchadnezzar has a dream. The image that appears to him has a head of gold, breast and arms of silver, belly and thighs of brass, and legs of iron. The feet of this image are made of iron and clay. A stone hits the feet and the whole image breaks into pieces. The prophet Daniel's interpretation of the dream is that Nebuchadnezzar was the head of gold (a great king), but after him would come weaker kingdoms (like the image with feet of clay).

38 Pamela M. Lee, "Pater Nauman," *October* 74 (Autumn 1995): 129–32.

39 Among others, I would add the artists Erwin Wurm, Urs Fischer, Ugo Rondinone, Mungo Thomson, and Sam Taylor-Wood to this list as well.

40 Lee, "Pater Nauman," 32: "By a dialectical turn, this work supersedes the virile expressionist artist of the eighties by dressing down in the persona of the loser."

41 Sillars cites Kraynak's formulation of this argument in the introduction to *Please Pay Attention Please* ("Bruce Nauman: Keeping Busy," 15). See also Bakhtin's "The Problem of Speech Genres," in Mikhail Mikhailovich Bakhtin, *Speech Genres and Other Late Essays*, translated by Vern W. McGee, edited by Caryl Emerson and Michael Holquist (Austin: University of Texas Press, 1986).

42 Anne Middleton Wagner, "Nauman's Body of Sculpture," in *A House Divided: American Art since 1955* (Berkeley: University of California Press, 2012), 145.

43 Despite the fact that UC Davis's art program was burgeoning and experimental (having been established in 1961), the foundation of the sculpture area was nevertheless highly traditional. Tio Giambruni initiated the metal-casting foundry and the curriculum that accompanied it. Anne Wagner discusses the impact this emphasis on bronze and the monument within the sculpture program at UC Davis likely exerted on Nauman, and the ways its "distinctly Renaissance methods and feel" were ripe material to be at once "the vehicle and the butt of the joke" (*House Divided*, 143).

44 Anna Dezeuze, "Bound to Fail," in *Bruce Nauman: Make Me Think Me*, edited by Lawrence Sillars (London: Tate, 2006), 48.

45 Michele De Angelus, "Interview with Bruce Nauman, May 27 and 30, 1980," in Kraynak, *Please Pay Attention Please*, 236.

46 Slifkin discusses this semantic confusion in his astute article "Now Man's *Bound to Fail*, More," 55. Slifkin persuasively problematizes the role of "figuration" in Nauman's early work in the context of the emergence of postmodernism.

47 Jane Livingston, "Bruce Nauman," in Livingston and Tucker, *Bruce Nauman*, 11.

48 Douglas Eklund, Department of Photographs, "Conceptual Art and Photography," 2004, in *Heilbrunn Timeline of Art History* (New York: Metropolitan Museum of Art, 2000–), http://www.metmuseum.org/toah/hd/cncp/hd_cncp.htm.

49 Roxana Marcoci, *Bruce Nauman: Disappearing Acts* (New York: Museum of Modern Art, 2018), 126.

50 Jane Livingston quotes Nauman as saying, "Now I wasn't just making shapes to look at; by saying 'these are templates of my body,' I gave them reason enough for their existence" ("Bruce Nauman," 11).

51 Nauman said in 1967, speaking about *Impressions of the Knees*, "I couldn't decide who to get for artists, so I used my own knees. Making the impressions of the knees in a wax block was a way of having a large rectangular solid with marks in it. I didn't just want to make marks in it, so I had to follow another kind of reasoning. It also had to do with trying to make the thing itself less important to look at" (quoted in Joe Raffaele and Elizabeth Baker, "The Way Out West: Interviews with 4 San Francisco Artists," *Art News*, Summer 1967, 5).

52 This cast piece by Nauman literalizes the cliché of artistic poverty and also alludes to

Duchamp's *In Advance of a Broken Arm* (1915), which uses displacement and uselessness as its fundamental strategies. Continuing the lineage and advancing the inherent postmodern critique, Mike Kelley photographed Nauman's piece in 2004, presenting it as his own work of art titled *Bruce Nauman, Hand to Mouth* (1967).

53 Anne Wagner, "Henry Moore's Mother," *Representations,* no. 65 (Winter 1999): 94.

54 Cordes, "Talking with Bruce Nauman," 26.

55 See Lee, "Pater Nauman," 129–32, and Isabelle Graw and Dorothea von Moltke, "Just Being Doesn't Amount to Anything (Some Themes in Bruce Nauman's Work)," 133–38, both in *October* 74 (Autumn 1995).

56 Considering the anecdotal relationship between Nauman's *Messes* and Jorge Luis Borges's famous narrative of the "map of the world with the 1:1 ratio" as well as his "library containing all knowledge" would also be fitting here. A map in any format will never actually be a territory but will always be an abstraction. Similarly, the possession of information is not the same thing as possessing knowledge.

57 Soutter, "Visual Idea," 70.

58 Ibid.

59 Slifkin, "Now Man's *Bound to Fail,* More," 53.

60 Soutter, "Visual Idea," 1.

61 Ibid., 70.

62 Using his studio activities as a trope for, and a challenge to, the notion of "artwork" continues to be a central device for Nauman. In a recent piece titled *Mapping the Studio I (Fat Chance John Cage),* a large-scale video installation, Nauman records the nocturnal activity in his studio of his cat and an infestation of mice during the summer of 2000. With seven projections and multiple audio tracks of ambient sounds, Nauman, in his words, "used this traffic as a way of mapping the leftover parts and work areas of the last several years of other completed, unfinished, or discarded projects" (Dia Center for the Arts, press release, December 14, 2001).

63 *Bruce Nauman* (New York: Leo Castelli, 1968), unpaginated.

64 Christine Hoffman, "Think-Thank / Denk-Dank," in *Bruce Nauman: Theatres of Experience,* edited by Susan Cross (New York: Guggenheim Museum, 2003), 55. See Kathy Halbreich, "Interview with Bruce Nauman," audio file (New York: Museum of Modern Art, January 9, 2012), https://www.moma.org/momaorg/shared/pdfs/docs/learn/archives/transcript_nauman.pdf.

65 See Robin Kelsey, "Reverse Shot: Earthrise and Blue Marble in the American Imagination," in *Scales of the Earth* (Cambridge, Mass.: Harvard University Graduate School of Design, 2011), 10–16.

66 Nauman attributed his turn to photography in the late 1960s as a desire to escape from aesthetic concerns associated with drawing and painting: "Somehow I think, I may be mistaken, I had the idea that I could just take a picture, and I wouldn't have to think about how to draw it or something. Of course, when you take a picture, you have to think how to take the picture, but in another sense I knew enough about painting to know that it would be a whole lot of work and I didn't really know enough about photography to get involved in trying to make a really interesting or original photograph" (Nauman, interview with Michele De Angelus, 77).

67 Richard Shaw, quoted in Lewallen, *Rose Has No Teeth,* 45; quoted in Marcoci, *Original Copy,* 130.

68 Only a year earlier, Nauman had seen "the first exhibition in the United States to present the full range of Man Ray's work," at the Los Angeles County Museum of Art (Lewallen, *Rose Has No Teeth,* 63).

69 Victor Burgin, "Situational Aesthetics," *Studio International* 178, no. 915 (October 1969): 120.

70 Godfrey, *Conceptual Art,* 205. Godfrey acknowledges the genesis of Burgin's piece in Wittgenstein's *Philosophical Investigations* but does not mention the connection to Nauman.

71 Soutter, "Visual Idea," 72.

72 "The objective nature of photography confers on it a credibility absent from all other picture making" (André Bazin, "The Ontology of the Photographic Image," translated by Hugh Gray, *Film Quarterly* 13, no. 4 [1960]: 7–8).

73 Benjamin H. D. Buchloh, "Process Sculpture and Film in Richard Serra's Work," in *Neo-Avantgarde and Culture Industry: Essays on European and American Art from 1955 to 1975* (Cambridge, Mass.: MIT Press, 2003), 414.

74 De Angelus, "Interview with Bruce Nauman, May 27 and 30, 1980," 250.

75 This work has been fodder for many artists, including most notably one of Bas Jan Ader's best-known works, *Primary Time,* commonly referred to as *Untitled (Flower Work)* from 1974. This piece, created as a film as well as a series of photographs, presents the artist arranging a vase of flowers. We see the artist's body, dressed in black, from the hips to the neck. No face is necessary, for the focus is on his actions rather than his expression. As he arranges the flowers, he carefully segregates them into the three primary colors: red, blue, and yellow. Through arranging and rearranging, the vase moves from being multicolored to being monochromatic and then back again to an arrangement that contains all three colors. As Thomas Crow writes in the exhibition catalog, "The performance was his wry homage to and mockery of Mondrian, Rietveld, and the floral clichés of his native country" (*Bas Jan Ader: A Bridge Too Far,* edited by Brad Spence [Irvine: Art Gallery, University of California at Irvine, 1999], 13–15). Ader shares a clear affinity with both Nauman and Burden in terms of investigating how the body is articulated in space and under states of duress. See also *Colour after Klein: Re-thinking Colour in Modern and Contemporary Art,* edited by Jane Alison (London: Barbican Gallery and Black Dog, 2005), 50.

76 Ludwig Wittgenstein, *Philosophical Investigations,* translated by G. E. M. Anscombe (New York: Macmillan, 1953), 20.

77 See, e.g., Sillars, "Bruce Nauman: Keeping Busy."

78 The exceptions are Eva Ehninger, "Bodies on Cool Surfaces," in *Bruce Nauman: A Contemporary* (Basel: Laurenz Foundation Schaulager, 2018), 117–48; and Roxana Marcoci, "Photography from the Studio to the Moon," *Bruce Nauman: Disappearing Acts* (New York: Museum of Modern Art, 2018).

79 Barthes, "Rhetoric of the Image," 200.

80 Patricia Norvell, "Robert Smithson, June 20, 1969," in *Recording Conceptual Art: Early Interviews with Barry, Huebler, Kaltenbach, LeWitt, Morris, Oppenheim, Siegelaub, Smithson, and Weiner,* edited by Alexander Alberro and Patricia Norvell (Berkeley: University of California Press, 2001), 128.

81 Ibid.

82 See Kraynak, *Please Pay Attention Please,* 10; and Frazer Ward, "Some Relations between Conceptual and Performance Art," *Art Journal* 56, no. 4 (1997): 36–40.

83 Benjamin H. D. Buchloh, "Conceptual Art, 1962–1969," *October* 55 (Winter 1990): 105–43.

84 "The Reception of the Sixties," roundtable discussion, *October* 69 (Summer 1994): 18.

85 Mel Bochner observed tellingly, "There is no art that does not bear some burden of physicality. To deny it is to descend into irony" ("Excerpts from Speculation [1967–1970]," in Meyer, *Conceptual Art,* 50).

86 Ward, "Some Relations between Conceptual and Performance Art," 39–40. Ward makes this connection in an extremely helpful analysis of Acconci's *Step Piece* (1970) as well as Burden's infamous *Shoot Piece* (1971). See also Ward, "False Intimacies, Open Secrets: Public and Private in the Performance Art of Vito Acconci and Chris Burden" (PhD diss., Cornell University, 2001).

87 Ward, "Some Relations between Conceptual and Performance Art," 36.

88 Ho, "One Thing: Viet-Nam," 17.

89 In Nauman's two-channel video *Jump* (1994), the artist takes on the challenge of gravity again. This time he has a succession of very short-lived victories.

90 In other works, such as *Walking in an Exaggerated Manner around the Perimeter of a Square* (1967–68) or *Bouncing in the Corner* (1968), Nauman set himself commonplace tasks, turned his obsessive-compulsive attention to his repetitive scheme, and filmed the result.

91 Nauman, interview with Brenda Richardson, June 21, 1982, quoted in *Bruce Nauman: Neons,* exh. cat. (Baltimore: Baltimore Museum of Art, 1982), 20.

92 Christy Lange, "Bound to Fail: Open Systems I," Tate, 2005, http://www.tate.org.uk/tate-etc/issue-4-summer-2005/boundtofail.htm

93 In *Tony Sinking into the Floor, Face Up, and Face Down* (sixty minutes, color, sound), the actor's task was to imagine himself sinking into the floor. The resulting images portray him stretched out on the floor, sometimes face up, sometimes face down, in a series of dissolves. Although the mental component of the exercise is not captured, Nauman has recounted the highly charged atmosphere of the shooting session: "He was lying on his back and after about fifteen minutes he started choking and coughing. He sat up and said, 'I did it too fast and scared myself.' He didn't want to do it again, but did it anyway. At another time we were watching his hand through the camera and it was behaving very strangely. We asked him about it later and he said that he was afraid to move his hand because he thought he might lose his molecules." See Electronic Arts Intermix online catalog, http://www.eai.org.

94 Hoffman, "Think-Thank / Denk-Dank," 57.

95 Cross, *Bruce Nauman: Theatres of Experience,* 14.

96 John Roberts, *The Intangibilities of Form: Skill and Deskilling in Art after the Readymade* (London: Verso, 2007), 71.

97 Ibid., 72.

98 Henri Bergson, *Laughter: An Essay on the Meaning of the Comic* (1900), translated by Cloudesle Brereton and Fred Rothwell (Copenhagen: Green Integer Books, 1999), 24.

99 Roberts, *Intangibilities of Form,* 73.

100 For an extensive discussion of the theoretical and practical contribution of the comedic to understanding life, see Alenka Zupančič, *The Odd One In: On Comedy* (Cambridge, Mass.: MIT Press, 2008).

101 Roberts, *Intangibilities of Form,* 74.

102 Another mocking example of this phenomenon would be Mike Mandel's *Making Good Time* (1989), a collection that pokes fun at scientific management studies by photographically producing a "good," i.e., humorous time, rather than a "good," i.e., speedy time.

103 Karl Marx, *Capital,* vol. 1 (London: Lawrence and Wishart, 1969), 336–38.

104 Robert Hirsch, *Seizing the Light: A History of Photography* (New York: McGraw-Hill, 2000), 218.

105 Joan Simon, "Breaking the Silence: An Interview with Bruce Nauman" (1988), in Kraynak, *Please Pay Attention Please,* 332. Kraynak's publication has been an invaluable resource and includes fourteen of Nauman's major interviews from 1965 until 2001.

106 In 1962 the Maharishi dictated his book, *The Science of Being and the Art of Living,* in California.

107 Lane Relyea, "Cast against Type," *Artforum* 33, no. 8 (1995): 62–69.

108 Fried, "Art and Objecthood."

109 The trope of the fountain, traditionally associated with knowledge, has been central to sculptural history, from the works of Gian Lorenzo Bernini to Duchamp. The culturally loaded and highly connotative theme of the fountain has recurred in Nauman's work since 1966, starting with his text piece *The True Artist Is an Amazing Luminous Fountain,* which comes with instructions on how this sentence could be installed in any space or translated (albeit with the chance of inexact interpretation) in any language.

110 "I would say my interest in Duchamp has to do with his use of objects to stand in for ideas" (Livingston, "Bruce Nauman," 11). In my study it is photographs that stand in for ideas. Similarly, the critical reading of Duchamp's oeuvre has been greatly informed by his performed and often-photographed persona.

111 For a deft critique of Kosuth in this regard, see Benjamin H. D. Buchloh, "Conceptual Art 1962–1969: From the Aesthetic of Administration to the Critique of Institutions," *October* 55 (Winter 1990); originally published in *L'art conceptuel: Une perspective* (Paris: Musée d'Art Moderne de la Ville de Paris, 1989).

112 In 1968 Nauman met the dancer-choreographer Meredith Monk and the composer Steve Reich, and he became aware of the work of John Cage, Merce Cunningham, and Karlheinz Stockhausen, all of whom influenced his experiments in time-based, performance work (Cross, *Bruce Nauman: Theatres of Experience,* 63). On the ontological similarities between performance and photography, see also Karen Henry, *Point and Shoot: Performance and Photography* (Montreal: Dazibao, 2004), 73.

113 Henry, *Point and Shoot,* 77.

114 Joan Simon, *William Wegman, Funney/Strange* (New Haven, Conn.: Yale University Press; Andover, Mass.: Addison Gallery of American Art, 2006), 91.

115 Hoffman, "Think-Thank / Denk-Dank," 52.

116 Rosalind Krauss, "Video: The Aesthetics of Narcissism," *October* 1 (Spring 1976): 50–64.

117 Ibid., 58.

118 Sillars, "Bruce Nauman: Keeping Busy," 34.

3. Everyone Who Is Anyone

1 Some people speculate that these iconic New York street signs lack the apostrophe in order to make them clearer and more immediate.

2 My translation. Douglas Huebler, interview with Irmeline Lebeer, "Le monde en jeu," first published in *Chroniques de l'Art Vivant,* no. 38 (April 1973): 20–23; reprinted in *L'art? C'est une meilleure idée! Entretiens (1972–1984)* (Paris: Editions Jacqueline Chambon, 1997), 113. Full quotation: "L'utilisation pléthorique de la photo dans le domaine de l'art introduit une énorme confusion. Employer la photo parce que la mode l'exige, c'est brouiller les pistes et ramener le problème à un niveau où je ne me suis jamais situé."

3 Huebler, interview with Lebeer; my translation. Full quotation: "La stratégie à laquelle je recours et qui consiste à libérer les choses, présentes dans le monde, du poids et de la pression de leur spécificité."

4 Huebler was included in the groundbreaking exhibition *Primary Structures: Younger American and British Sculptors,* April 27–June 12, 1966, Jewish Museum, New York.

5 Quoted in a statement accompanying the 1969 group show *Prospect '69* at the Kunsthalle Düsseldorf, curated by Konrad Fischer and Hans Strelow, n.p.

6 Kynaston McShine, introduction to *Primary Structures: Younger American and British Sculptors,* exh. cat. (New York: Jewish Museum, 1966), n.p.

7 Douglas Huebler, *Primary Structures,* n.p.

8 Donald Judd, "Specific Objects," *Arts Yearbook,* no. 8 (1965): 74–82; reprinted in Judd, *Complete Writings, 1959–1975* (Halifax, Nova Scotia: NSCAD, 1975).

9 Huebler, *Primary Structures.*

10 Roland Barthes, *Camera Lucida: Reflections on Photography* (New York: Hill and Wang, 1981).

11 Charles Stainback, *Special Collections: The Photographic Order from Pop to Now* (New York: International Center for Photography, 1992), 12.

12 Huebler, interview with Achille Bonito Oliva, New York, 1969, in *Encyclopedia of the Word: Artist Conversations, 1968–2008* (Milan: Skira, 2010), 23.

13 John Miller, "The Possibility of Knowing," in *Origin and Destination: Alighiero E Boetti, Douglas Huebler,* edited by Marianne Van Leeuw and Anne Pontegnie (Brussels: Société des Expositions du Palais des Beaux-Arts de Bruxelles, 1997), 177.

14 See Allan Sekula, "The Traffic in Photographs," *Art Journal* 41 (Spring 1981): 15–29; Sekula, "The Instrumental Image: Steichen at War," *Artforum* 14, no. 4 (1975): 26–34; and Sekula, "The Body in the Archive: The Use and Classification of Portrait Photography by the Police and Social Scientists in the Late Nineteenth and Early Twentieth Centuries," *October* 39 (Winter 1986): 3–64.

15 Huebler, *Origin and Destination,* 133–34.

16 "Douglas Huebler: Duration Piece #11, Bradford, Massachusetts" (2004.51a,b), in *Heilbrunn Timeline of Art History* (New York: Metropolitan Museum of Art, 2000–), http://www.metmuseum.org/toah/works-of-art/2004.51a,b.

17 Joshua Shannon, *The Recording Machine: Art and Fact during the Cold War* (New Haven, Conn.: Yale University Press, 2017), 56.

18 Hito Steyerl, "In Defense of the Poor Image," *e-flux journal,* no. 10 (November 2009), https://www.e-flux.com/journal/10/61362/in-defense-of-the-poor-image.

19 Susan Sontag, *On Photography* (New York: Farrar, Straus and Giroux, 1977), 3.

20 Marshall McLuhan, quoted in Marshall McLuhan and W. Terrence Gordon, *Understanding Media: The Extensions of Man* (Corte Madera, Calif.: Gingko, 2003), 266.

21 Ibid.

22 See Louis Kaplan, "Photo Globe: The Family of Man and the Global Rhetoric of Photography," in *American Exposures: Photography and Community in the Twentieth Century* (Minneapolis: University of Minnesota Press, 2005), 55–79.

23 Christopher Phillips, "The Judgment Seat of Photography," *October* 22 (Fall 1982): 46.

24 Kaplan, "Photo Globe," 79.

25 Allan Sekula, "The Traffic in Photographs," *Art Journal* 41 (1981): 15–25.

26 Blake Stimson, "Photographic Being and the Family of Man," in *Pivot of the World: Photography and Its Nation* (Cambridge, Mass.: MIT Press, 2006), 67.

27 Edward Steichen, Carl Sandburg, and Ezra Stoller, *The Family of Man: The Photographic Exhibition* (New York: Museum of Modern Art and Simon and Schuster in collaboration with the Maco Magazine Corp., 1955), 4.

28 See Stimson, "Photographic Being and the Family of Man," 71.

29 Steichen, Sandburg, and Stoller, *Family of Man,* 5.

30 Stimson, "Photographic Being and the Family of Man," 84.

31 Ibid., 85.

32 Michael Hardt and Antonio Negri, *War and Democracy in the Age of Empire* (London: Penguin Books, 2005).

33 Arthur A. Goldsmith Jr., "The Family of Man," *Popular Photography,* May 1955, 88, 147. Also quoted in Stimson, "Photographic Being and the Family of Man," 101.

34 Huebler, interview with Bonita Oliva, 22.

35 Ulrich Baer, "THE LESS SETTLED SPACE: Civil Rights, Hannah Arendt, and Garry Winogrand," *Aperture,* no. 202 (Spring 2011): 64.

36 Ibid., 63.

37 Hannah Arendt, *The Human Condition* (Chicago: University of Chicago Press, 1958), 57. Also quoted in Baer, "LESS SETTLED SPACE," 63.

38 Arendt, *Human Condition,* 37.

39 Baer, "LESS SETTLED SPACE," 65.

40 Gordon Hughes, "Game Face: Douglas Huebler and the Voiding of Photographic Portraiture," *Art Journal* 66, no. 4 (2007): 55. See also Hughes, "Exit Ghost: Douglas Huebler's Face Value," in *Photography after Conceptual Art,* edited by Diarmuid Costello and Margaret Iversen (Oxford: Wiley-Blackwell, 2010), 74.

41 Carol Armstrong, "Biology, Destiny, Photography: Difference according to Diane Arbus," *October* 66 (Autumn 1993): 29, 40.

42 Benjamin H. D. Buchloh, "Divided Memory and Post-Traditional Identity: Gerhard Richter's Work of Mourning," *October* 75 (Winter 1996): 69.

43 Michel Foucault, *Ceci n'est pas une pipe* (Montpellier: Editions Fata Morgana, 1973), 78.

44 Hughes, "Game Face," 61.

45 Sol LeWitt, "Serial Project No. 1 (ABCD)," *Aspen* 5–6 (Fall–Winter 1967), n.p.; quoted in Hughes, "Game Face," 58–59; and in Alexander Alberro, *Conceptual Art and the Politics of Publicity* (Cambridge, Mass.: MIT Press, 2003), 23.

46 Robert Morris, "Blank Form," 1961; reprinted in Barbara Haskell, *Blam! The Explosion of Pop, Minimalism, and Performance, 1958–1964* (New York: Whitney Museum of American Art in association with W. W. Norton, 1984), 101.

47 Soutter, "Visual Idea," 117. See Ludwig Wittgenstein and G. E. M. Anscombe, *Philosophical Investigations,* German text, with a revised English translation (Oxford: Blackwell, 2001). See also Rosalind Krauss, "Sense and Sensibility: Reflection on Post-'60s Sculpture," *Artforum* 12, no. 3 (1973): 43–52.

48 Roland Barthes, *S/Z* (Paris: Sevil, 1973), 16–17.

49 George Baker, "Photography between Narrativity and Stasis: August Sander, Degeneration, and the Decay of the Portrait," *October* 76 (Spring 1996): 74.

50 Fried, "Art and Objecthood."

51 The *Life* cover reads "The Faces of the American Dead in Vietnam; One Week's Toll," while the title inside the issue on page 20 is "Vietnam: One Week's Dead."

52 See John Gennari, "Bridging the Two Americas: *LIFE* Looks at the 1960s," in *Looking at Life Magazine,* edited by Erika Doss (Washington, D.C.: Smithsonian Institution Press, 2001), 262n1.

53 *Life,* June 27, 1969, 32.

54 Mike Kelley, "Shall We Kill Daddy?," in *Foul Perfection: Essays and Criticism,* edited by John C. Welchman (Cambridge, Mass.: MIT Press, 2003), 189.

55 Huebler, interview with Lebeer, 114; my translation, my italics. Full quotation: "Tout le monde est libre de concevoir tous les modèles imaginables pour exister dans un monde où nous sommes purement contingents."

56 See Victor Burgin, *Thinking Photography* (London: Macmillan, 1982).

57 Stainback, *Special Collections,* 9.

58 See Michael Fried, "Barthes's *Punctum,*" *Critical Inquiry* 31 (Spring 2005): 569. Douglas Hughes also notes this connection in his insightful article "Douglas Huebler and the Voiding of Photographic Portraiture," *Art Journal* 66, no. 4 (2007): 63.

59 See, e.g., Hughes, "Douglas Huebler," 63.

60 Ibid.

61 Rosalind Krauss, "Grids" (1979), in *The Originality of the Avant-Garde and Other Modernist Myths* (Cambridge, Mass.: MIT Press, 1985), 9.

62 Ibid.

63 Ibid.

64 Jeff Wall, "'Marks of Indifference': Aspects of Photography in, or as, Conceptual Art," in

Reconsidering the Object of Art, 1965–1975, exh. cat. (Los Angeles: Museum of Contemporary Art, 1995), 247–67.

65 Jeff Wall, "'Marks of Indifference': Aspects of Photography in, or as, Conceptual Art," in *The Last Picture Show: Artists Using Photography, 1960–1982* (Minneapolis: Walker Art Center, 2003), 38.

66 Huebler, interview with Bonito Oliva, 25.

67 Jeff Wall, "Conceptual, Postconceptual, Nonconceptual: Photography and the Depictive Arts," *Critical Inquiry* 38 (Summer 2012): 697.

68 Huebler, interview with Lebeer, 120; my translation. Full quotation:

Lebeer: Pensez-vous qu'un artiste puisse faire abstraction de milieu social et politique dans lequel il vit?

Huebler: Mais je n'ai pas du tout l'intention de me situer en dehors de la société!

Lebeer: En proposant des systèmes imaginaires, n'occultez-vous pas les vrais systèmes, politiques, sociaux, économiques?

Huebler: Absolument pas!

69 Michael Auping, "Talking with Douglas Huebler," *LAICA Journal* 15 (July–August 1977): 41.

70 Wall, "'Marks of Indifference'" (1995), 255.

71 Susan Sontag, "Shooting America," *New York Review of Books,* April 18, 1974.

72 See Mark Godfrey, "Across the Universe," in Witkovsky, *Light Years,* 61.

73 Huebler, interview with Bonito Oliva, 25.

74 Jeremy Gilbert-Rolfe, *Immanence and Contradiction* (New York: Out of London Press, 1985), 160.

75 Ibid., 158.

76 Krauss, "Grids," 21.

77 Ibid., 18.

78 Ibid., 19.

79 Meyer Schapiro, "Mondrian: Order and Randomness in Abstract Painting," in *On the Humanity of Abstract Painting* (New York: George Braziller, 1995), 28.

80 Ibid., 29.

81 See http://www.getty.edu/art/gettyguide/artMakerDetails?maker=1786.

82 Sontag, *On Photography,* 60.

83 The first posthumous publication appeared in 1980 and was realized by Gunther Sander, ed., *August Sander: Menschen des 20. Jahrhunderts. Portraitphotographien 1892–1952,* with text by Ulrich Keller (Munich: Schirmir/Mosel, 1980). A faithful reconstruction of the original in seven volumes, in accordance with the groups defined by Sander, was published in 2002 by the Photographische Sammlung / SK Stiftung Kultur, Cologne, since 1992 the owners of the August Sander Archive (edited and newly compiled by Susanne Lange, Gabriele Conrath-Scholl, and Gerd Sander).

84 Huebler to Dr. Giuseppe Panza di Biurno, November 3, 1981, Special Collections, Getty Research Institute for the History of Art and the Humanities, Panza Archive (90004, IIA. 133.22).

85 Quoted in Alberro (*Conceptual Art,* 99) referring to Jameson, "Periodizing the Sixties," in *The Sixties without Apology,* edited by Sohnya Sayres et al. (Minneapolis: University of Minnesota Press, 1984); reprinted in Fredric Jameson, *Syntax of History,* in vol. 2 of *The Ideologies of Theory: Essays 1971–1986* (Minneapolis: University of Minnesota Press, 1988), 197.

86 Petra Kuppers, "Visions of Anatomy," in *Scars of Visibility* (Minneapolis: University of Minnesota Press, 2007), 37.

87 Sontag, *On Photography,* 4.

88 Patricia Norvell, "Douglas Huebler, July 25, 1969," in *Recording Conceptual Art,* edited by Alexander Alberro and Patricia Norvell (Berkeley: University of California Press, 2001), 139.

89 See translation of text on page 5, *Film Quarterly* 13, no. 4 (1960).

90 Bazin, "Ontology of the Photographic Image," 6.

91 Ibid., 7.

92 Godfrey, "Across the Universe," 8.

93 Hughes, "Game Face."

94 Angela Grauerholz and Anne Ramsden, "Photographing Industrial Architecture: An Interview with Hilla and Bernd Becher," *Parachute,* Spring 1981, 18.

95 For more on this dynamic, see Hughes, "Game Face."

96 Douglas Huebler, catalog statement, *Origin and Destination: Alighiero e Boetti and Douglas Huebler,* edited by Marianne Van Leeuw and Anne Pontegnie (Brussels: Société des Expositions des Beaux-Arts de Bruxelles, 1997), 128.

97 John Miller, "Double or Nothing: The Art of Douglas Huebler," *Artforum* 44, no. 8 (2006): 220–27.

98 For an incisive discussion of Huebler's complex use of "documentation," particularly in relation to his *Location* pieces, see Christian Berger, "Douglas Huebler and the Photographic Document," *Visual Resources* 32 (2016): 3–4, 210–29.

99 Huebler, catalog statement, 128; also cited in Hughes, "Game Face," 56.

100 Barthes, *Camera Lucida,* 12.

101 Auping, "Talking with Douglas Huebler," 42.

102 Huebler, catalog statement, 133.

103 Norvell, "Douglas Huebler, July 25, 1969."

104 John Berger, "Understanding a Photograph," in *Understanding a Photograph,* edited by Geoff Dyer (New York: Aperture, 2013), 24.

105 See Eduardo Cadava and Paola Cortes-Roca, "Notes on Love and Photography," *October* 116 (Spring 2006): 3–34. Cadava and Cortes-Roca discuss the effects and affects of photography on and of the subject: "Photography—and the portrait as its genre *par excellence*—constitutes a radical and absolute destabilization of the Cartesian subject" (8).

106 Ariella Azoulay's evocative description of photography's referent is relevant here, as "deviant, jarring and devoid of any standard within the paradigm of modern art" (*Civil Imagination: A Political Ontology of Photography* [London: Verso, 2015], 58).

107 The "Wanted Poster" as a format for positing the artist as outlaw while playing on conceptual questions of criminality, aesthetics, and identity can be traced back to Marcel Duchamp's infamous *Wanted* poster of 1923. John Baldessari also used this trope as a conceptual strategy. Duchamp's precedent is discussed more explicitly in the following chapter on Baldessari.

108 Susan Sontag remarked something similar in 1977: "Photographs furnish evidence. Something we hear about, but doubt, seems proven when we're shown a photograph of it. In one version of its utility, the camera record incriminates" (*On Photography,* 5).

109 Huebler, catalog statement, 129.

110 Bazin, "Ontology of the Photograph," 8: "The photograph as such and the *object* in itself share a common being, after the fashion of a fingerprint."

111 See, e.g., John Tagg, *The Burden of Representation: Essays on Photographies and Histories* (Minneapolis: University of Minnesota Press, 1993).

112 Auping, "Talking with Douglas Huebler," 44.

113 I am evoking here the title of Richard Bolton's prominent and excellent edited volume, which grapples with the social and aesthetic consequences that emerge from the mobilization of photography as an art form as well as a mode of mass communication. See Bolton, ed., *The Contest of Meaning: Critical Histories of Photography* (Cambridge, Mass.: MIT Press, 1989).

4. This Is Not to Be Looked At

1 Peter Schjeldahl, "Wonderful Cynicism: John Baldessari," *Village Voice,* February 4, 1998.

2 "I thought, I'm not using paint, its photographic process, and so you can't claim that they're paintings. Rauschenberg had done overlaps of paint and screened photographic images, one over the other onto the canvas in a transfer method he had invented himself. But I wanted to be less artful than Rauschenberg and Warhol: this is a photograph, here's a text. That's it. And I thought, because they're done on canvas, they might be equated with art" (Baldessari, quoted in Coosje van Bruggen, *John Baldessari* [New York: Rizzoli, 1990], 29).

3 See Liz Kotz, *Words to Be Looked At: Language in 1960s Art* (Cambridge, Mass.: MIT Press, 2007).

4 See https://www.whitney.org/WatchAndListen/1092.

5 See ibid.

6 Christian Boltanski, "What Is Erased," *Blind Spot,* no. 3 (1994): 1–4.

7 Nicholas Mirzoeff, "The Right to Look," *Critical Inquiry,* Spring 2011, 474. Mirzoeff refers to Thomas Carlyle's lectures *On Heroes* (1840), published as *On Heroes, Hero-Worship & the Heroic in History: Six Lectures,* by James Fraser, London in 1841.

8 Nicholas Mirzoeff, "On Visuality," *Journal of Visual Culture* 5, no. 1 (2006): 67.

9 Mirzoeff, "On Visuality," 56; and Mirzoeff, "Right to Look," 474.

10 Bettina Riccio Henry, "Lights, Camera, Art: John Baldessari, Ed Ruscha, and Hollywood Film" (PhD diss., City University New York, October 2006), 24.

11 Quoted in van Bruggen, *John Baldessari,* 11.

12 Max Kozloff, "Pygmalion Reversed," *Artforum* 14.3 (1975): 30–37.

13 Ibid., 30.

14 Ibid.

15 Ibid.

16 Ibid., 37.

17 Kenneth D. Keele, *Leonardo da Vinci's Elements of the Science of Man* (New York: Academic Press, 1983), 254; cited on http://leonardodavinci.stanford.edu/submissions/clabaugh/history/ leonardo.html.

18 Thomas McEvilley, "I Think Therefore I Art," *Artforum* 23, no. 10 (1985): 75.

19 Van Bruggen, *John Baldessari,* 21.

20 Marie-Françoise Plissart and Jacques Derrida, "Right of Inspection," translated by David Wills, *Art and Text* 32 (Autumn 1989): 74. Derrida also cautioned against using the word *fragment* due to its problematic suggestion of a lost totality or one yet to come. See Martin Jay, "Phallogocularcentrism," in *Downcast Eyes: The Denigration of Vision in Twentieth-Century French Thought* (Berkeley: University of California Press, 1993), 519–20.

21 Max Kozloff, "American Painting during the Cold War," *Artforum* 11, no. 9 (1973): 43–54.

22 Peter Wollen, "Vectors of Melancholy," in *Scene of the Crime,* edited by Ralph Rugoff (Cambridge, Mass.: MIT Press, 1997), 32.

23 Ibid.

24 Rugoff, *Scene of the Crime,* 106.

25 Begun on May 10, 1968, and ended on September 17, 1979, *I GOT UP* consists of 4,160 pages in twelve volumes.

26 Lucy Lippard, *Six Years: The Dematerialization of the Art Object from 1966 to 1972* (New York: Praeger, 1973), 50.

27 Rugoff, *Scene of the Crime,* 77.

28 Rosalind Krauss, "Notes on the Index: Part 2," in *The Originality of the Avant-Garde and Other Modernist Myths* (Cambridge, Mass.: MIT Press, 1986), 211.

29 In his discussion of the shift from cult value to exhibition value, Walter Benjamin writes,

"But as man withdraws from the photographic image, the exhibition value for the first time shows its superiority to the ritual value. To have pinpointed this new stage constitutes the incomparable significance of Atget, who, around 1900, took photographs of deserted Paris streets. It has quite justly been said of him that he photographed them like scenes of crime. The scene of a crime, too, is deserted; it is photographed for the purpose of establishing evidence" ("Work of Art in the Age of Mechanical Reproduction," 226).

30 Rugoff, *Scene of the Crime.*

31 For example, see *Double Man and Seal* (1988) or *Two Stories* (1987). This tactic becomes a more prevalent device in Baldessari's work beginning in the 1980s. Since Baldessari's most common source material was appropriated and found photographs, this technique may have also developed out of a concern for copyright issues: "I think on the one hand I was a little bit worried about using someone's face, as I did not want to get sued, and I didn't know exactly where these photographs were coming from, so I used stickers I had lying around to obliterate the faces; and I felt so good I just kept on doing it" (quoted in van Bruggen, *John Baldessari,* 185). Baldessari has also connected his interest in blotting out or breaking up parts to an interest in ruptures of continuity inspired by his memories of the plaster fillings for missing shards in the Greek vases that he saw on his visits to the Metropolitan Museum of Art in New York in 1965 (see van Bruggen, *John Baldessari,* 184).

32 Jay, "Phallogocularcentrism," 521.

33 Jacques Derrida, quoted in Jay, "Phallogocularcentrism."

34 Van Bruggen, *John Baldessari,* 57.

35 Ibid.; quote from Baldessari also from this page.

36 Walter Benjamin, "Paris, Capital of the Nineteenth Century," in *Reflections: Essays, Aphorisms, Autobiographical Writings,* edited by Peter Demetz, translated by Edmund Jephcott (New York: Schocken Books, 1986), 155.

37 The clipping reads: "A free-rolling truck tire struck and killed a pedestrian in Delano, according to the California Highway Patrol. As Francisco Ramirez, 30, drove north on California 99, a tire came off his truck, crossed the north and southbound lanes, and hit Don Edwin Yarbrough, 21, of Denton, Tex., the CHP said. Yarbrough was reported dead at the scene."

38 Rugoff, *Scene of the Crime,* 82.

39 Quoted in van Bruggen, *John Baldessari,* 214.

40 Andy Warhol, *The Philosophy of Andy Warhol* (New York: Harcourt Brace Jovanovich, 1975), 123. For a further discussion of the death drive in Warhol's work, see Hal Foster, "Death in America," *October* 75 (Winter 1996): 37–59.

41 Kay Larson, "Death and Menace," *New York Magazine,* April 21, 1986, 89.

42 John Roberts, *Photography and Its Violations* (New York: Columbia University Press, 2014), 2.

43 Philip Kerr, *A Philosophical Investigation* (New York: Farrar, Straus and Giroux, 1993), 166.

44 John Tagg, "A Discourse with Shape of Reason Missing: Art History and the Frame," in *The Disciplinary Frame: Photographic Truths and the Capture of Meaning* (Minneapolis: University of Minnesota Press, 2009), 235–63.

45 See John C. Welchman, "'Don't Play It for Laughs': John Baldessari and Conceptual Comedy," *Black Sphinx: On the Comedic in Modern Art,* edited by John C. Welchman (Zurich: JRP Ringier, 2010), 245–68. Welchman discusses the prominence of gun iconography in Baldessari's work, linking it to the fetishization of personal weaponry in the United States, which he calls "the extraordinary and insidious longevity of the insemination of the gun into the North American popular unconscious, borne out by its omnipresence in film, comic, and now online cultures, and its inflection of the very language we speak" (258).

46 Welchman, "'Don't Play It for Laughs,'" 254–55.

47 Sol LeWitt, "Paragraphs on Conceptual Art," *Artforum* 10, no. 5 (1967): 79. The same issue contained Fried's "Art and Objecthood," 12–23. LeWitt followed his "Paragraphs" with his "Sentences on Conceptual Art," first published in the magazine *0–9* in January 1969, edited by Vito Acconci and Bernadette Mayer.

48 Jasper Johns, *Writings, Sketchbook Notes, Interviews* (New York: Museum of Modern Art, 1996), 410.

49 Benjamin H. D. Buchloh, Yve-Alain Bois, Hal Foster, and Rosalind Krauss, *Art since 1900* (New York: Thames and Hudson, 2005), 409.

50 See Michael Fried, "Shape as Form: Frank Stella's Irregular Polygons" (1966) and "Frank Stella" (1963), in *Art and Objecthood*, 77–99, 277–78.

51 Carl Andre and Frank Stella shared a studio in New York in 1959; see Carl Andre, "Preface to Painting," in *Sixteen Americans*, edited by Dorothy C. Miller (New York: Museum of Modern Art, 1959) 76.

52 The Museum of Contemporary Art, Los Angeles fortuitously owns both Baldessari's *This Is Not To Be Looked At* (donated by Joel Wachs in 2005) and Stella's *Union III* (donated by the collector Robert Rowan in 1980); see Jeremy Strick, "Director's Foreword," *This Is Not to Be Looked At: Highlights from the Permanent Collection of the Museum of Contemporary Art, Los Angeles* (Los Angeles: Museum of Contemporary Art, 2008), 8.

53 Jay, "Phallogocularcentrism," 518–19.

54 See Gwen Allen, *Artist's Magazines: An Alternative Space for Art* (Cambridge, Mass.: MIT Press, 2011), 23n34, citing a study titled "Periodicals in the Visual Arts" (1962).

55 Lucy Soutter, *The Visual Idea: Photography in Conceptual Art* (PhD thesis, Yale University, 2001), 137.

56 For a discussion of both *Artforum's* early editorial attitude toward conceptual art and the resentment of California artists, see Amy Newman, ed., *Challenging Art: Artforum, 1962–1974* (New York: Soho Press, 2000).

57 Jacques Derrida, "The Deaths of Roland Barthes," in *Philosophy and Non-Philosophy since Merleau-Ponty*, edited by Hugh J. Silverman (New York: Routledge, 1988), 91.

58 Tagg, "Discourse with Shape of Reason Missing," 246.

59 Walter Benjamin, "A Short History of Photography" (c. 1931), translated by Stanley Mitchell, *Screen* 13, no. 3 (1972): 25.

60 Numerous works by Baldessari problematize "directional looking" and invectives or signs on where to look, for example, *A Movie: Directional Piece Where People Are Looking* (1972–73), a montage composed of twenty-eight still photographs.

61 The centrality of Stella's work to the art world at this time is concurrent with the dominance of *Artforum*'s discourse. As David Antin has described retrospectively, "Pop Art, Minimalist Sculpture, and Hard Edge paining were trying to marry American commercial culture and were celebrated each month in the pages of *Artforum*." Contemporaneously, Baldessari jokingly advised Marcia Tucker that if she wanted to find artists working outside the modes of the central scene for the Whitney Biennial, all she would have to do is "look up all the people whose subscriptions to *Artforum* have lapsed." See David Antin, "Eight Stories for John Baldessari," in *John Baldessari: National City*, edited by Hugh M. Davies and Andrea Hales (La Jolla, Calif.: Museum of Contemporary Art San Diego, 1996), 16–17.

62 Fried, "Art and Objecthood," 168. Another Baldessari work of 1966–67 focuses on the right-hand corner of the *Artforum* cover featuring Stella's *Union III*; this corner is blown up and reproduced with photo emulsion on canvas.

63 Nietzsche, quoted in Crary, *Techniques of the Observer*, 97.

64 Benjamin H. D. Buchloh makes this observation about Friedrich's paintings in his essay on Gerhard Richter, "Readymade, Photography, and Painting in the Painting of Richter,"

Neo-Avantgarde and Culture Industry: Essays on European and American Art from 1955 to 1975 (Cambridge, Mass.: MIT Press, 2000), 384.

65 "Interview with John Baldessari," in Davies and Hales, *John Baldessari: National City,* 87.

66 Van Bruggen, *John Baldessari,* 29–30.

67 Abigail Solomon-Godeau, "The Rightness of *Wrong,*" in Davies and Hales, *John Baldessari,* 33.

68 See Lela Graybill, "Illegible Bodies: On Not Seeing in Goya's Disasters of War," *Stanford Journal of Archaeology* 2 (2003): 2.

69 Graybill, 3.

70 For a discussion of Goya's etchings, responsiveness to suffering in art, and their expressive phrases, see Susan Sontag, *Regarding the Pain of Others* (New York: Farrar, Straus and Giroux, 2003), 44–47.

71 Graybill, "Illegible Bodies," 4.

72 Amelia Jones, *The Artists' Body,* edited by Tracey Warr (London: Phaidon, 2006), 20.

73 Martin Jay, "From Empire of the Gaze to Society of Spectacle," in *Downcast Eyes,* 389; Jay refers to Rajchman, "Foucault's Art of Seeing," *October* 44 (Spring 1988): 93.

74 Jacques Derrida, "Restitutions of the Truth in Pointing ['Pointure']" (1978), in *Jacques Derrida: The Truth in Painting,* translated by Geoff Bennington and Ian McLeod (Chicago: University of Chicago Press, 1987), 255–382.

75 Graybill, "Illegible Bodies," 6.

76 Robert Hariman and John Louis Lucaites, "Public Identity and Collective Memory in U.S. Iconic Photography: The Image of 'Accidental Napalm,'" *Critical Studies in Media Communication* 20.1 (2003): 35–66.

77 Joseph Eszterhas et al., "The Massacre at Mylai," *Life,* December 1969, 41; "MyLai Massacre," *Time,* November 28, 1969, 17–19.

78 See W. R. Peer, *The My Lai Inquiry* (New York: W. W. Norton, 1979); and Seymour M. Hersh, *My Lai 4: A Report on the Massacre and Its Aftermath* (New York: Random House, 1970).

79 See Julia Bryan-Wilson, *Art Workers: Radical Practice in the Vietnam War Era* (Berkeley: University of California Press, 2011).

80 Claude Cookman, "An American Atrocity: The My Lai Massacre Concretized in a Victim's Face," *Journal of American History* 94.1 (2007): 154–62. See also Michal R. Belknap, *The Vietnam War on Trial: The My Lai Massacre and the Court-Martial of Lieutenant Calley* (Lawrence: University of Kansas Press, 2002); and James S. Olson and Randy Roberts, *My Lai: A Brief History with Documents* (Boston: Bedford, 1998).

81 Andy Grundberg, "Point and Shoot: How the Abu Ghraib Images Redefine Photography," *American Scholar* 74.1 (2005): 107.

82 Quoted in Cookman, "American Atrocity," 158.

83 Ibid., 158.

84 "Conceptual Alchemy: A Conversation with John Baldessari," *American Art* 19, no. 1 (2005): 68.

85 "The procedure: First I visited many art exhibits. When I discovered a painter I asked if he would do a painting on commission. Then I delivered a standard canvas with an area delineated to the proportions of a 35-mm transparency. The problem of providing interesting subject matter (to avoid their usual choice of Schooner ships, desert cacti, moonlit oceans, etc.) was solved by a series I had just finished which involved someone walking around and pointing at things that were interesting to him. I presented each artist with approximately a dozen of these slides from which to choose. They were asked to paint a rendition as faithfully as possible; the idea being that art would emerge. Upon completion, each painting was taken to a sign painter and the artists name affixed thus "A Painting by . . ." The entire set was exhibited in galleries in Los Angeles and New York that dealt in recent modern art. It was important that the paintings were exhibited as a group so that the spectator could practice connoisseurship, for example comparing how the extended forefinger in each was painted. In all, the point was to organize these artists in a different context and provide them with an unhackneyed subject that would attract the attention of a viewer interested in modern art" (*John Baldessari: A Different Kind of Order (Arbeiten 1962–1984)* [Cologne: König, 2005], 153).

86 Anne Rorimer, "Composing on/off a Canvas: Pictorial Innovation in the Early Work of John Baldessari," in *John Baldessari: A Different Kind of Order,* 73.

87 Dave Hickey, in Davies and Hales, *John Baldessari: National City,* 26.

88 Charles Sanders Peirce, *Peirce on Signs: Writings on Semiotic by Charles Sanders Peirce,* edited by James Hoopes (Chapel Hill: University of North Carolina Press, 1991), 25. See also Mary Doane, "Indexicality: Trace and Sign: Introduction," *differences: A Journal of Feminist Cultural Studies* 18 (2007): 1–6.

89 Quoted in Jeanne Siegel, ed., "John Baldessari: Recalling Ideas," in *Art Talk: The Early 80s* (New York: Da Capo, 1988), 40.

90 *Wrong* and *The Viewer Is Compelled . . .* are part of this series. Others from this time are even more blasé, however, such as *Ryan Oldsmobile National City, Calif.* (1967–68). See Robert L. Pincus, "'Quality Material . . .': Duchamp Disseminated in the Sixties and Seventies," in Clearwater, *West Coast Duchamp,* 93.

91 Baldessari, quoted in *John Baldessari* (New York: New Museum, 1981), 63. See also Andrea Hales, "National City Revisited," in Davies and Hales, *John Baldessari: National City,* 10–13.

92 A. D. Coleman, "'I'm Not Really a Photographer,'" *New York Times,* September 10, 1972.

93 Charles Desmarais, *Proof: Los Angeles Art and the Photograph, 1960–1980* (Laguna Beach, Calif.: Laguna Art Museum, 1992), 29.

94 Quoted in Desmarais, *Proof,* 30, from Robert Pincus-Witten, "Blasted Allegories! The Photography of John Baldessari," in *John Baldessari,* 51–52.

95 Desmarais, *Proof,* 30.

96 Rorimer, "Composing on/off a Canvas," 73.

97 Larisa Dryansky, *Cartophotographies: De l'art conceptuel au Land Art* (Paris: Institut Nationale de l'Histoire de l'Art, 2017), 301.

98 Quoted in ibid.

99 On display from October 31, 1992, to January 17, 1993, the exhibit traveled to five other locations across the United States over the next couple of years: the De Cordova Museum and Sculpture Park in Lincoln, Massachusetts; the Ansel Adams Center in San Francisco; the Montgomery Museum of Fine Arts in Alabama; the Tampa Museum of Art in Florida; and the Des Moines Art Center in Iowa.

100 Desmarais, *Proof,* 10.

101 Ibid., 11.

102 Douglas Crimp, "The Photographic Activity of Postmodernism," *October* 15 (Winter 1980): 91. Crimp bases his claim here on the use of the term in his 1979 essay "Pictures." See also Desmarais, *Proof,* 12.

103 Quoted by Douglas Fogle in the catalog of *The Last Picture Show: Artists Using Photography, 1960–1982,* (Minneapolis, Minn.: Walker Art Center, 2003), 17. See also Marie de Brugerolle, "John Baldessari, A Twist in Reality," *John Baldessari: A Different Kind of Order,* edited by Edelbert Kàb and Peter Pakesch (Cologne: Walther Konig, 2005), 108.

104 Quoted in Madan Sarup, *An Introductory Guide to Post-Structuralism and Postmodernism* (Athens: University of Georgia Press, 1989), 51. See also Friedrich Nietzsche, "On Truth and Lies in the Extra-Moral Sense" (1873), in *Friedrich Nietzsche on Rhetoric and Language* (New York: Oxford University Press, 1989).

105 Desmarais, *Proof,* 12.

106 Ibid., 13.

107 Quoted in Desmarais, 13. Many of Baldessari's works evidence the influence of Hollywood "staging," for example, his *Embed Series: Oiled Arm (Sinking Boat and Palms)* (1974) in which a close-up shot of the artist's arm covered in oil appears to be a sea in which a miniature boat and a couple of palm trees illustrate a constructed narrative that plays on the viewer's perception of scale. The title gives away the ruse, while the photograph amuses through its reference to Hollywood set productions.

108 As late as 1950, despite desperate attempts, Louise and Walter Arensberg could find no Los Angeles institution prepared to accept their spectacular collection of Duchamps, Brancusis, Ernsts, Légers, Mirós, and other modern works. See Naomi Sawelson-Gorse, "Hollywood Conversations: Duchamp and the Arensbergs," in Clearwater, *West Coast Duchamp,* 25–45.

109 Desmarais, *Proof,* 14.

110 Ibid., 17.

111 Ibid.

112 Ibid., 15.

113 Quoted in ibid.

114 Pincus-Witten, "Blasted Allegories!," 51–52.

115 For Robert Heinecken, "The photograph . . . is not a *picture of* something but it is an *object about* something." See William Jenkins, introduction to *Heinecken,* edited by James Enyeart (Carmel, Calif.: Friends of Photography, 1980) 11; Robert Heinecken, "The Photograph: Not a Picture of, but an Object about Something," *ADLA,* October 1965, n.p.

116 On the issue of the photograph as object, see Hilton Kramer's review of Peter Bunnell's MoMA exhibition *Photography into Sculpture* (1970). No catalog was published for the show, but there are articles from the time by Bunnell in the magazines *Art and Artist, Art in America,* and *Artscanada.* The exhibition traveled widely to eight additional venues, including the Otis Art Institute of Los Angeles County (January 24–March 5, 1972).

117 Desmarais, *Proof,* 18.

118 Ibid., 31–32.

119 Ibid., 31.

120 Ibid.

121 See Peter Plagens, *Sunshine Muse: Contemporary Art on the West Coast* (New York: Praeger, 1974).

122 Angela Y. Davis, "Other Landscapes," in *Art/Women/California, 1950–2000,* edited by Diana Burgess Fuller and Daniela Salvoni (Berkeley: University of California Press, 2002), 46; also quoted in Julia Bryan-Wilson, "To Move, to Dress, to Work, to Act: Playing Gender and Race in 1970s California Art," *State of Mind: New California Art circa 1970,* edited by Constance M. Lewallen and Karen Moss (Berkeley: University of California Press, 2011), 211.

123 Quoted in Desmarais, *Proof,* 33. See also Allan Sekula, "On the Invention of Photographic Meaning," *Artforum* 13.5 (1975): 37.

124 Sekula, "On the Invention of Photographic Meaning," 37.

125 Quoted in *John Baldessari: A Different Kind of Order,* 56.

126 Quoted in Thierry de Duve, "Echoes of the Readymade: Critique of Pure Modernism," *October* 70 (1994): 85.

127 Other versions included rhubarb rather than green beans, for example. The seeming randomness of these objects/things furthers the sense of the arbitrary and even the silly in these works.

128 Kàb and Pakesch, *John Baldessari: A Different Kind of Order,* 177.

129 Robin Kelsey, *Photography and the Art of Chance* (Cambridge, Mass.: Harvard University Press, 2015), 293.

130 Henry Martin, "Milan Letter," *Art International* 16.6 (1972): 106.

131 Kelsey, *Photography and the Art of Chance*, 290, 299.

132 *The Vietnam War Was Good for Something*, https://web.musicaficionado.com/main/article/The_Best_and_the_Rest_of_Vietnam_Protest_Songs_by_jkordosh web.musicaficionado.com.

133 Baldessari, quoted in van Bruggen, *John Baldessari*, 214.

134 Ibid., 36.

135 Andy Grundberg, "Point and Shoot: How the Abu Ghraib Images Redefine Photography," *American Scholar* 74.1 (2005): 109.

Epilogue

1 See David Wise, "Dilemma in 'Credibility Gap,'" *New York Herald Tribune*, May 23, 1965, 15; and Wise, *The Politics of Lying: Government Deception, Secrecy, and Power* (New York: Random House, 1973), 22–23, 290–91.

2 Quoted in Michael Leja, *Looking Askance: Skepticism and American Art from Eakins to Duchamp* (Berkeley: University of California Press, 2004) 16.

3 Lauren O'Neill-Butler, "Mind the Fact: Hannah Arendt's Clairvoyant Diagnosis of Post-truth Politics," *Bookforum*, Summer 1968, 35.

4 Hannah Arendt, preface to *Men in Dark Times* (New York: Harcourt, Brace & World, 1968), viii.

5 Hannah Arendt, *Eichmann in Jerusalem: A Report on the Banality of Evil*, rev. ed. (New York: Viking, 1965).

6 David Joselit, "Fake News, Art, and Cognitive Justice," *October* 159 (Fall 2017): 14–18. See Joselit for a perceptive discussion of how contemporary art might challenge the current state of cognitive disenfranchisement in the United States.

7 "Immerse yourself in such a picture long enough and you will recognize how alive the contradictions are, here too: the most precise technology can give its products a magical value, such as a painted picture can never again have for us. No matter how artful the photographer, no matter how carefully posed his subject, the beholder feels an irresistible urge to search a picture for the tiny spark of contingency, of the Here and Now, with which reality has so to speak seared the subject, to find the inconspicuous spot where in the immediacy of that long-forgotten moment the future subsists so eloquently that we, looking back, may rediscover it" (Benjamin, "Short History of Photography," 1931).

8 Teju Cole, "On Photography: Capital, Diplomacy and Carnations," *New York Times Magazine*, November 29, 2016.

9 Godfrey, *Conceptual Art*, 301.

10 Arthur C. Danto, introduction to *On Certainty*, by Ludwig Wittgenstein (San Francisco: Arion, 1991), n.p.

Index

Page numbers in *italics* refer to illustrations.

Heather Diack is assistant professor of contemporary art at the University of Miami. She is coauthor of *Global Photography: A Critical History.*